Storm over Iraq

*Air Power
and the
Gulf War*

Richard P. Hallion

*Smithsonian Institution Press
Washington & London*

This book was edited by Initial Cap Editorial Services.
Production editor: Jack Kirshbaum
Designer: Chris Hotvedt/Janice Wheeler
Maps: Blue Heron, Inc.

Library of Congress Cataloging in Publication Data
Hallion, Richard.
  Storm over Iraq / Richard P. Hallion.
  p.   cm.—(Smithsonian history of aviation series)
Includes bibliographical references and index.
ISBN 1-56098-190-3
  1. Air power—United States—History.   2. United States.   Air Force—History.   3. Persian Gulf War, 1991—Aerial operations, American.   I. Title.   II. Series.
UG633.H35   1992
358.4'03'0973—dc20   92-7034
                                                                            CIP
Printed in the United States of America
96 95 94 93 92   5 4 3 2 1

The paper used in this publication meets the minimum requirements of the American National Standard for Permanence of Paper for Printed Library Materials Z39.48-1984.

Unless otherwise stated, all photographs are courtesy of U.S. Department of Defense.

To the men and women who flew in Desert Storm, and, especially, to the memory of

       Lieutenant Colonel Bryant Dougherty, USAF

who rode their wings.

> *"You give wonderful comrades to me, the faithful who dwell in your land . . . "*

Contents

Preface

It is important to understand what this book is *not*. It is not an integrated, authoritative history of the Persian Gulf War, its origins, progression, and impact, for that history cannot yet be written—neither sufficient time has passed, nor are appropriate documentary materials (from all sides) available. It does not attempt to explain Saddam Hussein's rationale for invading Kuwait or his refusal to leave prior to conflict. It is not a history of the diplomacy of the Gulf crisis, nor does it examine such questions as the fate of the Kurds, the general state of Arab-American-European relations, the Israeli-Palestinian crisis, and the nature of Mideast diplomacy. It does not attempt to trace day-to-day decisionmaking by the civilian and military leaders of the nation. All of these deserve their own works, and all have already been the subject of various studies and undoubtedly will continue to be. Likewise, it is not a "you are there" combat narration in the style of the late S. L. A. Marshall; the anecdotes related are few, and were selected only because of their relevancy to larger issues.

Rather, this book is an attempt to come to an understanding about the military conduct of the Gulf war, to examine and frame some of the military issues of the war, and, in particular, to assess the impact of coalition air power and its implications for the future of warfare. (The term *air power* is used in the broadest possible sense, to mean *the various uses of airborne vehicles and forces to achieve national needs by the projection of military power or presence at a distance*.) To set the context of the Gulf war, the work begins with a discussion of how the United States rebuilt and then employed its military forces (particularly air power) in the years after Vietnam. Only by understanding this evolution prior to August 1990 can their role in the Gulf war be properly comprehended.

Every author is dependent upon a network of colleagues who have assisted in innumerable ways. I have benefited from many, but particular from the following—as brilliant a collection of individuals as have ever served in uniform: Gen. Mike Loh; Maj. Gen. Buster Glosson; brigadier generals James Cole, George Muellner, and Ed Robertson; colonels John Brooks, Philip Corbett, Mike Hayden, Doug Joyce, Dave Milam, W. Hays Parks, John Piazza, George Sumrall, and John Warden; lieutenant colonels Dave "Zatar" Deptula, Ben Harvey, Bob Hilton, Dan Kuehl, Phil Meilinger, Rich King, Barb McColgan, and Tom Smith; commanders Donald "Duck" McSwain and Bill Readdy; majors Steve Cullen, Bob Eskridge, Brian Hoey, Dave Klaus, Buck Rogers, and Chip Setnor; lieutenant commanders Debra Johnson and Greg Johnson; and captains Stan Alluisi, Bill Bruner, "Snake" Penchiney, Ray Grienke, and John Watkins. Royal Air Force group captains Andy Vallance and Neil Taylor offered valuable insight on lessons learned, as did Air Vice Marshal R. A. "Tony" Mason, RAF (ret.), and Col. Alan Gropman, USAF (ret.). Major T. M. Deane, British Army (ret.) furnished important information on the operations of British helicopters in the Gulf war. Colonel William Lawrence and Lt. Col. Troy Pennington provided a valuable perspective on Marine Corps air operations.

Former colleagues from the flight test community were helpful, in the past and present, notably major generals Peter "Peet" Odgers and Phil Conley; colonels Bob Ettinger, Pete Knight, Cal Jewett, and John Taylor; lieutenant colonels Ray Houle and Dave Spencer; Pat Henry (McDonnell-Douglas), Phil Oestricher (General Dynamics), Pete Adolph, Dr. Jim Young, and the late Chuck Sewell (Grumman). Dr. Robert Helmbold of the U.S. Army's Concepts Analysis Agency and Prof. Ken Werrell of Radford College furnished important insights. Colonel Rod Paschall, U.S. Army (ret.) was, as always, a fruitful source of information and insight, particularly on special operations forces. I am very grateful for information received from the various history offices of the U.S. Department of Defense, and thank particularly Brig. Gen. Hal Nelson and the staff of the Army Center for Military History, and Col. Tom Sweeney and the staff of the U.S. Army Military History Institute. Drs. Will Webb and Ron Cole of the JCS History Office were particularly helpful, as was Jack Neufeld, the director of the Center for Air Force History, and his colleagues, Drs. Rich Davis, Diane Putney, Perry Jamison, Tom Y'Blood, Al Misenko, Herm Wolk, and M. Sgt. William Chivalette.

Several individuals offered vital "sanity checks" of the manuscript, particularly Dr. Christopher J. Bowie and Dr. Rebecca Grant of the Rand Corporation, Ms. Ellen Piazza of the Secretary of the Air Force's Staff Group, Dr. Don Baucom of the Strategic Defense Initiative Organization (SDIO), and Dr. Wayne Thompson of the Gulf War Air Power Survey (GWAPS). Others offered important insights, information, and suggestions, including Dr. Steve Rearden, John Kreis, Dr. John Fozard, and, as always, Lt. Col. William "Flaps" Flanagan, USAF (ret.) of the Northrop Corporation. Others who have assisted are Dr. Dana J. Johnson and James A. Winnefeld of Rand, Mary C. FitzGerald of the Hudson Institute, Margaret Kane of Sidwell Friends Middle School, Gloria Mundo of the U.S. Bureau of the Census, Bonnie Mattingly of the Dulles Airport staff, Barbara Hartnett of British Aerospace, Inc., Terry Gordy of Rockwell International, Elissa Decker of Grumman Melbourne Systems, and Tom Forburger of Raytheon. I am grateful to Therese D. Boyd of Initial Cap Editorial Services, who edited the manuscript.

I profited from refreshing and informative discussions with colleagues at the National Air and Space Museum of the Smithsonian Institution during my year as the Charles A. Lindbergh Professor of Aerospace History, particularly Drs. Martin Harwit, Steve Soter, Tom Crouch, Gregg Herken, Peter Jakab, Allan Needell, and Tami Davis Biddle. Colonel Don Lopez, USAF (ret.), Air Vice Marshal Ron Dick, RAF (ret.), and Capt. Tim Wooldridge, USN (ret.) offered keen insights honed from years in the cockpit. Allan Janus, Mark Taylor, Patty Woodside, Brian Nicklas, Dana Bell, and the staff of the library and archives of the museum were extraordinarily helpful in furnishing access to materials and information, particularly as I grappled with curating a Desert Storm exhibit for the museum in the spring of 1991. My renewed contact with Prof. Wayne Cole of the Department of History, University of Maryland, was most welcome. As an aviator, author, and dean of American diplomatic historians, Wayne

Cole's perspectives were always timely, appropriate, and insightful. Finally, I thank the students and faculty of the Defense and Arms Control Studies Program, Center for International Studies, Massachusetts Institute of Technology, particularly professors Harvey Sapolsky, Barry Posen, and Ted Postal, for the opportunity to explore some of the ideas expressed in this book in two seminars characterized by a stimulating atmosphere of vigorous discussion and debate.

Selected portions of chapters 6 and 7 were excerpted by the Office of the Secretary of the Air Force for the publication *Reaching Globally, Reaching Powerfully: The USAF in the Gulf War—A Report,* issued in September 1991 as a "quick look" at what the air war had accomplished.

While many may assist, the author alone must accept responsibility for the final product. This book is a very personal view of the war, and does not seek to represent the view of any official body, agency, or individual of the U.S. government, the United Nations, or any other organization. Time will tell if it has enduring merit. For myself, I will be satisfied it has served its purpose if it stimulates and encourages the discussion, comment, and scholarship of others who follow.

Storm over Iraq

One

An Uncertain Legacy

Air Power from the Western Front through Vietnam

Today air power is the dominant factor in war. It may not win a war by itself alone, but without it no major war can be won.
Adm. Arthur Radford, USN (1954)

The Persian Gulf War will be studied by generations of military students, for it confirmed a major transformation in the nature of warfare: the dominance of air power. As Air Vice Marshal R. A. "Tony" Mason, RAF (ret.), wrote, "The Gulf war marked the apotheosis of twentieth-century airpower." [1] Simply (if boldly) stated, air power won the Gulf war. It was not the victory of any one service, but rather the victory of coalition air power projection by armies, navies, and air forces. At one end were sophisticated stealth fighters striking out of the dark deep in Iraqi territory. At the other were the less glamorous but no less important troop and supply helicopters wending their way across the battlefield. In between was every conceivable form of air power application, short of nuclear war, including aircraft carriers, strategic bombers, tactical and strategic airlift, and cruise missiles.

The success of air power in the Gulf war was neither universally predicted nor assumed in the weeks and months before Desert Storm broke. Indeed, while many analysts expected air power to influence the outcome of the war, few expected it to be the war's decisive force. In part this stemmed from air power's mixed record in previous conflicts. While military historians could argue that air had already been the single most important form of military power since 1939 and the outbreak of the Second World War, its application in wars since that time had often been haphazard, not sustained, disappointing, or obscured by equally complex and involved land and sea operations.[2] Only one previous war came close to being a decisive victory for air power alone: the June 1967 Arab-Israeli war—but this was the last "pre-missile era" air war, and, as such, one whose lessons had to be qualified in light of the experience in Vietnam and later conflicts. Few commentators discussed the June 1967 war or its successors when predicting potential outcomes of a Gulf conflict as the crisis escalated over the fall and winter of 1990–91. Even more surprising, few air power historians ventured to make any sort of predictions about what might happen in the Gulf. With the vast preponderance of media consultants being specialists either in land or sea warfare, it is not surprising that they consistently ignored or (at best) underestimated air power and its potentialities. Only rarely did someone speak favorably of air power, and in those few cases, moderators usually carefully sandwiched such remarks between ones much more critical or "realistic."

The vast reach of the media into the Gulf region subjected Saddam Hussein and his advisors to a daily barrage of information from the West stating, basically, that air power could not force Iraq out of Kuwait. It could punish and harass Saddam Hussein's military forces. But on its own, air power could not resolve the Gulf crisis, for air power had always failed to deliver on its promise. At some point, Iraqi troops would have to be forced out of Kuwait at the point of a bayonet. And with that, critics warned, American casualties would explode, morale would plummet, and a Vietnam-style antiwar movement would destroy the United Nations coalition. In the months before the UN coalition went to war, a seemingly endless succession of experts, consultants, and defense hangers-on predicted outright disaster or Pyrrhic victory in the Gulf. Harvard economist John Kenneth Galbraith offered up that Americans "should react with a healthy skepticism to the notion that air power will decide the outcome of a war in Kuwait and Iraq," magisterially intoning that "there's no issue to be regarded with such doubt as this."[3] Joshua Epstein of the Brookings Institution predicted 1,049 to 4,136 deaths and up to 16,059 total American casualties, thanks to a computer model of war.[4] Other statistical models predicted at least 9,000 casualties, based on Army doctrine for waging intensive ground-maneuver warfare.[5] Well-established and knowledgeable authorities painted equally dismal pictures. For example, former Army Chief of Staff Gen. Edward C. "Shy" Meyer estimated 10,000 to 30,000 American casualties against dug-in Iraqi troops.[6] Air power's ability to prevent such losses was repeatedly denigrated, particularly after the firing of Air Force Chief of Staff Gen. Michael J. Dugan.[7]

There were other arguments as well. A decade of partisan bickering over the Reagan-era defense buildup resulted in a resurrection of so-called defense reform arguments to the effect that America suffered from a short-sighted and inept military leadership that had produced dubious doctrines and initiatives resulting in the acquisition of weapons that didn't work for threats that didn't exist. Pentagon critics such as Gary Hart, Alexander Cockburn, Kosta Tsipis, James Fallows, Richard Gabriel, John Pike, and William Lind (and organizations such as the Center for Defense Information and the Union of Concerned Scientists) had so elevated these notions into canons of modern defense thought that virtually every weapon that subsequently fought spectacularly well in the Gulf—such as the F-117 stealth fighter, Tomahawk cruise missile, Abrams main battle tank, Apache attack helicopter, and the Patriot surface-to-air missile—was belittled. Cockburn, for example, warned that soldiers in the Gulf would have to fight "with weapons badly made by manufacturers colluding with the Defense Department in the padded invoice and the faked test."[8] As one general put it after the Gulf war, "If you had been reading press accounts of the American military for the past ten years, you would come away with the impression that we're the gang that couldn't shoot straight with weapons that don't work."[9] Worse, as former Army undersecretary and aerospace executive Norman R. Augustine subsequently wrote, "One can't help being reminded of those economists who, whenever any action works well in the business world, rejoin 'Yes, but would it have worked in theory . . . ' " Augustine concluded,

> In fact, we came perilously close to not having "invisible" airplanes, not owning the night, not having "smart" munitions that could select the room within a building to hit, not possessing some of the spacecraft that constituted the new high ground over the desert, and not having a "bullet that could hit a bullet."[10]

It should not be surprising, then, that Saddam Hussein, taking this climate to heart, stubbornly refused to leave Kuwait. One wonders to what degree his intransigence was strengthened by these multiple preachers of the old conventional wisdom that air power wouldn't work, technology would disappoint, and that eventually it would come down to a nineteen-year-old American in the open with an M-16 versus a dug-in nineteen-year-old Iraqi with an AK-47, with horrendous resulting casualties. Certainly they offered him presumptive evidence that he could withstand and even triumph over a coalition attack to liberate Kuwait, for they implied that eventually the war would degenerate into the kind of World War I–type attrition warfare slugfest that he had endured with Iran over nearly a decade, and which Iraqi troops had eventually won.

To arrive at an understanding of the Gulf air war, to comprehend why so many could be so wrong about so much, and to understand, on the other hand, how the air commanders of the Allied coalition could approach the prospect of war with Iraq with such confidence in the air weapon, requires journeying back through time, tracing as briefly as possible the relevant previous history of military air power. We must venture to the skies over Flanders, touch upon the bitter legacy of the Spanish Civil War, visit the strategic and tactical bombing campaigns in Europe, stop in Korea and Indochina, and wade through the morass of the Vietnam quagmire. Having done so, we must next journey into the air wars of the Middle East, and probe the minds of military strategists who reshaped Air Force, Army, and Navy doctrine after Vietnam. We must drop by the laboratories and flight test centers that rebuilt American air power after that war so that it could confront the wars of the future, cognizant always of the decisionmaking world and the world of popular opinion that influenced and shaped air power in the post-Vietnam era. Next we must review the military experiences of the 1970s and 1980s, some sobering tragedies, others encouraging signs of growing strength and confidence. Finally, then, we will be ready to examine the buildup to war and the war itself.

The Great War and the Origins of Air Power Thought

Air power, as a concept, is difficult to define; Winston Churchill took note of this when he stated, "Air power is the most difficult of all forms of military force to measure, or even to express in precise terms." [11] For the purposes of this work, air power shall be considered the *various uses of airborne vehicles and forces to achieve national needs by the projection of military power or presence at a distance*. The First World War generated the missions of air power as well as the first experimentation with comprehensive air doctrine. [12]

The first mission for air warfare, and the one from which all others sprang, was the need for reconnaissance. Before the First World War, various military aviators—usually officers within the cavalry, the traditional reconnaissance branch of the military—had suggested that airplanes could quickly supplant balloons and horses for reconnaissance purposes.[13] (Indeed, it was the anticipated suitability of the airplane for reconnaissance that had led to the U.S. Army Signal Corps specification resulting in the world's first military airplane, the 1908 Wright Military Flyer). Within two months of the opening of the war, aerial reconnaissance had proven its value in the two pivotal battles of the opening months: the battles that set the stage for the war of stalemate that would follow—the First Battle of the Marne, and the Battle of Tannenberg. The obvious value of overhead intelligence and the danger of allowing enemy reconnaissance aircraft to penetrate one's air space led to the introduction of the first rudimentary fighters in 1915, triggering an ever-increasing seesaw battle for air superiority that the Allies eventually won. This air superiority war generated a truth even more significant for our modern world than it was in 1915–18: without control of the skies, an air force cannot profitably fulfill any other mission (be it reconnaissance, support of one's own troops, or long-range bombardment), and no other form of military power—land or sea—can perform effectively either. Control of the skies is critical, and is necessarily the single most important mission for air power.

Before the First World War, apocalyptic literature had forecast that the Zeppelin airship would be used as a long-range bomber of civilian population centers. In fact, this did come to pass, but its city attacks were far less destructive than imagined, and they aroused the fury of bombarded populations rather than compelling surrender and mass demoralization.[14] The increasing vulnerability of these large hydrogen-filled dirigibles also resulted in its replacement by the multi-engine long-range bomber—itself an outgrowth of the long-range reconnaissance airplane.[15] The appearance of the combat airship and long-range bomber marked the emergence of "strategic" aviation—air power delivered at great distances to destroy an enemy's will to resist and means of resistance. (The vulnerability of both to antiaircraft fire and fighters during daylight attacks caused airmen to forego daylight bombing missions for nighttime ones.) If its strategic operations proved less significant than forecasters had predicted, the bomber proved more significant in what are now termed "strike" missions: attacks delivered closer to the front aimed at reducing an enemy's ability to resist by targeting stockpiled goods, shipment points, roads, and rail networks. The development of special-purpose battlefield attack airplanes—themselves outgrowths from frontline observation aircraft—coupled with the appearance of the swing-role bomb-dropping fighter in 1917 meant that air power now could exert an occasionally profound impact on land warfare right at the front itself. By 1918, troops at the front were supported by (or exposed to) close air support (then termed "trench strafing") and battlefield air interdiction (then termed "ground strafing"). Further, intelligence agents were inserted and extracted from enemy territory via aircraft. At sea, aircraft patrolled against submarines and were launched from primitive aircraft carriers in attacks against ships and shore targets. Only the transport for theater and long-range airlift failed to make its appearance in the war, though it did so shortly thereafter, when the Royal Air Force and French air service employed modified bombers for troop transport purposes in various colonial conflicts.

Together with giving military aviation its missions, the First World War triggered the initial explorations of air doctrine. Generally speaking, the Allies had pursued an offensive air doctrine throughout the war that emphasized conducting intensive air operations as deep into enemy territory as practicable. For its part, Imperial Germany followed a defensive air doctrine for its fighters, emphasizing patrolling over German-held territory to prevent Allied incursions, but holding to an offensive doctrine for its airships, long-range bombers, and battlefield attack aircraft—a curious, and fatal, doctrinal split. The Allied doctrine was the superior and more perceptive of the two, and, ironically, echoes of this "debate" can be found in the Gulf war. The United States and Great Britain, for example, had a long tradition of espousing *offensive* air operations, while Iraq clearly showed its Soviet–Warsaw Pact legacy of *defensive* air operations, emphasizing a strong integrated air defense system linking surface-to-air missiles, fighter aircraft, and antiaircraft artillery with comprehensive command and control facilities.[16]

Three major figures emerged in the years after the First World War as champions—indeed, some of their more enthusiastic followers considered them veritable prophets—of offensive air power: Italy's Giulio Douhet, Great Britain's Hugh "Boom" Trenchard, and America's William "Billy" Mitchell. Of these three, Douhet lacked the experience of running air campaigns that Trenchard and Mitchell possessed, but was clearly the most influential, thanks to his book *The Command of the Air* (although it seems to have been more often cited than actually read).[17] Trenchard, with the greatest wartime command experience, was the most perceptive and realistic, with Mitchell (who discussed air power extensively with Douhet during a postwar trip to Italy) the most enthusiastic, if intemperate.[18] Following a career-ending and highly publicized court-martial triggered by his speaking out on air power issues, Mitchell did not retire into obscurity. Rather, he continued to write, his visionary claims for what air power could legitimately accomplish regrettably ignoring the then-immature state of aeronautical technology. For example, he wrote in 1930:

> The advent of air power which can go to the vital centers [of gravity—a pointed reference to the work of the great theorist of war Carl von Clausewitz] and entirely neutralize or destroy them has put a completely new complexion on the old system of war. It is now realized that the hostile main army in the field is a false objective and the real objectives are the vital centers. The old theory that victory meant the destruction of the hostile main army, is untenable. Armies themselves can be disregarded by air power if a rapid strike is made against the opposing centers.[19]

Fifteen years later, one could advance that claim with greater assurance, but it was not until the marriage of long-range global air power with precision weaponry that this claim arguably became reality. Air power execution caught up with air power theory, as evidenced by the conduct and results of the Gulf war, over sixty years later.

Central to the thinking of all three of these men was the compelling vision of the long-range strategic bomber striking deep into enemy territory and destroying both the means and the will to resist. This vision had important results. It was the single, clearly definable mission that airmen could point to as a justification for making military aviation separate from armies and navies. To Trenchard and Douhet, it condoned (to a greater or lesser extent) the concept of terror-bombing civilian populations as a means to destroy morale, and thus set the stage for the horrors of city bombing in World War II. It focused military acquisition in the interwar years on procuring both long-range bombers and the short-range interceptor fighters needed to shoot them down. It tended to minimize other productive methods of air attack, specifically the kind of battlefield and interdiction attacks that had proven surprisingly useful in the First World War and which would prove vitally significant in the Second. As a result of this singular vision of air power, long-range strategic bombardment became endowed with the same apocalyptic exaggeration that had characterized the Zeppelin before the First World War—a dangerous attribute, for it resulted in tremendous overexpectations in the 1930s regarding its effectiveness. (British pre–Second World War estimates predicted fifty casualties per ton of explosive dropped by German planes, while subsequent experience indicated actual casualties averaged less than five.)[20] Finally, it enshrined forever the large, multi-engine strategic bomber as the international *symbol* of air power. This was an assumption fraught with harmful implications for the future. If the bomber proved disappointing and possessed clear limitations (as it must, given the technological limitations of aeronautics in the pre–World War II era), then could not air power itself be perceived as possessing *inherent* limitations? Further, it focused entirely too much attention on only one of air power's many possible roles in warfare.

There were a number of conflicts that served as testing points for air power in the years between 1918 and 1939, as well as profound changes in the nature of aviation technology. The most important of these wars was the Spanish Civil War of 1936–39, which afforded the first major test of post–World War I air power doctrine. The results were mixed. Terror bombing clearly did not crack civilian morale, but it did devastate urban areas. Bombers proved far more vulnerable to enemy defenses than had been originally thought. Fighters demonstrated more versatility than functioning as mere interceptors, and dogfighting—thought to be passé now that aircraft were flying faster than 250 MPH—was alive and well. Battlefield air missions—both what are now termed "close air support" (CAS) and "battlefield air interdiction" (BAI)—proved critically and decisively important throughout the war. Air transport likewise proved indispensable; indeed, Francisco Franco could not have staged his revolt had it not been for timely air transport of his forces across the Strait of Gibraltar.[21]

The Second World War: Much to Criticize, Much to Praise

On the heels of the experience in Spain came the Second World War. In this war, air power functioned at the strategic and tactical level, was integral to the plans of the various national and coalition high commands, was heavily technological in character, and was decisive—though not necessarily in the way that prewar doctrine had predicted. In particular, strategic bombing proved disappointing, characterized by mixed results.

This is an important point, for to most authorities, as well as the public at large, strategic bombing *was* air power; quite naturally, then, a dangerous and unwarranted overreaction occurred after the Second World War that increasingly minimized the importance of air power in future war, with the exception of atomic warfare. Basically, World War II strategic air power—except for the very end of the war—could not fulfill the Douhet-Trenchard-Mitchell over-promises of the 1920s and 1930s; it lacked the accuracy, sustainability, and precision of destruction to completely eliminate an enemy's means of waging war, and it did not shatter an enemy's morale. But although it may have *disappointed*, this is not the same as saying it *failed*.

Nothing so typified the frustration of true believers in air power than Air Marshal Arthur "Bomber" Harris's campaign to destroy Germany's will to resist by a series of ever-costly imprecise night air raids against German population centers by Royal Air Force Bomber Command. The raids—essentially a massive turnabout of the smaller night raids the Luftwaffe had sent over England in the winter of 1940–41—killed hundreds of thousands of German civilians (but precious few war workers and military forces). Brutally effective German air defenses, including radar-directed artillery and night fighters, claimed tens of thousands of RAF bomber crewmen. Late in 1944, when U.S. Army Air Forces's B-17 and B-24 crews demonstrated that precision daylight attacks against the German oil, power, and transportation industries were far more productive and had a demonstrable effect on the capabilities of German frontline forces, Harris still persisted in his belief that victory for Douhet-style air power was just around the corner—all it might take was one more big raid, one more city-gutting. So cathedrals continued to topple and bombers still dissolved in balls of flame, and all to little effect.[22]

Unlike the RAF and the Luftwaffe, the Army Air Forces had placed its faith in mass-formation daylight attacks using the Norden bombsight to hopefully achieve "bomb in a barrel" precision against industrial and military targets. In part, this stemmed from technological, cultural, and ethical influences. As late as 1926 (continuing First World War thought), U.S. bombing doctrine called for German- and British-style night attacks. Then came evidence of the accuracy that could be achieved in daylight attacks, advances in technology (such as the turbosupercharger) that enabled aircraft to fly well above the level of antiaircraft fire, and precise bombsights, particularly the Norden sight. There was the indirect cultural influence of the "American tradition of expert marksmanship," and the ethical "distaste for indiscriminate bombing of civilian areas." [23] Finally, there was a belief that precision air attack best fulfilled the classic principles of land war, which the Air Corps Tactical School (the forerunner of today's Air War College) fully embraced.[24] "Air strategists," historian James L. Cate stated after the war, "considered precision methods to be no more than a refinement of the principle of economy of force which was basic to the whole concept of strategic bombardment." [25]

Thanks to a summation of discrepancies—including the suitability of the bombing aircraft, accuracy limitations of the bombsight itself, the notoriously poor western and northern European weather, the confusion and dispersion that afflicted bomber formations when attacked by fighters as they neared their target, training, and the poor aerodynamic design of contemporary bombs—desired accuracy levels were only rarely achieved. "Precision" proved a relative word; for example, the average miss distance for a 2,000-pound bomb dropped over Germany was 3,300 feet off the aiming point. (Indeed, an Eighth Air Force assessment of its bombing from September through December 1944 concluded that only 7 percent of all bombs dropped hit within 1,000 feet of their aiming point. In contrast, in the Gulf war, "precision" meant hitting within 10 feet of a target.) Even so, however, America's European strategic bombing campaign proved very valuable, particularly in two unexpected ways. Whereas prewar doctrine had anticipated that bomber strikes against key industrial and military targets would be the most useful, the actual experience of the American bomber effort clearly demonstrated that its primary accomplishments had been, first, in luring the Luftwaffe into battle where escorting fighters destroyed it (1942–44), and, second, in targeting the German oil and power industries and transportation network (1944–45). (When the USAAF began the latter strikes, Nazi Armaments Minister Albert Speer wrote, "a new era in the air war began. It meant the end of German armaments production." [26])

In the Pacific, as Prof. Eliot A. Cohen has noted, American strategic bombers and naval aircraft came "remarkably close" to winning the war on their own, even without the atomic bomb. The entire Pacific campaign, in fact, could be interpreted as an effort to secure air bases ever closer to the Japanese home islands for the purposes of projecting long-range air power. "By the spring of 1945," Cohen has written,

American army and naval aviators had demolished Japan's civilian and military industries, sunk most of the Japanese fleet, and established a virtual blockade of the Japanese islands (with the aid of American submarines). Ground and purely naval forces had served mainly to seize and hold forward bases for the projection of air power.[27]

Cohen's conclusions are supported by two close-hand observers who had no doubts about the significance of air power. Japanese Prince Fumimaro Konoye stated bluntly that "the thing that brought about the determination to make peace was the prolonged bombing by the B-29s," and Premier Kantaro Suzuki stated that:

> It seemed to me unavoidable that in the long run Japan would be almost destroyed by air attack so that merely on the basis of the B–29s alone I was convinced that Japan should sue for peace. On top of the B-29 raids came the atomic bomb . . . which was just one additional reason for giving in . . . I myself, on the basis of the B-29 raids, felt that the cause was hopeless.[28]

Unfortunately, postwar critics missed these lessons and instead concentrated on the "failure" of strategic bombing and, by extension, air power itself. Their difficulties in perception seem to have stemmed in large measure from their backgrounds. Many were economists plucked from universities, seeking evidence in economic data to answer what were essentially operational questions demanding trained experts with strong military backgrounds. For example, they looked at large increases in German wartime production as evidence that the bombing campaign had failed, ignoring that much of this production (as revealed by the postwar U.S. Strategic Bombing Survey) went literally nowhere due to the effectiveness of the oil campaign and strikes against the German transportation network. Further, the strategic bombing campaign tied up hundreds of thousands of troops and thousands of antiaircraft weapons in the defense of the Reich that could have been more gainfully employed elsewhere, increasingly skewing German aircraft production toward fighters and interceptors—essentially forcing a *defensive* (i.e., reactive) air posture on Hitler's airmen—and away from the kind of *offensive* striking weapons (such as bombers) that the Nazis really needed as they fought desperately to "win" the war. Neither of these points were ones likely to elicit favorable interpretation by critics obsessed with costs and production numbers.

Further, over time, such continued criticism of strategic bombing led to a remarkably enduring myth: namely, that the postwar Strategic Bombing Survey had concluded that strategic bombing failed. In fact, the report (written by individuals who had no ties to the military aviation community that might have biased their views) concluded the opposite. "Allied air power was decisive in the war in Western Europe," the report summarized. "Hindsight inevitably suggests that it might have been employed differently or better in some respects. Nevertheless, it was decisive." [29] In the Pacific theater, the report stated that combat experience "supports the findings in Germany that no nation can long survive the free exploitation of air weapons over its homeland. For the future it is important fully to grasp the fact that enemy planes enjoying control of the sky over one's head can be as disastrous to one's country as its occupation by physical invasion." Indeed, the report argued that "prior to the European war, *we underestimated the predominant role that air power was to play* and allocated to it too small a share of even the inadequate resources then available to the Army and Navy" (emphasis added). [30]

One use of air power that did prove disappointing in the war was the inability, except under special circumstances, to interdict an enemy's supplies moving toward a front. Air proved most successful in doing this when operating in an antishipping role, coupled with excellent intelligence; the best examples here are the destruction of tankers resupplying Erwin Rommel's Afrika Korps, the Battle of the Bismarck Sea, and the continuous antishipping campaign directed against the Japanese merchant marine. But on land it was a different story. Operation Strangle, an attempt in 1944 to interdict supplies moving down the Italian peninsula, failed to inflict supply denial. Even though large amounts were destroyed, the supplies that did get through were generally sufficient to maintain *Wehrmacht* strength. Its successor, Operation Diadem, combined air- and ground-maneuver warfare much more productively, since the level of fighting forced the Germans into using those supplies that did get through, and the ground-maneuver threat forced German units to come out from cover and reposition themselves, where subsequent air attacks devastated them. The lesson here was an important one, for it demonstrated a synergy between offensive maneuver and air interdiction: in the pre–precision weapon era, the combination of the two was necessary to make each work more effectively. [31]

There was one aspect of Second World War air power that worked extremely well—the concept of the tactical air assault to destroy an enemy's means and will to resist *at the front*. [32] Throughout the war, ground commanders were astonished at how air attack both assisted and hurt them. One commentator remarked that "the air force has become the hammer of modern warfare on land." [33] France's former air minister wrote that the collapse of France "proved that an army can do nothing without the support of an adequate air force." [34] Erwin Rommel, reflecting on the disastrous collapse of his forces in North Africa, wrote that "anyone who has to fight, even with the most modern weapons, against an enemy in complete command of the air, fights like a savage against modern European troops, under the same handicaps and with the same chances of success." [35] His naval aide wrote after the Normandy invasion that air warfare "is the modern type of warfare, turning the flank not from the side but from above." [36] (For his part, invasion commander Gen. Dwight Eisenhower remarked to his son while driving through Normandy, "If I didn't have air supremacy, I wouldn't be here." [37])

Each nation developed its own distinctive style for control and delivery of tactical air power, and the United States, inspired by the British example, issued a document of profound significance in the summer of 1943: field manual FM 100-20, *Command and Employment of Air Power*.[38] It governed the use of air power for the rest of the war, including the extraordinarily successful air-land campaign across France in the late summer of 1944. FM 100-20 lauded the "co-equal and interdependent" nature of both air and land power, and pointedly stated that "neither is an auxiliary of the other." It established three "priorities" of air missions, a ranking basically still followed by the U.S. Air Force today: air superiority, strike, and battlefield air support. As a War Department product, and not just the product of the USAAF, FM 100-20 has been called the Air Force's "Declaration of Independence," and not without good reason. The combination of this document, the AAF's wartime performance, popular pressure encouraged by zealots such as the prolific writer-airman Alexander P. De Seversky, and astute political maneuvering by Gen. Henry H. "Hap" Arnold and the other "visible saints" of American air power meant that the postwar creation of the U.S. Air Force was all but a foregone conclusion.[39]

Douhet Triumphant: The Atomic Era

In 1947, while giving the Lee Knowles Lectures at Cambridge University, Lord Tedder, Eisenhower's former Deputy Supreme Commander, boldly proclaimed the credo of the airman at mid-century when he stated that "I am utterly convinced that the outstanding and vital lesson of the last war is that air power is the dominant factor in this modern world and that, though the methods of exercising it will change, it will remain the dominant factor as long as power determines the fate of nations."[40]

Above all else, World War II had been a technological war; the jet engine, radar, infrared detection devices, long-range radio navigation, pressurized cabins, air-to-ground and air-to-air rockets, the ballistic missile, and the atomic bomb were just some of the numerous technologies introduced, refined, or tested in the crucible of combat. The shocking destructiveness of the atomic bomb, coupled with the evident significance of the long-range airplane, the turbojet revolution, and the new era of electronic warfare just dawning led to some assumptions about the postwar world that proved seriously flawed. One was an overemphasis on *speed* and *atomic weapons.* While most advanced nations suffered from this, the United States proved particularly vulnerable, lured, in the words of one student of air power doctrine, by "technology's Siren song."[41] This song became manifest with the appearance in 1946 of a seminal multivolume document, *Toward New Horizons,* issued by the AAF's scientific advisor, the distinguished Hungarian scientist Theodore von Kármán, at the express request of Hap Arnold.[42]

Whatever else it might have done, the von Kármán report could not substitute for the absence of a realistic planning process for the postwar Air Force. Unfortunately, that is what happened.[43] In the late 1940s, the Air Force became more and more wedded to an atomic and speed-driven future. The strategic bomber fantasies of the 1920s and 1930s returned, now substituting nuclear weapons for chemical and conventional ones. The atomic bomb could achieve the destructive impact upon an enemy government that prewar enthusiasts had forecast for conventional precision attack, though at the price of horrendous civilian casualties. With the turn toward atomic warfare, American military air power doctrine took a profound step away from the thoughtful legacy of Mitchell, embracing instead the terrible visions of Douhet (and not fully returning to the Clausewitz-based Mitchell model until the late 1980s). As a result, the United States essentially disestablished its tactical air forces in the years between 1945 and 1950. Air power enthusiasts intemperately predicted a new world of air power in which long-range missiles, "robot aircraft," and bombers would decide future wars, armies would exist to occupy atom bomb–devastated territory, and navies would exist to get them there. (Such arguments proliferated in the bitter roles and missions debates of the late 1940s when the Navy and Air Force went to battle to secure control of the atomic power projection mission.) A number of popular works brought this message to the public, particularly De Seversky's *Air Power: Key to Survival,* which, if it did not achieve the popularity of his earlier *Victory through Air Power,* nevertheless received widespread attention and flamboyantly carried the torch for strategic air power into the nuclear age.[44]

One might have expected that Korea would have restored a measure of rationality to postwar defense thinking, but, alas, it did not. Although it did result in a brief renewed interest in tactical air power issues—for example, Tactical Air Command was established at the end of 1950—the war generally was considered as the "exception" to the anticipated normative war of the future—atomic conflict.[45] The rapid proliferation of atomic and eventually thermonuclear weapons within the stockpiles of the United States and the Union of Soviet Socialist Republics (USSR), and the urgency accompanying development of the first American nuclear-tipped ballistic missiles tended to confirm this expectation.[46] Professional journals issued by the various military services drove the message home with articles that extolled the use of atomic weapons in a wide range of conflict situations, including what would now be considered limited wars.[47] Indeed, atomic enthusiasm even encouraged thinking about developing nuclear-powered aircraft, a multi-billion-dollar technological dead-end as well as a project of dubious safety and utility.[48]

Thus, after Korea—which had involved a whole range of air power issues demanding World War II–style solutions—there was a "return to normalcy" within air power circles, normalcy being defined as a renewed emphasis on atomic air war, postulation of a "robot aircraft" future, emphasis upon intercontinental ballistic missiles and bombers, research aimed at futuristic multisonic exotic aircraft such as the Mach 3 + XB-70A strategic bomber and F-108 interceptor, and the Dyna-Soar orbital boost-glider, which grew out of futuristic global rocket bomber studies. Interservice cooperation and doctrinal development, such as that undertaken since 1975 by the joint AirLand Forces Application (ALFA) agency established by the U.S. Air Force Tactical Air Command (TAC) and U.S. Army Training and Doctrine Command (TRADOC), were essentially unknown. The carefully honed expertise of air support faded from disuse, to be rediscovered at no little cost in Southeast Asia a decade later. Under the rubric "New Look," nuclear warfare contingency planning predominated. By 1955, as some noted ruefully, TAC had been "SACumcized," itself taking on a nuclear attack mission. (Indeed, in 1957, Gen. Curtis E. LeMay proposed combining Strategic Air Command [SAC] and TAC into a single nuclear-oriented "Air Offensive Command.")[49]

Naturally, this afflicted the aircraft acquisition process as well. The swing-role air-to-air and air-to-ground fighter that had proven so valuable in the Second World War all but disappeared; the post-Korean "Century series" fighters of the 1950s—the first American supersonic jet fighters—increasingly diverged from the realities of doctrinal and military need, ultimately being split between antibomber interceptors and atomic-bomb-armed "strike" fighters. Of the 5,525 Century series produced—the F-100, F-101, F-102, F-104, F-105, and F-106—only the very first, the F-100, was a true swing-role fighter, designed with the real lessons of the Second World War and the fresh experience of Korea in mind.[50]

The real-world "normalcy" of the post–Korean War era was, of course, more of the same: disturbing and nagging limited wars unsuited to the massive employment of air power on the lines of the World War II experience, let alone atomic weaponry. In these conflicts, air power proved disappointing. In Korea, it had been unable to prevent the delivery of supplies from China and North Korea to the front. Further, there were no real "strategic" targets worthy of the name. In battlefield air support and tactical air power, it was a very different matter; UN air power over the battlefield contributed significantly to saving the South from two major invasions in 1950–51, and helped reduce UN casualties along the front to the armistice in 1953.[51] But in Indochina, air power was simply not present in the strength necessary to assist meaningfully the French fighting to hang on and, in any case, the French cause was dubious from the start. Dien Bien Phu fell in 1954 following a desperate air resupply and support effort that collapsed in the face of withering antiaircraft fire.[52] Combined air and ground action proved significant, though not overwhelming, in ending terrorist threats in Malaya and Kenya, and in the French struggle in Algeria where, for the first time, armed helicopters made an appearance over the battlefield. While all of these actions drew attention in the United States, the fixation on strategic nuclear war remained paramount long after it should have faded and, in fact, remained in place until well after the onset of the Kennedy administration in 1961. At that time, President Kennedy and his secretary of defense, Robert McNamara, began a reshaping of American defense policy. McNamara boosted the expansion of conventional forces, made the Air Force acquire more suitable multimission aircraft than the overspecialized and limited

Century series—this resulted in the excellent McDonnell F-4 Phantom II and Vought A-7 Corsair entering Air Force service, as well as the troublesome F-111—and emphasized development of a so-called counterinsurgency philosophy in the American military. It would be nice to be able to state that all this worked out very well, but, of course it did not. The result was a major shock that spawned further (and often unjust) denigration of air power: the war in Vietnam.

Vietnam: Misuse Generates Misunderstanding

It is a truism to state that the long and tortuous war in Vietnam profoundly wounded the United States.[53] It shattered one administration, triggered the greatest national wave of protests since the Civil War, profoundly demoralized the American military establishment, and left behind what some called a "Vietnam syndrome," others a "paradigm," that nearly two decades later threatened to cripple any attempt to halt Saddam Hussein's aggression in the Gulf. Central to this notion was the idea that Vietnam had demonstrated the futility of military action; as Joshua Muravchik has written, the Vietnam paradigm

> included the idea that the use of force had lost its utility. Even small countries, it seemed, could find the means to thwart large ones. This was held to be especially true for America because of the peculiar ineptness of our armed forces, which were hopelessly top-heavy and paralyzed by inter-service rivalry. And even in the unlikely event that America could employ force successfully, we would so alienate other people that the victory was bound to be pyrrhic. Further, economic power had become more important than military power, and the costs of arms and war made the whole undertaking almost inevitably self-defeating.[54]

When critics of action in the Gulf spoke out over the fall and winter of 1990−91 (particularly in Congress), they talked less in terms of the Gulf crisis itself and more in reference to Vietnam. Vietnam dominated the debate and was the yardstick by which the Gulf was measured. Would the military do better than . . . *Vietnam?* Would we become bogged down as in . . . *Vietnam?* Would the Gulf trigger massive antiwar protests as had . . . *Vietnam?* Would the Gulf war trigger casualties on the order of . . . *Vietnam?*

Vietnam revealed very disturbing problems within the military establishment: increasing drug and alcohol abuse; profound deterioration of race relations leading, in some cases, to outright riots and mutinies aboard ship; "fragging" incidents of unpopular officers and NCOs; poor military and civilian leadership; and (fortunately very infrequently) ethical breakdowns such as My Lai. As a result, while many in America's military came out of the Vietnam War with supreme confidence in their own abilities and those of their comrades, they had profound uncertainty about the ability of their service, the Department of Defense, and/or the government in general to achieve military goals, and little or no confidence in the American people to support them. Their experiences, the existing political climate, and fashionable social opinion all reinforced their fears and, indeed, bred disillusionment. Although too much can be made of it, it is nevertheless important to remember that returning Vietnam veterans were advised to change out of uniform before they arrived back in the States lest they be vilified.[55] Occasionally, violent protests ranged across college campuses, and prudent ROTC students and instructors generally wore their uniforms only when inside their own classrooms. Such experiences inculcated an attitude of mistrust that manifested itself in bitterness toward senior military and civilian leadership. But those same experiences also drove a zealous desire for internal reform. One Vietnam-era officer, when asked by a prominent American military correspondent whether he would stay in the Army, said "I'm going to stay with the Army, but if I have anything to do with it, it's going to be a different Army. Vietnam had one good result: It's made us question the way things have been done." [56]

So Vietnam's impact on the American military was dramatic. One had only to lecture or teach in the professional military schools in the 1980s—the Army War College, the Air War College, and Naval War College, for example—to immediately sense how their experiences had convinced most professional soldiers, airmen, and sailors to never expect subordinates to fight in the circumstances they themselves had fought in. Simply put, most military professionals believed that the Vietnam War had been ineptly conceived and badly run. Worse, many believed that their senior commanders had broken faith with their own services in not taking issue with some of the more egregious presidential, state, and defense decisions regarding the conduct of the war.[57]

One key point of contention was the issue of gradualism; nowhere was this more criticized than among the airmen who had flown in the war, for they were the ones who paid the price—sometimes with their lives, sometimes with years of brutal captivity, sometimes with both. Every major strategist and theorist of war, from Sun Tzu through Carl von Clausewitz and Henri Jomini, recognized that military force should be applied decisively, not as a means of sending signals. Yet that is what happened in Vietnam, and particularly in the case of air power: Lyndon Johnson, Robert McNamara, Dean Rusk, and George W. Ball—respectively the president, secretary of defense, and secretary and undersecretary of state—fought an air war to send signals and messages (all the while being overly concerned that U.S. actions not cause the North Vietnamese an excessive loss of prestige!) while the North Vietnamese fought to win.[58] (This led to a cynically apt Air Force aphorism after Vietnam: "If you want to send a message, call Western Union.") So air power was misused in Vietnam, with that misuse often clouding results attributed to the limits *of* air power when they really stemmed from limits *on* air power. Air power therefore was subjected to further belittling and denigration in the years after the war, and (perhaps even worse) was not recognized for what it *had* done well in the war.[59] Over two decades later, decisionmakers—both military and political—were still arguing whether or not air power could actually be relied upon should the UN coalition go to war against Iraq, failing to recognize that it was its misuse—a product of the purposes to which it was employed in Vietnam and the organization and tactics of its usage—that created this image of "failure."

There was another serious problem: officials thousands of miles away from the scene of combat directed the active day-to-day conduct of air warfare at the operational and tactical levels of war. This reflected the managerial style of both Lyndon Johnson and his secretary of defense, and, unfortunately, set a pattern and established a legacy for subsequent management practices that lasted through the 1970s and even into the first years of the 1980s, as Desert One and the Marine bombing in Beirut showed. Individual targets and rules of engagement were selected and established at White House luncheons each Tuesday, and seemingly added, dropped, restricted, or qualified for the most ephemeral of reasons. In one case, as a result of a Tuesday luncheon, "pilots learned that they had authority to strike moving targets such as convoys and troops, but could not attack highways, railroads, or bridges with no moving traffic on them." [60]

Not all problems were caused exclusively by the political climate, however. It was in Vietnam that the shortsightedness of overemphasizing nuclear war–fighting became most apparent. Aircraft designed for a nuclear war environment—such as the Republic F-105, intended to carry a single nuclear bomb deep into enemy territory—now had to be hastily modified to fulfill conventional missions. How to run a strategic air campaign day after day in the face of intensive enemy opposition had to be relearned for the war in the North, as did the operational art and techniques for a tactical air support campaign in the South. To prosecute the counterinsurgency war in the South, the Air Force modified trainers as strike airplanes, upgraded World War II–vintage bombers and transports, and bought quantities of the Navy's propeller-driven A-1 attack airplane. Planners divided North Vietnam into a series of "route packages," for which the various services had strike responsibility, contributing to a dilution of the air effort and the perception of "Air Force" and "Navy" targets. There was a severe bomb shortage, for in the nuclear era, many conventional "iron" bombs had been sold for salvage. At one point, the United States had to buy 5,000 discarded 750-pound bombs back from West Germany, which had purchased them as scrap for $8,500; the Department of Defense bought them back for *$105,000.*[61]

Obsessed with measures of merit, Defense Department officials and service chiefs settled on two that quickly became goals in and of themselves: body counts for the ground war and sortie rates for the air war. Artificial means were pursued to inflate both; to keep sortie rates high in the midst of the bomb shortage, aircraft were sometimes launched with a single bomb or two, unnecessarily endangering multiple crews and reducing the amount of lethal force an individual aircraft could bring to bear on its target. High-performance jet aircraft proved vulnerable to antiaircraft fire and surface-to-air missiles (SAMs). (So unanticipated had this latter threat been—even though a SAM had claimed Francis Gary Powers's U-2 in 1960—that when American strike aircraft began operating over the North, they lacked even rudimentary radar and SAM warning receivers.) The SAM threat forced an increased reliance on electronic protection and suppression, coupled with antiradar missiles to destroy launch sites.[62] Worse, in the air war over North Vietnam, both the Air Force and Navy experienced disturbing losses to enemy fighters. In comparison to an 8 to 1 victory-loss ratio in World War II and a 10 to 1 ratio in Korea, the United States mustered no better than a 2.4 to 1 ratio over North Vietnam, and for a while it was roughly 1 to 1. These losses stemmed from three reasons: fighting under the limitations of politically determined rules of engagement; the poor air-combat training of American pilots (in one fighter squadron, only four of thirty pilots had ever had any aerial gunnery practice); and the unsuitability of many American aircraft, designed for anticipated nuclear war interception or strike missions, to engage in the swirling "furball" dogfights of Southeast Asia.[63]

What Went Right

There were a number of things that went right in the Vietnam air war that critics often missed or chose to ignore. In the spring of 1972, decisive use of air power (including antitank missile-firing helicopters and laser-guided bombs) destroyed North Vietnam's hopes for victory during the Easter invasion of the South.[64] Then, of course, came the December 1972 Linebacker II offensive (an integrated air offensive of a sort never previously tried in the war). It shattered North Vietnam's air defense network; more significantly, its results, combined with the failure of the Easter invasion earlier, compelled the North Vietnamese government to return to the Paris peace talks and sign an agreement within a month.[65] The introduction of helicopter gunships and the unquestionable success of heliborne air assault tactics resulted in a reshaping of Army thought and started a process of doctrinal examination that would eventually lead to the Army's notion of AirLand Battle in the 1980s.[66] Airlift within the war zone and to Southeast Asia from the United States worked extremely well. Tactical airlifters—C-123s, C-130s, and ex-Army C-7s, with a smattering of helicopters—moved 7 million tons of cargo and passengers over the ten-year war, including 42,000 tons in a one-month period in May 1967.[67] "Smart weapons," experimented with during the Second World War and Korea, made a major appearance midway through the war, proving their ability to destroy targets precisely and thus obviating the need for often costly return sorties. (Nowhere was this more evident than when laser-guided bombs destroyed the infamous Thanh Hoa bridge in May 1972; its defenses had claimed many strike aircraft dropping conventional bombs over the previous seven years.) Reputedly, of 21,000 laser-guided bombs dropped in Vietnam, 17,000 scored direct hits on their targets, generating an impressive 80-percent success rate for this innovative weapon.[68]

Throughout the war, air-ground warfare was a standout success. On a number of occasions, battlefield air support saved hamlets and outposts that might otherwise have fallen to the Viet Cong. The most notable of these was the Marine encampment at Khe Sanh; had it fallen, it would have had the same devastating political impact as Dien Bien Phu fifteen years earlier.[69] When the extensive involvement of American ground forces in Vietnam began, there were precious few air-support resources available for them; within several years all this had changed. The Army went to battle by helicopter, and those helicopters were themselves protected by attack helicopters. The Air Force, Navy, and Marines supported ground operations with a wide range of aircraft, including the A-1, A-4, A-6, A-7, and A-37 attack aircraft; F-4, F-5, F-8, F-100, and F-105 fighter-bombers; B-52 and B-57 bombers; AC-47, AC-119, and AC-130 gunships; and orbiting O-1, O-2, and OV-10 forward air control (FAC) aircraft directed air strikes. Virtually every spot in South Vietnam was within a fifteen-minute jet flight by aircraft, for the countryside contained a number of jet bases: Binh Thuy, Bien Hoa, Tan Son Nhut, Phan Rang, Phu Cat, Chu Lai, and Da Nang. So great was the volume of aerial firepower present that when ground forces were engaged in combat, they often elected to hunker down, call in all available air support (both from their own service, and from the Air Force, Navy, or Marines), artillery as well, and wait for the dust to settle.[70] In a post-Vietnam Army survey of generals, only 2 percent rated Army–Air Force cooperation "unsatisfactory"; instead, fully 60 percent rated it "excellent."[71]

Perhaps the best words on what timely air intervention could mean are those of an Army troop commander and an unidentified "grunt," both of whom had personal experience with what air power could do. "I learned after a while," the officer stated, "that my casualties were tremendously decreased if I used the air power and air strikes and used [them] properly. And it was there to use."[72] The GI put it on a more personal level:

> When you're . . . pinned down under fire, and here comes the Air Force and they just drop the bombs right where they belong and they knock out what they are supposed to knock out . . . It's a fantastic feeling. It's more than thanks. You just can't express it, really.[73]

Two major concepts of air-ground warfare received their "baptism of fire" in Vietnam: the "airmobile" movement of troops on a large scale, and the helicopter and fixed-wing "gunship." Further, for the first time, air attackers routinely directed precision-guided weapons against ground forces, including tanks. In 1962, the Army established the Army Tactical Mobility Requirements Board, presided over by Lt. Gen. Hamilton H. Howze, and thus known to history more familiarly as the Howze Board. Rather than view his mandate from the secretary of defense as just to find a new means of shipping soldiers to battle, Howze chose instead to see if advanced air mobility could enable Army forces to assume the functions of flying cavalry, emphasizing shock and firepower. In an era of generally lackluster leadership, Howze and his board (including the distinguished aircraft designer Edward H. Heinemann) were extraordinarily prescient, and forecast many of the critical technology items that appeared in time for the Gulf war—"drone" observation systems (now termed "unmanned air vehicles"), airborne targeting and location systems, and precise position-fixing systems and high-resolution radars (for the latter, think of the present Global Positioning System and the JSTARS system that functioned so well in the Gulf). But more significantly than these, the Howze Board structured a series of theoretical airmobile units that could function as the cavalry traditionally had: exploiting, pursuing, counterattacking, delaying, and protecting flanks. The Howze Board's work eventually led to the operational testing of two formations (an air assault division and an air transport brigade) in 1962, their war game evaluation in 1964, and deployment to Vietnam in 1965 of the air assault division as the 1st Cavalry Division (Airmobile).[74]

The "Air Cav" baptized itself in the bloody and protracted Ia Drang Valley battle, and its success both in that battle and subsequent engagements went a long way toward establishing a permanent airmobile cast upon the U.S. Army.[75] To give some example of how prominently air figured in the Army's scheme of maneuver and operations, one need only note that the service's 1st Aviation Brigade at one point had no fewer than 641 airplanes, 441 Bell AH-1 Cobra attack helicopters, 311 Boeing Chinook cargo helicopters, 635 observation helicopters, and no fewer than 2,202 Bell UH-1 utility helicopters. Indeed, when one thinks of the Army presence in Vietnam, it is not so much the World War II image of the "grunt" in the mud, but the image of the airborne assault that comes to mind.[76]

That the Army could rely as much as it did upon the helicopter was due to remarkable advances in the capabilities of these awkward-looking machines. The development of the lightweight gas-turbine helicopter engine in the late 1950s vastly increased the power available to helicopters, making possible longer range and higher payload. The Army settled on two basic types: the Bell UH-1 utility helicopter (dubbed the "Huey"), and the heavier and larger Boeing-Vertol CH-47 Chinook. (Later models of both of these workhorse machines served in the Gulf war.) The Huey served as a troop transport, medical evacuation helicopter, and armed "gunship," carrying rocket pods and machine guns. But the armed Huey lacked the speed and agility to be a true attack helicopter, and therefore Bell modified the basic design extensively, creating a two-seat streamlined gunship called the AH-1 Cobra that first flew in 1965. The Cobra had a gunner and a pilot, a swiveling nose turret with a minigun and grenade launcher, and stub wings that could carry rocket or gun pods. In every respect the Cobra can be considered the direct ancestor of the multitudinous antiarmor helicopter gunships in the world's armies today. As with the Huey, later models of the Cobra served in the Gulf with the Marines and the Army.[77]

The Cobra gunship, although vulnerable to automatic weapons fire and (later) SA-7 shoulder-fired missiles, proved a devastating fire support system in Vietnam (particularly during the bitter fighting in 1972), and its early and rapid success encouraged the Army to proceed with development of an "Advanced Aerial Fire Support System." The AAFSS became the abortive Lockheed AH-56A Cheyenne gunship, an important interim step on the road to the present-day Hughes-McDonnell-Douglas AH-64A Apache that worked so well in the Gulf war. Equally devastating, though very different, were the fixed-wing gunships introduced in Vietnam: the AC-47, AC-119, and AC-130. These modified transports, initially intended as hamlet defenders using batteries of side-firing machine guns, gradually evolved into sophisticated aerial-fire support systems carrying a variety of optical and electronic sensors, light cannon, and even modified 105mm howitzers, operating deep into enemy territory on interdiction missions against the Ho Chi Minh trail network. The four-engine AC-130E Pave Spectre was one of three weapons singled out as unqualified successes by Army Gen. Creighton W. Abrams, Jr., commander of the U.S. Military Assistance Command in Vietnam, when he commented on the efficacy of air support during the 1972 North Vietnamese spring invasion (the others were the helicopter-fired TOW antiarmor missile, and the guided "smart" bomb). Like the helicopter gunship, the fixed-wing gunship continued in service and development after the Vietnam War, seeing combat in such subsequent engagements as the *Mayaguez* rescue mission, Grenada, Panama, and the Gulf war.[78]

Reinforcement of Misperception: The Middle East

Before American involvement in Vietnam ended, a number of changes were underway to reshape military aviation; these did not occur in an isolated fashion within just the United States, for the Vietnamese air war was one that drew the worldwide attention of military establishments.[79] Critics unfavorably compared it to another air war of the 1960s, one that went profoundly differently—the Arab-Israeli war of 1967. Numerous differences existed in the basic conditions under which the Vietnam and Middle East wars were fought; Vietnam really was *two* air wars, a counterinsurgency war in the South and a limited Korean-style (but with even more constraints) air war "up North." In contrast, the 1967 Middle East war was a war of national survival. Israel's small (but superbly equipped, led, maintained, and trained) air force destroyed the air forces of three Arab states—Egypt, Syria, and Jordan—in essentially a day of concentrated air attacks, shooting 58 out of the air and blasting approximately 450 others on the ground. Then, having secured air supremacy, Israel went on to devastate their land forces with tactical air strikes and combined arms air-land warfare.[80] Critics simplistically compared the performance of the Israelis with the United States in Southeast Asia and snidely belittled the abilities of American soldiers and airmen; it was unfair, of course, for these same critics neglected to compare the rules of engagement and circumstances under which the United States fought in Asia and the Israelis fought in the Middle East. For example, the Vietnam War was already an intensive electronic and antimissile air war, and the Middle East war was a largely nonelectronic, nonmissile one. In effect, the 1967 Arab-Israeli war had been the last great pre–missile era air war, for even though Egypt and Israel had substantial numbers of missile batteries, they played virtually no role in the war.[81] Therefore, the war had demonstrated how, in the absence of the new surface-to-air and air-to-air missile threat, conventional air power could devastate land forces in a manner that calls to mind the recent success of the UN coalition operating—in the missile era—against Iraqi forces in the Gulf.

The Middle East conflict made evident a larger truth not lost on airmen in many nations. The success of the Israeli air force indicated what could be accomplished when a nation's decisionmakers authorized a modern, properly led, equipped, and maintained air force to go to war *as it saw fit* even against multiple strong opponents. Another was a lesson for the losers: seeing how vulnerable they had been, Egypt and Syria opted to reform and reshape their military according to the tightly structured Soviet–Warsaw Pact model. In particular, both emphasized creating elaborate integrated air defense networks, with internetted warning and control stations; multiple-layered fixed and mobile SAM sites using a diverse group of missiles; massive amounts of conventional antiaircraft artillery; and interceptors following Soviet-style ground-controlled inter-cept (GCI) procedures. Looking to the relative success of North Vietnam in constraining American air operations over the North—and underesti-mating the degree to which that constraint was self-imposed by bad American decisionmaking—the two Arab nations determined to rely upon their new integrated air defense networks to confront future Israeli attackers.[82] (The relative success Egypt and Syria subsequently enjoyed as a result of this air defense reshaping inspired the even more formidable air defense network Saddam Hussein installed in Iraq.) Things would be very different in the future.

But the intricacies and differences of the 1967 Arab-Israeli war to that of Vietnam, as with the successes of the Southeast Asian air war, were not evident to the public, and were unappreciated or ignored by the media (they remain so, for the most part, even today).[83] Largely unaware of the on-again off-again nature of the Vietnam air war and its serious organi-zational problems (at least up to 1972), the public could hardly be blamed if they accepted simplistic interpretations: namely, that "technol-ogy" had "failed," that U.S. bombing (including false allegations of B-52s "carpet-bombing" downtown Hanoi in 1972) was indiscriminate, had accomplished nothing, and unforgivably killed large numbers of innocent civilians. Historians have generally and uncritically accepted this view themselves; consider Loren Baritz's statement that "over and over again we have to learn the lesson that air power cannot win wars, and having learned it we immediately forget it."[84] This latter view became a veritable article of faith among anti–air power extremists, and was dusted off again in the weeks and months before Desert Storm.[85]

Two

Rebuilding Air Superiority

The contest for air superiority is the most

important contest of all, for no other

operations can be sustained if this battle is

lost. To win it we must have the best

equipment, the best tactics, the freedom to

use them, and the best pilots.

Gen. William W. Momyer, USAF (1978)

In the years between Vietnam and the mid-1980s, the military services totally rebuilt American air superiority, with profound changes in training and technology. Vietnam shocked the American fighter community because it demonstrated the basic unsuitability of the Century series (and the newer F-4 Phantom II) for hard-maneuvering air combat against even older generation MiGs, such as the MiG-17, and revealed serious inadequacies in weapons, training, and tactics. After every previous war, "experts" had predicted that the era of dogfighting was over, that future aircraft would use speed and weapons to render maneuvering dogfights a thing of the past. And in each case, they were proven wrong.[1] During the Korean War, the Navy relied upon Air Force F-86 fighters to protect their strike forces from marauding MiG-15s. After the war, shocked by the technological superiority of the MiG (which had been offset only by superior Navy and Marine pilot training), Navy planners pushed development of two superlative aircraft. These, the F-8 Crusader for air superiority fighting, and the F-4 Phantom II for fleet air defense and secondary strike duties, represented the two sides of a doctrinal divide beginning to split the fighter world: whether to build highly maneuverable "traditional" gunfighters (the F-8), or whether instead to build "missile plat-forms" (the F-4) designed to take missile shots against relatively benign targets such as intercontinental and maritime patrol bombers. Ironically, the Air Force, which had functioned superbly in Korea (its F-86s estab-lished a 10 to 1 victory-loss ratio over the MiG-15, and sometimes it approached 14 to 1), turned away from the notion of dogfighting in the years after the war. The F-104, which began in response to Korean fighter veterans' calls for a cheap, lightweight, maneuverable high-performance fighter to confront future generations of MiGs, evolved instead into a specialized Mach 2+ interceptor on one hand, and a low-level nuclear strike fighter on the other. Such was true of the majority of the Century series. Only the F-100 was a true fighter-bomber in the tradition of the P-47 or F-84 of previous wars, because it had been developed during the Korean War specifically to fulfill the swing-role air-to-air and air-to-ground mission.[2]

By the early 1960s, however, the F-100 was rapidly aging; further, even in its heyday, it constituted only a marginal match for its nearest Soviet equivalent, the MiG-19, which itself, by 1960, was giving way to the later MiG-21. The Tactical Air Command (TAC) had wanted to re-place the F-100 with the F-105, but McNamara wisely recognized that the service really required a much more flexible multirole airplane. He directed the Air Force to acquire the F-4 and, eventually, the Air Force would purchase 2,675 of this big twin-engine two-seat Mach 2 fighter-bomber for its own use. Complementing the F-4 would be Air Force squadrons of a Navy-developed light attack aircraft, the Vought A-7, also to replace the F-100, but for the close air support of Army forces. Tactical Air Command took to the F-4 and A-7 with some initial reluctance that soon disappeared as the capabilities of the two warplanes became appar-ent.[3] Vietnam demonstrated that the acquisition of the F-4 had come just in time, for the F-4 bore the brunt of the air-superiority war over the North, both for the Air Force and for the Navy. Initially, the results were anything but encouraging. While the F-8 had a 6 to 1 victory-loss ratio over North Vietnamese fighters, the F-4 had a 2 to 1 ratio early in the war, and—even after drastic improvements in pilot training—only a combined USAF-USN exchange rate of 3.38 to 1 at the end of it. Discon-certingly, all too many of the losses of F-4s, F-105s, etc., were coming at the hands of Korean War–vintage MiG-17s.[4]

What had gone wrong? Some problems were clearly related to design, others to weapons, and still others to training and tactics. Together they produced a synergy of disappointment. Phantom II crews attempting to maneuver with a transonic fighter such as the MiG-17, not surprisingly, found that their big fighter, designed for supersonic performance, simply was neither as maneuverable nor as agile as the lighter, smaller MiG. Further, if they did manage to close on a MiG, the systems operator in the aft cockpit (called a radar intercept officer [RIO] in the Navy, and a weapons system officer [WSO] in the Air Force) had an extremely difficult time setting up a missile shot, thanks to poor equipment location. Even the pilot had to go back and forth between a "heads down" and "heads up" scan. The pilot lacked a cannon to fire at his opponent unless his F-4 was carrying drag-inducing external gun pods. (The F-4E model, introduced toward the end of the war, rectified this shortcoming, and also introduced other aerodynamic and equipment improvements to make it a better dogfighter.) Finally, the F-4's J79 engines were notorious smokers—the smoke trail of an F-4 pointed like an accusing finger at the fighter, robbing it of inconspicuousness.

If the F-4 was the bow, its air-to-air missiles were the arrows: the radar-guided or infrared (heat-seeking) models of the AIM-4 Falcon, the radar-homing AIM-7 Sparrow, and the infrared AIM-9 Sidewinder. An F-4 could carry four Sparrows, and either four Falcons or four Sidewinders. Only Air Force F-4s carried the Falcon, designed primarily as a weapon to be used against bombers; it proved unsuitable for fighter-versus-fighter air combat and quickly disappeared. Eventually, like their Navy and Marine counterparts, Air Force F-4s carried four Sidewinders in addition to their four Sparrows, but even these had their share of problems. Sparrows and a few Falcons accounted for approximately 60 percent of all missiles launched against North Vietnamese fighters, but achieved only 42 percent of the kills. The better-performing Sidewinder accounted for approximately 40 percent of all missiles launched, but claimed 58 percent of all North Vietnamese fighters destroyed.[5]

Undoubtedly, the missile results were a disappointment. The Sidewinder, Sparrow, and Falcon had been under development since the early 1950s, and much was expected of them—but once again, planners had anticipated that they would be used primarily against relatively gently maneuvering large radar-reflective and bright heat–source targets such as Soviet Bear, Bison, and Badger bombers. The "one missile, one kill" expectation that governed their development went by the board in Vietnam, and even public affairs officers stopped automatically fixing the appellation "deadly" before their names. The Sidewinder had the distinction of being the world's first air-to-air guided missile to see combat service, debuting spectacularly during the 1958 Taiwan Straits crisis when Chinese Nationalist Air Force F-86s emerged victorious from dogfights with vastly larger MiG-17 formations. But the Nationalists had been aided by the obvious poor training and tactics of their adversaries, who neither maneuvered much (thus allowing the Sidewinder's infrared sensor to "dwell" on them long enough to establish a lock) nor showed discipline or teamwork.[6] The North Vietnamese were very different. A hard-maneuvering MiG-17 taxed the ability of a tracking Sparrow or Sidewinder to follow it. The missile generally had to pull at least four times the "g" of a maneuvering fighter to intercept it; therefore, a missile tracking a MiG pulling 6.5g would have to pull over 25g, risking stalling itself out and tumbling.[7] Further, the MiG-17 and MiG-21 presented small radar targets for Sparrows and Falcons, and the MiG-17's high tail location shielded its infrared emissions from homing Sidewinders approaching from above and behind.

So it is not surprising that many fighter crews fired missiles at MiGs and then watched in frustration as the missiles "went stupid." In many cases they had been launched out of parameters, or were defeated by the agile MiG. Others, disturbingly, failed to track for seemingly no reason; some stemmed from quality control failures during production, or from poor maintenance and handling procedures—for example, loading trailers of fragile missiles and then driving them over washboard-style roads on their way to "loading up" on fighters.[8]

No Second Place: Rediscovering Air Combat Fundamentals

Training and tactics constituted more easily remedied difficulties, but still offered plenty of challenges. Phantom II crews learned not to dogfight on the MiG's terms, but instead to use the Phantom's strengths, particularly tremendous power that enabled it to excel in the vertical plane. F-4s switched to slashing attacks in much the same fashion that P-38 pilots in the southwest Pacific learned how to deal with the nimble Zero in World War II. (The situation was directly comparable; at first the P-38 had not done particularly well against the Zero, but after adaptation of what would now be called energy maneuverability, the P-38 became a fearsome opponent.) In 1968, the Navy took the first steps toward revamping the curriculum of American fighter pilot training. Naval Air Systems Command requested that Capt. Frank Ault, a distinguished Navy fighter and attack pilot, study the causes for the Navy's poor performance over North Vietnam. The resulting Ault Report faulted missile performance, rules of engagement, and training. It recommended a return to basics: practicing air combat maneuvering (ACM). VF-121, a F-4 fighter training squadron, developed an interim curriculum and graduated its first "Fighter Ph.Ds" in March 1969. Over the next three years, its graduates proved the program in the skies over Hanoi, their victory-loss ratios reaching 12 to 1 at war's end. Out of this modest beginning came the formalized "Top Gun" Fighter Weapons School at Miramar Naval Air Station, opened in 1972, which has graduated classes of superbly trained fighter crews ever since.[9]

The Air Force followed the Navy's example and established an "aggressor" training squadron as part of the Air Force Fighter Weapons School in October 1972, just months before the end of the war; before this, the service made do with exchange training visits between Navy and Air Force fighter squadrons. The results at times were disconcerting. One F-8 pilot detailed to an Air Force Phantom II base in Thailand in August 1972 to play "MiG" found the experience disturbing:

> The sight that remains in my mind from this experience is a chilling one, for any number of MiG pilots must have seen identical views: the pitiful spectacle of four super aircraft in front of you all tucked in close finger-four [formation], pulling a level turn. An Atoll [Soviet heat-seeking missile] fired anywhere in parameters would find itself in the position of the proverbial mosquito in the nudist colony. It would hardly know where to begin.[10]

Air Force training changes went into effect too late to have a major impact on the service's own performance in the war, but in the post-Vietnam era, the service aggressively revamped and reemphasized air combat training at the Tactical Fighter Weapons Center at Nellis Air Force Base. Both the Air Force and Navy curriculums stressed training fighter crews to function together as a team and to deal with "1 v 1" and "2 v many" air combat situations. In this quest for basics, the fighter instructors at Miramar and Nellis ranged across the spectrum of air combat history, drawing tactics and perspective from the fighter greats of previous conflicts: Oswald Boelcke, Edward "Mick" Mannock, and Manfred von Richthofen of the First World War; Johnnie Johnson, John Thach, Werner Moelders, Dick Bong, and Erich Hartmann of the Second; Frederick "Boots" Blesse of Korea; and Robin Olds of Vietnam. Of particular value was the rediscovery and reimplementation (allowing for changes forced by the missile era) of Boots Blesse's legendary fighter manual, *No Guts, No Glory.*[11]

The Air Force may have been slower than the Navy to implement a revised training curriculum for its fighter pilots and WSOs, but it went considerably beyond its sister service in establishing mass strike package training for attack forces with the creation of "Red Flag." TAC commander Gen. Robert Dixon established the so-called Red Flag program in 1975 at the suggestion of then-Lt. Col. Richard M. "Moody" Suter, an innovative fighter tactician. The Air Force's "Red Baron" combat evaluation study program in Southeast Asia and historic examinations of previous air wars had indicated that an air crew was at its most vulnerable within the first ten missions. Therefore, Red Flag sought to eliminate the "beginner" syndrome from air combat, by giving air crews the kind of experiences that they would see within the first ten missions of an air war. Crews faced multiple air and ground threats, including attacks by aggressor aircraft selected for their similarity to the performance of contemporary Soviet MiGs which were flown by pilots schooled in Soviet-style tactics, and "Smokey SAMS" (harmless missiles that could be fired at them to simulate the smoke trail and visual cues of hostile surface-to-air missiles). Red Flag emphasized "train as you fight" instruction, pitting air crews against realistic scenarios, rather than merely flying, say, F-4s against F-4s with both defenders and aggressors following American tactics. The Air Force has run an average of five Red Flag "air wars" per year over the Nevada desert since November 1975; their success inspired Maple Flag, a Canadian-based program simulating the European environment, and Cope Thunder, a Red Flag–style program run by the Pacific Air Forces (PACAF).[12]

Although the Navy participated in Red Flags, the service only really matched the Red Flag experience when in 1984 Navy Secretary John Lehman established "Strike University," the Strike Warfare Center at Fallon Naval Air Station, following a disastrous mission launched against Lebanon the previous year.[13] The U.S. Marine Corps likewise participated in Red Flags and Top Gun but, because of the specialized relationship between the Marine air and ground arms, also created its own "postgraduate" air warfare training program at Yuma Marine Corps Air Station.[14] When the U.S. Army established its own National Training Center (NTC) at Ft. Irwin in January 1982, it created a kind of land-warfare "Red Flag." In fact, Red Flag directly inspired the Army to create the NTC, located in the heart of the Mojave Desert. Prior to the NTC, Army training had emphasized dealing with "generic" nonspecific threats—imaginary weapons and unimaginative aggressors. But with the issuing of Army field manual FM 100-5, "Operations," in 1976, the Army identified the Warsaw Pact as the anticipated enemy, and spelled out clearly that, in the future, the service would train to take on the Warsaw Pact and win. This gave a focus and direction to Army aggressor training. The Army trained selected personnel to "fight" a Soviet-style "war" against American forces, using ingenious representations of actual Soviet equipment, coupled with Red Flag– and Top Gun–like electronic tracking of "firing" and "kills." The NTC went considerably beyond mechanized warfare, actively incorporating airborne threats for both offensive and defensive operations, including helicopters and tactical aircraft.[15] The Marine Corps created its own land-warfare desert training center, the Marine Corps Air-Ground Combat Center at Twenty-Nine Palms, California, to furnish the kind of intensive aggressor training available to the Army.

Taken together, by the mid-1980s, these five centers constituted the finest and most sophisticated military training facilities in the world. Thus, almost a decade before the Gulf war, the U.S. military was able to run massive air-ground exercises over a number of interlinked ranges equipped with sophisticated tracking, threat, and analysis equipment, over a geographical area closely approximating many countries, involving diverse organizations and services. Further, the lessons learned from much of this training were disseminated in reports and articles within the "warrior" community via publications such as the Air Force's *Fighter Weapons School Review* at Nellis AFB, and the Army's *Military Review* published by the Command and General Staff College at Ft. Leavenworth. These journals, and others like them, increasingly featured articles by enthusiastic, articulate, and unquestionably professional junior officers who were taking their work very seriously indeed. The applicability of this training, and the climate of thought and discussion produced by it, to the recent war in the Gulf is obvious.

Changing Mind-set: Returning to the Air Superiority Fighter

Stopgap modifications to aircraft such as the F-4 were one way of trying to improve the air superiority situation for the future, and training was another. But the third was the most demanding of all: developing new air superiority fighters. At the time of the First World War, the average high-

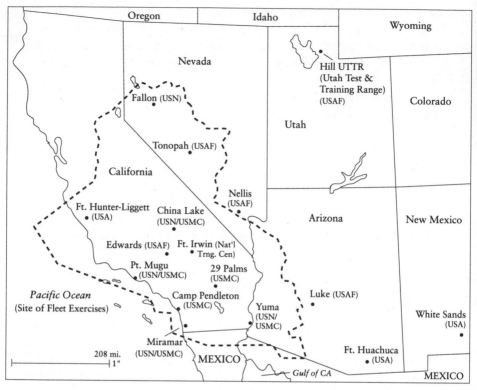

2.1 Major American Test and Training Ranges By the mid-1980s, American land, sea, and air forces could conduct theater-wide training exercises. (Iraqi border shown for comparison.)

performance fighter design had a useful life of eleven months before obsolescence. By the middle of the Second World War, the average fighter family—a Spitfire, a P-51 Mustang, a Messerschmitt Bf 109—had a useful frontline life of about five years, but individual sub-models (say, a Spitfire Mk I or a Mk V, or a P-40B or a P-40E) might have a considerably shorter life—a year or two before obsolescence caught them. In the early 1950s, jet fighters had a "first-line" life of up to a decade or so. By the late 1950s, this had increased so that new fighter designs—for example, the F-4 Phantom II family—were being acquired not for years of service, but for at least a decade or more. The increasing sophistication of new aircraft technology permitted designs to maintain a period of relative superiority far greater than previously. The ever-increasing development times of new aircraft designs (which, by the end of the 1950s, were already averaging almost five years from program onset to first flight) constituted the downside to this. Planners and decisionmakers clearly recognized that any future fighter aircraft designs following the F-4 would take years to place in service, and then would likely have to serve for decades.[16]

Given the military's traditional preference for sophistication, any such fighters would have to use a *quality* edge to offset an anticipated *quantity* disadvantage—but Vietnam showed that what quality edge contemporary American fighters possessed was not sufficient to guarantee the kind of victory-loss ratios that had prevailed in previous wars. Things would have to improve in the future. Further, the very cost of new fighters would almost certainly limit the number the United States could field, and thus force them to have "more bang for the buck." Reflecting "then-year" money, at the time of the First World War, a fighter cost about $5,000. By World War II this had climbed to $50,000, and it went to $500,000 in the Korean era. At 1970 prices, the cost of a fighter had increased yet again to about $5 million.[17]

Several circumstances and problems combined to make the search for an F-4 successor a difficult yet promising one. The first of these was the fallout from the ill-conceived Tactical Fighter Experimental (TFX) program, the F-111, which primarily hurt the Navy. Another was the acquisition community's continued fixation with "bigger, faster, heavier, more complex" notions for future fighters. But offsetting these difficulties were some catalysts as well: potential threats; the growing frustration of World War II– and Korean War–generation fighter pilots now moving into senior command positions within the U.S. military (who mentally compared their experiences with what was happening in Southeast Asia) and a reformist group of "Fighter Mafia"; and the rapidly improving state of aviation technology (typified by advanced avionics and electronic flight controls, and better performing engines) coupled with the emergence of "energy maneuverability" (P_s) theory (these technology issues are examined in detail in Appendix A). Each of these needs brief mention in turn for from their confluence and interplay came the "super-fighters" of the 1970s and 1980s: the Grumman F-14 Tomcat, McDonnell-Douglas F-15 Eagle, General Dynamics F-16 Fighting Falcon, and the McDonnell-Douglas F-18 Hornet.

The TFX-F-111 controversy constituted the most visible example of Robert McNamara's stewardship of the Department of Defense, and its obvious failure obscured genuine accomplishments of his tenure—the acquisition of the F-4 and A-7 for the Air Force, and increasing the number of tactical fighter wings from eighteen to twenty-four.[18] Essentially, McNamara and his staffers (against the best advice of the uniformed service chiefs and their senior technical staffs) took two contradictory operational requirements—a F-4 replacement requirement from the Navy for a new fleet air defense fighter, and a F-105 replacement requirement from the Air Force for a next generation deep-strike nuclear fighter-bomber—and merged them together. Seduced by the false economy of commonality, they ignored a fundamental law: it is extremely difficult to take a land-based aircraft and modify it for operation from a ship without undertaking extensive revision and redesign of the airplane. (The reverse is relatively straightforward, as the story of the F-4 and A-7 demonstrates.[19]) Compounding this, of course, were the wildly differing performance requirements. Not unexpectedly, from the outset of flight testing in 1965, the plane itself was immersed in controversy. The Air Force version, the General Dynamics F-111A strike airplane, had numerous developmental problems, but these paled in significance to those afflicting the Navy's model, the Grumman-General Dynamics F-111B fleet air defense fighter. Whereas the F-111A had undeniable potential for fulfilling a supersonic low-level strike mission requirement, the F-111B could not even safely operate from an aircraft carrier. Overweight, sluggish, and unresponsive, the F-111B was anything but a fighter and, in fact, had a performance considerably inferior to the existing F-4 it was supposed to replace. (Asked in a Congressional hearing if more thrust might help the plane, one admiral ruefully answered, "There isn't enough thrust in all Christendom to make the F-111B a good airplane.") It did not even look like a fighter; it had poor visibility, awkward lines, and its two-man crew sat side by side, as in a bomber. Ultimately, it cost the service twelve years of fighter time, from the first flight of the F-4 (1958) to the first flight of the F-14 (1970).

Unfortunately, while fighter development in the United States had stagnated after the F-4, the same was not true elsewhere. Vietnam demonstrated that the latest generation of American jet fighters had their hands full fighting even older generation MiG-17s. The newer supersonic MiG-21, armed with air-to-air heat-seeking missiles and a back-up cannon, was a dangerous opponent, for it had a superlative rate of climb and good maneuverability. Then, the "next generation" Soviet fighters appeared in the 1967 Tushino air show outside Moscow, where the aerodynamic prototype of the MiG-23 made its appearance, together with swing-wing variants of the Su-7 family and the Mach 3 + MiG-25. This tremendous diversity of types indicated a massive effort by the Soviet Union to re-shape its tactical and air superiority forces away from the first genera-tions of transonic and supersonic fighters that it had fielded in the 1950s. As serious a threat as this was, there was yet another concern for Ameri-can air planners: the rising number of potentially hostile post-colonial "Third World" air forces fielding equipment of Western origin, including aircraft of British and French manufacture. In particular, when the super-sonic delta-wing Mirage III and V family entered service with an increas-ing number of air forces starting in the mid–1960s, the danger of "blue on blue" combat became a very real one (as indeed happened in the Falk-lands war where British-, American-, and French-origin aircraft all fought each other, and later in the Gulf as well). The enhanced Soviet threat and that posed by allies having very loose arms sales policies ob-viously demanded that the United States emphasize acquisition of new fighters that could master all these products, be they from the design bu-reaus of friends or foes.

In the early to mid-1960s, a number of Air Force career fighter pilots reached general officer rank. These individuals had been schooled in the skies over Germany, Italy, and the South Pacific, and many had gone on to the Yalu. Their notions of what constituted a fighter differed consider-ably from then-currently accepted ideas of long-range low-level nuclear-armed penetrators, or multisonic interceptors, and they were increasingly disturbed at how the acquisition community had become fixated on such aircraft. For example, even after the Vietnam War clearly indicated the unsuitability of such designs for the real-world of air combat, some engi-neers at Aeronautical Systems Division, the Air Force's famed "bicycle shop" at Wright-Patterson Air Force Base, Ohio, still proposed a "super F-111," a 60,000-pound, Mach 2.7, experimental fighter concept, the F-X, having a thrust-to-weight ratio of only 0.75—high by U.S. stan-dards, but nowhere near what the Air Force fighter community wished in a new fighter. (Fortunately, Air Staff Fighter Mafia reformers rejected it, starting the ball rolling toward the F-15 Eagle, and, in a roundabout way, to the YF-16/YF-17 that led to the subsequent F-16 and F-18.)[20]

The American aerospace industry, normally a source of innovative ideas, was itself wedded to the "bigger, heavier, faster" notion. In the late 1950s, only Northrop had gone boldly in the other direction (though somewhat too much so), with a basic design that spawned the immensely successful T-38 trainer and F-5. It had taken the F-111 experience to shake up the aerospace community, but, even so, this "corporate culture" issue largely still had to be resolved within the military services (preferably by people with a cockpit perspective or, at least, an "operator's" attitude) and then, if necessary, imposed upon the industry. Disturbed by what they saw as the misdirection of the Air Force fighter force (and, one suspects, more than a little embarrassed that the service had to turn to the Navy for a suitable general-purpose fighter for the 1960s), reformers set out to find an alternative course. One of these men was Maj. Gen. Arthur C. Agan, the Air Staff's director of plans. Agan, an unsung hero in the reshaping of American air superiority, put together a distinguished study team of former Air Force fighter pilots and aces. Armed with their report, which argued forcefully for more maneuverable, agile fighters carrying both missiles and guns, Agan went to the Air Force chief of staff, Gen. John P. McConnell, with a draft memo provocatively entitled "Air Force Doctrine on Air Superiority" which "the Chief" subsequently issued on May 3, 1965, to all Air Force commands and operating agencies. It stated, in part, "For air-to-air combat we should seek advantages in such performance parameters as acceleration, climb, maximum speed, ceiling, maneuverability, sighting equipment, and armament capability."[21] This ringing endorsement of air superiority thought, of course, eventually resulted in the F-15.

Complementing the work of Agan and his aging colleagues was a coalescing group of mid-level advocates dubbed the "Fighter Mafia": Maj. John Boyd, Chuck Myers, Pierre Sprey, Col. Everest Riccioni, and Maj. John M. "Mike" Loh. Aggressive, opinionated, and totally dedicated to ending the status quo of fighter development, these men transformed the Air Force's approach to air superiority between 1966 and 1972.[22] Boyd rejected the Aeronautical System Division's F-X proposal in October 1966, after he joined the Tactical Division of the Air Staff Directorate of Requirements, on the basis of energy maneuverability theory. Boyd's work, coupled with that of Agan, the other fighter mafioso, and a group of reformist engineers within the plans and programs office at Aeronautical Systems Division, triggered the drastic reshaping of the F-X study effort, which, in October 1968, became the F-15 program. By that time Boyd and his cronies had clearly won their point. In an influential article in the *Air University Review* appearing that spring, the Air Force vice chief of staff, Gen. Bruce Holloway (himself a distinguished World War II fighter ace), had written, "With the exception of the F-4, we do not even now have a first-line tactical fighter that was designed primarily for air-to-air combat . . . *We now see quite clearly the need for one*" (emphasis added).[23]

The Super-fighters: Aircraft for the 1970s and Beyond

Once Air Force and Navy air superiority fighter proponents had convinced the senior leadership of their respective services to change the course of fighter development, the services moved very quickly, as brief development histories of the F-14, F-15, F-16, and F-18 indicate:

The Grumman F-14 Tomcat: Given what was happening in Southeast Asia, it was inconceivable that the Navy could live with such a miserable airplane as the F-111B. Grumman's leadership was equally displeased, for the firm had a superb reputation (Adm. John McCain had once stated that "the name Grumman on a plane or a part is like sterling on silver") and their design team understandably felt they could do much better on their own, unconstrained by another company's design.[24] Quietly, beginning in September 1966, they examined a series of increasingly promising alternative studies, encouraged by the Navy itself. Eventually, made aware of these studies, and convinced by the ardent and forceful persuasiveness of George Spangenberg, the chief designer of Naval Air Systems Command, Congress canceled the F-111B program in April 1968. Relieved, the Navy issued a request for proposals (RFP) to the aerospace industry for a VFX, an experimental naval fighter, two months later. The RFP stipulated a twin-engine two-seat design; an armament of long-range Phoenix, medium-range Sparrow, and short-range Sidewinder missiles, plus an internal 20mm cannon; and a sophisticated Hughes AWG-9 fire control system that could scan and track multiple targets simultaneously. Five companies responded. Grumman and McDonnell-Douglas made the short list, and then, in January 1969, the Navy awarded Grumman the contract for what became the F-14A Tomcat, the first of a new breed of high-performance fighters. In December 1970, the first F-14A took to the air from Grumman's Calverton, Long Island, plant, and production deliveries began in May 1972.

The Mach 2+ F-14 immediately demonstrated superlative performance, and the sophistication of its weapons suite obviously made it a particularly potent fighter. A variable-sweep wing gave it excellent maneuverability over its entire speed range, and, in fully swept configuration, ensured that it had extremely high dash speed as well. Compared to the F-4, it had a 40-percent tighter turn radius, 21-percent higher acceleration (and acceleration had been one of the F-4's strong points), a 20-percent better rate of climb, and twice the radar search and tracking range. In only one area was it disappointing—its TF30 jet engines, the same design that powered the F-111, constrained it from achieving even greater performance. The Navy had planned that the initial production F-14A would give way very quickly before a F-14B model with more advanced engines, but this, unfortunately, proved illusory, a victim of 1970s cost-cutting (as did a similar program to re-engine the airplane in the 1980s, though small numbers of this "Super Tomcat"—the F-14A + — were placed in service). Navy plans to re-equip its entire fighter force with the F-14 fell apart as 1970s budget realities dictated reducing the Tomcat program. Eventually, the service settled on a "high-low" mix of F-14s and F/A-18s.[25]

The McDonnell-Douglas F-15 Eagle: The stories of the F-15, F-16, and F-18 are intertwined. Air Force Systems Command—the service's research, development, test, and evaluation command—had begun studies for a new tactical fighter in April 1965, and out of this effort came a "Preliminary F-X Concept Formulation Package" presented by Aeronautical Systems Division in September 1966, which Major Boyd rejected the following month. The Air Force did not settle on a final concept until June 1967, and it took another year before the service issued requests for proposals on the airplane, its pulse-doppler radar, and its engines (for, unlike the F-14, it would incorporate the latest in engine technology). The aircraft RFP went to eight manufacturers on September 30, 1968; four responded, and on December 31, 1968, the Air Force narrowed this down to three: North American–Rockwell, McDonnell-Douglas, and Fairchild. Eventually, on December 23, 1969, the Air Force selected the McDonnell-Douglas aircraft as the better proposal. Pratt & Whitney won the F-15 engine competition with their F100 design the following March. The F-15 passed its critical design review in April 1971, and made its first flight on July 27, 1972. The next year (as will be discussed below, in the F-18 section), the F-15 faced a serious challenge from the Navy, which attempted to reduce F-14 acquisition costs by forcing it on the Air Force. Fortunately, as subsequent events over the Bekaa Valley and the Gulf would prove, the F-15 weathered this challenge. First production delivery came in November 1974, and in September 1975 it achieved "IOC" (initial operational capability) with the Tactical Air Command.

In contrast to the two-seat variable-sweep F-14, the F-15 had a single seat, and a fixed wing. Its 1970s-technology engines gave it extraordinary power, thus endowing it with a significant performance advantage over the Navy's F-14, let alone an aircraft such as the F-4. Its mix of four Sparrows, four Sidewinders, and a 20mm gun made it a formidable foe. Refined fuselage design and cockpit location gave it superb visibility, better than any other fighter in the world. To accelerate the service's "learning curve" with the plane, the Air Force sent the Eagle to Red Flag in July 1976, deliberately risking logistics failures as the price that might have to be paid for operational experience and training benefits. Encouragingly, the Eagle performed very well, and became a "regular" at Red Flag from that point onward. Some potentially serious engine problems remained, however, particularly the susceptibility of the F100 engine to momentary stall stagnation—a transitory condition of engine overtemperature and thrust loss caused by an aerodynamic disturbance that, in effect, chokes the compressor. In just one month (July 1977), F-15s experienced 223 stall stagnations, most during afterburner operation. The stall problem, and others as well—such as engine thermal stress from rapid throttle transients (going from low to high power setting and back again, more frequently than with previous engines), and turbine blade, fuel pump, and control system reliability—were eventually overcome by a mix of redesign, careful maintenance, and changed operating procedures.[26]

As a result of the careful attention paid to the Eagle, the later F-16 experienced very few of the difficulties encountered and resolved with the F-15. Instead, both fighters went on to set dramatic new standards for safety, reliability, and performance. (For example, as of this writing, not a *single* F-15 or F-16 has crashed at Edwards during flight testing in all the years that both airplanes have been flying—an unthinkable statistic by the standards of the 1950s or 1960s.) The F-15, at least to the end of the seventies, remained "true" to its air-to-air mission, but even that would change in the 1980s as deep-strike increased in importance, resulting in the F-15E Strike Eagle that performed so well in the Gulf war.[27]

The General Dynamics F-16 Fighting Falcon: Even before the F-15 flew, the more extreme members of the Fighter Mafia—the very community that had launched it—had decided that it might be just another big fast sled, and were ardently championing instead a lighter, single-engine, even more agile, and less-than-Mach-2 air superiority fighter. In 1968,

Boyd, Sprey, and several others proposed as an alternative to the F-X an "austere" fighter carrying just two Sidewinders and a 20mm cannon, which they dubbed the "F-XX," but failed to win Air Staff support for the idea. Whatever merits the F-XX might have had, it made little sense to derail the F-X, a much more capable machine, in favor of such a single-purpose solution. But F-XX had undeniable promise as a complementary effort, and that promise seemed even more attractive and compelling after the Air Force Aeronautical Systems Division concluded a favorable study entitled "The Application of the Theory of Energy Maneuverability to Fighter Aircraft Design."[28]

F-XX blossomed after establishment of Pres. Richard M. Nixon's "Blue Ribbon" defense panel headed by David Packard. When the panel issued its final report in June 1970, recommending an end to NcNamara-era Total Package Procurement in favor of "fly-before-buy" competitive prototyping, Boyd and Major Loh saw an ideal opportunity to press for F-XX. A year of careful work generated the so-called Lightweight Fighter (LWF) Program in September 1971, a technology demonstration effort to evaluate two alternative designs. Though few mentioned "production" openly, there was a tacit understanding that the "winner" would likely enter large-scale production with the Air Force, the NATO air services (replacing the F-84, F-100, and F-104) and, possibly, with the Navy as well. Boyd and Loh wrote an RFP released to five aircraft companies on February 18, 1972. Over a month later, on April 1, the Air Force awarded LWF development contracts to General Dynamics and Northrop. The resulting aircraft, the YF-16 and YF-17, first flew on January 20, 1974 and June 9, 1974, respectively. Six months of intensive comparative air-to-air and air-to-ground flight testing followed, and although both were superlative "hassling" airplanes, the YF-16 clearly had an edge. On January 13, 1975, the Air Force declared the YF-16 the winner, and two months later, the Defense Systems Acquisition Review Council approved full-scale development of a slightly larger derivative, the F-16A.[29]

The following June, NATO's defense chiefs picked the F-16 as the alliance's next standard tactical swing-role fighter. Thus, after having been justified as an air-to-air machine, the "austere" F-16 now found itself saddled with NATO's traditional tactical fighter-bomber ground-attack mission as well. The NATO selection did not come easily, for France's Marcel Dassault offered a modified version of the Mirage F-1 fighter, the F-1/M53, and Northrop pushed a YF-17-like fighter proposal called the Cobra. Performance clearly favored the F-16; a dramatic and spectacular "fly-off" between the YF-16 and the F-1/M53 during the 1975 Paris air show left no doubt that the F-16 was the better aircraft.[30]

The first full-size F-16A flew on December 8, 1976, and the Air Force activated its first F-16 squadron in January 1979, roughly a decade after the Fighter Mafia had first called for its development. Unlike the F-15, the F-16 demonstrates true "fly-by-wire," using computers constantly "voting" on each other's performance to maintain control over the airplane. Deliberately made unstable in the "unaugmented" mode (and, hence, uncontrollable should its electronic control system fail), the F-16 features superlative maneuverability, with foreign designs only approaching its performance nearly two decades after the YF-16s first flew. It completely fulfills the expectations of energy maneuverability enthusiasts, as quickly became evident when it flew "against" an F-4 on comparative flight trials. Indeed, so agile is the F-16 that it can induce "G-LOC" (g-induced loss of consciousness), despite an inclined seat for greater g tolerance, for a pilot can virtually instantaneously command 9g or more using his side-stick flight controller, sufficient to result in immediate blackout. The F-16's combination of refined aerodynamic design and a digital electronic flight control system endow it with generally excellent (if artificial) handling qualities. For example, while a 1950s-vintage jet fighter (such as the F-104 that the F-16 replaced in NATO service) might buffet so badly in transonic turns as to seriously degrade its tracking ability, the F-16, even above 9g, is rock-steady. Subsequent aircraft development led to heavier aircraft relying upon the same basic structure as the original F-16A, with the result that, in the immediate post–Gulf war period, the Air Force discovered a potentially serious fatigue crack problem. It afflicted many F-16 aircraft and demanded intensive maintenance fixes—a hazard historically associated with lightweight air superiority fighters that evolve into heavier strike fighters.[31]

The McDonnell-Douglas F/A-18 Hornet: Had the U.S. Navy had its way, the Hornet never would have come out of its nest. The service preferred equipping its entire fighter force with F-14s. But questions over the total cost of F–14 procurement caused concern within the Navy as early as 1971, resulting in a series of alternate studies, including reducing the F-14 buy and making do with a "navalized" F-15, improved F-4s, or derivatives of the Air Force's LWF prototypes, the YF-16 and YF-17. The F-4 option made no sense, and the F-15 would have to be so extensively modified to meet the Navy's mission and carrier-landing requirements as to be an essentially new airplane. In 1973, recognizing that the F-14 had already been designed to meet carrier standards, then-Secretary of Defense William Clements ordered examining another alternative—scrapping the F-15 program in favor of reducing F-14 costs by acquiring it for the Air Force as well. The Navy enthusiastically joined in this last effort to torpedo the Air Force's F-15. Service representatives floated press releases suggesting (with questionable solicitousness) that the Eagle was too risky for the Air Force because it involved simultaneous development of the airframe, engine, and radar, and that the F-14 could more reliably do the Eagle's job. Dispassionate comparative analysis clearly refuted this claim, and the F-15 continued onward.[32]

The Navy now had little choice but to concentrate its efforts on the outcome of the LWF Program. By April 1974, Naval Air Systems Command had launched a study effort called VFAX, for a naval fighter-attack aircraft to replace the F-4 and the A-7. Over the next six months the Navy briefed the aerospace industry on VFAX, and six potential manufacturers responded. In late August, Congress terminated the VFAX program, and the Navy responded by issuing an operational requirement for a new multimission airplane called the NACF, for Navy Air Combat Fighter. What was occurring did not sit well with all elements within Naval Air Systems Command. George Spangenberg, for example, saw the halving of F-14 production as a false economy issue, for any new aircraft would have its own built-in costs that would eat away any anticipated savings over a straight F-14 buy, and the F-14s that were bought would, of course, have a much greater unit price. Further, Spangenberg and many others believed that the resulting aircraft would have few of the attributes of the F-14, since it would be a smaller and less sophisticated vehicle, and thus, the ground made up by the F-14 after the F-111B debacle would now be lost to an emasculated lightweight. Nevertheless, the anticipated cost savings issue played well within Congress, and the legislative body directed, in the fall of 1974, that the Navy look to derivatives of the existing YF-16 and YF-17 to fulfill the NACF mission.[33]

The YF-16 never had many Navy friends because it was a single-engine aircraft and the service increasingly preferred twin-engine designs because of their inherently greater reliability for over-water operations. Further, General Dynamics had never been a supplier of Navy carrier aircraft. Northrop, designer of the preferred YF-17, likewise had a negligible record of supplying the Navy with aircraft, and thus, in October 1974, the company had teamed with McDonnell-Douglas, a firm second only to the Grumman "Iron Works" itself in naval aircraft design experience. In January 1975, the YF-16 won the Air Force LWF fly-off, but that decision did not distract the Navy, which understandably pressed on with studies of a YF-17 derivative. On April 28, 1975, the Navy selected McDonnell's Model 267, to be built by McDonnell-Douglas as the prime contractor, and Northrop as a subcontractor. On November 21, 1975, the Navy issued an engine development contract to General Electric for the new F404 engine planned for the new fighter, now designated F-18; the service followed the engine contract with one for full-scale development (FSD) of the F-18 on January 22, 1976. The first F-18 flew on November 18, 1978, the last of America's "super-fighters" developed in the 1970s. The plane reached initial operational capability with the fleet in March 1983, by which time, in deference to its dual-role fighter-attack mission (replacing the F-4 and A-7 in the Navy, and the F-4 and A-4 in the Marine Corps), it had received the designation F/A-18.[34]

Like the F-16, the F-18 had a fly-by-wire flight control system, but the F-18's greatest innovation lay in its imaginative use of three cathode-ray tube (CRT) multifunction displays in the cockpit. One functioned as a radar display, another as a weapons and external stores management display, and the third (depending on fighter or attack requirements) as either a horizontal situation indicator, or a moving map, although all three CRTs were interchangeable in an emergency. Unlike the F-15 and F-16, which progressed in relatively tranquil fashion from test to service, the F/A-18 had some teething troubles with its aerodynamic design, range, and high-angle-of-attack stability and control, particularly approaching "departing" from controlled flight. Range was a serious concern; during flight testing at Patuxent River, for example, it was not uncommon for F-18 test aircraft to go "bingo fuel" (reach minimum fuel to return to base) before their fuel-gulping F-4 chase aircraft. But compared to previous fighter aircraft—for example, the naval fighters of the 1950s, or even the F-4 itself—the F/A-18's problems were small. (The most serious subsequent technical problem the F/A-18 experienced was structural cracks—not unlike those discovered later with the F-16 family—which threatened to limit the service lives of early production American Hornets, and a good many more Canadian ones.) Balancing this somewhat was its popularity with both pilots and maintenance crews, from performance, reliability, and maintainability standpoints. (Of far more serious concern were the program's rising costs, which caused Secretary of the Navy John Lehman to threaten program cancellation in the early 1980s until McDonnell-Douglas and Northrop reached a more favorable contract settlement with the government.[35])

The Missile Issue

By 1980, the F-14 and F-15 had already been in service for several years, the F-16 had just entered service, and the F/A-18 was edging ever closer to the fleet. The airplane side of re-establishing American air superiority was well in hand. But one of the serious shortfalls of the Vietnam experience had been the poor performance of air-to-air missiles. At the time, many partisans had pointed to the missile results as a compelling argument for the retention of cannon in fighters, a wise point. But the cannon obviously was a short-range weapon, and thus considerable changes had to be made in air-to-air missile development to ensure that the new fighters appearing on the ramps and decks of American airfields and aircraft carriers would have a decent punch at a distance.

Among the critical problems afflicting Vietnam-era air-to-air missiles were reliability and tracking; thus, not unexpectedly, these two issues dominated much of the missile development in the 1970s and into the 1980s. Developers had only two options: create improved derivatives of existing missiles, or develop totally new weapons. They chose to do both. The Sidewinder and Sparrow family underwent continuous improvement in this time period, and two other major missile programs proceeded apace, the very long range AIM-54 Phoenix (which first entered service in 1973), and the experimental AIM-120 AMRAAM (see below).

Critical to any new or improved air-to-air missile development would be realistic test and evaluation procedures. Missile trials in the 1950s basically consisted of "captive carry" tests, in which a missile flew attached to its launch pylon under the wing of some fighter, while engineers evaluated how it held up under the dynamic conditions of flight, and how its presence influenced the airplane carrying it; and launches of the missile in either an unguided mode—that is, just to validate that it could "come off the rail," or against relatively passive targets. There was little attempt to make the tests combat-realistic, for example, evaluating the behavior of the missile and fighter in a mock-combat environment. By the 1970s, with the experience of Vietnam behind them, a number of fighter test pilots and flight test engineers recognized that such benign tests would not do for the era of the super-fighters. The critical measure of a missile's effectiveness was its probability of achieving a single-shot kill, or, in engineering shorthand, P_{ssk}.[36] The best way to ensure that the probability of a single-shot kill was as high as possible would be to ensure that missile tests had as great a fidelity to combat as possible.

The post-Vietnam development of comprehensive test ranges and instrumentation in the 1970s—particularly the Yuma and Nellis ranges that supported Top Gun and Red Flag—offered an opportunity previously unavailable to missile testers to evaluate missiles as fully integrated elements of warplanes. This recognition that the missile had to be considered within the context of a fighter maneuvering in air combat was one of the key factors that led to a series of tests in 1977 dubbed AIMVAL/ACEVAL (for Air Intercept Missile Evaluation and Air Combat Evaluation). Ordered by the secretary of defense as a result of a Congressional mandate that called for the Air Force and Navy to team on joint missile definition studies, AIMVAL/ACEVAL went considerably beyond merely examining certain kinds of missiles. AIMVAL examined the operational utility of existing and hypothetical short- and medium-range air-to-air missiles as carried by "Blue Force" (friendly) F-14As and F-15As versus "Red Force" (hostile) F-5E aggressors, under conditions where the friendlies were outnumbered 2 to 1 50 percent of the time. ACEVAL involved force-structure issues, looking at how the number of aircraft on a side influenced likely air combat outcomes, ranging from 1 v 1 to 4 v 4. During all of the trials, the aircraft had data transmitted to a specialized test facility at Nellis Air Force Base, a space positioning system developed by the Cubic Corporation that enabled thorough analysis and even reconstruction of the engagements for further study. Over 4,000 individual sorties were eventually flown by 27 different test aircraft. The results generally confirmed that modern missiles were increasingly dangerous to the point that if a fighter got into position to fire one under conditions where it could acquire and track an opponent, the opponent's expectations of surviving the dogfight were considerably reduced.[37]

AIMVAL/ACEVAL established a major missile database that developers could draw upon when improving existing missiles or designing new ones. Two of the missiles that most directly benefited from these tests were missiles that themselves participated in them: the AIM-7 Sparrow and the AIM-9 Sidewinder, and a brief history of each of these is in order, together with two other missiles, the AIM-54 Phoenix and the AIM-120 AMRAAM.

The AIM-7 Sparrow: As mentioned previously, the Sparrow had proven a serious disappointment in Southeast Asia, and as early as December 1965 the Navy had launched a development effort to improve its performance. In July 1966, the Navy awarded a development contract to Raytheon for this improved version, the AIM-7F. Like its predecessors, the AIM-7F was a semi-active radar-homing missile, but otherwise it constituted a virtual total redesign, and its creators intended it from the outset to arm the new generation of fighters then under discussion or development. Its warhead increased in size from 44 to 86 pounds, and moved ahead of the missile's wings. Solid-state electronics (including a Raytheon doppler radar) allowed the missile's overall dimensions to remain the same, despite the larger warhead. A lengthened high-impulse solid-fuel rocket motor increased the missile's range to well over 25 miles. Finally, it had more powerful hydraulic controls, enabling it to maneuver more aggressively. Developmental testing began in August 1969. Operational testing followed, beginning in January 1972, and on October 1, 1974, it reached DSARC III (Defense Systems Acquisition Review Council Milestone III—production approval). Raytheon delivered the first AIM-7F in January 1976 (with an improved fuze design), and it entered operational service the following April. DSARC III had directed development of a new so-called monopulse seeker to improve missile guidance even in conditions of extreme electronic countermeasures and ground-radar-return "clutter." Eventually this led to the AIM-7M, which underwent joint Air Force and Navy testing beginning in June 1980, operational testing in February 1981, and entered production at the end of 1982. AIM-7M was the Sparrow variant used in the Gulf war.[38]

The AIM-9 Sidewinder: Sidewinder came out of Vietnam with a much better reputation than the Sparrow, but improvements still needed to be made. A series of missile updates eventually resulted in the AIM-9J/P, L, and M series. The J series were rebuilt AIM-9Bs and -9Es for both the Air Force and Navy that had much higher acceleration (to kill "fast movers"), larger canard control surfaces, and partially solid-state electronics. Most subsequently upgraded to AIM-9P standard, with seeker, motor, and smoke-reduction improvements. But the "Lima" was very different, a third-generation Sidewinder intended to use advances in chilled infrared sensor technology to give it an "all-aspect" engagement ability, in contrast to its predecessors, which had been exhaust-seekers. The AIM-9L, developers hoped, could detect an airplane against the ambient signature of the sky or ground and still destroy it. Further, it would have an improved warhead and advanced proximity fuse design. AIM-9L development began in June 1971, and the first prototype flew captive-carry in July 1972, with firing following in August. Joint Air Force and Navy technical evaluation began in August 1974. The AIM-9L joint test force flew 680 operational test and evaluation sorties, flew 5,000 captive-carry flight hours to assess its reliability and maintainability, and fired thirty missiles against a range of hard-maneuvering fighter-type drones (including the QF-9, QF-4, QF-86, PQM-102, QT-33, and QT-38) from all aspects—such as nose, beam, and tail—and up to 8g. "A high degree of realism was achieved in the firings against these targets," two project pilots reported later, "and the launch conditions and intercepts were frequently very dynamic. Our ground rules were clear—maximum maneuvering performance whenever possible."[39] The AIM-9L passed its own DSARC Milestone III in January 1976, and low-rate initial production commenced that summer, followed by full production in 1978. As with the AIM-7F/M, the Lima underwent continuous improvement; in February 1976, work began on an advanced Lima that would have enhanced abilities to defeat enemy infrared countermeasures, a "low smoke" solid-fuel rocket engine, and improved cooling of the IR seeker-head. This advanced model made its first flight in February 1978, being redesignated the AIM-9M the next month. It entered production in May 1981. Other advanced Sidewinder models subsequently followed.[40]

The AIM–54 Phoenix: The Phoenix, begun in 1960, was not a "dog-fighting" missile but, rather, one intended to destroy Soviet maritime patrol bombers and antiship cruise missiles at very long range (launching in excess of 100 miles from its targets) and at speeds over Mach 4. Over 13 feet long, with a weight of nearly 1,000 pounds, the AIM-54 is the most sophisticated air-to-air missile in the world, and one of the world's largest. Intended for the abortive F-111B, it made its first successful intercept in September 1966, demonstrating simultaneous attack capability exactly three years later. With the cancellation of the F-111B, Phoenix passed on to the F-14A. Hughes delivered the first production Phoenix in March 1973, the Phoenix entering service with the fleet the following December. In 1976, Hughes began an improvement program on the Phoenix, increasing its speed to over Mach 5, replacing its analog electronics with digital units, and giving it better overall mission performance against so-called stream raids, electronic counter-countermeasures (ECCM), and better high and low altitude performance. The new version, designated the AIM-54C, entered flight testing in July 1979, initial production in 1981, and fleet service in 1984. Serious manufacturing quality control problems at the Hughes plant briefly forced the Navy to halt acceptances of missiles and, after Hughes's performance improved, the Navy resumed accepting missiles in 1985. At approximately $500,000 per missile, the Phoenix is obviously a weapon to be used with great deliberation and forethought.[41]

The AIM-120A AMRAAM (Advanced medium-range air-to-air missile): AMRAAM began in October 1975 when the Department of Defense convened a joint Air Force–Navy tactical working group to study advanced air-to-air missile needs specifically for the F-14, F-15, F-16, F/A-18, and any new advanced fighter beyond them. Out of this came a requirement for an active radar-guided (i.e., the missile would carry its own radar) over-30-mile-range Mach 4 + missile to replace the Sparrow. Originally dubbed BVR (for "Beyond Visual Range"), and, subsequently AMRAAM, the new missile, unlike the Sparrow, was a "launch and leave" weapon that a pilot could fire without having to continue to illuminate the target with his fighter radar. A variety of government and contractor studies followed, and in February 1979 both Hughes and Raytheon received prototype development contracts. The test program began that November, with first flights of the competing missiles taking place the following June. The test evaluation concluded in April 1981; Hughes received the AMRAAM contract in September 1982.

Subsequent AMRAAM refinement proved long and involved; its development stretched from 54 to 79 months, due, in part, to the demanding nature of AMRAAM requirements. In 75 scored test shots against targets, AMRAAM logged 58 successful intercepts, including 19 direct hits, giving it a success rate of 77 percent. The steadily encouraging test results forestalled possible cancellation of the troublesome program, particularly when the missile triumphed on a so-called Third World War shot in May 1990 when four simultaneously fired AMRAAMs destroyed or passed within lethal distance of a series of widely divergent drones. The missiles accomplished this despite intensive electronic countermeasures directed against them, and the results greatly heartened program proponents, for the missile had failed just such a test the previous year. Quality control and reliability problems, as with the Navy's AIM-54C, caused the Air Force to temporarily suspend accepting production missiles, but a "get well" program restored the service's confidence in Hughes and its suppliers. Only slightly smaller than the AIM-7M Sparrow but a full 160 pounds lighter, the AIM-120A AMRAAM deployed to the Gulf, though not in time for F-15s to launch it "in anger."[42]

The development of improved and advanced air-to-air missiles in the 1970s was a critical aspect of the entire air superiority story; aircraft on their own would not have been enough. Because of advances in electronics technology and solid-state physics, improved test techniques and facilities, and a better appreciation of the kind of environment in which these missiles would have to be utilized, the missiles resulting from this effort were vastly different than their predecessors. At the same time, the increasingly complex nature of air-to-air missiles—they really *were* miniature aircraft, in many respects—is evident in their lengthy development times: ten years for the AIM-7F Sparrow, approximately eight years for the "simple" AIM-9L Sidewinder (compared to four years for the AIM-9B); thirteen years for the AIM-54A Phoenix; fifteen years for the AIM-120A AMRAAM. Indeed, the development times of each of these missiles equalled or exceeded the development times of the much larger and more complex fighters designed to launch them! In return for this complexity, cost, and care of development, the advanced AIM-7, AIM-9, AIM-54, and even the experimental AIM-120 demonstrated the kind of performance missile advocates had always claimed for their weapons, but which had previously been lacking: the potential of first-shot, first-kill performance. Now it was a reality, as the British would demonstrate over the Falklands in 1982, and the Israelis over the Bekaa Valley later that same year.

Of Super Fighters, Austere Fighters, and Fighter Reformers

The "super fighters" and their associated missile armament gave the United States a convincing technological lead in fighter technology over both the Soviet Union and the Western alliance. With the development of the F-14, F-15, F-16, and F/A-18, one might have expected that criticisms of American air superiority initiatives after Vietnam would have been stilled. In fact, they were not. Defense critics, including several of the key individuals in developing the aircraft above, rejected even these as being too complex, costly, and sophisticated. Arguing that quantity offset sophistication so that, say, six MiG-21s could defeat a single F-15, they suggested building large numbers of even less sophisticated ("austere") smaller single-seat single-engine fighters, which some called "Blitzfighters." (Advocates then proposed the same notion for ground-attack, urging the development of cheap single-seat "Mudfighters" to go after tanks.) The extreme austerity sought by their proponents was reflected in one of these design studies submitted to Air Force Systems Command, which had but a single Sidewinder missile and a 20mm cannon.[43] This quantity versus quality, costly versus cheap, sophisticated versus austere, argument (publicly articulated by critic James Fallows) continued well into the 1980s. Echoes of it were heard when, in the fall of 1990, the Air Force had its fly-off between the two competitive prototypes for the Advanced Tactical Fighter (ATF), an air-superiority fighter intended for service well into the next century.[44]

The argument sounded reasonable, at first. Proponents promised that smaller, austere fighters would have higher sortie generation rates, would be less likely to be detected, more lethal against opponents because they would have greater agility and surprise, and so cheap as to offset any losses by their larger numbers. Very often, the aircraft they chose for examples of excellence were the F-86 of Korea and the P-51 of the Second World War, a choice smacking more of nostalgia than hard thought. In reality, their arguments were seriously flawed. In their day, both the F-86 and P-51 were considered very sophisticated, and costly. The F-86, for example, had advanced hydraulically boosted flight controls and a radar-ranging gunsight, and the P-51 possessed at least as much sophistication as its most sophisticated propeller-driven opponents, the German FW 190D and Japanese Ki-84. Both dominated less sophisticated opponents such as the MiG-15 and the Bf 109G. Sortie generation rates for these earlier aircraft were not impressive either; at the end of the Second World War, for example, American fighters had mission availability rates around 45 percent (compared to over 90 percent for Air Force and Navy fighters in the Gulf war). Accident rates were tremendous; the reformers who argued for F-86-like attributes for their austere fighters would have done well to reflect on the F-86's reputation as a "lieutenant eater"; in the early 1950s, an F-86 crashed somewhere in the world every week, and accidents sometimes approached one per day. At Nellis Air Force Base in early 1953, for example, twenty-two Sabre pilots died in eleven weeks.[45]

One of the major attributes of the newer post-Vietnam super-fighters was, in fact, their flight safety—the ability to sustain flight in what would have been considered "out of control" conditions a few years earlier. One example suffices of the tremendous controllability and survivability that the new high-performance fighter generation possessed, thanks to their highly augmented flight control systems. During a 1982 Israeli air strike over Lebanon, an A-4 pulling off the target collided with an F-15, slicing into its right wing. The Skyhawk pilot ejected safely from his own austere airplane, but the F-15 pilot found, by maintaining full opposite controls, he could keep his grievously wounded Eagle aloft. He gingerly turned back for Israel, picking up a heading taking him to an emergency landing strip. He approached at almost twice the speed of a healthy Eagle, touching down at or above 200 MPH. The gear held up, and he taxied safely to the ramp—with almost all of the right wing sheared off as with a knife, except for a stub extending no more than two or three feet from the fuselage![46]

Safety was one issue, but military effectiveness and combat survivability were others. Critics made much of the "Sherman versus Tiger" argument, an allusion to the fighting across France in the Second World War, when large numbers of inferior Allied Sherman tanks overwhelmed smaller numbers of much more heavily protected and deadly Nazi Tigers, which typically took a heavy toll until one of the more numerous Shermans would get in a lucky shot. (The analogy was flawed in that most German tanks in 1944–45 operated from defensive ambush against Allied forces having to advance in the open; under these circumstances, any antitank artillery piece would have inflicted heavy losses. Lessons from two-dimensional war can only rarely be applied to three-dimensional air war.) In fact, with their often minuscule armament, the Blitzfighters and their like could hardly be expected to sweep the skies of enemy airplanes, and their light structure and nonredundant and largely nonelectronic systems gave them dubious survivability. Further, by overstressing one combat mission—maneuvering air combat—they were constrained in their ability to perform other missions, including other air superiority ones.[47]

If military aviation history teaches any lessons, it is that when sophisticated aircraft take advantage of the force-multiplying qualities that their greater technology gives them, and do not negate these advantages (as had happened to a large degree in Vietnam) by fighting to an enemy's strengths, the unsophisticated opposition is generally quickly defeated. General Alton Slay, commander of Air Force Systems Command in the late 1970s and a formidable military leader, reputedly stated that austere fighters would darken the skies with their numbers, and then, once war broke out, whiten the skies with their pilots' parachutes. Six austere fighters might destroy one sophisticated opponent at a cost of, say, four of their number; while this might count as a "successful" engagement, at the price of four men likely killed, it would not encourage aggressiveness. Put another way, would any Blitzfighter advocate really have wanted to be in the lead Blitzfighter as it ingressed into Iraq at H-hour on Day 1 of the Gulf war?[48]

That the military services of the United States had identified, pursued, and acquired the technology and systems needed to address the shortfalls in air superiority so glaringly evident from Vietnam so quickly is a measure of the zeal with which air superiority partisans pursued the goal of rebuilding America's fighter forces. But such technical improvement was not enough. A major task was getting meaningful numbers of these newer aircraft into service. At the end of the 1970s, the United States was in somewhat the same position as the French air force on the eve of the Second World War: large numbers of older and aging aircraft, and much smaller numbers of newer and very advanced ones just entering service. In 1980, over 60 percent of Air Force fighters consisted of F-4 Phantoms, first introduced in 1963. In contrast, over half of the fighters in service with the Soviet Union that same year were designs that had entered service after 1972.[49] So developing new fighter aircraft and air-to-air missiles, together with improvements in training and tactics, would not be enough to redress the problems with America's military air power that Vietnam had highlighted. Many other tasks needed to be fulfilled, including developing new or improved systems for strike warfare; clarifying the relationships between air, land, and sea forces; rethinking the style of command and control between the military services and the world of political decisionmaking; and addressing doctrinal issues posed by the changing nature of the 1970s–1980s world. All this would take time. Restoring American air superiority via technology, training, and attitude certainly could not be considered achieving the total of what needed to be done, and it did not even constitute, to paraphrase Winston Churchill after the Battle of Britain, "the beginning of the end." But it was "the end of the beginning."

Three

Reforging
Forces for
General War

You can shoot down all the MiGs you want,

but if you return to base and the lead Soviet

tank commander is eating breakfast in your

snack bar—Jack, you've lost the war.

A-10 pilots' motto, Nellis AFB (1982)

Once squandered, a military force is difficult to rebuild, yet that is what confronted the American defense establishment in the years after Vietnam: the military services had to reshape and recast themselves. It was neither a simple process nor one that led to immediate changes in military effectiveness. Instead, numerous changes had to occur before planners could be confident that the services had the kind of forces, body of thought and doctrine, and weapons to confront various levels of warfare ranging from support of client states in Third World conflict to actual large-scale commitment of American forces in combat against numerically superior forces in, for example, a NATO–Warsaw Pact war. While this time period witnessed many significant doctrinal and technological changes, lingering traces of Vietnam-era defense leadership and management remained, as typified by the Desert One debacle of 1980 and, in 1983, the disastrous Marine bombing in Beirut, the troublesome Grenada intervention, and a botched naval air strike over Lebanon. The structural changes that were made profoundly affected the military of the 1980s. What is less remarkable than it might seem—for losers usually learn more and are goaded to do more than winners, a danger to be remembered for the present Gulf war—is that they occurred in very troubled times. The nation experienced an era of severe budgetary limitations that further reduced military readiness; unfocused, discredited, and distracted national leadership; a political climate hostile to defense expenditures and high technology initiatives; and a social and cultural environment highly critical of the military in general and Vietnam veterans in particular. Yet during this time the various services nevertheless profitably examined their performance in Southeast Asia, rethought their role in national defense, and embarked upon the new generations of weapons and systems that, roughly two decades later, functioned so decisively in the Gulf war.

The Reagan-era defense buildup after 1980 greatly accelerated, expanded, and encouraged this "get well" process. While it would be both inaccurate and unfair to state that national defense policy and the condition of the various services were ignored in the years prior to the 1980 election, the pre-1980 national political leadership undoubtedly did not take national defense as seriously as the post-1980 leadership did. What good was done in the 1970s seemed at times to spring almost exclusively from within the military services themselves, and, to a great degree, at what might be termed the "mid-level manager" level—initiatives pushed by combat veterans of Southeast Asia who were already working as best they could (and with a "never again" mindset) to ensure that the procedural, organizational, doctrinal, and equipment shortcomings of the Vietnam era were redressed. Two combat experiences in the early 1970s—the 1972 North Vietnamese spring invasion across the optimistically named Demilitarized Zone (DMZ) into South Vietnam, and the 1973 Arab-Israeli war—and the continuing threat to NATO posed by the Warsaw Pact greatly influenced Army and Air Force thinking about air power requirements and the nature of future war.

The North Vietnamese Spring Invasion

On March 30, 1972, encouraged by the partial withdrawal of American troops from South Vietnam, Gen. Vo Nguyen Giap (the victor of Dien Bien Phu) launched a bold conventional offensive against the South, consisting of fourteen divisions (including hundreds of T-34, T-54, and PT-76 tanks), and mechanized infantry units supported by extensive heavy artillery fire. To counter Allied armored vehicles, his troops had large numbers of rocket-propelled grenades (RPGs) and Soviet-made AT-3 wire-guided antitank missiles. To substitute for the lack of a strong air force, Giap hoped that massive use of conventional antiaircraft artillery (a mix of 23mm, 37mm, 57mm, and 100mm cannon) and surface-to-air missiles would inflict air denial upon the South Vietnamese and the United States, as Viet Minh antiaircraft defenses had done to the French a generation before. He moved SA-2 surface-to-air missiles into the DMZ to provide a SAM "umbrella" over his troops, and frontline units operated Soviet-supplied SA–7 shoulder-fired missiles to shoot down tactical airplanes. Had the United States not responded as vigorously as it did, it is possible that North Vietnam would have achieved the success denied it for another three years; at the very least, Giap would have retained Military Region I, the northernmost portion of the country. In any case, Pres. Richard M. Nixon responded with a concentrated air campaign, called Linebacker (later, after Linebacker II in December, renamed Linebacker I) involving Air Force, Navy, Marine, and South Vietnamese aircraft, many of which were deployed from the United States.[1]

Fighting went on from the end of March into June before the North Vietnamese offensive finally collapsed. The bitter fighting on the ground—in which South Vietnamese forces generally fought far better than postwar accounts would suggest—was, as former Navy Secretary James Webb has written, "more reminiscent of Passchendaele in World War I, or the Battle of the Bulge in World War II than any previous fights in Vietnam."[2] Altogether, the combined air forces flew nearly 56,000 strike sorties (not including helicopter sorties) to blunt the offensive, including carrier strikes and over 6,700 B-52 strikes.[3] Over 17,000 of these strikes occurred in April 1972 alone. Thanks to aggressive anti-SAM measures, including extensive use of electronic combat aircraft such as the EB-66C Destroyer radar jammer and the F-105G Wild Weasel (a converted Thunderchief fighter-bomber used as a SAM-killer), the SA-2 proved far less useful than Giap had hoped. But the SA-7 proved a very nasty surprise; with a range of two miles and a reach up to 10,000 feet, the SA-7 posed a serious problem for attack aircraft and, especially, forward air controllers and helicopters loitering over the battlefield. Flares proved useful in distracting the SA-7, but speed and height were better. On average, it took 135 SA-7s to destroy an F-4, 10 for slower attack aircraft such as the A-1, but only 1.8 per helicopter—a dangerous sign. "The SA-7's major impact," historian Kenneth Werrell has written, "was to force American aircraft to fly higher where they were less effective and to put some aircraft, such as the [Douglas] A-1, out of business."[4]

If this was the down side to the 1972 spring invasion, the other side was extremely encouraging. Air attacks had inflicted an estimated 120,000 casualties upon the North Vietnamese by mid-summer, and the North Vietnamese themselves had concluded that because of their "prodigious" losses, "the territorial advances could not be sustained."[5] The B-52 had proven highly successful in shattering North Vietnamese formations (as it would in the Gulf war nearly twenty years later). It made an indelible impression on survivors; one Communist official who came under B-52 attack wrote that "one lost control of bodily functions as the mind screamed incomprehensible orders to get out."[6] But it was three other weapons that captured the attention of Gen. Creighton Abrams and military analysts: the AC-130 gunship, the TOW-firing antitank helicopter, and the "smart bomb." All had devastated North Vietnamese armored formations. The gunship, though vulnerable under some conditions to the SA-7, had performed surprisingly well. One Spectre, near Dak To, had located a column of T-54 tanks, silenced enemy antiaircraft fire with its cannon, and then had destroyed at least seven of the tanks.[7] An experimental detachment of two Army Bell UH-1B Hueys carrying the Hughes BGM-71A TOW (tube-launched, optically tracked, wire-guided) antitank missile arrived in Vietnam; firing eighty-one TOWs, they destroyed twenty-six tanks and thirty-three other targets in what was essentially an operational test and evaluation exercise.[8] The laser-guided smart bomb made the most dramatic impression, for it routinely devastated bridges and vehicles, striking as close as six feet from its aiming point or even less, and clearly indicating its potential in the years ahead.[9]

The 1973 Arab-Israeli War: A Critical Watershed

In October 1973, Israel and the Arab nations plunged into their fifth Middle East war, one that the Israelis referred to as the Yom Kippur War, and the Arab nations as the Ramadan War. This war went considerably differently than its predecessors. Egypt and Syria (profiting from careful planning, preparation, deception, and training) surprised Israel, breached the vaunted "Bar Lev line," defeated successive attacks by Israeli armored forces by using antitank missiles, and so dominated the skies over the Golan Heights by imaginative use of surface-to-air missiles and antiaircraft artillery that they inflicted, at least briefly, "air denial" on the Israeli air force. It was the latter point—the temporary neutralization of the Israeli air force—that shocked not merely Israel, but air forces around the world. After nineteen days of intense, bitter fighting, a ceasefire went into effect; over time Israeli military superiority reasserted itself but it had been, as Wellington said of Waterloo, "the nearest-run thing you ever saw in your life."[10]

The 1973 Arab-Israeli war gave both the Soviet Union and the United States some important lessons for future conflict, for the war, better than any other post–World War II conflict, constituted a microcosm of the kinds of issues that might be involved in a high-technology war of movement in Europe. Both sides had made imaginative use of antitank weapons as well as armored thrusts. Egyptian forces used RPGs and AT-3 antitank missiles to decimate Israeli armored formations; in less than one day, Israel lost 180 of 290 tanks—fully 62 percent of its Sinai tank forces. TOWs achieved the same kind of results against Egyptian armor.[11] Overall, attrition soared. Israel lost approximately 420 tanks (25 percent of its total armor force, and equivalent to *three years* tank production by the United States), while Egypt and Syria lost approximately 1,270 (about 36 percent of their inventory, equivalent to *eleven weeks* of Soviet tank production). When tanks did come into combat with each other, the increased precision of their sighting systems and the lethality of their projectiles resulted in near "one shot, one kill" results. In the Second World War, guaranteeing a 50-50 chance of hitting an enemy tank at 1,500 meters required an average of thirteen rounds from a tank's cannon. In the Sinai, it required but one.[12] After the war, some analysts argued that in terms of overall equipment and human casualties, the 1973 Arab-Israeli war was less "deadly" than previous conflicts. But what they failed to note is that, in this war, when a high-visibility target (such as a tank) did come under fire, it faced vastly increased chances of being destroyed, thanks to the accuracy and lethality of modern antitank weapons.

Even more ominous than the land conflict lessons were ones from the air war.[13] Overconfident from its performance in previous wars, the Israeli air force blundered into high-threat SAM areas, apparently under the presumption that SAMs would not be a problem. Immediately, losses generated by the combination of the SA-2, -3, and -6 missiles forced attackers down into lower altitudes where they encountered SA-7s, or, in particular, the ZSU-23-4, a highly effective antiaircraft gun carriage coupling tank-like mobility with radar fire control and four rapid-firing 23mm cannon. In the first three days of the war, the Israeli air force experienced a loss rate of 4.1 percent—that is, 4.1 percent of all sorties ended in the destruction of an Israeli airplane; while seemingly low, this loss rate, accumulating over several days, threatened to gut Israel of its proven air shield. So serious were losses over the Golan Heights that the Israeli air force temporarily suspended operations until land- and sea-based artillery fire and armor-infantry assault destroyed or forced abandonment of Syrian SAM sites. (The first Skyhawks arriving over the Golan encountered fifty SAMs in the air simultaneously.) SAMs cost the Israeli air force 42 airplanes, and, in conjunction with conventional anti-aircraft fire, six others; 32 of these 48 were A-4 attack aircraft. Altogether, Israel lost 109 aircraft—more than one-third of its prewar total force structure of 309—in nineteen days of combat. Sixty-one of these losses occurred in close support missions of Israeli troops. As a result, "the [Israeli air force] was unable to offer close support upon request," one analysis concluded, "and could not fulfill its own expectations and those of the ground forces."[14]

The 1972 North Vietnamese invasion of the South and the 1973 Arab-Israeli war offered cautionary experiences to both air and ground warriors. First, a new generation of missile systems—antitank and antiaircraft—endangered the freedom of movement over the battlefield of both armored fighting vehicles and aircraft. Second, intense conflict with such weapons produced high attrition of equipment and personnel in very short order, for with the new generation of guided and, indeed (in some cases at least), "smart" weapons, if a target could be seen, it could be hit, and if it could be hit, it could be killed. Both conflicts demonstrated that once defenses were breached, an opponent on the offensive tended to gain ground rapidly, making the task of defeating him even more difficult. For armies, there were two shocks: the ability of aircraft to hit precisely targets such as tanks, artillery, and bunkers with unprecedented accuracy—accuracy beyond that even achieved with carefully directed and observed artillery fire. The second was the vulnerability of the tank to missile-armed infantry and aircraft, a vulnerability that had been predicted as early as 1949 by Vannevar Bush, former head of the wartime Office of Scientific Research and Development.[15]

Avraham "Bren" Adan, one of Israel's most successful and resourceful tank commanders in the 1973 war, addressed the implications of this second shock when he wrote:

It cannot be denied that in the Yom Kippur War there appeared effective and relatively simple weapons whose continued development must signal and warn of serious dangers that will be posed in future wars to aircraft and especially to tanks: mines that can be scattered in the twinkling from planes, helicopters, or by rockets to block tanks' avenues of approach; short- and long-range antitank missiles fired by infantry or from assault helicopters; high-precision bombs and missiles that can be fired from afar—from planes, helicopters, various types of launchers, and even from field guns, and which "ride on laser beams" or home in via laser-illuminated targets. Armor's enemies are growing. Will the tank survive on the battlefield of the future? . . . *It may be assumed, though, that these developments will mean that the blitzkrieg tactics of World War II (and of the battles in Sinai in 1956 and 1967)—when armor exploited its qualities to the full, gaining the shock of surprise—are largely over* [emphasis added].[16]

Subsequently, the Gulf war experience confirmed Adan's fears regarding the tank's vulnerability to the kinds of precision weapons first encountered in the 1973 Arab-Israeli war. Questioned after World War II, battered in the Sinai, the old armored warfare adage that "the best defense against a tank *is* a tank" would be completely discredited and overturned in Kuwait and Iraq at the hands of smart-bomb and missile-armed attack aircraft, fighter-bombers, and helicopters.

Yet, at the same time, armies could take comfort in the discomforture of air forces, for mobile SAMs and mobile radar-directed antiaircraft fire clearly hindered the operation of strike aircraft over a battlefield. As a result of the Yom Kippur War, various nations accelerated development of SAMs and mobile flak. More serious to air forces even than this were the hazards evident in undertaking deep strikes into densely defended air space. Before the Israelis fought in such circumstances in 1973, only the United States had encountered internetted radars, SAMs, AAA, and fighters, in the 1972 air war against North Vietnam. The density of the threat had forced ever-increasing numbers of electronic warfare support aircraft to accompany strike aircraft. For example, during Linebacker II, the ratio of support airplanes (not including tanker or reconnaissance aircraft) to strike airplanes was roughly 4 to 1. By the time of the Gulf war, in an even more intensive air defense environment, this had risen to almost 5 to 1 for conventional (i.e., nonstealthy) strike airplanes.[17]

While this electronic warfare support seriously degraded the ability of the SA-2 to engage and destroy American aircraft, losses still occurred. Even with extensive ECM (electronic countermeasure) protective efforts, for example, the United States lost fifteen B-52s to SAMs, eleven in only four days, a loss rate that recalled the Eighth Air Force over Germany in 1943. The tenacity with which the North Vietnamese and their Soviet advisors approached electronic and missile warfare clearly indicated that any future conflict against the same or different opponents could be expected to tax both technical and tactical ingenuity, as well as the courage and steadfastness of the air crews. The overall success of electronic warfare protection efforts in the Vietnam War cannot be doubted, however; estimates of how many losses were prevented by the ECM campaign vary from 25 percent (an Air Force estimate) to 80 percent (a Navy one); regardless of which figure is more accurate, the implications of not having had anti-SAM ECM in Vietnam are obvious.[18] This success understandably inspired expansion and diversification of electronic warfare research after the Vietnam and 1973 wars that resulted in advanced stand-off jammers such as the EF-111A Raven, more capable "Wild Weasel" SAM suppressors typified by the F-4G, and improved antiradar munitions such as the AGM-88 High-Speed Anti-Radiation Missile (HARM) first used in the Libyan strikes.

The Vietnam and Middle East air wars also spawned one truly radical approach to defeating an enemy's air defenses: minimizing the radar and infrared signatures of an aircraft by careful attention to shaping, use of radar-absorbent materials, and use of "cool" two-dimensional sheet-like exhausts. The result was the world's first "stealth" attack aircraft designed from the ground up to defeat an enemy's defenses: the Lockheed F-117A. *In sum, experience encountering integrated air defense networks over Vietnam and the Middle East compelled the West to invest in technology, training, and tactics that would result in integrated air assaults to crack such defenses. The success of that effort, hinted at in Lebanon and Libya, would be obvious in the skies over Baghdad on the opening night of Desert Storm.*

The Airlift and Tanker Impact

The Soviet Union and the United States actively supported opposing sides in the 1973 conflict. The Soviets delivered replacement surface-to-air missiles and antitank weapons, and the U.S. Air Force mounted Operation Nickel Grass, a major airlift from the United States, flying in ECM equipment that greatly reduced SAM effectiveness and thus increased Israeli aircraft survivability, critical aircraft spares (including A-4 tail sections to replace those on survivors damaged by SA-7s), "smart" munitions such as the AGM-65A Maverick missile (which subsequently claimed 87 hits out of 99 launches), radars, trucks, and M-60 main battle tanks. Airlift delivered critical items far faster than sealift; a massive sealift resupply got underway at the same time as the airlift, but the first shipment did not arrive until several days after the war was over, and would have taken even longer had not the first ship of that sealift been diverted from its original destination to Israel. Altogether the resupply airlift delivered 22,395 tons in 567 missions by C-5 and C-141 transports. The airlift, Israeli Prime Minister Golda Meir subsequently stated, "meant life to our people."[19]

Overall, the war showcased the vital and continuing necessity for heavy airlifters able to operate over long ranges, and for increased air refueling capacity as well. Further, it signaled a continuing need for the projection of decisive combat air power over global distances and, to that degree, stimulated long-range-bomber thought, if not actual development. In part, these were lessons not related so much to technology shortfalls as to political realities. The European nations (with the exception of Portugal) refused to allow the United States to land at NATO bases before continuing on to Israel. This meant, for example, that when tanks were taken out of stocks in Germany, the transports flying them had to go first to the Azores and then on to Israel, rather than direct from Germany. The 1973 war stimulated the equipping of all Military Airlift Command (MAC) C-5s and C-141s for aerial refueling, for in the uncertain world of the 1970s, no one could be certain that future wars would be fought without equally foolish overflight and landing limitations, and air refueling would dramatically increase operational flexibility. (And indeed they weren't, as exemplified by France's refusal in 1986 to allow U.S. strike aircraft to overfly that country on their way to Libya.)

It also stimulated airlifter development, but this had mixed results. One that did not see production was the on-going AMST program (for Advanced Medium Short Takeoff/Landing Transport), which had generated two rival widebody prototypes for a C-130 replacement, the Boeing YC-14 and McDonnell-Douglas YC-15. AMST died in part because of the declining strength of relative defense spending in the late seventies, but primarily because the 1973 Arab-Israeli war highlighted shortfalls in long-range high-payload airlift, not medium-lift "theater" airlift. One interim solution to meet this latter need was the stretching of 1960s-era C-141As into longer-fuselage C-141Bs to give them greater cargo capacity. The overpowered C-141A had more than enough reserve power to accommodate the stretching without any degradation of its performance; MAC received its first C-141B in 1979. The collapse of the Shah's government in 1979, which removed one of the "Two Pillars" (the other being Saudi Arabia) that the United States had always relied upon for regional stability in the Persian Gulf, further accelerated the drive for improved long-range high-capacity airlift. One interim solution involved reopening the C-5 production line (which had shut down in 1972) pending the development of a new airlifter. The new Galaxy, the C-5B, was a somewhat more simplified airplane, but with improved avionics and a greater strength wing (also being refitted to the original C-5As) that boosted both its range and payload. The first of fifty C-5Bs entered MAC service in late 1985. The preferred Air Force solution was development of an entirely new long-range airlifter, the McDonnell-Douglas C-17, which drew heavily on AMST technology. Briefly deferred for cost reasons by the C-5B buy, the C-17 entered full-scale development in 1985, making its first flight in September 1991.[20]

Increasing tanker support was equally as important to long-range power projection as was airlifter development. Air refueling appeared before the Second World War, employed by Imperial Airways flying boats on transatlantic flights. It had proven critical in the postwar years, first ensuring Strategic Air Command's long-range bombers could maintain an airborne alert posture and reach far-flung targets and bases, and then enabling Tactical Air Command's fighters to deploy around the world. In the 1950s, the Air Force purchased 732 Boeing KC-135 Stratotankers, the world's first jet tanker (though it could carry passengers and cargo as well), which entered service in 1957. KC-135s proved invaluable during their subsequent service, particularly in Southeast Asia, during the first air-refueled jet war. By the late 1970s, the tanker was showing its age, particularly because its old J57 jet engines did not offer very good performance. Accordingly, in the late 1970s, the Air Force began re-engining the tanker with much more advanced large turbofans. Boeing flew a demonstrator powered by four CFM-56 engines in 1982, and the first of the "production" re-engined aircraft, designated KC-135R, entered service in 1985. KC-135A, R, and other derivative models served extensively in the Gulf war with American and coalition forces.

As with airlifters, however, the ideal solution was an entirely new tanker-transporter. Fortunately, the development of commercial widebodies offered an opportunity to acquire relatively cheaply much more capable and modern aircraft. After evaluation of several types, the Air Force selected a variant of the DC-10 airliner called the KC-10 Extender. The KC-10 entered service in 1981, and the last of sixty aircraft was delivered in 1988. With four times the range of the earlier KC-135, the KC-

10 was an extraordinary force-multiplier for the Air Force, enhancing airlift, bomber, and fighter operations.[21]

The Bomber Dimension

An aspect of both the 1972 Vietnamese air campaign and the 1973 Middle East war not altogether appreciated is the degree to which both experiences impacted thinking about long-range bombers. At the time of both wars, the major American strategic long-range bomber was the already aging eight-engine Boeing B-52 Stratofortress. The history of this remarkable and gigantic airplane, which participated significantly in the Gulf war, is one of constant adaptation to meet changing employment strategies and threats, coupled with a remarkable ability to outlive successors.

The Strategic Air Command originally envisioned the B-52 as a long-range high-altitude bomber carrying the massive multimegaton hydrogen bombs of the mid-1950s and dropping them directly over their targets. Then the Soviet Union developed the SA-2 SAM, which dramatically claimed Francis Gary Powers's U-2 in 1960, forcing changing the B-52 from a high-altitude penetrator to a low-altitude one, using stand-off weapons such as the Hound-Dog (an early cruise missile), and the later short-range attack missile (SRAM), which entered SAC's inventory in 1972. Ultimately, when Soviet defenses grew so strong as to prevent B-52 incursions, its purpose switched to that of stand-off air-launched cruise missile (ALCM) carrier. ALCM entered SAC's operational inventory in 1982. In 1965, the B-52 went to war, but as an "iron bomb" dropper over Vietnam. During the Vietnam War, the B-52 flew 126,615 sorties, primarily by Ds, Es, and Fs, earning a reputation as the airplane that North Vietnamese and Viet Cong troops feared the most. They flew on battlefield support missions (for example, during the siege of Khe Sanh), and strikes against logistics and supply routes along the Ho Chi Minh trail. In the 1972 Linebacker II campaign over the North, B-52s experienced serious losses from SAMs, losing fifteen to SA-2s during 724 sorties, a loss rate of 2.1 percent (planners had estimated a 3-percent loss rate prior to the raids). In part, the method of bombing—level runs at high altitudes in the face of a missile designed specifically to confront the B-52—played into the hands of Vietnamese air defenders, but deficiencies in the electronic defenses of B-52Gs also contributed as well.[22]

Even before the first B-52 entered operational service, SAC was planning its successor, an exotic Mach 3 + high-altitude penetrator called the B-70. The B-70 had questionable value after the Powers shootdown (though in anticipation of its employment, the Soviets developed the MiG-25 Foxbat), and the Kennedy administration canceled it in 1961. Another evocative airplane, the Mach 2+ B-58 Hustler, was dubbed the "James Dean bomber"—living fast, dying young—entering operational service in 1961 and being retired before the end of the decade. In the late 1960s, SAC introduced the FB-111A, a nuclear bomber variant of the F-111, as a replacement for the B-47, America's first strategic jet bomber, but the FB-111 had much less range and payload than either the B-52 or, for that matter, the B-47 it replaced. (The FB-111A eventually left service in 1991.) Thus, by the early 1970s, SAC had only one genuine strategic bomber in its arsenal, the subsonic Stratofortress. The increasingly deadliness of air defense networks, as indicated by the Vietnamese and Arab-Israeli experience, encouraged arguments for the B-52's successor, the Rockwell B-1A, and led (via the small but growing interest in stealth technology) to studies for what would eventually emerge as the advanced technology bomber, the B-2.[23]

In contrast to the B-52, the proposed B-1A was a shapely four-engine supersonic on-the-deck swing-wing penetrator armed with SRAMs and nuclear bombs. Development of the B-1A began in 1962. Any notions that the B-1A would have a smooth transition from flight testing (which began in late 1974) to production were shattered when the Carter administration canceled it in 1977, in favor of deploying strategic cruise missiles from bombers, land bases, submarines, and surface craft. So, into the early 1980s, the B-52 continued to reign supreme. Under the Reagan administration, the Air Force procured 100 advanced B-1s, the B-1B, although profound difficulties existed within its defensive countermeasures system (thanks to poor design by the system's manufacturer) that seriously compromised the B-1B's ability to fulfill its strategic mission. The B-1B entered service with SAC in 1986, and did not go to war in the Gulf, primarily due to its alert requirements as part of the nuclear triad and the weapons it was cleared to use, rather than from any significant shortcoming of the airplane itself. Procuring the B-1B permitted considerably broadening the B-52G's responsibilities, freeing it for missions such as sea control and conventional bombing.[24]

Thus, throughout the seventies and well into the eighties, had the United States gone to total war against the Soviet Union, the available weapon would have been the B-52, a disturbing commentary on the history of efforts to replace this versatile if ancient airplane. When Saddam Hussein invaded Kuwait, the B-52 constituted the available "big stick"; some went into combat with crews younger than the plane they were flying. Though G model B-52s did not have the massive capacity that the earlier D, E, and F models did in Southeast Asia, they were, nevertheless, a unique resource in terms of the number of bombs—over fifty—that they could carry. Perhaps even more than this, however, was their psychological impact. Even in the 1990s, as symbol, the B-52 *is* air power in a way no other air system matches, at once ironic and fitting for a system whose first conceptual requirement dated to 1944.[25] The threat of sending the B-52 to war signals the seriousness with which American leadership views a crisis.

Meeting Brezhnev's Challenge: Re-equipping for NATO's Needs

In 1968, at the height of the war in Vietnam, Soviet and Warsaw Pact forces invaded Czechoslovakia, bringing a tragic end to a "Prague Spring" of increasing liberalization. The event shocked the West, both for the Soviet leadership's matter-of-fact assumption that they could do so without regard to what the West thought or did, and the suddenness and the skill with which the Soviets and their Warsaw Pact allies carried out a mass incursion by both land and air. Further, after the invasion, the Soviets abruptly boosted the offensive character of their forces in Europe, in keeping with the philosophy of party leader Leonid Brezhnev, aided by "the naivete of the Western governments and negotiators."[26] Vain and corrupt, Brezhnev was a dedicated Communist who saw military power as the guarantor of Soviet influence and prestige, and whose policies governed the Soviet Union from the time he assumed power after the fall of Nikita Khrushchev until his own death in 1982.

Brezhnev saw three major goals for Soviet defense policy: to build military forces strong enough to defeat the combined strength of any potential adversaries; to dominate Eastern Europe both by a permanent Soviet troop presence "in country" and by actual intervention, if necessary (as with Czechoslovakia); and to encourage revolution in the Third World as a means of building Communist states and/or weakening the West. For the most part, his successors followed those same policies even into the Gorbachev era. The rapid expansion of Soviet offensive forces built up not only the Soviet and Warsaw Pact militaries, but those of client states in the Third World, including Iraq. By mid-1989, on the eve of the Eastern European revolution that eventually led to the collapse of the Warsaw Pact and Soviet communism, this had generated truly gigantic disparities between NATO and Warsaw Pact forces (see Table 3.1).[27]

To achieve the kinds of force disparities evident from these statistics, Soviet military production flowed at an intense pace. At one point, for example, the USSR was producing well over 50,000 SAMs each *year*. In the area of strategic modernization, between 1960 and 1989, the Soviets introduced three new or derivative bombers, eleven different classes of strategic missile-firing submarines, thirty-six different kinds of new or derivative ballistic missiles, and two kinds of cruise missiles. The figures for the United States were, respectively, two new bombers, four classes of ballistic missile submarines, fourteen new or derivative ballistic missiles, and two kinds of cruise missiles.[28] Table 3.2 indicates production of major weapon systems by the U.S./NATO alliance and the Soviet Union/ Warsaw Pact, between 1979 and 1988.[29]

Even with the substantial increase in defense that accompanied the Reagan years there were some extraordinary contrasts between the West and the Soviet bloc. For example, in the 1979–89 *decade,* the NATO nations and the United States together produced roughly as many SAMs as the Soviet Union produced in a single *year* in the mid-1980s. The threat to the West did not involve just the Warsaw Pact and indigenous Soviet forces, for much of the Soviet Union's production went into the unstable Third World. Between 1980 and 1988, for example, the Soviet Union delivered the following quantities of arms to Third World nations: 7,985 tanks and self-propelled guns; 14,100 light armored vehicles; 20,470 artillery pieces; 50 major surface warships; 194 minor surface

Table 3.1. NATO and Warsaw Pact Forces, Mid-1989

Weapon	NATO	Warsaw Pact	Ratio
Tanks	16,424	51,500	1:3.14
Armored vehicles	23,340	55,100	1:2.36
Artillery	14,458	43,400	1:3.00
Combat aircraft	3,977	8,250	1:2.07
Helicopters	2,419	3,700	1:1.53
Ground forces	2,213,593	3,090,000	1:1.40

Table 3.2. Production of Major Weapon Systems by the U.S./NATO Alliance and the Soviet Union/Warsaw Pact, between 1979 and 1988

Weapon	U.S./NATO	SU/WP[a]	Ratio
Tanks	11,000	31,400	1:2.85
Armored vehicles	19,100	55,100	1:2.88
Artillery pieces[b]	16,200	25,300	1:4.08
Bombers	103	400	1:3.88
Fighter/attack aircraft	5,900	7,100	1:1.20
Helicopters	3,900	5,000	1:1.28
Major surface warships[c]	175	107	1:0.61
Submarines	69	79	1:1.14
ICBM/IRBM/MRBM[d]	65	925	1:14.23
Surface-to-air missiles[e]	58,700	121,700	1:2.07

Note: It should be noted that the NATO figures shown here reflect the results of the Reagan-Weinberger-Carlucci defense buildup; otherwise, the disparities would have been even greater.
[a]SU/WP = Soviet Union/Warsaw Pact
[b]Consists of tube artillery greater than 100 mm, mortars, and rocket artillery
[c]Having displacements greater than 900 tons
[d]Intermediate- and medium-range ballistic missiles
[e]Excluding man-portable SAMs such as the SA-7 and Stinger

warships; 17 submarines; 37 missile attack boats; 2,620 supersonic military aircraft; 210 subsonic military aircraft; 1,705 helicopters; 690 other military aircraft; 32,210 surface-to-air missiles. Thus, the United States and friendly nations around the world had to be ever-ready to fight against Soviet-trained and -advised forces equipped with modern Soviet weaponry and following Soviet military doctrine and tactics.[30]

The primary area of anticipated conflict was, of course, Europe. Planners worried constantly about defending the West from a rapidly unfolding Soviet blitz through the Fulda Gap into the heart of Germany. So powerful and deterministic was this vision of future conflict that it distracted the American and European nations from more likely conflicts in traditional hotspots, particularly the Middle East. (For example, in 1990, after the Eastern European revolution and the decline of the Warsaw Pact, many European and American legislators wondered why NATO and the United States needed to maintain large military forces; some academics even proclaimed a new millennial age of peace. Less than a year later, the United Nations were at war in the Gulf.)[31] So military professionals and popular commentators alike forecast a major war in Europe involving massive use of armor and air forces, high casualties, and possible use, even in a limited fashion, of nuclear weapons and chemical-biological warfare.

Such thinking gave rise to a new form of fiction, the "techno-thriller," in which authors (with varying success) tried to play general using the high-tech weaponry in both the American and Soviet arsenals.[32] In each, NATO's armies shattered bold Soviet invasions by devastating use of precision-guided high-technology weapons. In one case, however, the plot outline of one of these works had been considerably changed. In 1978, Gen. Sir John Hackett and several other seasoned ex-NATO commanders—individuals far more cognizant of war than most novelists—collaborated on a book entitled *The Third World War, August 1985*. They intended their novel to warn the European nations to better prepare for their defense. The book postulated a general world war arising from a European conflict, a war the United States and its Allies eventually won after Western high-technology overcame Soviet and Warsaw Pact numbers. The collapse of the Soviet government followed, and while there had been a brief nuclear exchange (essentially a "city-swap"), the war did not escalate to a general nuclear conflagration. In fact, when planning the book, the authors apparently had a very different scenario in mind: a surprise Soviet offensive overwhelmed NATO and *destroyed* it! Hackett et al. had solicited the assistance of several other active-duty general officers in NATO forces, and at least two of them refused to help so long as NATO lost; one recalled later that he had no wish to make the Europeans think the NATO–Warsaw Pact situation "even more hopeless." The authors revised their outline accordingly, and the book emerged with a *deus ex machina* NATO triumph, although the ending seemed forced.[33]

More than military services might like to believe, they are driven by "replacement" requirements: a system in service ages and undergoes constant improvement, but at some point it must be replaced—unless the need for such a system disappears altogether. Thus, even before the Arab-Israeli war, the U.S. Army had already settled upon the systems for the 1980s and 1990s that it wanted to replace those first developed or ordered for the 1960s and 1970s. The Army's senior leadership had done so at the direction of the assistant vice chief of staff of the Army, Lt. Gen. (subsequently Gen.) William E. DuPuy, a distinguished combat veteran who had commanded the 1st Infantry Division in Vietnam. DuPuy had to reduce the size of the post-Vietnam U.S. Army from 1.6 million soldiers to 800,000 (together with an equivalent reduction in resources), and he approached it with vigor. (In one case, he cut 100,000 wheeled vehicles out of the service after discovering that the Army had a proportion of one wheeled vehicle per two soldiers.) Extraneous and "might be nice" acquisitions had to go. In 1972, DuPuy and a select group of general officers went into seclusion and evaluated all planned weapon programs.[34]

The result was a short-list of key systems the Army believed it urgently needed for the future. All were ideally suited for a major force-on-force NATO–Warsaw Pact clash. Aside from a need for an improved Pershing tactical nuclear missile (which became Pershing II) to counter the Soviet SS-20, the "Big 5" items were a new main battle tank, a new "infantry fighting vehicle," a new utility transport helicopter, a new attack helicopter, and a new surface-to-air missile that could defend high-value targets in rear areas against both aircraft and tactical ballistic missiles. Additionally, the service leadership supported acquisition of a new forward air defense mobile SAM system, a new shoulder-fired SAM, a new antitank missile for attack helicopters, an upgraded scout helicopter for surveillance and laser target–designation in conjunction with attack helicopters, a mobile division air defense gun system, mobile general support battlefield rocket system, and a laser-guided "smart" 155mm artillery shell. Table 3.3 gives a comparison of the requirements the Army had in 1972 with the new weapons that resulted from decisions on those requirements reached by DuPuy and his colleagues, which clearly indicates how their work profoundly influenced what the Army could field for the Gulf war nearly two decades later.

In the interests of accuracy, it is necessary to note that three of these systems were failures or disappointments. The "Sergeant York" gun system was intended to kill Soviet attack helicopters and other low flyers, and followed the example of the ZSU-23-4: it joined a radar to twin 40mm cannon and a M48 tank chassis. What might have seemed a simple integration exercise turned instead into an acquisition nightmare, for its developers totally underestimated the difficulties they would encounter. The system soared in cost and failed repeatedly in testing; as time went on, missiles seemed a far better weapon, in any case. With little choice, the Department of Defense eventually canceled the York in the mid-1980s. The Roland, intended as an American version of a proven European surface-to-air missile system, likewise rose in cost and complexity,

Table 3.3. Army Replacement Strategy after Vietnam

Requirement	Old System	Resulting System
Main battle tank	M-60 family	M-1 Abrams
Infantry fighting vehicle	M-113 family	M-2/M-3 Bradley
Utility transport helicopter (UTTAS)	UH-1 Huey family	UH-60 Blackhawk
Advanced attack helicopter (AAH)	AH-1 Cobra family	AH-64 Apache
Rear-defense SAM	Nike Hercules, I-Hawk	MIM-104 Patriot
Forward-defense SAM	Chaparral	Roland
Shoulder-launched SAM	Redeye	FIM-92 Stinger
Helicopter antitank missile	TOW	AGM-114 Hellfire
Upgraded scout helicopter (AHIP)	OH-6 Cayuse	OH-58D Kiowa Warrior
Mobile division air defense cannon	M-163 Vulcan	M-998 Sergeant York
General support rocket system (GSRS)	N/A	MLRS
Laser-guided 155mm artillery	N/A	M-712 Copperhead

forcing drastic reductions in the scope of the program. Copperhead, a laser-guided 155mm "smart" artillery round with popout wings and fins, was intended as a cheap tank-killer. Proponents claimed it could be threaded through the open hatch of a moving tank at a range of 16 kilometers. Though promising, Copperhead's costs rose so much that eventually the Army could only afford 8,750, stockpiled for the Rapid Deployment Force. (Army units fired ninety Copperheads during Gulf war combat, reportedly with "high success."[35]) The rest of the list were each extremely and undeniably successful, and were on hand in sufficient numbers to be used in the Gulf war.

Renewing Air Force–Army Cooperation

In the early and mid-1970s, NATO's air commanders had grave concerns whether they could achieve even local air superiority over the battlefield, given the large numbers of MiG-21s and MiG-23s confronting NATO's F-104s and F-4s. The new super-fighters were still in flight test, and would not reach Europe for several years. But there was a more serious problem still that ground commanders recognized first and the air commanders a little later—the potential *irrelevancy* of an air superiority war. Given the huge Warsaw Pact ground forces, and the growing size of Soviet tactical aviation, equipped with deep-strike and support aircraft such as the Su-24, MiG-27, and Su-17 family, it was not inconceivable that the Pact could overrun the Alliance even if NATO's fighters were holding their own. (Such a situation occurred in Korea in the summer of 1950, when the North Koreans came close to inflicting air denial on the United Nations coalition simply by seizing all the airfields in the South.) The only option in such a case might be a resort to nuclear weapons, a daunting step. A popular cartoon making its way around defense councils in the mid-1970s highlighted this concern: it showed two Soviet generals sipping their aperitif in a little bistro off Brussels's main square, their tanks parked in the background. "Tell me, comrade," one asked idly, "who won the air battle?"[36]

Critical to any chance the NATO alliance might have against the Warsaw Pact was the air-ground partnership between the Air Force and the Army. Ever since Gen. George Marshall had issued FM 100-20 (the Air Force's "Declaration of Independence") in 1943, an uneasy relationship existed between the Air Force and Army, highlighted by the issue of close air support. The Air Force saw its primary mission as securing air superiority, followed by deep strike, followed by battlefield support. The Army thought this relegated them to, at best, a tertiary status. In fact, during the campaigns in Italy and across northern Europe—both after FM 100-20—air support had worked generally very well, and, at times (such as the breakout across northern France, when tactical air devastated German forces in front of Omar Bradley and guarded George Patton's flanks) spectacularly so.[37] Korea was a somewhat different story, at least at first, for too many "tacair" lessons had been lost in the five years after V-E day. After their rediscovery, and goaded by the success of the Marines in furnishing close air support during the bitter fighting of 1950, the quality of Air Force support improved noticeably.[38]

Over fifteen years later, Vietnam witnessed massive use of tactical air power, and, indeed, so widespread and successful was its utilization that its future availability and desirability both virtually became "givens" in the minds of many Army veterans of the Vietnam War. Such a diversity of air power resources did not exist in Europe in the 1980s and it certainly did not exist a decade earlier. With the unpleasant discoveries in

Vietnam and the Middle East of both Army and Air Force vulnerabilities to high-tech weaponry, the traditional skepticisms that accompanied the relationship between any army and its brother air force, and the undeniable magnitude of the threat confronting the NATO alliance (particularly the huge force disparities), one question dominated air support thought in the mid-1970s: How could the smaller available Air Force work together more efficiently and productively with the U.S. Army to confront the Pact and other threats worldwide? The answer came with a strengthening of tactical air doctrine within NATO; the development of increasingly close ties between the senior leadership of the Air Force and Army, and the Air Force's Tactical Air Command and the Army's Training and Doctrine Command; the development of a new Army doctrine that eventually emerged under the rubric "AirLand Battle"; and, eventually, adaptation of a series of thirty-one initiatives for joint Army-Air Force cooperation.

In the summer of 1970, NATO began a search for a new air support doctrine to confront the growing Soviet and Warsaw Pact buildup, entrusting the task to a multinational Tactical Air Working Party (TAWP) established that year. Out of this eventually emerged two key NATO policy statements: ATP-27A, *Offensive Air Support* (1975), and ATP-33, *NATO Tactical Air Doctrine* (1976). The latter was a new creation, while the former represented a revision of an existing NATO policy statement, which itself would be more completely revised in a "B" version issued in 1980. These doctrinal developments did not come easily; ATP-33 took six years of effort before being ready for release, and ATP-27B took three, from 1977 to 1980. Often conflicting notions of how to command and control air power (essentially representing different doctrinal emphasis by the RAF and the USAF) had to be worked out, together with the views of the NATO nations over whose territory any war would be fought. Eventually, in 1979, the TAWP began investigating yet another doctrinal change—deep attack against advancing Soviet ground forces, which eventually crystallized in the NATO-derived notion of Follow-on Forces Attack (FOFA) of 1983, which bore close resemblance to the ideas incorporated within two uniquely American notions: the Army's AirLand Battle doctrine of 1982, and the TAC-TRADOC ALFA idea of J-SAK, "Joint Attack of the Second Echelon," issued that same year. While ATP-33 addressed major overall command and control issues, ATP-27A emphasized standardized terminology and common employment strategies for the NATO air forces during offensive air support operations. Its successor, ATP-27B, introduced the notion of battlefield air interdiction (BAI), differentiating it from traditional close air support (CAS) by noting that while BAI required joint planning and coordination, it did not necessarily require the kind of coordination during execution that typified CAS operations. It would certainly be a mistake to imply that this NATO work went smoothly, with no or even few disagreements among the various parties. But it is certainly true that by the mid-1980s, within the alliance most directly threatened by the Soviet–Warsaw Pact system, there was a coherent body of thought on tactical air power that had been sorely missing a mere decade before.[39]

TAC-TRADOC ALFA, AirLand Battle, and the "31 Initiatives"

Within the United States, an ideal circumstance existed in the early 1970s to improve Air Force–Army cooperation: the proximity of the Army's Training and Doctrine Command at Ft. Monroe to the headquarters of the Air Force's Tactical Air Command at Langley Air Force Base. In actuality, this proximity was not accidental. In 1946, before the Air Force became a separate service, Gen. Dwight Eisenhower (a strong supporter of both strategic and tactical air power) directed the essential co-location of Army Ground Forces (AGF, TRADOC's predecessor) and the AAF's Tactical Air Command. Eisenhower's intent was that both would cooperate with each other and with the Navy's Atlantic Fleet at Norfolk. In the mid-1960s, increasingly bitter roles and missions debates between the Air Force and the Army had resulted in a uneasy compromise. The Army was stripped of most fixed-wing combat aircraft, and the Air Force in turn gave up its opposition to helicopter gunships and agreed to undertake development of a new aircraft specifically for the close support of Army forces, the A-X (which became the A-10). Not willing to rely completely upon the Air Force for its support, the Army pressed ahead with the Lockheed AH-56 Cheyenne advanced gunship program. This led, indirectly (for the Cheyenne program collapsed from cost and complexity), to the later AAH, which became the AH-64 Apache. These were not duplicative systems; each had a strong role to play, and dispassionate members of both services recognized that each made perfect sense. But they did spark a brief and intense interservice spat, and drew attention to the danger of doctrinal and organizational differences leading to costly and duplicative weapons and forces. In the 1970s, with a demoralized military recovering from Vietnam, with declining defense budgets, and with an ever-increasing Soviet threat, such a situation would be intolerable.[40]

In 1973 the chiefs of staff of the Air Force and Army, generals George Brown and Creighton Abrams, endorsed unofficial joint Air Force–Army staff studies that had examined dividing Air Force and Army responsibilities over a battle area. Abrams notified Gen. William DuPuy, who now served as the first commander of TRADOC, to continue this dialogue, which coincided with overtures made to DuPuy by the outgoing commander of TAC, Gen. William Momyer. After this charismatic fighter pilot left, his place was taken by the new TAC commander, Gen. Robert Dixon; DuPuy and Dixon began a series of increasingly productive meetings. Finally, courtship complete, in June 1975 the Air Force and the Army formally established the AirLand Forces Application (ALFA) agency to address the problems and issues involved in joint combat operations.[41]

Happily, the subsequent relationship went well. Creation of ALFA coincided with DuPuy's revision of Army war-fighting doctrine, resulting in the issuance of field manual FM 100-5, *Operations,* in July 1976. The new "100-5" drew upon lessons from the Arab-Israeli war, the concerns of German military leaders, and the recognition of the absolute necessity of strong Air Force support (it stated bluntly "the Army cannot win the land battle without the Air Force"). Overall, FM 100-5 emphasized mobility, firepower, and tactical defense. It demonstrated greater appreciation for integrating new weapons into the Army, arguing that when new weapons came out, the Army must examine its force structure and those of its opponents to determine how to exploit the best qualities of its new weapons against identified weaknesses of the enemy. Perhaps most important, it was the first of a series of new and more hard-edged "how to fight" manuals. Instead of speaking in the previously fashionable vague generalities of confronting a nonspecific "aggressor," FM 100-5 clearly identified the enemy as the Warsaw Pact.[42]

As valuable as the new FM 100–5 was, in the fluid conditions of the 1970s and 1980s it could not remain constant long. It had emphasized a defensive posture, using firepower-dominated combined-arms attacks by air and land forces to destroy Warsaw Pact forces lured into NATO-favorable killing zones. Ironically, for DuPuy was a strong proponent of maneuver, some critics now saw it as not allowing enough maneuver warfare, and opening up NATO forces to vulnerability from second-echelon Warsaw Pact units. When Gen. Donn A. Starry replaced the retiring

DuPuy as TRADOC commander in 1977, he expanded its doctrinal studies, supported by the workings of ALFA, and postulated a modified battlefield in the 1980s characterized by simultaneous engagement of enemy forces close-in, deep in enemy territory, and in one's own rear areas. This thinking resulted in a new FM 100-5 issued in 1982 that scrapped the DuPuy doctrine of "active defense" in favor of a new buzzword: "AirLand Battle."[43] The new manual drew fire, however, for seeming to overemphasize nuclear and chemical warfare (which made the European nations very nervous), and, as a result, four years later TRADOC issued a revised FM 100-5 that the Army still fought to in the Gulf war.[44] This third post-Vietnam 100-5 emphasized that AirLand Battle took place at the operational (i.e., large unit) and tactical (small unit) levels of war, not the strategic level, and that one had to view battles as complex, integrated conflict systems decided by combinations of operational maneuver and a series of tactical actions—for example, if one were fighting either an offensive or defensive close-in battle, deep operations against the enemy could disrupt, delay, and disorganize him.

The Army has to have forces ready to fight across the spectrum of conflict, from terrorism (lowest national risk but highest probability of occurrence) through unconventional warfare, minor conventional warfare, major conventional warfare, theater nuclear warfare, and on to strategic nuclear warfare (highest national risk, but lowest probability of occurrence). AirLand Battle ideally addressed the requirements of mid- to high-intensity war, and, specifically, the challenge of confronting rapidly advancing Soviet forces attacking in depth. It anticipated that up to 75 percent of attacking Soviet/Warsaw Pact forces would be so-called follow-on forces that Soviet commanders would employ to maintain the tempo of an offensive. Therefore, AirLand Battle sought, via land action supported by air attack, to disrupt that tempo before Soviet second-echelon forces arrived at the front.[45]

To do this would require "shaping" or "preparing" the battlefield to NATO's advantage. AirLand Battle emphasized four basic traditional military principles: initiative, depth, agility, and synchronization. *Initiative* meant maintaining an offensive spirit, not in the foolish sense of the French army in 1914, but, rather, in the constant effort to seize or retain independence of action. It emphasized that subordinates must be able to act independently within the framework of an overall plan. *Depth* meant combining elements of time, distance, and resources across the entire spread of a battlefield to prevent an enemy from concentrating his firepower and maneuvering freely. *Agility* emphasized being more responsive, anticipatory, and flexible in decisionmaking and movement than an enemy to avoid enemy strengths and exploit enemy vulnerabilities. Finally, *synchronization* emphasized coordinated action and an all-pervading unity of effort; "Synchronized, violent execution," AirLand Battle doctrine held, "is the essence of decisive combat."[46]

Perhaps not surprisingly, much of this involved traditional conflict formulation. Indeed, one could place AirLand Battle tenets alongside the classic principles of war governing the Army and have a virtually one-for-one comparison (see Table 3.4).[47]

ALFA supported AirLand Battle's continuing evolution with a series of initiatives keyed to critical aspects of air-land combat operations: JAAT, J-SEAD, and J-SAK. JAAT, "joint air attack team operations," teamed Army gunships and designator/scouts with Air Force A-10 attack aircraft and fighter-bombers such as the F-16. J-SEAD, "joint suppression of enemy air defenses," used a mix of aircraft, helicopters and, if necessary, ground artillery fire. J-SAK stood for "joint attack of enemy second-echelon forces." Second-echelon forces typically operated at least 15 kilometers behind the front, and were potentially less risky and more vulnerable targets because they usually were still in vehicles and not yet deployed for combat. These attacks were termed "battlefield air interdiction," as distinct from close air support, which implied attacks so close to one's own troops that the missions had to be carefully integrated into the fire and movement of friendly forces.[48] Further, the agency distributed a

Table 3.4.   Classic Principles of War versus AirLand Battle Tenets

Classic Principles	AirLand Battle
The Objective	Designate, sustain, and shift the "Main Effort"
The Offensive	Press the fight
Mass	Combined arms/services; concentrate combat power
Maneuver	Move fast, strike hard, and finish rapidly
Economy of Force	Conserve strength
Security	Use terrain, weather, deception, operational security
Surprise	Anticipate events
Unity of Command	Achieve unity of effort
Simplicity	Emphasize direct, simple planning; avoid complexities

"how-to" bulletin for Air Force and Army crews that discussed the latest in doctrine, technology, and technique related to AirLand Battle.[49]

In April 1983, the chiefs of staff of the Air Force and Army, generals Charles A. Gabriel and Edward C. Meyer, signed a joint memorandum of understanding pledging that each would work to enhance the joint employment of AirLand Battle doctrine. Out of this goodwill came a study group of hand-picked Army and Air Force officers with extensive joint service experience (and thus "purple" rather than "blue" or "green" outlooks), the Joint Force Development Group (JFDG). The following March, they presented a series of recommendations to both chiefs, who considered them for a month, approved them, and then, on May 22, 1984, held a press conference. The result of months of study by the JFDG were a series of thirty-one initiatives that addressed issues in air defense, rear area operations, suppression of enemy air defenses, special operations forces, joint munitions development, joint combat techniques and procedures, and fusion of combat information. Eventually four more were added in the mid-eighties raising the total number to thirty-five. These were:[50]

1. Area SAMs/Air Defense Fighter

2. Point Air Defense

3. Counter Heliborne Assault

4. Tactical Missile Threat

5. Identification Friend or Foe Systems

6. Rear Area Operations Centers

7. Host Nation Support Security Equipment

8. Air Base Ground Defense

9. Air Base Ground Defense Flight Training

10. Rear Area Close Air Support

11. Mobile Weapon System

12. Ground Electronic Combat vs. Enemy Attack

13. Airborne Radar Jamming System

14. Precision Location Strike System

15. J-SEAD

16. Combat Search and Rescue

17. Rotary-Wing Support for Special Operations

18. Joint Tactical Missile System

19. Army/AF Munitions Research, Development, Test, and Evaluation

20. Night Combat

21. Battlefield Air Interdiction

22. Joint Target Set

23. Theater Interdiction Systems

24. Close Air Support

25. Air Liaison Officers and FACs

26. Manned Aircraft Systems

27. JSTARS

28. Lockheed TR-1

29. Manned Tactical Reconnaissance Systems

30. Intratheater Airlift

31. Program Objective Memorandum (POM) Priority List

32. Rapid Targeting Capability

33. Future Close Air Support

34. Validating Joint Force Development Process

35. Joint Low Intensity Conflict Center

Less than a month after announcing the initiatives, the Air Force and Army chiefs created a Joint Assessment and Initiatives Office to formalize the Joint Force Development Process and assist the implementation of the "31 Initiatives." The "31 Initiatives" became the skeletal framework on which the Air Force and the Army have since based their cooperation on air support doctrine and planning.[51]

Given the disproportionate numbers of Warsaw Pact forces and

NATO, even at the end of the 1980s, it would not be accurate to state that NATO ever developed overwhelming firepower advantages over the Pact, but it had acquired the technical, doctrinal, and training means to ensure that the Pact could not overwhelm it, something it sorely lacked in the early to mid-1970s. The political situation in the 1980s had benefited the NATO alliance, for in Pres. Ronald Reagan and Great Britain's Prime Minister Margaret Thatcher, NATO's leadership possessed powerful and constant friends. All these strategic and political changes were significant, but it must be remembered that, at some point, if NATO and the Warsaw Pact *had* come to blows, it would have had to be decided in the air and on the land in brutal combat amid the European heartland. To win that battle required air, ground, and naval power of the first rank. Preparing for that unpleasant possibility was the battle that the Air Force and Army had to fight and win in the 1970s and 1980s. As has been seen, by the intense efforts of both the Air Force and the Army, the air warfare short-falls confronting NATO after the Soviet invasion of Czechoslovakia eventually were overcome. The great irony, of course, is that less than a year after the European revolution of 1989, some of those very forces developed to confront the Pact were now deployed to the desert of Saudi Arabia awaiting the launching of Desert Storm, where they would be confronting an enemy—Iraq—that had been a constant friend and beneficiary of the Soviets, whose military machine was modeled on the Soviet style of command and tactical doctrine, and which was equipped overwhelmingly with the products of Soviet technology. In any major force-on-force encounter, one could expect the outcome to be a worthy test of whether the air and ground reforms and developments undertaken by the NATO nations—and, specifically, the U.S. Air Force and Army—in the 1970s and 1980s had been effective.

There were more than enough critics to suggest they were not. Given the obvious intense mutual interest in improving Army–Air Force abilities to work together, it is worth noting the lengths to which some of them went to allege that the Air Force had no interest in helping its Army compatriots. One such article, written on the eve of the Air Force's fortieth anniversary (in 1987), intoned that "the irony of one service staging a public festival to celebrate its bureaucratic escape from having to cooperate with another may be lost on the media, but it will not be lost on U.S. soldiers in future combat."[52] (The author also belittled attack helicopters, laser-guided bombs, the Maverick missile, the F-111, the F-15E—in short, all systems that worked well in the Gulf war.) The best response to such articles, of course, would come with the whirlwind of destruction unleashed upon Iraqi forces by the Air Force in the first weeks of 1991, for it demonstrated beyond all doubt what the service *had* done for its compatriots on the ground in the years since Vietnam.

F o u r

Renewing Military Confidence

It is not big armies that win battles; it is the good ones.

Maurice de Saxe (1732)

Technology, equipment, logistics, doctrine, and training are all-important and necessary aspects of any military organization, but there are others that are at least equally significant: *experience* and *confidence*. There is something of a chicken-and-egg relationship between the two: to a degree, an inexperienced military force can approach a conflict with a justifiably high level of confidence if it is proficient in the other areas of combat readiness. But the actual experience of war itself is always the final arbiter. War invariably imparts a strong sense of either confidence or uncertainty, and the results of that remain in the soul of soldiers for a long time. Such, of course, was particularly true after Vietnam, which left the services—and the nation as a whole—shaken and dismayed. The military experience of the United States after Vietnam (as distinct from the "homefront" activities in air and land warfare previously discussed) can be divided into roughly three "recovery" periods: first, a retrospective licking of wounds immediately after the war, including absorbing of the lessons of Vietnam and both wars in the Middle East; then, a period of imperfectly conceived or executed military operations (from the *Mayaguez* through Desert One, Beirut, and Grenada, some acceptable, and others terrible) reflecting lingering leadership problems from the Vietnam era; and, finally, a period of steadily improving performance, from 1986 through the Gulf war in 1991. The improving performance reflected changed leadership philosophies (particularly the Weinberger doctrine of 1984 and, to a lesser degree, the subsequent Congressional Goldwater-Nichols initiative of 1986), vastly improved training, and the fruits of doctrinal and technological innovation. The borders between these periods were not clearly defined; for example, 1983 witnessed two failures— the Marine bombing at Beirut and a botched Navy air strike over Lebanon—but also one very important qualified success: Grenada.[1] More than anything else, however, the experience of the military in the late 1970s and into the 1980s demonstrated the importance of having clearly understood objectives, commonsense lines of authority and responsibility, and appropriate use of the forces necessary to get the job done. At Desert One and Beirut that philosophy did not exist; at Grenada it was imperfect; finally, at Libya, Panama, and the Gulf it did exist. The results speak for themselves.

The Bitterness of Defeat: From Vietnam to Desert One

The U.S. military of the 1970s reflected Vietnam and that reflection fed a dichotomy of thought within the service community. On one hand, many—particularly those at the senior enlisted and midlevel officer ranks—recognized their own professional expertise, had confidence in their abilities, and had confidence that the new technology and structural changes taking place would prevent future Vietnams from occurring. But on the other hand, profoundly disturbing signs existed as well: the continued bitterness left from the war; public distrust of the military (both of its motives and abilities); weak Congressional support for military spending; poor leadership (both within the civilian and military communities); overly complex and top-heavy management of day-to-day defense and national security decisionmaking; the debate over the merits of certain defense initiatives such as the "all-volunteer Army" of Secretary of Defense Melvin Laird; and the fracturing of relations between the Legislative and Executive branches in the Nixon, Ford, and Carter years. While most military professionals believed the nation could win on the tactical and operational levels of war, they were less certain that the United States could win on the strategic level, particularly against enemies that might have a better overall appreciation of what strategic objectives they were fighting for, how to achieve them, and the willingness to pursue them. And that, given the Vietnam experience, was sobering. "You know," Army Col. Harry G. Summers, Jr., had remarked to a North Vietnamese colonel in Hanoi on April 25, 1975, a scant five days before South Vietnam collapsed, "you never defeated us on the battlefield." "That may be so," the colonel replied thoughtfully, "but it is also irrelevant."[2]

Vietnam was a war of powerful images, none more so than that of helicopters lifting off the U.S. Embassy rooftop hours before Saigon fell to the Communists. This image of "American" failure lingered after the war and would be, unfortunately, reinforced by even worse front-page images in 1980: "Desert One" littered with abandoned helicopters, blackened wreckage, gawking Iranian Mullahs and Revolutionary Guards, and the bodies of dead airmen and Marines who had perished on an abortive rescue mission to free hostages held by the Khomeini government. Nothing—not even the Watergate crisis—so profoundly shook America's national self-confidence after Vietnam as the failure of that rescue attempt. It came during the administration of an "outsider" Americans had elected as president precisely because they blamed Washington "insiders" for all that had gone wrong before. Yet it smacked of all the familiar Vietnam elements—disorganization, terrible planning and insight, and inability to achieve a goal. In both the civilian and military communities, the Desert One disaster created a serious setback in the national recovery from the lingering trauma of Vietnam. Worse, it came at a time when the United States seemed thwarted at every turn by totalitarian movements—typified by resurgent leftism and Islamic fundamentalism—in countries such as Afghanistan, Angola, Iran, Mozambique, Nicaragua, El Salvador, and, soon, Grenada. In 1977, Pres. Jimmy Carter had pronounced that Americans had an "inordinate fear of communism"; now the Communist threat seemed all too real.[3] For their part, genuine and would-be revolutionaries saw American drift, malaise, and incompetency as further proof of the inevitable "historical" decline of capitalism in general and the United States in particular, mandated by prevailing Marxist dogma.[4]

America's experience with prisoner and hostage rescue attempts previous to Desert One was not the most encouraging. In November 1970, a joint-service team had raided the Son Tay prison camp outside Hanoi, hoping to find American POWs. Executed brilliantly, this heroic effort failed because the camp had been abandoned and intelligence had failed to detect the transfer of the prisoners.[5] Then, some good news: in May

1975—two weeks after the South Vietnamese government capitulated, and less than a month since Cambodia collapsed to the Khmer Rouge—the United States acted decisively to rescue the crew of the American container ship *Mayaguez,* taken prisoner by Cambodian Communists. Air Force, Marine, and Navy elements attacked Cambodian installations and facilities, and although many questions remain (for example, the exact relationship between the Cambodian government and the individuals who seized the ship in international waters), the seamen were freed though, regrettably, with more American casualties than there were prisoners. What is clear is that land-based air power, including that of naval patrol airplanes, "first stabilized the crisis and then modified [Cambodian] behavior in such a way as to terminate the crisis on terms satisfactory to the United States."[6] Coming so quickly on the heels of the war in Southeast Asia, any outcome, however favorable, could hardly affect the long-term malaise growing out of the Vietnam experience, but it was a good start. Unfortunately, the United States muffed a third opportunity to try a hostage rescue in 1980, following the collapse of the Shah's government in Teheran, the establishment of an Shiite Islamic fundamentalist state under the Ayatollah Ruhollah Khomeini, and, finally, the seizure of the American embassy and its personnel in November 1979 by the Iranian government.

In retrospect, it is difficult to imagine that the United States could have rescued its hostages from Iran, no matter how bold, audacious, and carefully such a mission was planned, without grave losses of both rescuers and captive diplomats. The challenges went considerably beyond Vietnam's abortive Son Tay POW raid, the *Mayaguez* experience, and that of the Israeli government at Entebbe, where Israeli commandos rescued a planeload of citizens from Ugandan dictator Idi Amin. Defense Secretary Harold Brown reportedly confided to Carter chief-of-staff Hamilton Jordan after Carter left office that the Iran rescue mission would have worked only "six or seven times out of ten," but even so, he considered the mission "well planned, well organized and well led," and basically victimized by "some bad luck."[7] In reality, the plan *was* haphazard, complex, characterized by fragmented Vietnam-style management practices (there was no single commander, and troops in the field had little freedom for individual action and decisionmaking), and overly dependent on good fortune.[8]

Good fortune may enhance a good plan, but it can never salvage a bad one. Even had everything else been appropriate, the choice of rescue helicopters would not have been. Instead of using the supremely capable Sikorsky MH-53H Pave Low III special operations helicopter acquired for just this kind of contingency, planners stipulated that the Navy supply RH-53Ds originally developed as aerial minesweepers, simply because the RH-53D had a foldable rotor that enabled it to be sent below deck via a carrier's elevators, and had a slightly greater payload capacity. Little effort seems to have been made to investigate whether these "reasons" were so overwhelmingly significant as to rule out attempts to incorporate the Pave Low. Further, apparently without great thought, they determined to select Marine pilots used to flying conventional CH-53 assault helicopters and train them en route on the nuances of the Navy RH-53D. After the debacle at Desert One, the Holloway board, which investigated the operation at the behest of the Joint Chiefs of Staff (JCS), concluded it would have made more sense to use Air Force special operations helicopter crews with the Navy helos, for "a pilot could learn to fly another helicopter model much more easily than he could acquire a new psychological attitude to cope with the dangers of special operations."[9]

Uninformed as to why the helicopters were needed, the individual at Norfolk tasked with providing them assumed it was just another routine request and thus deliberately sent his "hangar queens"—the worst ones he could unload—rather than his best. The Marine pilots did not join the RH-53Ds they were to fly until on board the Nimitz en route to the rescue attempt. Spare parts shortages and maintenance failures—another legacy of 1970s-era defense mismanagement—plagued the rescue attempt. During the rescue mission itself (called Operation Eagle Claw), three of the eight helicopters—nearly 38 percent of the force—broke down, forcing cancellation of the mission before a possibly even more disastrous arrival in Tehran, and abandonment of the Desert One landing site. Then a helicopter collided with a fuel-laden C-130, turning mere disappointment into horrible tragedy; eight men died, and the survivors took off in disillusionment and shock, leaving sensitive classified materials and their dead comrades amid the blazing wreckage of their aircraft.[10]

Desert One represented the absolute nadir of the military's self-confidence in the post–World War II era, occurring as it did at a time of greatly increasing international instability, explosive domestic inflation, the continuing questioning of American institutions after Vietnam and Watergate, and the realities of late 1970s–era military life. After Desert One, a poll revealed that only 25 percent of American citizens trusted their government "to do what is right"; even in the worst days of Vietnam, confidence in the government had remained above 50 percent. At the time of Desert One, Air Force air crews wore fire-resistant flight suits so old and purged of their fire-resistance properties by repeated cleanings that, in fact, they were as flammable as older nylon garments and would readily burn like a torch; the money wasn't in the budget to replace them. Planes down for maintenance were cannibalized and their parts "swapped out" to keep others aloft; at any one time, over 7 percent of the Air Force's fleet was grounded for supply shortages. By carefully husbanding resources, vital test programs on systems such as the F-15 and F-16 went ahead, but at slow rates.[11]

Enlisted members of all services were so poorly paid—entering soldiers received only 84 percent of the federal minimum wage—that many had no choice but to put their families on food stamps or hold second and third jobs so as to cope with the economy. They were poorly educated as well: only about half had graduated from high school (by Desert Storm, the figure had risen to 95 percent, an increase of a remarkable 90 percent). The Navy faced perhaps the worst problems. Ships missed sailing dates because they did not have enough crewmen. The size of the Navy had shrunk by half over ten years, cut to 479 ships. Even so, not enough munitions were on hand to fill all ships' magazines even once. Morale plummeted, leading to poor retention rates; only 28 percent of Navy pilots, for example, remained in service, dramatically reducing the skill level available to the fleet. In contrast, superbly equipped by the careful ministrations of Adm. Sergei Gorshkov, the Soviet navy went from strength to strength, extending its operations worldwide, operating from ports in both hemispheres with ever-newer vessels and increasing professionalism. And what was true for the Soviet navy was, as has been related, true also for Soviet land and air forces as well.[12]

Less a Breeze than a Gale: Weinberger Ushers in the Reagan Defense Era

In 1933, Franklin Roosevelt took office in the midst of the Great Depression. Throughout his first two terms, he tried a variety of ideas and solutions to confront the economic disaster afflicting the country. Roosevelt's buoyant optimism and that of his "Brain Trust" masked a genuine lack of consensus about what to do and what direction the country should take. His greatest strength lay in his experimentation, for he believed that time would determine which of the initiatives he began—including some contradictory ones—would pan out.[13] The same could be said of Ronald Reagan's approach to government in general and defense in particular. There was no underlying strategy, only the recognition that something had to change over what had gone on before. The incoming administration had, at best, vague commitments to specific weapons—for example, it did not harden on the B-1B for well over a year—and no specific doctrines or strategy, aside from an equally general commitment to support anti-Communist movements in the Third World (what became known as the Reagan Doctrine).

The Reagan defense revolution arrived in January 1981 in the person of Caspar Willard Weinberger, a tough, no-nonsense veteran of infantry combat in New Guinea's fetid jungles during the dark early days of the Second World War.[14] Weinberger, a Harvard Law School graduate, had enlisted in the U.S. Army months before Pearl Harbor, inspired by the infantry's grim nobility as portrayed in the novels of Siegfried Sassoon. (Weak eyesight had prevented him from joining the Royal Air Force.) He never forgot the "total lack of preparedness for war" that he encountered.[15] After taking office as secretary of defense, Weinberger wasted no time in letting both American bureaucrats and foreign diplomats know that a new era had dawned. He took seriously Ronald Reagan's campaign promises to strengthen national defense, once bluntly telling Soviet ambassador Anatoliy Dobrynin that the United States had and "will acquire, much greater strength as well as greater firmness and resolve during this Administration, and that there is also great concern here about the Soviet actions in Afghanistan and around Poland."[16]

Despite critics who derided him as a proponent of intervention and any military weapons system, no matter how fanciful or costly, Weinberger had the combat veteran's innate sense of caution when it came to using military force. He believed especially that the Department of State and the National Security Council were ever-ready to advocate military presence or intervention, and continuing debates within the administration between Weinberger and Secretary of State George Schultz confirmed his sense that Defense had to keep its own counsel lest it be propelled into inappropriate conflicts. But it was the National Security Council (NSC) that really bothered him. In particular, he found the NSC

> seeming to me, and to the Joint Chiefs [of Staff], to spend most of their time thinking up ever more wild adventures for our troops ... The NSC staff's eagerness to get us into a fight somewhere—anywhere—coupled with their

apparent lack of concern for the safety of our troops, and with no responsibility therefore, reminded me of the old joke "Let's you and him fight this out."[17]

Out of both this cautious approach and the bitter experience of Beirut came the so-called Weinberger Doctrine, first spelled out in November 1984, that proposed six tests before the committing of troops overseas: (1) Were American vital interests at stake? (2) Are the issues so important that we will commit enough forces to win? (3) Are the political and military objectives clearly defined? (4) Are the forces sized to achieve the objectives? (5) Do the American people support the objectives? (6) Are forces to be committed only as a last resort?[18]

As for his alleged proclivity to accept unquestioningly the services' justifications for new weapons, during a career of increasing responsibilities in private, state, and federal government, Weinberger had, in fact, displayed a tenacity, thriftiness, and strong will that earned him, when he was Nixon's chief of the Office of Management and Budget, the nickname "Cap the Knife." If anything, he could be fearsomely abrupt and draconian in demeanor when dealing with acquisition issues.[19] Given this kind of individual at the helm of national defense, it is not surprising that profound changes in the defense community followed almost immediately.

Several major issues and interventions defined the Reagan-Weinberger defense era, sending strong signals to the Kremlin's aging but still formidable leadership. Three major international interventions—directly in Grenada, and indirectly in Nicaragua and Afghanistan—coupled with four positions taken by the Reagan administration on weapons development sent unmistakable messages to the Soviet Union that America's defense leadership crises of the 1970s had passed, and that the high tide of uncontested Communist expansion and influence had crested. The four weapons issues were:

1. The decision to embark on a dual-track "low risk" and "high risk" strategic bomber modernization program, leading to the conventional B-1B and stealth B-2. The B-1B subsequently proved anything but low risk, experiencing serious difficulties with its defensive electronic countermeasures and flight control systems. Nevertheless, all 100 of the planned aircraft eventually entered service to stand nuclear alert as part of America's strategic "triad" of submarine, bomber, and silo-launched missile nuclear forces. In contrast to the troublesome B-1B, the higher-risk, higher-payoff stealth program moved steadily along. The F-117 (which entered service in 1983), B-2, and work on a stealthy advanced cruise

missile demonstrated the Reagan administration's willingness and ability to develop new aircraft systems using revolutionary design approaches that would render forty years of Soviet investment in radar defenses obsolete, directly challenging Soviet military security. It also indicated a pragmatic willingness to continue a program that, before the 1980 election, had been perceived as a "Democratic" one, though, in fact, the actual stealth program made manifest by the F-117, B-2, and ACM considerably predated the Carter administration.[20]

2. The deployment of the Pershing II medium-range ballistic missile and the ground-launched cruise missile (GLCM) in Europe. The Soviet Union and its allies fought that decision very strongly, but the NATO alliance held firm and, despite some carefully orchestrated protests, Pershing II and GLCM stayed, before eventually being bargained away in mutually satisfactory treaty talks with the Soviet Union. Had they not been deployed, the character of Soviet forces remaining in Eastern Europe would likely have been very different, as would have been the resulting political climate in western Europe.

3. Launching the Strategic Defense Initiative (SDI), popularly dubbed as "Star Wars." SDI sent several powerful messages. One was the Reagan administration's resolve to depart from the notion of the McNamara-Kennedy era's "Mutual Assured Destruction." Another was the surprising confidence SDI proponents showed in their chances of developing a system that could generate enough uncertainty about whether or not a Soviet first strike could succeed that Soviet planners would not be tempted to confront it. Their confidence was buoyed subsequently by unexpectedly strong technical successes accompanying SDI's research, to the discomforture of its critics. These ranged from a variety of ballistic missile intercept tests, to the ASAT test of 1986 (when a F-15 shot down a satellite orbiting the earth with a special antisatellite homing missile), and to routine laboratory work. SDI continued to face an uncertain future into the Bush years, but, interestingly, critics challenged it less on technical merit than on grounds that it was either strategically destabilizing or unnecessary.[21]

4. The continuance and acceleration of intercontinental ballistic missile modernization. The best known was the Air Force's MX, designed to hit strategic targets at 6,000 nautical-mile ranges with a probable circular error of only 400 feet. The MX concept dated to 1971, but it did not make its first flight until June 1983. It went operational in December 1986 as the LGM-118A Peacekeeper, sixteen years after its predecessor,

the LGM-30G Minuteman III. Concerted efforts to cut the MX program resulted in its production being reduced, but the program went forward. The Reagan administration likewise endorsed the Navy's Trident II ballistic missile and submarine program to upgrade the survivability and capability of the Navy's submarine-launched ballistic missile effort. Trident II signaled to the Soviets that, as with the B-1, B-2, cruise, and MX ashore, the United States was determined to modernize all three legs of the nuclear triad.

One of the constant criticisms of the Reagan era was alleged overspending on defense at the expense of social programs such as Social Security and Medicare. In fact, as a review of gross national product (GNP) and national defense spending patterns indicates, defense spending in the Reagan-Bush era fell well within historical patterns established in previous administrations and, in fact, was less than many. Post–Second World War defense spending peaked thirty years before the Reagan era, during the Korean War. In 1953, defense spending constituted 14.5 percent of GNP. Table 4.1 lists GNP, taken at two-year increments from 1960 to 1990, outlays on defense, social security and medical programs, and includes defense spending expressed as a percentage of GNP.[22]

As can be seen in Table 4.1, Reagan-Bush defense spending remained consistent with previous defense spending patterns from the end of the Eisenhower administration through those of presidents Kennedy, Johnson, Nixon, Ford, and Carter. Outlays on Social Security and medical programs (with the exception of one year, 1986) exceeded defense spending throughout the period. As a percentage of GNP, it averaged far lower than the 1960s, *before* Vietnam became a serious concern, and significantly lower than the peak years of the Vietnam War. It was less than half of the postwar peak years of 1952 (13.5%), 1953 (14.5%), and 1954 (13.3%).[23]

Nevertheless, this level of defense expenditure sufficed to place the Soviet Union in an increasingly untenable position. Though possessing immense military power, the Soviet Union was unable to overcome the multiple challenges posed by the West in the 1980s, for it was, as Soviet expert (and emigré) Dimitri Simes perceptively pronounced, "a Colossus with many contradictions."[24] Faced with a reinvigorated West, confronting growing economic distress and insufficiency at home, and experiencing political discontent within the Soviet "republics" and in the Eastern European countries, Mikhail Gorbachev had little choice but to ride the winds of liberalization. However reformist he might be, he was less the

Table 4.1. Defense Spending Trends, 1960–1990

Year	Gross National Product	Defense	Social Security/ Medicare	Defense Spending as Percentage of GNP
1960	$507.8	$48.1	$11.6	9.5%
1962	556.7	52.3	14.4	9.4
1964	629.4	54.8	16.6	8.7
1966	740.5	58.1	20.7	7.8
1968	852.4	81.9	28.5	9.6
1970	990.5	81.7	36.5	8.2
1972	1,151.2	79.2	47.6	6.9
1974	1,417.0	79.3	65.5	5.6
1976	1,699.6	89.6	89.7	5.3
1978	2,173.4	104.5	116.6	4.8
1980	2,667.7	134.0	150.6	5.0
1982	3,141.5	185.3	202.5	5.9
1984	3,695.7	209.9	235.8	5.7
1986	4,184.3	273.4	268.9	6.5
1988	4,792.8	290.4	298.2	6.1
1990	5,446.7	296.3	345.1	5.4

Note: Monetary units are expressed in billions of "then-year" dollars.

new democratic Soviet man and more the last Communist: the bills, literally, came due on his watch.[25] Genuine democrats—the Lech Walesas, the Vaclav Havels, that every Eastern European country had—forced him at last to abandon the corrupt governments that had kept their own people in a Marxist-Leninist thrall for over forty years. Dictators fell in disgrace and derision, with one genuine tyrant—Nicolae Ceausescu (a hunting partner, incidentally, of Saddam Hussein)—shot down by his own troops. Statues of Lenin, Stalin, and Brezhnev toppled like tenpins. Arms agreements reduced the nuclear forces in both the Pact and NATO (though Soviet military spending continued above 25 percent of the Soviet GNP level). The Berlin Wall fell and the two Germanys reunited. The formal dissolution of the Warsaw Pact, which coincided with the end of the Gulf war, quickly and inevitably followed.

Then came the Gulf war, which further exacerbated relations between Soviet hardliners and moderates, adding its own pressures upon those who sought a return to the days of Brezhnev, or even Stalin. In August

1991 came the last spasmodic attempt of Soviet stalwarts to reassert power; they sought legitimacy for their coup not by appeals to Marx but by reliance on coercion and force. Massive public protests, coupled with resolute defiance of the coup leaders by the Soviet military, ended this last attempt to rekindle a return to Soviet totalitarianism. Nothing could so dramatically illustrate how greatly communism had been discredited than this: at its most dire moment, it had no defenders. Soviet communism did not even reach its diamond anniversary.

First Experiences: The Gulf of Sidra, the Falklands, and the Bekaa Valley

Proof that the new administration had dramatically shifted the direction of national defense came seven months after Ronald Reagan took his oath of office, in the far from tranquil waters of the Gulf of Sidra. The malaise and drift of executive leadership in the late 1970s had nurtured the roots of the Gulf of Sidra episode. For years, Libyan dictator Muammar Qaddafi had baited the United States, and evidence indicated that, at one point, he had gone beyond mere rhetoric: his fighters apparently had fired an air-to-air missile at an Air Force EC-135 flying over international waters, fortunately without hitting it.

In the late 1970s, the Carter administration suspended Navy operations below the line of 32°30′ north latitude rather than contest Qaddafi's claims to the Gulf of Sidra, which were without foundation under international law. Reagan and Weinberger, on the other hand, approved plans of Secretary of the Navy John Lehman (himself a naval aviator) to undertake Sixth Fleet exercises in the Gulf in August 1981 even if this put the Navy "in harm's way." They did so both because the Gulf's waters were off major shipping routes and thus ideal for running maneuvers, and because it would assert an important right to free navigation under international law. For several days, Qaddafi's airmen (including some Syrian, North Korean, North Vietnamese, and East German pilots in his air force) attempted to sneak up on the fleet, but each time the combination of airborne warning aircraft (the carrier-based E-2C Hawkeye) and the Grumman F-14 fighter with its powerful 200-mile range AWG-9 radar generated a number of F-14 intercepts and "photo opportunities." On August 19, two Sukhoi Su-22s came out; from the moment the Su-22s had begun their takeoff role 60 miles away, two patrolling F-14s from the carrier *Nimitz* had had them "locked up" in their fire control radar. The

Libyan fighters had been ordered to shoot, and so, from a head-on aspect, one foolishly fired an early model Atoll heat-seeker. The two Tomcats promptly maneuvered behind them and shot both down with AIM-9Ls; for the rest of the exercise, Libya backed off. (Near the end of the decade, in January 1989, in a case of "*déja vu* all over again," F-14s shot down two MiG-23s that approached the Sixth Fleet and then injudiciously maneuvered as if to attack the Tomcats, leading some wags to allege that getting a Libyan fighter over the Gulf of Sidra was now the Navy's final exam for Top Gun.) Confidence in America's military, low since the Desert One debacle, rose to 52 percent—better, but still shaky.[26]

In the spring of 1982, the United States involved itself in another conflict, one that had profound implications for strengthening Anglo-American relations and, in turn, the American-European NATO alliance. It was one that also offered some important lessons for future combat: the Falklands war. It is difficult to write about the Falklands conflict without feeling a great deal of sympathy, respect, and no small heartache for the combatants of both sides, particularly the British and Argentine airmen who flew with unswerving courage and unfailing élan. It was inconceivable that the Thatcher government could let the aggression go unchallenged once Argentina invaded the islands, and it was equally inconceivable that the United States could stand on the sidelines and claim neutrality, as much as some might have wished it to. American support removed any lingering onus of bitterness from Suez a quarter-century earlier (when Eisenhower roundly criticized the Anglo-French chastisement of Nasser), and demonstrated at the same time that Americans harbored no resentment for Britain's decidedly disapproving attitude toward America during Vietnam. From the outset, the logistical and power-projection challenges faced by Great Britain were formidable, and many American military figures, perhaps reflecting the demoralization of the post-Vietnam years, were quick to write off the Thatcher government's chances. Not so Reagan, Weinberger, and the new defense leadership, notably John Lehman. At their direction, the services provided weapons, technical advice, and equipment to the British who, on their own, were already doing a remarkable job modifying their aircraft and converting commercial vessels to go to war.[27]

The delusions under which the Argentine military community suffered, which mirrored the delusions afflicting their political leadership, supported the decision to go to war, although planning was chaotic. In one notable case, a very senior member of the Army's planning staff only heard of the occupation of the "Malvinas" (as Argentina referred to the islands) as he listened to the radio on his way to work![28] This unreality carried over into a lack of training and preparation so that, when the British naval task force arrived in the vicinity of the islands some weeks later, Argentina was still far from ready. Its military forces were largely poorly trained conscripts, and while naval and air force airmen were undoubtedly more competent, they too lacked the kind of intensive operational training available to British soldiers, sailors, and airmen. A short and bitter war followed. Handicapped by having to operate their fighters and strike aircraft from the South American mainland, Argentina's airmen arrived over the Falklands with minimal fuel and weapons. Further, their French-supplied Mirage and Israeli-supplied Mirage-derivative Dagger fighters and aging Douglas Skyhawk attack bombers were inferior in avionics, maneuverability, and weaponry to the British Sea Harrier vertical-and-short-takeoff-and-landing (V/STOL) fighters. For their part, the British had eliminated large-deck fleet carriers and long-range F-4s from their navy, and thus had to make do with much smaller helicopter carriers which, fortunately, carried the superb Harrier. To make up for the lack of any airborne warning and control aircraft such as the U.S. Navy's E-2C Hawkeye or the Air Force's E-3B Sentry AWACS, the British made do with modified helicopters lugging small radars to altitude; their own early warning Gannets had likewise disappeared with the retirement of their large fleet carriers. Both sides used air-launched antiship missiles: Argentina fielded the French Exocet, and the British had the Sea Skua. Both sides made extensive use of surface-to-air missiles.[29]

In the fighting that followed, each side lost six vessels (either sunk or so badly damaged as to be abandoned), the Exocet and Sea Skua both proving particularly dangerous and effective weapons. Argentina's courageous Skyhawk pilots achieved notable antishipping successes dropping "dumb" bombs in the face of intense flak and SAM fire. This lesson greatly increased interest in point-defense systems such as rapid-firing guns or fast-reacting SAMs. Small arms and surface-to-air missiles took a toll of both Argentine and British strike aircraft. But it was the air-to-air combat results that generated the greatest interest. The all-aspect AIM-9L carried by the Sea Harrier proved to possess a terrible deadliness, achieving a success rate of nearly 83 percent (compared to less than 20 percent in the Vietnam War), meaning that when a Harrier pilot fired a "Lima" at an opponent, he already had an 83-percent chance of scoring a hit. It destroyed nineteen Argentine aircraft in twenty-three engagements, although there were no true dogfights per se, at altitudes between 50 and 500 feet. Overall, Harrier pilots shot down twenty-five Argentine aircraft without loss; for the record, they did so without using engine thrust vectoring. The age of the reliable and deadly all-aspect air-to-air missile—and the practical V/STOL strike fighter—had clearly arrived.[30] More important than any of this, however, was the cross-fertilization between the United States and Great Britain. American technology had helped Britain win a difficult war, but the demonstration of British resolve considerably strengthened those within the American government who believed that the United States should not shrink from taking a more active role in confronting aggression around the world. As Christopher J. Bowie has written, "The Falklands conflict . . . revealed a hidden strength of a united democracy—its ability to focus its hard-won intellectual and industrial power to cope with the unexpected."[31] It was this moral lesson that was the most important of all.

Shooting had not yet stopped in the South Atlantic when a much more intensive and instructive conflict erupted in the Middle East: the Bekaa Valley air campaign. In this case, Israel needed minimal if any advice from the United States. Instead, even more than the Gulf of Sidra or the Falklands, the lessons and example from this conflict offered profound encouragement that the institutional and technological changes implemented after Vietnam were working. In early June 1982, several terrorist events worldwide triggered an ill-considered if long-planned Israeli offensive into southern Lebanon to destroy the infrastructure of the Palestine Liberation Organization (PLO) and increase the security of northern Israeli settlements endangered by PLO shelling and rocket attacks. This offensive, dubbed "Operation Peace for Galilee" for political reasons, immediately aroused the Syrian government, which reinforced nineteen existing SAM sites located in the Bekaa Valley, a long valley approximately the size of Luxembourg, nestled between the Lebanon and Anti-Lebanon Mountains that separate Lebanon from the sea and from Syria. Israel decided to attack the SAM sites, and the resulting air strikes generated intensive air combat between dozens of opposing Syrian and Israeli fighters over the next several weeks. When the smoke plumes had dissipated, the results were clear: Israeli F-15 and F-16 fighters had destroyed eighty-four Soviet-built fighters (a F-4 had shot down an eighty-fifth) without loss. The principal weapon had been the AIM-9L, although Israeli pilots had also used the AIM-7F.[32]

What attracted more attention than even the air-to-air results—the most lopsided air combat victory in the history of military aviation—was that the campaign, as brief as it was, was a fully integrated mini–air war, the first of its kind since Vietnam. The Israelis had made superb use of airborne warning aircraft (American-built E-2C Hawkeyes that literally detected Syrian fighters even before they went "wheels up" after takeoff); had used F-15s as radar "gap fillers" to assist the less-radar-capable F-16s; had flown sorties of small unmanned remotely piloted vehicles (RPVs) to force Syria to use their radars so that signature information could be acquired for Israeli SAM-killers; had blended air strikes with imaginative use of ground artillery and rocket fire; and had used electronic intelligence, deception, and jamming techniques to totally paralyze Syria's Soviet-style air defense system. As a result, the Syrians generally wandered around the sky in their MiG-21s, MiG-23s, Su-20s, and even MiG-25s until shot down by marauding Eagles and Fighting Falcons; F-15s claimed forty, and F-16s claimed forty-four. Sixty-four of these (and all nineteen SAM sites) were destroyed in the first two days of the campaign. Israel had clearly learned the lessons of the 1973 war.[33]

There is always a danger of reading too much significance into a conflict (and that danger is certainly present in analyzing the Gulf war of 1991 as well). Thus, the Falklands and Bekaa Valley experiences have to be considered within the context of what they were: limited wars over small geographic areas against opponents deficient in training and leadership and who, circumstantially, possessed sanctuaries beyond the reach of attackers. Nevertheless, there were some important lessons in both that attracted attention in the world military aerospace community and, particularly, within the Soviet Union. One was the obvious significance of new generations of deadly munitions (such as the AIM-9L, the Exocet, and antiradar missiles). Another was the growing importance of electronic warfare and airborne warning aircraft. A third was the significance of relatively cheap battlefield drones; after Lebanon, interest in RPVs (which had languished in the United States after Vietnam except for a few zealots) greatly increased. A fourth was that sophisticated SAMs such as the SA-6 could be killed by creative anti-SAM tactics. A fifth was the validation of the V/STOL fighter against the pronouncements of all its critics who had alleged such aircraft would never be better than curious freaks. A sixth was, of course, the obvious dominance of the new generation of super-fighters, particularly the F-15 and F-16.

No sooner had the Bekaa shooting stopped than the Soviets dispatched a team under the First Deputy Commander of Soviet Air Defense Forces,

Col. Gen. Yevgenii Yurasov, reportedly followed by another visit by no less a personage than the then-chief of the Soviet General Staff, Marshal N. V. Ogarkov. What comrades Yurasov and Ogarkov said back in Moscow may best be imagined. In any case, they replaced those arms lost by the Syrians, added a new "tiered" SAM system of SA-8, SA-9, and long-range SA-5 missiles, attempted to shore up their lost international prestige by a propaganda blitz claiming a great Syrian-Soviet victory, and quietly undertook a more detailed analysis that appeared over the next year. They had good reason to be concerned, for the West would demonstrate even more completely what its technology could do against much more extensive Soviet-style air defenses when the United States took on Qaddafi in the night skies over Libya in 1986, and the UN coalition went to war over Kuwait and Iraq in 1991.[34]

Uncertain Steps Down the Road to Recovery: Beirut, Grenada, and a Botched Air Strike

In the fall of 1983, U.S. forces engaged in three combat operations that produced mixed results, indicating that much work still remained to be done before the deficiencies of Vietnam-era military thinking were totally expunged. The first of these was genuine tragedy: a Marine force sent to Beirut as part of a multinational peacekeeping force suffered 341 casualties (241 of whom died) to a terrorist truck bomb on October 23. What made this even more horrible was that they had been sent there without clear purpose in response to pressure from the UN, the NSC, and the Department of State, in direct opposition to the wishes of the secretary of defense and the Joint Chiefs of Staff. They operated under such vaguely drawn rules of engagement and complicated control that their commanders did not even believe the troops had permission to have rounds chambered in their weapons. For that reason, when the truck bomber accelerated his vehicle toward the barracks housing the Marines, the guards were not in a position to stop him. The remaining troops stayed on for several more months before finally pulling out at the end of February, 1984. This episode crystallized Weinberger's thinking on what emerged the following November as the Weinberger Doctrine, with its tests for legitimate U.S. military involvement overseas.[35]

The reaction of the American public to the Beirut disaster might have been far worse had it not been for the second event in 1983: a coincidental, simultaneous crisis far closer to home, on the island of Grenada, in the southeasternmost corner of the Caribbean. In 1979, a pro-Communist revolutionary group under Maurice Bishop deposed Sir Eric Gairy, a quixotic and eccentric leader, while he was in New York lecturing the UN on unidentified flying objects and their connection with voodoo. Bishop and his cronies quickly entered assistance agreements with Cuba, East Germany, the Soviet Union, Bulgaria, North Korea, and Czechoslovakia, received massive amounts of military equipment, and began construction of a large military airport.[36] With the contemporaneous consolidation of power by the Sandinistas in Nicaragua and the Castro government firmly in place in Cuba, the shift of Grenada into the Communist orbit promised to create a Cuba-Nicaragua-Grenada nexus that could, in times of international crisis, effectively close off the shipment of goods and supplies throughout the Caribbean Basin and far out into the Atlantic as well.[37] In 1983, Bishop's relationship with his cronies deteriorated, and in October he was overthrown and killed by even more radical elements in an episode so bizarre that even the Cuban government protested.[38]

The Reagan administration, embroiled in Lebanon, watched this new crisis nervously, and prepared a contingency plan for invasion. Finally, with Bishop dead, Reagan authorized Operation Urgent Fury on October 23, the same day as the Beirut bombing. Urgent Fury had three goals: rescuing a thousand Americans, mostly college students, who were likely targets for an Iranian-style hostage-taking; restoring order; and returning Grenada to the democracy it once had been. The subsequent military action to seize Grenada was, on the whole, successful, although it came at the cost of eighteen American dead, ninety-three wounded, and sixteen missing. It also highlighted lingering deficiencies in planning, command, control, and execution. The invasion began before dawn on October 25 when American forces, aided by multinational Caribbean defense forces, landed on Grenada. Occasionally sharp fighting lasted through the twenty-eighth.[39] Air Force C-5, C-141, and C-130 transports flew 991 sorties, some under enemy fire, delivering over 15,000 tons of cargo and 36,000 troops and passengers. The students were rescued without loss, and came home loudly praising the intervention and the military, stifling criticism of the operation and helping to dramatically swing public opinion in favor of the administration. The military quickly restored order, and the Grenadans—the overwhelming majority of whom were profoundly grateful for the intervention—moved quickly to install a democratic leadership.

Still, some problems did reveal themselves, though not as many as some critics subsequently alleged.[40] Although the command structure was an improvement over Vietnam, Desert One, and Lebanon, there was still a demarcation between "Army" and "Marine" sectors that caused unnecessary complexity, and planning was characterized by a gradualist approach that prevented the rapid achievement of the classic *coup de main* and, indeed, necessitated substantial reinforcement of combat forces to confront a nagging and determined resistance. Helicopters took high losses from unexpectedly strong antiaircraft fire; 30 of 100 involved were hit, and 9 were lost. Grenada marked the baptism of the new UH-60 Blackhawk helicopter, which performed generally well, although it did not prove immune to losses. Marine AH-1T Cobra gunships contributed significantly to the success of the Marines' ground campaign, but two of four were shot down, with a loss of three of their four crewmen (one of whom Cuban troops murdered on the ground). The antiaircraft fire—especially from 23mm cannon—particularly endangered C-130s carrying in the Ranger assault force. As Grenada veteran Richard D. Hooker, Jr., has written, "Several of the 23 C-130 transport aircraft used in the airborne assault of Point Salines airport were holed . . . and only a courageous decision to descend to 500 feet (the minimum jump altitude for the assaulting Rangers) averted the probable loss of several of the aircraft, each filled with over 60 troops."[41] (An Air Force AC-130H Spectre gunship contributed significantly to Urgent Fury's success—as gunships would later in Panama—by silencing antiaircraft batteries firing at troop transports and undertaking general support missions.) Close air support strikes by naval aircraft produced friendly casualties. Some vestiges of peacetime thinking remained; at one point, Vice Adm. Joseph Metcalf, commander of the invasion forces, noticed two helicopters on the deck of his helicopter carrier were taking a long time to refuel and rearm. He inquired why and found the Marine crews arguing with a petty officer insisting that they have the properly signed accountable form for the fuel they were getting. "The biggest problem I found," he related later, "is getting people to shed their peacetime way of thinking and realize they are at war."[42]

Communications, intelligence, and planning all came under justifiable criticism. So urgent—literally—was the invasion requirement that planners duplicated each other's activities, kept details "close hold" among themselves for security reasons, and failed (on occasion) to share necessary intelligence among all key players. A split occurred in senior defense leadership between the John Lehman camp, which believed a naval task force with embarked Marines could handle the crisis, and Weinberger, who believed that the operation had to be broader and should involve Army Rangers supplied by Air Force airlift. While one can sympathize with Lehman's fear of unnecessary "jointness," the presence of larger-than-perhaps-necessary forces proved necessary and guaranteed success. Throughout his tenure as defense secretary, Weinberger followed a simple rule: "My invariable practice was to double, at least, any Joint Chief recommendations as to the size of a force required, *since I always had in mind that one of the major problems with our attempt to rescue our hostages in Iran in 1979 was that we sent too few helicopters*" (emphasis added).[43] Given the high helicopter losses—particularly a full 50 percent of the Marine attack helicopters available for troop support—his decision was prudent.

Despite some commentary by critics, the majority of participants, planners, and the public at large were satisfied, if sobered.[44] War is not tidy, and there are always discontinuities. Coming after the demoralization of Vietnam, the bitter experience of Desert One, and the shock of Beirut, Grenada was a welcome relief, for it demonstrated that the post-Vietnam U.S. military could do something right on a large scale. By prompt large-scale military action, the Reagan administration demonstrated resolve and overthrew a Marxist state, preventing the development of a dangerous three-cornered "triangle of influence" between Cuba, Nicaragua, and Grenada. For these reasons, its significance must not be underestimated. Certainly, Deputy Undersecretary of Defense Dov S. Zakheim was absolutely correct when he wrote:

> The cumulative impact of Grenada on America's self-image should not be underestimated. It represented a clearcut military success—something that the American public had not witnessed since before Vietnam. It marked the expression of American vigor in foreign policy, and signified an understanding of the role of force as a vehicle for the support of U.S. foreign policy objectives when all other options are closed except passive resignation to the whims of fate.[45]

The third event in 1983 ensured that the U.S. Navy would end the year on a somber note, courtesy of a Lebanese air strike that got out of hand. In response to antiaircraft missiles fired at low-flying reconnaissance aircraft, the Sixth Fleet launched a two-carrier air strike on December 4 against Syrian gun and radar positions. Two airplanes went down from

SAMs, an A-6 and A-7; one airman died, one was rescued immediately, and one was held as a prisoner by the Syrians for a month. Bad planning, poor leadership, unrealistic time schedules, haste to meet schedules imposed by individuals thousands of miles from the scene, abysmal tactics, poor target selection, and poor weapons selection all contributed to losses that caused Navy Secretary John Lehman to react in fury. He immediately ventured to the two carriers involved, and after receiving unsatisfactory answers from the on-scene commanders, he "went down to the squadron ready rooms to begin finding out what really had happened."[46] What he discovered led him to conclude that even had the system worked perfectly (which it certainly hadn't), the Navy was fundamentally unprepared to undertake modern, post–Vietnam era strike missions without suffering serious losses. "Left to their desires," he concluded, "the task force simply would have added more aircraft and loaded more bombs and gone later in the day, with possibly greater losses."[47] As a result, in May 1984, Lehman ordered the establishment of the Strike Warfare Center at Fallon Naval Air Station, Nevada. "Strike University" basically emulated the kind of intensive threat training that had been available to the Air Force since the creation of Red Flag nearly a decade before. Experienced instructors taught attack aviators how to plan and execute air strikes with minimal risk to their own forces, and then let them fly the missions they planned to assess whether or not they worked. The creation of the Strike Warfare Center redressed the last great shortfall in institutionalized tactical air warfare training within the American defense community: training naval attack aviators to confront the threat environment of the 1980s. It ensured that the next time the Navy went "across the beach" in anger—in Libya in 1986—it would be more than ready.[48]

These episodes—the costly *Mayaguez* rescue, the tragedy of Desert One, the disastrous Marine intervention in Beirut, the successful (if imperfect) Grenadan intervention, and the terrible Navy air strike over Lebanon—constituted at times tragic and painful experiences on the road toward institutional competency. Once secured, that competency more typically characterized American military actions from the middle to the end of the decade, such as the Libyan air strikes (1986), Panama (1989), and the Gulf war (1991). At the end of 1983, the defense experiences of the United States since Vietnam could be viewed as a "glass half full, glass half empty" issue: one interpreted optimistically or pessimistically, depending on one's viewpoint. Many critics saw evidence of profound institutional failures that would continue to doom the American military to further defeat, unless, as one reformer put it, "some program for radical reform is adopted."[49] Others saw lingering tatters of Vietnam-era mismanagement that were already being expunged in favor of structural changes within the defense establishment—such as the Weinberger Doctrine, enunciated in 1984—that promised a better future. In this interpretation, those experiences offered cautionary warnings that nothing in military affairs should ever be taken for granted—for example, the notion of complex, long-distance command, the safety of a Marine force in garrison, the ease of seizing an island, and the survivability of a hasty air strike—but did not constitute evidence of pervasive institutional rot.

In 1986, driven by a mix of good motives, including the results of these operations, Congress mandated a major restructuring of the Department of Defense via the bipartisan Goldwater-Nichols Defense Reorganization Act. In retrospect, for all its changes to the nature of the Joint Staff and the relationship between the chairman of the Joint Chiefs and the commanders (the "Cincs") of the unified and specified commands, it seems to have been nice but hardly necessary to the success that accompanied American arms in the last half of the 1980s. Rather, by 1986, the American military establishment had already passed through the most demanding two of its three post-Vietnam stages, growing stronger and being tempered along the way. As a result, now it was ready to act with decisiveness.

A New Assurance: Prairie Fire, Eldorado Canyon, and the Taming of Qaddafi's Terrorism

In 1986, the air services of the United States embarked on their greatest test since the conclusion of the Vietnam War: the penetration of a dense air defense network at night by both naval and Air Force aircraft. What triggered this was a series of increasingly violent terrorist incidents sponsored, condoned, or encouraged by Libya's Muammar Qaddafi. In 1985, allusions to violence against the West, Arab "traitors," and alleged pro-"Zionists" increased dramatically in Qaddafi's speeches and pronouncements. The distinction between friend and enemy blurred. In March, Qaddafi called Lebanese militia leader Nabih Birri "the hero of the liberation of southern Lebanon." In June, a little over two months later, Qaddafi declared, "This man called Nabih Berri, it is right to kill him . . . The one who kills him will enter heaven."[50] In October 1985, the most infamous occurred: terrorists hijacked the cruise ship *Achille Lauro* and murdered an elderly American Jew confined to a wheelchair, then dumped his body overboard. Excellent intelligence enabled Navy F-14s to intercept an Egyptian airliner carrying the terrorists to Algiers and force it to Sicily, but Italian authorities refused to let American special operations forces take the terrorists into custody, a black episode in the fight against terrorism. Other episodes followed, including two particularly brutal airport attacks in Rome and Vienna in late December during which sixteen people fell victim to terrorists. The Reagan administration determined that the time had come to face down Qaddafi. In February, American C-141s supported French forces fighting a Libyan-sponsored insurgency in Chad, and French Jaguar fighter-bombers attacked a Libyan air base in the northern Chad. In March 1986, the Navy began Operation Prairie Fire, a series of fleet exercises in the Gulf of Sidra, with three carriers supported by two AEGIS-class radar cruisers, and 122 other ships. The Libyan air force (500 strong, with a mix of MiG-23s, MiG-25s, Su-22s, Mirage Vs, and Mirage F-1s) attempted to close on the fleet, but the combination of Aegis, airborne early warning E-2Cs, F-14s, and the new F/A-18s kept the Libyans at bay. Sixth Fleet commander Adm. Frank B. Kelso II—confident that Libya would react to this assertion of international rights, that his forces could confront the Libyans and win, and that he had the full backing and support of the Reagan administration for any course of action he might pursue—took the Sixth Fleet across Qaddafi's self-proclaimed "Line of Death" deep into the Gulf of Sidra. That was too much for the Libyan dictator. In the early afternoon of March 24, 1986, Libyan SAM sites at Sirte launched at least two long-range SA-5s—the most sophisticated and dangerous SAM in Qaddafi's inventory—at two Hornets. (The F/A-18s avoided the SAMs, thanks to timely intelligence from the radar cruisers.) Next, Libya sent out three small missile boats to engage the fleet. The two events triggered a series of intensive Navy attacks. A-7s carrying AGM-88 HARM antiradar missiles blew away the SA-5 radar sites (the first combat use of HARM, which had only gone into full-scale production in 1983), and A-6s, firing AGM-84 Harpoon air-to-surface missiles and dropping Rockeye cluster munitions, sank or mortally crippled all three boats. The stage was now set for the next—and potentially most dangerous—phase of America's confrontation with Libya.[51]

In early April, additional terrorist attacks claimed American lives in a Berlin disco and on a TWA jetliner; it was the last straw for the Reagan administration, which believed Qaddafi behind the attacks, although some evidence pointed to Syrian and Iranian involvement. Weinberger and the president authorized a retaliatory night air strike against five terrorist and airfield targets within Libya. The force would consist of eighteen F-111Fs and three EF-111A electronic warfare airplanes from England striking the Tripoli area, and fourteen A-6Es, six A-7Es, and six E/A-18As, covered by EA-6B EW aircraft from two Sixth Fleet carriers striking the Benghazi area, supported by a variety of naval electronic warfare aircraft, AWACS, and tankers. The incorporation of the "one-elevens" from England was a sore spot with Lehman, for he believed (as he later wrote) that the Sixth Fleet could have done it on its own, and that inclusion of the Air Force aircraft was merely a reflection of the administration's obsession with "jointness." There were, in fact, powerful reasons for incorporating the F-111s, the most important of which was that the small force of precision-attack A-6s available to the carriers could not cover all proposed targets. Admiral William Crowe, chairman of the Joint Chiefs of Staff, requested that the F-111s be added to the force, a decision that echoed an idea for a joint Air Force–Navy strike that then-Chief of Naval Operations Adm. James Watkins had first proposed immediately after the Rome and Vienna airport attacks. Further, with the memory of the botched Lebanon carrier strike still fresh in the minds of Washington planners, it was understandable that the JCS, the National Security Planning Group (NSPG), Weinberger, and, ultimately, the president, favored a joint Air Force–Navy strike, Operation Eldorado Canyon, as offering the best expectations for success.[52]

To fully appreciate what the strike forces were up against, it must be remembered that the NATO allies, with the exception of Great Britain, offered precious little assistance to the United States. Italy, Spain, and Greece bluntly refused use of their bases. France, though fighting Libyan forces in Chad, would not allow the strike forces to overfly its territory (yet French president François Mitterand then had the chutzpah to advise Weinberger to hit Qaddafi hard, and not inflict "a mere pinprick"). Mitterand's decision forced the F-111s to fly for seven hours, 2,700 miles one way, to the target, refuel four times (off France, Portugal, Algeria, and Tunisia), and thread the Straits of Gibraltar on their way to downtown Tripoli. Then, of course, they had to repeat the process on the way back. Libya itself hardly qualified as an undefended Third World nation; in fact, it had an air defense network much more complex and layered than North Vietnam's, the toughest the United States had ever faced until Desert Storm broke over Iraq less than five years later. Reflecting on the Libyan raids, Lehman subsequently wrote:

> After the raids, the air force and the navy compared [the air defenses around Tripoli and Benghazi] in studies with target complexes in Russia and the Warsaw Pact countries. *Only three targets behind the Iron Curtain were found to have thicker defenses than the Libyan cities.* Libyan defenses, in addition to the five-hundred-aircraft air force, included a massive network of surveillance and fire control radars, all netted together and controlling integrated SAM [sites] consisting of French Crotale missiles and Soviet SA-2s, 3s, 4s, 5s, 6s, 7s, and 9s. It included a large number of mobile ZSU-23 radar-guided antiaircraft guns and 57mm antiaircraft guns. The system was operated under the direction of three thousand Soviet air defense technicians [emphasis added].[53]

Operation Eldorado Canyon launched on April 15, 1986, timed so that when the F-111s arrived in the area, the Navy's strike force would be on its way, and support aircraft would be jamming, shooting, and capping Libyan defenses. Radar operators in France, Spain, and Portugal had spotted the F-111s but kept silent. Italian radar operators apparently detected the F-111s on their run across the Mediterranean, and, in contrast to their European brethren, alerted Malta. Then run by an unfriendly government sympathetic to Qaddafi (it has changed since), Malta promptly passed a warning to Libya about a half-hour prior to the attack. But no matter. The F-111s went deep and low into Libya before hooking back and striking Tripoli from behind, and the A-6s, also low, went "feet dry" on their way to Benghazi. At exactly 2:00 A.M. local time, Air Force and Navy bombs simultaneously hit their targets; thirteen minutes later, the last strike airplanes went "feet wet," leaving behind shattered debris, a literally shaken dictator, and, regretfully, an F-111 that crashed into the sea, perhaps from antiaircraft fire, taking its crew to their deaths. For hours afterward the night sky of Libya reverberated to the sounds of crackling antiaircraft fire fired by jittery gunners (what goes up must come down, and the steel rain from this barrage might well have claimed its own victims). SAMs launched willy-nilly and glaring tracer rounds produced an almost festive air, a foreshadowing of similar scenes over Baghdad a few years later.[54]

Overall, the Libyan raid was an encouraging one; post-strike reconnaissance showed all of the five targets selected were severely damaged or destroyed. In one case, the Pave Tack targeting system in one F-111F recorded bombs destroying a row of Soviet-built Il-76 transports at Tripoli's airport. A-6 strike crews saw HARM missiles "smothering" SAM sites as the Intruders went inbound and destroyed over twenty Libyan aircraft at Benghazi. Nevertheless, there were some problems. A combination of deficiencies, including generator failure, a refueling mixup, the crash of one plane, last-minute avionics failures, a cracked engine bleed duct, and mistaken identification of a targeting offset point meant that only two of nine F-111s were available to bomb the Bab al-Aziziyya terrorist compound. (Three others struck the Sidi Bilal training establishment as scheduled.) Five F-111s hit Tripoli Airport, although a sixth had to abort due to a systems failure. (Overall, six out of sixteen F-111s that made their targets had to abort, either from the rules of engagement established for the strike, or from systems and equipment failures.) Of the fourteen A-6Es, six hit the Jamahiriyah Barracks at Benghazi (a seventh aborted), though, as Lehman recollected, a civilian building was also accidentally bombed because the crews mistook it for a commando training center. Five Intruders bombed Benina airfield, but two others had to abort from systems failures. Overall, fortunately, civilian casualties in Benghazi and Tripoli were low, although misplaced bombs hit an apartment building and some homes; another bomb blew away a portion of the French embassy in Tripoli. Numerous Libyan homes were seriously damaged from antiaircraft shells that failed to detonate until they fell to earth, and, in at least one case, from a descending SA-3 SAM.[55]

Although some predicted dire terrorism consequences for the West as a result of the attack, in fact such a massive outpouring of violence did not take place, and the focus of the United States in the Middle East shifted from the central Mediterranean and North Africa to a region of growing instability, the Persian Gulf in Southwest Asia. Despite whatever small disappointments and discrepancies accompanied the Libyan strike, it obviously marked a major success for the United States. As Brian L. Davis has written, the Libyan strike "was probably the most controversial discrete foreign policy action undertaken by the Reagan administration."[56] The Reagan administration had shown its willingness to strike a heavily defended nation in the face of bellicose threats of retaliation, and do so with a self-confidence that did not demand a consensus of approval from its allies. It disregarded the foreign press criticism that accompanied the raid; within the United States, the administration's approval rating rose to 70 percent.[57] The U.S. military came away from Libya with the confidence that it *could* execute the sudden bold stroke, even (as had been the case in Libya) against a formidable opponent with a modern and deadly air defense system. It could do this because of training, maintenance, equipment changes, and the traditional courage of its members, but also because of other factors as well. Ably led, the services understood the business they were about and thus increasingly structured realistic plans for execution by individuals having both responsibility and authority. The services could do this because America's executive leadership in the 1980s had a steadily increasing faith in the military, and thus allowed the services to operate with increasingly less bureaucratic restrictions and "Mother may I?" management than had previous administrations. This interplay back and forth of experience, confidence-building, and goodwill created the climate that produced the Desert Storm victory a few years later.

USCENTCOM, Ernest Will, and Combat Operations in the Persian Gulf

The collapse of the Shah of Iran in 1979 removed one of the "two pillars" (the other being Saudi Arabia) that the United States had relied upon for regional stability in the Persian Gulf since the time of the Nixon administration. Southwest Asia immediately descended into a period of political instability characterized by a brutally authoritarian regime in Iran; increased terrorism sponsored by Iran against its neighbors, Western interests, and the United States in particular; the Soviet invasion of Afghanistan (which literally became a Russian nightmare as Vietnam had been an American one); and the outbreak of the Iran-Iraq war. The Iran-Iraq war witnessed savage land combat wherein late twentieth-century technology devastated soldiers largely following nineteenth-century tactical doctrine, a sea war involving attacks on supertankers and oil terminals by aircraft and naval forces operating like well-equipped pirates; a "battle of the cities" where both sides callously used civilian populations for missile practice; and an air war where both sides fitfully employed air power though it could not, in any sense, be said to have contributed meaningfully, except against shipping. This tremendous instability provoked three significant responses: the enunciation of what came to be called the Carter Doctrine, the creation of the regional Gulf Cooperation Council (GCC), and the establishment of a Rapid Deployment Force (RDF) that led eventually to U.S. Central Command (USCENTCOM).[58]

In his January 1980 State of the Union address, Pres. Jimmy Carter had enunciated the Carter Doctrine, which affirmed that the Gulf was an area of vital interest to the United States and that the United States would, if necessary, fight to prevent the Gulf from falling under the control of a hostile power. Later that year he established the so-called Rapid Deployment Force, a paper tiger until the Reagan administration gave it genuine teeth. (Senator Henry "Scoop" Jackson, a member of Carter's own party, echoed the famous *bon mot* applied to the Holy Roman Empire when he remarked that the RDF was "neither rapid, nor deployable, nor a force.")[59] In 1981, as a result of the Iran-Iraq war, the terrorist seizing of the mosque at Mecca (an unthinkable blasphemy to the Saudi government, the guardian of the two most holy shrines of Islam) and the Soviet invasion of Afghanistan, the Gulf states—Saudi Arabia, Kuwait, Qatar, Bahrain, Oman, and the United Arab Emirates (UAE)—formed a Gulf Cooperation Council. Ironically, this body had pronounced pro-Iraqi sympathies, a natural result of the vitriolic nature of the Iranian revolutionaries and their attempts at subverting the Gulf states, though, of course, it eventually became an important bulwark in the struggle against Saddam Hussein in 1990–91.[60]

The GCC, possessing immense wealth, nevertheless had little military strength. That was where USCENTCOM came in. An RDF Joint Task Force—the nation's first peacetime four-service (Army–Air Force–Navy–Marines) rapid reaction force headquarters—spawned the U.S. Central Command, which the Department of Defense established on January 1, 1983. Headquartered at MacDill Air Force Base, Florida, USCENTCOM's area of responsibility spanned no less than nineteen nations, from Egypt across the Horn of Africa, the Red Sea, the Arabian peninsula, the Persian Gulf, and across Iran, Afghanistan, and Pakistan. To function well, the command demanded reliable airlift (the United States being no less than fourteen hours away), sealift, and pre-positioning of critical supplies. USCENTCOM subsequently became the key Gulf player in the preparations for and conduct of Desert Storm. That year, American military forces engaged in Operation Bright Star, a rapid force and air power deployment to Egypt, including B-52 missions and joint Egyptian–Air Force air combat exercises. Bright Star was a valuable training introduction to the Middle East and the challenges of dealing with Arab military forces.[61]

The creation of USCENTCOM sent an important signal to the international community that America's leadership viewed the Persian Gulf as so critical as to warrant the possible expenditure of American lives to defend vital interests. But the command's mission was really to deter direct conflict, and to ensure that mideastern sea lanes remained open. For that reason, when Kuwait asked the United States in January 1987 to help it get its tankers through the Gulf unmolested, the United States quickly gave its assent. Iran had launched a wave of air and naval attacks specifically against Kuwaiti tankers by aircraft, antiship missiles, mines, military vessels, and speedboats, and other nations' tankers came under frequent attack as well. Out of this was born the so-called reflagging of Kuwaiti tankers and their escort by American and Allied naval vessels, Operation Earnest Will.[62] This activity, coupled with intensive multinational minesweeping operations, destruction of selected Iranian military forces by the United States, and the end of the Iran-Iraq war, eventually restored a brief measure of sanity to the Gulf before Saddam Hussein unleashed his own peculiar brand of *realpolitik* in August 1990.

Unfortunately, the brief tranquility in the Gulf came with a price. On May 17, 1987, an Iraqi aircraft fired two Exocet antiship missiles into the USS *Stark,* a frigate patrolling the Gulf. Evidence at the time suggested that the Iraqi pilot had mistaken the *Stark* for an Iranian ship, and nothing since then has changed this interpretation. Unfortunately, in part because of confusion over rules of engagement and inattention, the ship did not get its defenses together in time, and, as a result, thirty-seven Americans died. The *Stark,* badly damaged, survived because of the professionalism and dedication of its damage-control crew. Unlike the Navy in the 1970s, the oft-belittled "quality force" of the late 1980s was just that, and they proved it amid the hellish inferno ravaging the *Stark.* A second serious attack took place on May 14, 1988, not quite a year later. The USS *Samuel B. Roberts,* another frigate, ran across an Iranian-laid mine, breaking its back and nearly splitting the ship in two. Again, heroic ship-handling and brilliant damage-control improvisation saved the ship, which returned to service in time for Desert Storm. Frank Carlucci (who had replaced Weinberger as secretary of defense), Lehman, and Reagan all recognized that the Iranians had not laid this field by accident. Accordingly, on April 18, 1988, naval aircraft and ships attacked Iranian oil platforms and naval vessels (one of which cheekily fired a Harpoon missile acquired during the Shah's days, fortunately without effect). They destroyed half the Iranian navy in a single day, including a frigate nailed by a Skipper guided bomb launched from an A-6.[63]

One more terrible act had to be played out in the Gulf before the brief peace began that lasted until Saddam Hussein's invasion of Kuwait—the accidental shootdown of an Iranian Airbus commercial airliner by the USS *Vincennes,* an AEGIS-class guided-missile cruiser. On July 3, 1988, in the midst of a running surface battle with various Iranian small boats, the *Vincennes* detected an aircraft taking off from Iran and flying a direct course toward the engagement, "squawking" a Mode II (i.e., military) Identification Friend or Foe (IFF) code like an Iranian F-14, and flying on the edge of a permitted flight corridor. By tragic coincidence, the *Vincennes* was reading the IFF of an Iranian military airplane (a C-130 turning up at Bandar Abbas). The oncoming plane ignored repeated warnings and finally, fearing an attack, the cruiser launched surface-to-air missiles and downed the airliner. Within the Navy, an explosive exchange of professional views followed regarding the *Vincennes*'s actions; some sarcastically dubbed the ship "Robocruiser," and others leapt to the defense of the ship, its radar system, and its crew. Other critics immediately made a tragic situation worse by drawing inaccurate and misleading parallels to the Soviet shootdown of a Korean 747 airliner several years before, ignoring that the ship was in the midst of a battle, a battle in which five Iranian vessels were apparently sunk, and was itself taking fire from those vessels. The whole tragic, distasteful episode is best summarized by Weinberger, who wrote, "Captain Will Rogers of the *Vincennes* made efforts to identify the aircraft and only fired when warnings went unheeded. In my view, he was fully justified in his actions."[64]

American operations in the Gulf, the establishment of USCENTCOM, cooperation with the GCC, and the expansion of American presence and influence in Southwest Asia via use of the combined air-sea base at Diego Garcia in the Indian Ocean resulted in amelioration of the tense relations that had previously characterized American–Gulf Arab relations in the wake of the 1967 and 1973 Arab-Israeli wars. Few more dramatically different cultures existed, one Judeo-Christian, liberal, and Western, the other Islamic, conservative, and Middle Eastern. But the forced working together brought on by the Iranian revolution and its aftermath, together with American help to the guerrilla fighters in Afghanistan, did much to dampen belief in the United States as a "Great Satan," and established the foundations for cordial and supportive relationships in the future. It even offset, fortunately, the inanities of the Iran-Contra affair and its aftermath. American actions in the Middle East demonstrated important resolve as well to both the Soviets (bogged down in Afghanistan, and finding their aircraft and helicopters vulnerable to American-supplied Stinger missiles) and the Iranians, who previously had tended to regard the United States as little more than a blusterer. The key to supporting all of this, of course, was a well-honed, confident, and expert military system—

which, by late 1989, the United States clearly possessed. The military services had come a long way from the doldrums of the late 1970s, and an even longer way from Vietnam. It is ironic, of course, that all this was missed by Saddam Hussein, for the growing evidence of American confidence, expertise, and capability was everywhere to be seen. He fell victim to the old conventional wisdom. There was still one remaining chance for him to get the message, however: the overthrow of the Noriega government in December 1989. Unfortunately for Iraq, he missed that as well.

Just Cause: The Bush Administration Meets Its First Challenge

As of the writing of this work, the final outcome of the Panamanian intervention remains in the wings. The former dictator of Panama, Manuel Antonio Noriega, has been in detention since January 3, 1990, when he left the Papal Nuncio in Panama City for American custody. Shackled and seemingly in shock, he was transported by an Army helicopter to a nearby airbase, arrested there by an agent of the Drug Enforcement Agency, and then flown on an Air Force transport into captivity in the United States. The Panama incursion, Operation Just Cause, had its roots in growing disenchantment with the government of Noriega, a government that preyed upon its own citizens and served South American drug cartels shipping their lethal wares to the United States. Presiding over all this was Noriega himself, who, in an earlier and less tolerant era of American life, might have served as the archetype of the cinematic Latin dictator. Partial to voodoo, prostitutes, and the intimidation, torture, and murder of his enemies—defined loosely as anyone who got in his way—Noriega was, undoubtedly, one of the singularly unappealing international figures of the 1980s. Unfortunately, he had also at one time been an intelligence source for the United States, while a junior officer. But those days of wary collaboration were long over. After a series of increasingly violent incidents, including the overturning of legitimate election results and the brutal, televised beating of the rival candidates, an abortive coup, the murder of a American Marine, and the beating and assault of a naval officer and his wife, the U.S. government determined to remove him and the para-military forces that kept him in power.

The Panamanian intervention constituted the first major military test of the new Bush administration, and the defense leadership that had succeeded that of the Reagan years—Secretary of Defense Richard "Dick" Cheney and Chief of Staff Gen. Colin Powell.[65] The Bush-Cheney-Powell leadership style showed a strong continuity on defense basics: to see force as a last, not first, resort in international affairs, and to use its implicit threat whenever possible instead of conflict itself; but to unhesitatingly use it in the pursuit of national security objectives when other options would not work. Two pre-Panama cases illustrated this: the use of American airplanes flying over the Philippines to intimidate rebels from attacking the troubled government of Corazon Aquino, and the decision not to support a coup in Panama against Noriega sponsored by Panamanian officers of dubious background and abilities.

This latter decision gained the Bush administration a great deal of criticism, criticism that, in retrospect, seems ill-founded, since had the United States acted, the results might have been merely the replacement of one dictator by another. Instead, Bush ordered extensive planning and preparation so that the United States could be ready to intervene should circumstances require it. Those circumstances came in mid-December 1989. Noriega declared his regime "at war" with the United States, and the murder and brutalization of American military personnel followed. At 12:45 A.M. on December 20, Army, Navy, and Air Force special operations forces undertook the boldest military action of the United States since Vietnam—the deliberate overthrowing of a hostile regime.

The military campaign that followed was sharp, swift, and decisive, characterized by occasional bitter fighting, and culminating in a manhunt for Noriega that forced him into temporary sanctuary offered by the Vatican's personal representative, and then into American custody. The new Apache helicopter gunship demonstrated its value as a battlefield support system, and old favorites such as the AC-130 showed their continuing worth. The F-117 made its combat debut, two dropping bombs near a Panamanian barracks to intimidate and stun Noriega's troops. (Some misunderstandings resulted in the bombs dropping near but not precisely on the intended targets, although Army Rangers waiting nearby expressed their satisfaction with the strike.) The incursion had been accompanied by a massive airborne drop of troops sent directly from Ft. Bragg, North Carolina, the largest night combat air-drop since the Normandy invasion forty-five years before. In less than thirty-six hours, Air Force airlifters delivered 9,500 troops to Panama. Well-trained, highly motivated special operations forces—the Army's Delta Force, and Navy SEALs, for example—had quickly seized key objectives (though the SEALs took heavy losses from stiff resistance), liberated an American held for months in Panamanian captivity, and paved the way for conventional assault forces to follow. Achieving this cost the United States twenty-three killed and over three hundred injured. As for the Panamanians, they greeted American troops with wild demonstrations of support, cheering and encouraging U.S. forces wherever they appeared. It was Grenada writ large; 92 percent of Panama's citizens polled by CBS News supported the American intervention in their country. As the New Year dawned and Noriega left Panama in custody and disgrace, America's support of its military reached a new post-Vietnam high.

Invigorating Military Thought and Doctrine: Summers, Warden, Lehman, Rice

As defense analyst Maurice A. Mallin has perceptively noted,

> It does not appear that the Reagan administration assumed office with a clear vision of future military strategy. Yet the Reagan years saw a renaissance in military thought . . . As a collection of global policies, strategies, and doctrines, the Reagan administration's initiatives serve as conclusive evidence that the United States had broken from the self-imposed shackles of Vietnam.[66]

In the mid- to late 1980s, two powerful books by distinguished officers appeared that had profound impact on the American defense establishment. These were Harry G. Summers, Jr.'s *On Strategy: A Critical Analysis of the Vietnam War*, and John A. Warden III's *The Air Campaign: Planning for Combat*.[67] Both were products of senior defense colleges, the former written at the Army War College and the latter at the National War College. Both represented a rediscovery and re-emphasis of the teachings of Carl von Clausewitz but with some critical rethinking. After its extraordinary combat successes in the Spanish-American War dramatically counterpointed equally extraordinary deficiencies in logistics and supply, the Army had established the Army War College. After Vietnam, where a superb logistics and supply system dramatically highlighted failures in the conduct of the war itself, the Army War College had Summers investigate why. Summers placed the blame upon too little appreciation for the classic Clausewitzian principles of war, concluding that "the quintessential 'strategic lesson learned' from the Vietnam War is that we must once again become masters of the profession of arms."[68] The resulting book became a military masterpiece, taught throughout the professional military schools of the United States. Warden did the same kind of analysis for the Air Force while a student at the National War College, emphasizing air combat at the operational level of war, and how an air commander must plan and structure an air campaign. (Ironically, when he went to the college, his initial thought had been to write a military biography of Alexander the Great; what opportunity classical scholarship lost, modern air power scholarship gained.) Out of this came the clearest American expression of air power thought since the days of Mitchell and Seversky, though considerably more concise, cogent, and balanced.

Central to the thinking of both Summers and Warden was the Clausewitzian notion of "centers of gravity." To Clausewitz, an enemy possessed centers of gravity that an opponent should disrupt and destroy; these centers, Clausewitz had stated, were "the point against which all energies should be directed."[69] Both Summers and Warden took this to heart. Warden emphasized identifying the centers of gravity and structuring an air campaign to destroy them, drawing on experience derived from previous air wars and warfare in general. Military objectives, he concluded, could be the destruction of some or all of an enemy's forces, an enemy's economy, or the enemy's will to resist. The latter did not call for indiscriminate attacks against civilian population centers; rather, it might be achieved by targeting forces and the economy, or by demonstrating the resolve to continue fighting until victory was won. Further, proper identification of a center of gravity was critical (and Summers echoed this as well), and did not merely involve securing control of enemy territory. "Territory," Warden argued,

> is a dangerous enchantress in war. Serious wars are rarely won by capturing territory, unless that territory includes a vital political or economic center of gravity, the loss of which precludes continuing the war . . . Territory may well be the political objective of a campaign, but it rarely should be the military objective.[70]

Warden argued convincingly that, in several important regards, air warfare constituted a mirror-image of ground warfare: defensive air operations were always much more fraught with risk, difficult, and less productive than offensive air operations. Further, whereas classic Clausewitzian thought envisioned attacks directed against an enemy's fielded forces (the "shell" protecting the fragile nation-state)—for only in this manner could one army force another to combat—Warden recognized that air attack could wage war from the "inside out," against what he termed (in other writings) the "Five Strategic Rings": simultaneous attacks against a nation's leadership (the innermost target), key production, infrastructure, a population's support for its government, and fielded military forces (the outermost shell). To this degree, Warden's analysis could be considered "post-Clausewitzian" in contrast to Summer's "neo-Clausewitzian" approach.

Warden concluded his analysis by examining the process of air campaign planning. He stressed that, except under the most extraordinary circumstances, an air commander should emphasize achieving theater-wide air superiority, since placing air on the defensive imposed too many risks and generally allowed an enemy air force the ability to concentrate.[71]

Air superiority did not necessarily imply exclusively relying upon air power; land and sea forces could contribute significantly to the gaining and holding of air superiority (as, indeed, happened with the partnership of Air Force and Army special operating forces attacking Iraqi radars in the Gulf war). But without air superiority, all other missions—particularly ground operations, CAS, and air interdiction—would be degraded or prevented.

Given air superiority, an air commander next had to apportion the rest of the air effort: responding to emergency situations, playing off interdiction versus CAS, and determining the sequencing and/or synchronicity of air superiority, interdiction, and close support missions. Warden believed that the natural tendency to drop all other missions and assist ground forces by direct attack should an enemy launch an unexpectedly strong offensive must be tempered by appraisal of whether or not the enemy air force could still fight effectively. If it could, the temptation should be avoided; if it could not, then air could go to the immediate assistance of ground forces, particularly if the battle was likely to be the war's decisive encounter. As to interdiction versus CAS, Warden recognized that, historically, interdiction (both distant, intermediate, and close) has been far more productive; if no suitable interdiction targets existed, then an air force could be applied to CAS. Finally, rather than trying to fulfill all air missions simultaneously, the air commander should remember the importance of concentration and emphasize first air superiority; then, as the air superiority campaign was well on its way to succeeding, interdiction, and then, finally CAS. (This, again, was basically the progression followed in the Gulf war.) Warden concluded his work with a general examination of the problem of reserve forces, and knowing when to commit them, and the importance of clearly delineated command and control.[72]

At the time that Warden undertook his study, the service was in the midst of one of its periodic struggles over revising Air Force Manual 1-1, *Functions and Basic Doctrine of the United States Air Force*. In the absence of consensus regarding the direction that AFM 1-1 should take, Warden's book, blending creative thought with tenets echoing the venerated Clausewitz and Mitchell, assumed the de facto role of doctrinal guide and, indeed, air power "bible." Like Summer's earlier book, Warden's *The Air Campaign*—with its cautious, realistic, yet essentially hopeful appraisal of air power application—provoked widespread discussion, controversy, and review throughout the Air Force. It catapulted Warden into the first rank of modern air power theorists, on a level with individuals such as Great Britain's R. A. "Tony" Mason.[73] Not surprisingly, Warden received assignment to the Pentagon as deputy director of plans for Air Force headquarters. In that capacity, he would play a vital role in planning the air campaign against Saddam Hussein, an air campaign that reflected virtually all the salient points he had made in his book. Indeed, it is not too extreme to state that Warden was the Hal George and Haywood Hansell of the Gulf war: just as Lt. Col. Hal George and Major "Possum" Hansell had been the principle architects of A.W.P.D./1 (the conceptual plan created in the spring of 1941 that structured the Army Air Forces's strategic bombing campaign against Nazi Germany) John Warden structured the thinking and approach that subsequently crystallized in the Desert Storm strategic air campaign plan.[74]

The widespread acceptance of Summers's and Warden's interpretations generally coincided with the enunciation of the previously discussed Army's AirLand Battle doctrine, the Maritime Strategy of Navy Secretary John Lehman, and came just a little before the release of the *Global Reach—Global Power* White Paper by Air Force Secretary Donald Rice in 1990. Lehman, an articulate and forceful proponent of what might be termed a neo-Mahanistic view of the world, developed the *Maritime Strategy* in response to the decline of creative naval thought in the years after Vietnam. He revitalized the Navy by launching an ambitious program to rebuild naval forces and reassert a realistic and strong naval presence around the globe. Central to his strategy were a number of key ideas, including denying an enemy the use of the seas; and ensuring unimpeded use of the seas by the United States and its allies to support the land battle; carrying the fight to the enemy; and terminating a war on favorable terms.[75]

Lehman believed strongly in integrating maritime, land, and air forces, and, to that end, worked with the other services, particularly the Air

Force, to achieve a degree of jointness that had not been seen since the Second World War. As a result—analogous to the Army–Air Force's "31 Initiatives" effort—the Navy and the Air Force integrated planning and various weapon systems into their routine operations. For example, AWACS supported fleet air defense, and B-52s, armed with Harpoon missiles as long-range antishipping aircraft, undertook sea surveillance missions. By 1989 Lehman could write, correctly:

> The fact that U.S. Air Force AWACS, B-52 bombers, and fighters are now integral parts of every significant naval exercise and theater strategy attests to the fact that while interservice rivalry is strong on the playing fields of service academies, it does not interfere with the effective integration of our operating forces. The unrehearsed yet fully integrated U.S. Navy/U.S. Air Force strike on facilities that supported terrorism in Libya in 1986 put the lie to the myth that the services do not work well together.[76]

Unfortunately, what the *Maritime Strategy* did not address was warfare at the *operational* level of war—the level of decisionmaking and conflict between the tactical and strategic levels. Lehman made notable contributions to both of these—with the tactically focused Strike Warfare Center and the strategically oriented *Maritime Strategy*. This operational shortfall, regrettably, would become apparent with the Navy's subsequent experience in Desert Storm.[77]

The Air Force's *Global Reach—Global Power* White Paper, issued in June 1990, represented a bold departure point for the service, thanks to the forceful decisiveness of Secretary Rice, a former president of the Rand Corporation. In fact (and rather incredibly), it constituted the first senior-level official enunciation ever issued of just how the U.S. Air Force contributed to national security. Previous Air Force secretaries had rarely taken so direct a role in shaping a coherent framework for the service's future, preferring to leave this to the "blue suit" community. The *Global Reach—Global Power* initiative (which functioned as a strategic planning document) grew out of the recognition that air power offered clear advantages unavailable to other forms of land or sea power: the ability to reach anywhere on the globe within hours with decisive military force, thanks to five unique characteristics inherent within modern air power. These were *speed, range, flexibility, precision,* and *lethality*.

Air power seemed particularly well suited to the uncertain world of the post–Warsaw Pact era, by fulfilling five main objectives. First, it could *sustain nuclear deterrence*, for even in the post–Warsaw Pact era, the Soviet Union would be the only power in the world capable of destroying the United States in minutes. Second, air power could *provide versatile combat forces* for power projection and combat operations faster and with greater response than any other options. Third, it could *supply rapid global mobility* via airlift and tanker forces. Fourth, via surveillance, communications, and navigation systems, air power ensured *control of the high ground* to provide global knowledge and situational awareness. Finally, air power could *build U.S. influence* via airlift, crisis response, shows of force, and the like.[78]

Issued on the verge of Saddam Hussein's invasion of Kuwait, *Global Reach—Global Power* attracted immediate attention within the national defense community, provoking an immediate debate between air power modernists and sea power traditionalists, particularly over its recognition that land-based air power now constituted the dominant form of national presence and power projection. *Global Reach—Global Power* did not, in fact, actually attack traditional sea power precepts, but this was often lost in the dialogue between pro and con spokesmen that immediately broke out, a dialogue that reflected deeper battles over budget cutbacks and the attendant scrambling for resources.[79] What many missed in the dialogue that accompanied the release of *Global Reach—Global Power* was the careful and strong emphasis made within it for joint and "purple" approaches to war-fighting and international power projection, recalling the "co-equal and interdependent" language in FM 100-20 of 1943 or, for that matter, the intent of the Goldwater-Nichols Defense Reorganization Act of 1986. Land-based air power, the document clearly stated, could greatly enhance the combat power and combat efficiency of traditional land and sea forces. In retrospect, read after the Gulf war, it set forth in straightforward fashion many of the attributes of land-based air power made manifest in that conflict. This synergy of air-land-sea operations—an effective coupling of the notions of *Global Reach—Global Power,* the AirLand Battle doctrine, and the legacy of Lehman's Maritime Strategy—promised that in the uncertain world of the 1990s, the military strength of the United States would be flexibly, effectively, and decisively utilized whenever and however it might be required.

Five

The Road to War

*There is no merit in putting off a war for a
year if, when it comes, it is a far worse war or
one much harder to win.*
Winston Churchill (1948)

When Manuel Noriega entered prison in January 1990, not quite fifteen years had passed since South Vietnam had fallen to the Communists. The world had witnessed many major developments in that time: the opening of a peaceful dialogue between Egypt and Israel; the uncomfortable ending of the Indochina war, including boat people adrift on the South China Sea and fields of shattered skulls in Cambodia; continued conflict in the Middle East; the collapse of the Shah and the revolutionary terror that followed; the protracted and brutal Iran-Iraq and Afghanistan wars; the increasing liberalization of China and then its descent, once again, into repressive tyranny; the discrediting of the Sandinista revolution in particular and communism in general in Central America; the economic near-collapse of the Soviet Union, the outbreak of protest in Eastern Europe, and the de facto collapse of the Warsaw Pact system. Fixated on the U.S.-Soviet relationship and the welcome events in Europe, many idealistically argued that the time for military force was past; clearly, humanity had evolved beyond it.[1] They saw the constant military investment and preparation of the United States since 1945 as evidence of squandered wealth, not as proof that pressure continually applied had finally worn down a potentially aggressive hostile alliance system until it had collapsed.

At the same time, there were others more than willing to use force to coerce their citizens and neighbors, however "immature" it might seem. For this reason, and because the changes of the 1970s and 1980s had induced far more instability than stability, defense decisionmakers generally agreed that strong and well-prepared military forces would be as necessary in the 1990s as they had been at the height of the Cold War. Fortunately, those military forces were not only well prepared, but well led. In the decade between Desert One and the invasion of Panama, the nature of the national leadership and the capabilities and motivations of its military forces had changed as dramatically as from night to day. From conflict to conflict, America's military establishment had gone from strength to strength. The men and women of the all-volunteer forces were well equipped, well led, well motivated, well trained, experienced, and confident. Their motto might have been taken from the title of one of Richard Nixon's post-presidential books—*No More Vietnams*—for no stronger article of faith inspired them more than this.

The National Defense Report Card

The clock has almost run down; all that remains is the Kuwait crisis and the outbreak of war itself. There is no more time to restructure, reform, and reshape the American military; what has not been done cannot now be done. How ready, one wonders, is the American military at this point in its existence? In a hypothetical report card, Table 5.1 illustrates the results of the grades the United States defense establishment would have achieved over the last twenty-year grading period.[2]

At the end of July 1990, on the eve of the Gulf crisis, then, the American military establishment possessed the following advantages over any potential opponent. It had military and civilian leaders dedicated to avoiding the problems of leadership that had afflicted the United States and its military forces in the Vietnam era. It had combat forces with experience in realistic training at specialized training facilities, equipped with excellent, high-technology force-enhancing weapons and combat support systems. It had realistic doctrinal notions for conducting air-land-sea combat operations. It had highly motivated, well-trained volunteer military personnel (both officers and enlisted personnel, both men and women) supported by a strong civilian work force, and drawing

Table 5.1. The National Defense Report Card

Subject	1970	1980	1990
National civil/political leadership	C	D	B+
DoD/service leadership	C	C−	A
Military training	C−	B	A
Military equipment	B	B	A+
Maintainability and supportability of U.S. forces	A	D	A
Military doctrine and thought	C	C	A
Morale	C	C−	A−
Ability to undertake military tasks	B−	C	A
Civilian perception of military competence	C−	F	B
Military perception of military competence	C−	C+	A
Allies' perceptions of U.S. military competence	C	D	A
Quality of incoming military trainees	C	C	B+
Race relations	D	C	B
Relations between sexes	C	C	B
Drug/alcohol abuse	D	C	B+
Average Grade	C	C−	A−

upon the talents and abilities of a nationwide science, technology, and industrial work force. It had strong, mutually supportive relations with sister services in other allied countries. It had the confidence and experience coming from actual combat.

There is one irony regarding the American military establishment and its capabilities that should be noted—Saddam Hussein's timing of the Kuwaiti invasion. The military establishment had restructured itself and been built up to confront the challenges of international communism, focused on (some would say mesmerized by) the prospect of a NATO–Warsaw Pact war. By mid-1990, international communism was in total disarray, and critics were calling for massive cuts in defense spending. Realistically, given domestic concerns and international relations, the U.S. military could look forward to lean years in the decade of the 1990s, with dramatic force reductions. The irony is this: had Saddam Hussein waited three to five years before attacking Kuwait, the United States and the allied nations may not have been in a position to intervene. Further, had he curbed his ambitions toward Iran and, instead, attacked Kuwait in 1980, it is entirely likely that he could have gotten away with it, because of the poor state of the American military, the support he undoubtedly would have received from the Brezhnev government, and the national demoralization within the United States accompanying changes in the Middle East. Timing, in international relations as in life, is everything.

Iraq's Rise as Regional Troublemaker

We come now to Saddam Hussein, a strong, charismatic, ruthless, and ambitious dictator with a penchant for seeking violent solutions to real or imagined problems, whether personal or public. At the time of the Gulf war, Pres. George Bush compared him to another such individual, Adolf Hitler; many criticized Bush on the grounds that Saddam was not really in Hitler's league. In fact, there are many similarities (even sociological ones) in the backgrounds of both Hitler and Hussein, and, in personal violence toward others, Saddam Hussein appears even more reprehensible. Both participated in failed coups subsequently mythologized to enhance their leadership image. Both ruthlessly purged their parties and "old guard" shortly after rising to power; as Hitler purged the Nazi Party and *Sturm Abteilungen* (SA), establishing the more reliable *Schutz Staffeln* (SS), so did Saddam purge the Baath Party and Iraq's Revolutionary Command Council, and create the Republican Guard. Both Nazi Germany and Iraq armed themselves on a massive and disproportionate scale to their neighbors, with the full intent of going to war at some future time. Both espoused strongly expansionist philosophies; Hitler believed in a "Gross Deutschland," Saddam Hussein in restoring the power and influence of Iraq to the glories of Babylonia. Both justified their egregious behavior by accusing their neighbors of all sorts of imagined slights and desires. Both shared a virtually bottomless capacity for violence, personally participating in the extermination of their enemies. But whereas Hitler emphasized institutional violence, Saddam Hussein relished personal violence; at one point, before his rise to national power, he reputedly served as a torturer for the Baath government, in the cellars of the so-called *Qasr-al-Nihayyah,* the "Palace of the End," where political prisoners were abused and killed. Then, after becoming ruler of Iraq, he allegedly murdered political opponents by his own hand on at least several occasions.[3]

Baathism itself enshrined a cult of violence within the Iraqi state, being a mélange of twisted historical myths and philosophies blended to endorse and conform with the cult of the strong ruler. As Thomas Boylston Adams noted, the Baath movement "is founded on a serious belief in the virtue of violence as the catalyst of civilization."[4] Saddam Hussein took control as leader of Iraq and head of the Baath Party in 1979 after his predecessor retired, immediately ensuring his personal security and rule by purging likely political rivals, in the grand tradition of the Abbasid dynasty in the tenth century, or the toppling of the Hashamite monarchy two decades previous. He faced formidable challenges in ruling Iraq, for its population is roughly one-fifth Sunni Muslim Kurdish tribesmen, one-fifth Sunni Muslim Arab, one-half Shia Muslim Arab, and one-tenth non-Muslim and/or non-Arab. The Baath leadership, for the most part, comes from the minority Sunni Muslims. His solution, not surprisingly, was a draconian mix of domestic spying, communications monitoring, intimidation, and outright terror by the *Mukhabarat,* his secret police, and creation of an organized praetorian force called the Republican Guard. Like Hitler's SS, the Republican Guard had significant domestic and national security functions, and their privileges, equipment, training, and status reflected their importance to Saddam's state. To this degree, they were "elite" (a word much overused when describing them) but, as Gen. H. Norman Schwarzkopf remarked subsequently (comparing them to American forces), "Elite is a relative word."[5]

Situated at the top of the Persian Gulf, Iraqi leaders had always perceived Iran as their natural rival, and Iran certainly returned the complement. Indeed, such suspicion reflected a traditional animosity between Persia and Babylonia in antiquity; both the Baathist party and the Shah's government used their Babylonian or Persian heritage as important empowering symbols, thus keeping this feeling alive. When Iraq came increasingly under Soviet influence in the 1960s and 1970s, the Shah of Iran turned to the United States and Europe for equipment to offset the massive Soviet aid going to the Baath regime. When Iran collapsed in a Shia Islamic fundamentalist revolution, Iraq sensed both a danger and an opportunity. The danger was that traditional Iranian animosity toward Iraq would now exploit the religious sympathies of the Iraqi Shia population. The opportunity was that the revolution had wreaked havoc with Iran's military structure, which the fundamentalists saw as anti-Islam, oriented to the West, and supportive of the *ancien régime.* With a bold masterstroke, Iraq could seize control of key Iranian facilities, particularly the

Shatt al-Arab waterway dividing the two countries, and the Faw peninsula. With other Arab states looking nervously toward Teheran, Saddam Hussein could count on considerable support from the Gulf states, including, ironically, his future victim, Kuwait.[6]

Saddam Hussein launched his war on September 22, 1980, quickly discovering that instead of the planned two-week Iraqi *blitzkrieg,* he had opened up an Iranian hornets' nest that would eventually last for nearly eight years. While the fundamentalist purges of the Iranian military had obviously taken their toll (much as Stalin's had of the Red Army in the 1930s), the Iranian military and citizenry rallied against the Iraqis, fought them back to Iraq's borders, and then threatened to overwhelm them. Saddam Hussein purged his military of incompetents, promoted the professionals, and pinned his hopes on defending Basra, a critical city in southern Iraq. Relying upon First World War frontal assault tactics with which Sir Douglas Haig would have been quite comfortable, the Iranians took appalling losses for no appreciable gain, even though they held the offensive throughout much of the war, thanks to a 3 to 1 advantage in combat forces. After horrendous casualties, Basra held. A series of increasingly futile Iranian ground actions followed; Hussein's regime countered by ordering full mobilization, which Iran's clerics subsequently matched. Casualties soared on both sides, but Iraq's better-trained and -equipped forces took a steady and grim toll of Iranian troops. To increase his advantage, Saddam Hussein then employed chemical weapons, in violation of a 1925 Geneva protocol signed by both Iran and Iraq. Further, the Iraqi military abandoned static defenses for more active ones that would allow the Iranians to advance, channel them into killing zones, and then unleash chemical and air attacks and the Republican Guard upon them. The war expanded from the Iraq-Iran border to the home front, with a series of missile attacks by both the Iranians and Iraqis against each others' cities: in 1988 alone, Iraq fired 189 Scuds at Iran.[7] To destroy Iran's economy, Iraq targeted Iranian oil shipments through the Gulf using air attacks by Exocet-carrying aircraft, in the course of which the USS *Stark* was nearly sunk in May 1987. So successful were these attacks (which one analyst termed "the sole example in history of a successful economic blockade essentially carried out by air power alone") that Iran retaliated with attacks against tankers going to Gulf states helping Iraq, notably Kuwait.[8] In January 1987, Iran launched Karbala V: one last disastrous attack on the Shatt al-Arab. Using active defense coupled with massive firepower, the Iraqis decisively defeated Iranian forces, forcing the Khomeini regime completely on the defensive. Then, in April 1988, Iraq unleashed a blitz that seized the critical Faw peninsula at the mouth of the Shatt al-Arab, establishing unquestioned dominance over the Iranians. Iran, demoralized and effectively shattered as a regional military power, accepted a ceasefire the following July.

It might be expected that Saddam Hussein, having nearly lost the war, would have learned his lesson and set about rebuilding a country with a devastated economy and massive casualties. But instead he launched a series of violent assaults on his political opponents, singling out the Kurds for special attention, including bombing with chemical weapons. Far from curbing his aggressive tendencies, the end of the Iran-Iraq war seemed to have accelerated them; he pressed ahead with research on nuclear weapons (despite a crippling Israeli air strike), chemical weapons, and biological ones as well. Iraq's military budget in 1990 was $12.9 billion, an average of $721 per Iraqi citizen, in a country that had an annual per capita income that year of $1,950.[9] The Soviet Union had been a steadfast ally of Iraq's during the Gulf war (in fact, there were indications that Iraqi aircraft refueled at Soviet bases when attacking Iranian targets along the Caspian Sea) and had furnished massive military support, including thousands of tanks and hundreds of aircraft, and at least 819 Scuds.[10]

But Saddam Hussein also received extensive foreign assistance as well, some of it paid for with money from the Gulf Cooperation Council (GCC), who feared that Iran might succeed in exporting its Islamic revolution. A total of $40 billion—roughly 40 to 50 percent of Iraq's total military expenditures in the 1980s—was on foreign credit, enabling Iraqi military forces to shop widely. As a result, Saddam's was a truly international military force, with French, Soviet, Swiss, Czech, and Chinese combat aircraft; Soviet, French, German, Italian, and American helicopters; Soviet, Polish, Brazilian, Czech, Chinese, and French tanks and armored vehicles; Soviet, South African, Austrian, French, and Brazilian tube and rocket artillery; Soviet and French surface-to-air missiles supported by British, Chinese, French, and Swedish equipment; Soviet, German, and French antitank missiles; Soviet, Chinese, Italian, and French antiship missiles; and Soviet-supplied Scud and Frog surface-to-surface missiles, bolstered by Iraqi copies and derivations.[11] France was especially helpful to Iraq, thanks in part to the workings of the Franco-Iraqi Friendship Association (which, at the time of the Kuwaiti invasion, counted the French minister of defense, M. Chevenement, among its founders). Thirteen leading French arms manufacturers continued to sell weapons to the Hussein regime, despite Iraqi unwillingness to make payments on its previous French purchases. Additionally, French technicians reputedly made guidance modifications to Iraqi Scuds, and married the French Thomson-CSF Tiger radar to a Soviet-built Il-76, creating the Iraqi Adnan AWACS.[12]

Some sense of the Iraqi arms buildup may be gained by comparing just a few approximate variables of Iraqi military strength in 1980, on the eve of the Iran-Iraq war, and in 1990, on the eve of the Kuwait invasion:[13]

Force structure	1980	1990
Troops	180,000	900,000
Tanks	2,700	5,700
Artillery pieces	2,300	3,700
Combat aircraft	332	950

In sum, by the summer of 1990, Iraq possessed the world's fourth largest army (the U.S. was third), and the sixth largest air force.

Above all other countries, the Iraqi military machine patterned itself upon that of the Soviet Union. Although Saddam Hussein's regime bought widely on the international arms market, it consistently relied upon the Soviets. Between 1982 and 1989, Iraq reportedly purchased $23.5 billion in arms from the Soviet Union, roughly one-quarter of all its arms purchases, incurring a $6 billion debt to Moscow.[14] Its air operations drew heavily upon Soviet-style integrated air defense management, with a controlled network of SAMs, antiaircraft artillery, and fighters; its ground operations generally followed Soviet-style tactical employment and combat doctrine. But the Iran-Iraq war had failed to present the kind of opportunities for the Iraqis to learn whether such a system worked. The Iranians did not pose a serious air attack threat to Iraq, and the terrain along the border with Iran generally prevented the Iraqi army from gaining much combat experience with Soviet-style armored and mechanized forces.

The Iran-Iraq air war likewise had not really blooded the Iraqi air force (IQAF), which Saddam Hussein referred to as his "angels." From the creation of the Iraqi state until the mid-1950s, the Iraqi air force had been modeled on that of the Royal Air Force of Great Britain. (This lingering RAF tradition of chivalry manifested itself in the 1967 Arab-Israeli war, when Israel raided airfields in western Iraq to preempt Iraqi intervention in that war; captured Israeli air crew were treated with a measure of respect, comradeship, and humanity the Iraqi military totally lacked nearly a quarter-century later.) Then, with the rise of the Baathist movement, the model switched to the Soviets; Soviet equipment replaced British equipment, Soviet air doctrine replaced British air doctrine. The IQAF, always a creature of politics, established a reputation as a service prone to produce revolutionaries. In 1963, a group of air force officers launched yet another coup, the first Baathist revolt. While this might have been expected to win for the IQAF the undying affection of the Baathist movement, it seems to have worked the reverse. Exactly why is unclear, but it may have been because air forces traditionally require a degree of cosmopolitan knowledge and sophistication beyond that of traditional military forces. Bluntly stated, while Saddam Hussein could rely on like-thinking unsophisticates from his hometown of Tikrit to run his army, finding equally doctrinaire individuals who could also fly an airplane was a far more difficult task. (Hitler and Goering had the same problem with the Luftwaffe in the Second World War, which always lacked the political orthodoxy of the SS or even the German Army.) Thus, Saddam Hussein, whether he liked it or not, found himself having to rely on people he otherwise would never have raised to political power. As a result, after the establishment of Baathist control over Iraq, he placed the IQAF under increasing pressure to conform to the wishes of the Baathist leadership, who valued political correctness far more than military ability. Reflecting this, the IQAF academy moved from the suburbs of Baghdad to Tikrit, home of both the Baathist movement and Saddam Hussein himself.[15]

Short on experience (although an Iraqi Hawker Hunter squadron performed well during the 1973 Arab-Israeli war, attached to the Egyptian air force), the IQAF did not distinguish itself during the Iran-Iraq war, even though the GCC nations offered Iraqi aircraft "safe haven at airfields throughout the region."[16] Instead, it would only attack when not confronted directly in the air, and preferred to let ground-based air defenses attempt the destruction of the Iranian air force. Hussein himself seems to have played a major role in this policy. At first, the IQAF had attempted strategic air attacks against Teheran and Iranian airfields, using militarily insignificant two-, three-, and six-plane formations. After initially high losses to Iranian aircraft and defenses (the Iranians, after all, were equipped with modern American jet fighters and SAMs, and trained to U.S. doctrine), the IQAF essentially stood down from aggressive air combat operations. Hussein stated that the air force would be kept in reserve for decisive use later in the war; it is this "let's wait until tomorrow" attitude that eventually resulted in Iraq having a well-equipped air force with leaders who had absolutely no idea of how to run it.[17] In part this also stemmed from a desire never to appear to be usurping the powers of "the Minaret of All Mankind" (as Saddam Hussein styled himself). Individual initiative, far from being a desirable trait among the Iraqi military, was a sure way to wind up dead.[18]

An event occurred in June 1981 that had implications which, in retrospect, Saddam Hussein should have considered over the summer of 1990: the Israeli air force destroyed a nuclear reactor facility at the Baghdad Nuclear Research Center. Nuclear proliferation in the Middle East was nothing new; Israel had begun its own program to develop an atomic bomb in the middle 1950s and, by the end of the 1970s, had such weapons available for its use.[19] There were, however, significant qualitative differences between the Israeli leadership (even at its most extreme) and that of the two Arab states most interested in acquiring atomic weapons at the end of the 1970s, Libya and Iraq. Iraq had entered the atomic age courtesy of a small reactor (dubbed "Sov") supplied by the Soviets in 1968. Then, in 1975, France offered to sell Iraq a 1-megawatt research reactor and a 70-megawatt reactor capable of processing weapons-grade enriched uranium (although oil-rich, Iraq ostensibly wished the reactor for peaceful power generation purposes only), in return for Iraqi purchases of major French weapons such as the Mirage F-1. Saddam Hussein quickly assented. Despite international protests, the new reactors (the research one named "Isis," also "Tammuz II"; and the large one named "Osiris," later "Osirak," and also "Tammuz I") went up at Al Tuwaitha, outside Baghdad. Through a variety of complex arrangements presaging the kind they would undertake in the 1980s to attempt to build ultra-long-range cannon and acquire nuclear bomb detonators, Hussein's agents acquired substantial stocks of uranium from overseas sellers, as well as a German-Brazilian package deal for the construction of nine other reactors. Not a country to stand idly by, Israel certainly watched and presumably acted on the growing evidence of Iraqi interest in nuclear energy; mysterious accidents plagued the Franco-Iraqi project, and Vahia al-Mashad—a key Egyptian-born scientist—turned up dead.[20]

Saddam's first bad moment came on September 30, 1980, when two Iranian F-4 Phantoms bombed the incomplete facility, causing little damage and none whatsoever to the reactors. He responded by installing a dense network of antiaircraft defenses around the facility, using 23mm and 57mm cannon, and SA-6 SAMs. The month after the Iranian attack, the Israeli government secretly voted to stage an air raid of their own, to destroy the reactor before it was fueled and "went critical," although, apparently, Israel examined the air strike option even before the Iranian attack. The Israelis decided to employ the new General Dynamics F-16A fighter-bomber, equipped with long-range fuel tanks. They rejected smart bombs as too complex (the F-16s could not do their own laser target designation, which would force using an F-4E as a designator), preferring to rely on two conventional 2,000-pound bombs per plane released from a diving attack. Selected pilots began a series of rigorous training flights emphasizing low-level navigation and accurate bombing from "pop-up" maneuvers. The Israeli attack, called Operation Babylon, launched on June 7, 1981, with eight heavily laden F-16s covered by six F-15s as an anti-MiG combat air patrol (MiGCAP). After flying a long, circuitous, low-level route, the strike package ingressed to the reactor site, the F-15s popped up to cap the mission, and the eight F-16s rolled in and bombed the Osirak reactor. Fifteen of the sixteen bombs were direct hits, with the sixteenth a near miss.[21]

Saddam Hussein was out of the nuclear business for at least several years, thanks to high technology coupled with an imaginative plan and courageous pilots. What lessons Saddam ostensibly learned from the Israeli strike are hard to fathom. The results seem to have accelerated his tendencies to rely even more on densely arrayed air defenses. Further, he began an intensive program to place critical command and control facilities and other high-value targets deep beneath the earth, and to place his aircraft under shelters designed to exceed Warsaw Pact criteria for surviving even nuclear bursts. Communication systems were duplicated and "layered" to prevent severing of key nodes. (Any serenity he might have possessed as a result of these decisions was literally shattered on the first night of Desert Storm.) Beyond this, one cannot say that the Israeli raid dissuaded him from pursuing atomic research. Indeed, by the middle of the 1980s, Iraqi nuclear technologists were busily rebuilding Hussein's nuclear facilities, researching producing fissionable materials for atomic weapons, beginning studies on extracting lithium-6 to create hydrogen weapons, manufacturing increasingly sophisticated ballistic missiles that could be fitted with atomic warheads when and if they became available, accelerating development of multistage satellite launch systems, trying to develop ultra-long-range cannon with Canadian ballistics expert Dr. Gerald Bull, and vainly seeking to buy nuclear triggers from American companies.[22] In his grotesque obsession for and single-minded pursuit of exotic and fanciful weapons, Saddam Hussein could have been a character from fiction—but less an Arthur Conan Doyle's Moriarty than an Ian Fleming's Drax or Blofeld. Such efforts earned him international enmity, with several countries seizing suspect shipments of specialized scientific and military equipment bound for Iraq. For his part, Bull was assassinated while entering his apartment in Brussels, probably at the behest of Israel's hard-edge government.

Iraq Opts for War: Kuwait's Fall Threatens Saudi Arabia

Writing in March 1986, at the height of the Iran-Iraq war, Sudanese Air Force Brig. Gen. Osman A. Eisa stated perceptively that "the war has shown that Kuwait's geostrategic importance has mixed blessings . . . Even if it wanted to," he went on,

> Kuwait would have difficulty resisting Iraqi demands for access to port facilities and land transit rights. At the same time, Kuwait has not been able to defend itself against the limited Iranian military attacks . . . The war has demonstrated the importance of a coastline for Iraq. The Iranian navy has been able to bottle up Iraq easily, in part because of the limited Iraqi coastline . . . The war, graphically, demonstrated to Iraq the importance of Kuwait. Although an overt Iraqi seizure of Kuwait is unlikely, eventually Iraq may try to establish [a] special relationship with Kuwait.[23]

In fact, Iraq had long coveted Kuwait. During the Lebanon crisis of 1958, following the overthrow of the Iraqi premier Nuri Said and the murder of Crown Prince Emir Abdul Illah by Iraqi communists and followers of Egypt's Gamal Abdel Nasser, the potential threat of the new Iraqi regime to Kuwait caused then-president Dwight Eisenhower to order a Marine Regimental Combat Team into the Persian Gulf even as other troops rushed to Lebanon.[24] After this crisis passed, Iraq tried to seize Kuwait in 1961, but the presence of a combined Arab-British force had thwarted this ominous attempt before Iraq could invade. By mid-1990, such an incursion had become very likely indeed, although a surprising number of professional Middle East watchers failed to appreciate the nearness of conflict, even in late July, as Iraqi tanks were assembling on the Kuwaiti border.[25] Saddam Hussein clearly posed a considerable threat to the Persian Gulf region. He had $40 billion in debts from the war, much of the money being owed to the oil-rich sheikdom of Kuwait, a nation with essentially no military (its army was but one-sixtieth that of Iraq). He wished to improve his access to the Gulf, though it was by no means as poor as he would subsequently imply. His public and private pronounce-ments left little doubt that he had decided to extend his influence, either directly or indirectly, over the entire Arabian peninsula. He had a power-ful and combat-tested military equipped with first-rate military systems, and he had embarked on a vigorous weapons development program. It was in this climate of growing tension that the Air Force's *Global Reach—Global Power* White Paper, issued in June 1990, stated bluntly: "In the Persian Gulf, our objectives will remain to support friendly states and prevent a hostile power—any hostile power, not necessarily the So-viet Union—from gaining control over the region's oil supplies and lines of communication."[26]

But Saddam Hussein was not likely to listen. Isolated by a coterie of yes-men who dared not quibble with his judgments, and unfamiliar with the changes in the United States over the 1980s, he was a believer in the old post-Vietnam conventional wisdom—that the United States was im-potent, afraid of conflict, and unwilling to risk American lives for foreign commitments. "Yours is a society that cannot accept 10,000 dead in one battle," he bluntly told Ambassador April Glaspie, in a meeting on July 25, three days after he moved his armored units toward Kuwait's bor-der.[27] By that time, of course, the United States and the Gulf states were pondering intelligence information that Saddam had massed hundreds of tanks and thousands of troops along the Kuwaiti border. As the nations of the region hoped it was a bluff, Saddam Hussein, having already fate-fully decided for war, made his move.

War came to Kuwait at 2:00 A.M. on the morning of August 2, with a classic armored assault. Three armored divisions spearheaded by Soviet-built T-72 tanks broke across the border and raced toward Kuwait City down a modern superhighway ironically built as a symbol of Kuwaiti-Iraqi friendship. Simultaneously, Iraqi artillery pounded Kuwait's north-ernmost base at Ali Al-Salim, rendering it unusable, although fifteen Mi-rage F-1s escaped south to Bahrain and Saudi Arabia. As the sky light-ened, dozens of Soviet-built Mil Mi-24 Hind helicopter gunships covered the tanks and escorted dozens more Mi-8 Hip troop-carrying helicopters. MiG fighters and Sukhoi ground-attack aircraft appeared overhead, scouting for pockets of Kuwaiti resistance. For a brief while, Kuwait's three batteries of American-built Hawk surface-to-air missiles took a heavy toll of Iraqi aircraft, destroying twenty-three. American techni-cians on contract to the Kuwaiti government watched with a mixture of satisfaction and anxiety as the large radar-guided missiles erupted noisily off their three-missile launchers, briefly weaved back and forth as they homed on low-flying jets, and then shattered them in violent blasts. But the launchers eventually exhausted their ready supply of missiles and the Iraqis overwhelmed them. The Kuwaiti air force's A-4KU Skyhawk squadron at Ahmad Al-Jabir hastily launched some aircraft (despite an Iraqi heliborne assault on the field), fighting as long as possible against the advancing armored and mechanized infantry columns until they had to withdraw to Saudi Arabia for lack of fuel or weapons. In four hours, the Iraqis reached Kuwait City, where they attacked the emir's palace, leaving it in flames. Organized resistance quickly came to an end. Iraqi troops began mopping-up operations, even as the first members of the Iraqi internal security apparatus arrived to supervise the destruction of any vestiges of Kuwaiti individualism, culture, and identity. Kuwaitis entered their dark night as members of Iraq's "Nineteenth Province"—to the general rejoicing of the Iraqi population. Given their future, Iraq's citizens would have done better recalling Khalil Gibran's prophetic words, "Pity the nation that acclaims the bully as hero, and that deems the glittering conqueror bountiful."[28]

The invasion of Kuwait triggered intensive discussions among the American and allied foreign governments over suitable courses of action, for, if one accepted the view of Saddam Hussein as a regional Hitler, Kuwait might well be Poland to Saudi Arabia's France—just an hors d'oeuvre on the path to the main course. Saudi Arabia had always loomed large in American Middle East thought; as early as 1943, Pres. Franklin Roosevelt had proclaimed, "The defense of Saudi Arabia is vital to the defense of the United States."[29] The nature of this diplomatic maneuvering and the domestic discussions within the White House–Department of State–Department of Defense nexus fall largely beyond the scope of this work, however interesting and valuable they otherwise might be. Much has been made regarding "differences" and "hesitancies" between the uniformed military leadership and the civilian leadership over whether or not to pursue a military solution to the Kuwaiti invasion, with an implication that it reflected a disorganization or lack of unified purpose in the government's handling of the crisis.[30] But it must be remembered that it is in the nature of discussions between senior governmental personnel to have frank and open dialogue, with both small and large disagreements thrashed out. While unity is necessary for the execution of policy, diversity is desirable for the input of opinion so that when a consensus is reached, it is not the consensus of unthinking conformity, but a consensus tempered and tested by exposure to a broad range of viewpoints and interpretations. That such diversities of opinion were presented, discussed, and considered is de facto evidence that the decision-making process worked well, and as it is intended. The participants, whatever their views, deserve commendation for their forthrightness.

The greatest fear of the U.S. government decisionmakers was that Saddam Hussein's tankers, having overrun Kuwait, would turn south and attempt to seize Dhahran, securing control of Saudi oil fields and a significant portion of the Saudi coast. Debate abounded on what rate of advance invading Iraqi forces might be able to achieve. In 1941, during the invasion of Russia, a German armored corps covered 100 miles in two days. In 1944, the First U.S. Army briefly exceeded 30 miles per day during the breakout across France. In 1945, a Soviet tank army averaged 50 miles a day for 10 days during the invasion of Manchuria.[31] While few believed Iraq's forces could match these historic rates, Iraq clearly had an opportunity, if it chose to do so, to expand the war into Saudi Arabia at a time when its potential opponents were understrength—but this "window of vulnerability" was fleeting, thanks to the mobility of air power. (Subsequently, after the war, General Schwarzkopf concluded that Iraq had stopped in Kuwait only for a pause, not appreciating that the West would confront Hussein's aggression. "I don't think there is any question at all," he told interviewer David Frost, "that he would have attacked Saudi Arabia." What Saddam Hussein's likely timetable was—if indeed he had one—is unknown.)[32]

From the outset, land-based air power was the only significant immediate option open to decisionmakers, a powerful trump card against any ground force moving south. Discussing options immediately after the invasion, retired admiral William J. Crowe, immediate past chairman of the Joint Chiefs, stated bluntly, "There's not much the U.S. Navy can do. We'd have to get land-based air power into Saudi Arabia."[33] As a precautionary response, on August 2, the administration ordered the carrier USS *Independence* from the Arabian Sea into the Gulf of Oman, ordering the carrier *Eisenhower* two days later to transit the Suez Canal from the Mediterranean to the Red Sea. The next day, as Iraqi troops and tanks massed on the Saudi Arabian border, Bush warned Iraq not to invade its southern neighbor. On August 6, King Fahd bin Abd al-'Aziz Al Sa'ud of Saudi Arabia invited friendly nations to reinforce its defenses with their troops, and Bush ordered immediate deployment of F-15s from Langley Air Force Base, the 82nd Airborne Division from Ft. Bragg, and the movement of Maritime Prepositioning Ships from Diego Garcia and Guam to Saudi Arabia. Thus began Operation Desert Shield, a defensive deployment to protect the Gulf states from further Iraqi aggression. By August 8, both carriers had moved into position where they could, if necessary, deliver air strikes. But the natural limits attendant to naval air operations (particularly their lack of large-capacity long-range air refueling aircraft) seriously constrained their potential effectiveness; as Crowe recognized, the best solution would be the delivery of land-based air power, and quickly.[34]

Fortunately, land-based air was on its way, and in quantity. Even before the war, the Air Force had prepositioned $1 billion worth of fuel, ammunition, and other equipment in Saudi Arabia, as part of its commitment to USCENTCOM; Air Force Lt. Gen. Charles Horner later referred to the prepositioning program as "our term insurance." This prepositioned equipment included sufficient munitions for confronting Iraq's tanks and mechanized forces: sufficient GBU-10 and GBU-12 smart bombs to destroy 3,000 tanks, nearly two million 30mm cannon rounds for the A-10, 20,000 cluster bombs, and over 45,000 Mk.-82 500-pound "dumb" bombs.[35]

On August 7, at 5:25 P.M. East Coast time, twenty-four F-15C air superiority fighters of TAC's 71st Tactical Fighter Squadron thundered aloft from Langley AFB in Tidewater Virginia. They landed at Dhahran on the afternoon of August 8 (Saudi time), having completed a 15-hour, 8,000-mile, nonstop journey from the United States involving up to twelve in-flight refuelings. None of the Eagles had developed major problems, a tribute both to the technology advances since the 1950s and their maintenance crews. (In contrast, during the Lebanon crisis of 1958, of the first twelve F-100s launched, four arrived as planned, but eight diverted to alternate bases because of refueling difficulties, and one of the eight ran out of fuel and crashed.)[36] When the F-15s arrived, they were fully armed with eight missiles and full ammunition because no one knew if the Iraqis would stop at the Saudi border, and the Eagle pilots might have to fight their way in.[37] Only 38 hours after having received their initial notification of deployment, the F-15s were in Saudi Arabia, sitting alert. That same day, two commercial DC-10s under contract with the Military Airlift Command left Pope AFB for Dhahran with 520 troops of the 82nd Airborne Division. Two days later, the Royal Air Force matched the initial American response, sending twenty-four Tornadoes and Jaguars to the Gulf, the first of what would eventually become a seventy-three-plane force. The rapid reaction of the RAF after having been ordered to the Gulf earned the Tornadoes the nickname "my 600-knot gunboats" from Britain's foreign secretary.[38]

Within five days, C-5 and C-141 airlifters had moved five fighter squadrons (120 fighters), an AWACS contingent, and a brigade of the 82nd Airborne to Saudi, and the total number of Allied aircraft in-theater stood at 301. By August 21, the date when Secretary of Defense Dick Cheney announced that sufficient forces were in place to defend Saudi Arabia, the Air Force had moved in more F-15Cs from Langley and Eglin AFB; F-16C/D fighter-bombers from Shaw AFB; F-15E Strike Eagles from Seymour-Johnson AFB; F-4G Wild Weasels from George AFB; F-117A stealth fighters from Tonopah, Nevada; and A-10A attack aircraft from Myrtle Beach AFB. Supporting these "shooters" were E-3A AWACS, RC-135 reconnaissance aircraft, KC 135 and KC-10 tankers, and C-130 transports for theater airlift. Airlift had also delivered the Army's 11th Air Defense Artillery Brigade equipped with Patriot and Stinger SAMs. A month into the crisis, 1,220 Allied aircraft were in theater, ready for combat.[39]

Airlift proved critical, for it was the only rapid mobility tool that could deliver significant combat strength at long ranges within hours; sealift, while capable of carrying more, would obviously take weeks if not months. Altogether, Desert Shield/Desert Storm required 80 percent of the Air Force's C-141 fleet, and 90 percent of the C-5 fleet. These two aircraft systems moved nearly three-quarters of the air cargo and one-third of the personnel airlifted into the Gulf region. So great was the airlift that, as one airlift pilot put it, "You could have walked across the Mediterranean on the wings of C-5s, C-141s, and commercial aircraft moving across the region."[40] Within the Gulf region, the C-130 met theater airlift needs. By October 1, C-130s were providing daily airlift to every major USCENTCOM base through an intratheater channel airlift system. "Camel" missions moved cargo, and "Star" missions moved passengers. Approximately 32 percent of the Air Force C-130 fleet was in the Gulf, and, through Desert Shield/Desert Storm, they flew nearly 47,000 sorties, delivering over 300,000 tons of cargo and 209,000 troops. To meet additional airlift needs, the government activated the Civil Reserve Air Fleet (CRAF) for the first time in its 38-year history. American airline companies furnished cargo and passenger aircraft to support Allied airlift requirements. Eventually, a second-stage CRAF expansion took place when Desert Storm commenced, and the total number of civilian aircraft assigned for military use reached 158. By the middle of December 1990, sixteen different airfields were receiving up to 8,000 troops daily, delivered by 65 aircraft, an average of one landing every 22 minutes. During Desert Storm, this would peak at 127 aircraft per day, an average of one landing every 11 minutes. The tremendous experience gained during 1980s military exercises, particularly the REFORGER (Return of Forces to Germany) troop transport exercises now paid handsome dividends as, for example, when Air Force airlifters moved the Army's VII Corps from Germany to Saudi Arabia.[41]

By six weeks into the deployment, airlift had already flown more ton-miles than the entire Berlin airlift—an operation that took ten times longer: over 65 weeks. In the first 18 weeks, the airlift moved the equivalent of 2½ Berlin airlifts, a total of over 200,000 people and 210,000 short tons of cargo. Some measure of the Desert Shield airlift effort can be gained by comparing the Gulf airlift with other historical airlift examples, using, as the basis of measurement, million ton-miles (MTM) of cargo flown per day, during the peak period of each airlift effort (see Table 5.2).[42]

The tremendous productivity of the airlifters would not have been as impressive were it not for the synergistic interaction of tankers and transports. The advent of large-scale aerial refueling transformed the U.S. Air Force in the 1950s into a true global striking force; the expansion of air-refueling capability to transport aircraft in the 1970s had an equally significant impact on readiness and rapid deployment. Tanker support in Desert Shield was no less significant than it was during Desert Storm itself. During Desert Shield, Air Force tankers flew 4,967 sorties totaling nearly 20,000 flight hours, refueling 14,588 airplanes (including 5,495 Navy and Marine aircraft); "boomers" off-loaded 68.2 million gallons of

Table 5.2. The Gulf Airlift in Historical Perspective

Airlift	MTM/day	Primary Aircraft Type
World War II (CBI Hump)	0.9	C-46, C-47, C-54
Berlin Airlift	1.7	C-47, C-54, C-74, C-82, C-118
Operation Nickel Grass	4.4	C-141A, C-5A
Operation Desert Shield	17.0	C-141B, C-5A/B

Note: MTM = Million ton-miles

fuel. Without the timely investment in tanker technology made in the late 1970s, the burden of tanking would have fallen exclusively on the KC-135A Stratotanker, an aircraft dating to the mid-1950s. As it was, the newer KC-10 Extender tanker-transporter and the re-engined KC-135R contributed significantly to the total force capabilities of the air units placed in the Gulf, complementing the earlier Stratotankers in the Gulf. Fully 75 percent of the Air Force's KC-10 fleet and 44 percent of the KC-135 fleet were committed to the Gulf crisis.[43]

The Navy contribution to the growing Desert Shield effort was important. Three carrier battlegroups from the United States and Japan departed for the Gulf region, two to replace the *Eisenhower* and *Independence* (both scheduled for return). The *Saratoga* departed the East Coast on August 7 and arrived in the Red Sea on August 22. The *John F. Kennedy* departed on August 15 and arrived in the Red Sea on September 14. (By that time, the *Eisenhower* had already left the theater.) *Midway* left Yokosuka for the Gulf on October 2, arriving on November 1, replacing the *Independence*. Subsequently, in December, the Navy deployed the carriers *Ranger, Theodore Roosevelt,* and *America. Ranger* left port on December 8 and arrived on January 15, and the other two departed on December 28, arriving, respectively, on January 14 and 15, just in time for the opening of Desert Storm. Sealift proved vital, not surprisingly delivering the vast bulk of supplies sent to the Gulf. One significant movement began on August 17, when the two fast sealift cargo ships *Altar* and *Capella* left the East Coast with the 24th Infantry Division (Mechanized) embarked; they arrived in Saudi Arabia ten days later. Thereafter, sealift continually built up, and was particularly useful for delivering extra heavy and outsize cargo; over two million tons of equipment and supplies were shipped to Saudi Arabia by early December.[44]

One area in which the Navy contributed very significantly was in enforcing an embargo on Iraq. The Navy acted in accordance with UN Resolution 661 (passed on August 6), which imposed sanctions on all trade to and from Iraq with the exception of medicines and (if established by humanitarian need) food, and UN Resolution 665 (passed on August 25), which authorized the use of naval force to ensure that the sanctions were effective. The first Iraqi ship that fell afoul of the embargo was the *Al Karamah,* boarded off Jordan by a team from the cruiser *Biddle.* Assisted by air patrols that located possible contraband carriers, naval vessels subsequently undertook nearly 6,000 intercepts by Christmas 1990; of these, 713 resulted in actual boardings by American and multinational teams.[45]

With the situation in the Gulf stabilized, and with more supplies, personnel, and air power arriving literally every day (including that supplied by the regional GCC as well as the members of the UN coalition), thought could turn to the next likely step: switching from a strictly defensive posture to an offensive one to effect Iraq's withdrawal from Kuwait via persuasion or force. Planning had to consider all possibilities of combined arms warfare, with roles to be played by air, land, and sea power. Sea power was obviously limited in what it could accomplish, for Iraq and Kuwait were not in auspicious locations for amphibious landings or naval air attack, but the coalition navies obviously could play a key role in controlling the waters of the Persian Gulf and act as the stopper in the Gulf bottle. Coalition land forces could find themselves engaged in deadly armor and infantry assaults, with massive artillery bombardments; the expectation of such land warfare caused shudders among defense experts and generals alike, for casualties could be high—perhaps intolerably so, given the rising antiwar sentiments in both Europe and America.

Land-based air power offered the possibility of preventing this nightmare scenario: devastating air attacks could destroy the Iraqi air force and army, their supplies, and their command and control. But first, air power advocates would have to overcome an even more formidable foe: the old conventional wisdom of air power's alleged lack of effectiveness that caused many to now question whether it could be decisive. For example, Gen. H. Norman Schwarzkopf, the USCENTCOM commander, had reservations, recalling after the war that "Colin Powell and I understood very early on that a strategic-bombing campaign in and of itself had never won a war and had never forced anybody to do anything if they wanted to sit it out. I don't think he and I ever believed exclusively that that would be it."[46] Then, on the eve of the war itself, a key Army War College study concluded gloomily that

> we do not believe that air power alone will suffice to bring a war with Iraq to an early or decisive conclusion. In the final analysis, ground forces will be required to confront the Iraqi Army and either dig or drive it out of Kuwait.[47]

Much more likely, the study implied, was a long, drawn-out, and bloody war. "If we fight Iraq," the authors stated,

> we should be prepared to defeat it as quickly as possible, since the Iraqi military has shown that it fights well on the defensive. If the Iraqis do not capitulate in the first days of the conflict, we can expect them to "hedgehog." *They*

will wrap themselves around Kuwait and force us to pry them loose—a hideously expensive prospect, in lives as well as in resources [emphasis added].[48]

Such sentiments—reflecting the confusion between what air power actually *is* and *could do* in contrast to what it is *perceived* to be and *thought to have done* (based largely on the outdated World War II model, and serious misinterpretation of wars since that time)—required drastic revision before the war was over.

Orchestrating the Air War: Checkmate and Black Hole Write the Music

As USCENTCOM commander, responsibility for formulating a theater campaign plan for a possible war in the Gulf rested with Schwarzkopf, a forceful, humane, and personally courageous officer whose abhorrence for the mismanagement of the military during Vietnam and the 1970s had given him a determination never to go to war under such circumstances again.[49] Intriguingly, as befitted his canny and shrewd nature, he had a great enthusiasm for the artwork of Bev Doolittle (an artist who specialized in presenting deceptive Western scenes and landscapes that weren't what they first appeared to be), particularly an unforgettable painting from grizzly country called "Doubled Back." In peacetime, US-CENTCOM was a paper command, headquartered at MacDill AFB, Tampa, Florida. Its air component was the Ninth Air Force, commanded by Lt. Gen. Charles A. Horner, based at Shaw AFB, South Carolina. Its Army component was the 3rd U.S. Army, under Lt. Gen. John Yeosock, headquartered at Ft. McPherson, Georgia. In wartime, both forces would deploy to Southwest Asia, the Ninth Air Force forming the nucleus of U.S. Central Command Air Forces (USCENTAF), and the 3rd Army forming the basis for U.S. Army Forces Central Command (USARCENT).

USCENTCOM, new and thus unlike other commands, lacked a long tradition of planning that permitted it the luxury of merely updating some long-established document; in fact, planning at USCENTCOM had only really evolved in the mid-1980s. Fortunately, since its primary peacetime mission was, in fact, wartime contingency planning (in contrast to many other commands that had large numbers of units assigned to them in peacetime), USCENTCOM's planners were very aggressive in assembling contingency plans to meet possible crises, including one to confront a Soviet invasion of Iran. Thus, despite the newness of the command, USCENTCOM received high marks from planning analysts. A 1988 Army War College study team concluded admiringly that "participation in campaign planning in USCENTCOM is pervasive, detailed, and results in close coordination."[50]

When the Soviet Union underwent its dramatic transformation in the late 1980s, at both the suggestion of the Defense Department's policy planning staff and from his own perceptions, Schwarzkopf urged his air and land chieftains—the Air Force's Horner and Army's Yeosock—to shift their focus to Iraq, for, after the Iran-Iraq war, Iraq was the only other power in a position to pose a threat to the region.[51] (Interestingly, the same idea had occurred to war gamers at the Naval War College, which offered an Iraqi assault on Saudi Arabia as one of the study options for NWC students in the 1990–91 class, and to Air Staff and RAND study groups in the 1988–90 time frame). Horner and Yeosock met at Yeosock's headquarters; out of this meeting came a tentative plan to confront Saddam Hussein that Horner presented to Schwarzkopf in March 1990. He subsequently recollected:

> We looked at what kind of things would be important from an air standpoint if there were going to be a conflict in this part of the world.
>
> At that time, we talked about Patriots defending against Scuds. We talked about how we would provide close air support to the Army in a very fluid desert maneuver battle. We talked about chemical weapons and how we could counter chemical weapons. Also during that time we talked about attacking [Saddam Hussein's] war-making potential—strategic targeting, if you want to call it that.[52]

That July, a month before the crisis, Horner and Yeosock went to Eglin AFB in Florida, where they wargamed this tentative planning concept with Schwarzkopf, Iraq being cryptically dubbed "Country Orange."[53] Thus, when the crisis broke out, thanks to the timely foresight of the three men, rudimentary ideas already existed on what USCENTCOM's response might be. While Schwarzkopf organized the deployment in the United States before venturing to his command in the Middle East, Horner and Yeosock went ahead, arriving on August 5, to deal with the issue of force "bed-down" and to orchestrate the intricate details involved in establishing operations and working relations with the Saudis.[54]

Air Force contingency planning began virtually immediately upon the outbreak of the crisis. After hastily returning from a vacation cruise to the Caribbean, Col. John A. Warden III of the Air Staff Plans Directorate assembled a team of twenty experts who, like him, were "true believers"—the kind of airmen who spell *air power* as one word. On Monday, August 6, they gathered in "Checkmate," a crowded basement office area in the Pentagon, and, on their own initiative, began planning possible air campaign options for confronting Iraq. On August 8, recognizing the magnitude of the time, effort, and attention to detail required for beddown of the deploying air and ground forces and associated defensive planning, and cognizant that this was tying up most of Horner's time and manpower, Schwarzkopf formally turned to the Air Force, requesting inputs on offensive air options from the vice chief of staff, Gen. John M. "Mike" Loh, because the chief of staff, Gen. Michael J. Dugan, was out of town. Over the next two days, Air Staff planners rapidly sketched out a concept for a "focused and intensive" offensive air campaign, which they presented to Schwarzkopf at MacDill AFB on Friday, August 10. Called "Instant Thunder," this concept won Schwarzkopf's endorsement; its name was intended as a clear signal that any air campaign would be quick, overwhelming, and decisive—not a gradualist approach as had been the case with Vietnam's "Rolling Thunder" 15 years before. Further refined, and with inputs from Navy and Marine representatives, it subsequently formed the basis for what became Desert Storm's first phase.

Horner, as commander of U.S. Central Command Air Forces (US-CENTAF) and Joint Force Air Component commander, put the planning effort under the direction of Brig. Gen. Buster C. Glosson, an individual he knew well. Both Horner and Glosson were career fighter pilots and veterans of the air war over North Vietnam. Determined to prevent the kind of absentee air war management and abysmal operational tactics that had characterized the war in Vietnam, Horner directed Glosson to transform the Instant Thunder concept into executable reality. Glosson formed a secretive strike planning cell eventually known as the "Black Hole" (an allusion to astrophysics because, like a gravitational sink, information would get in, but nothing would get out), located in a basement storage area of Royal Saudi Air Force headquarters in Riyadh. The Black Hole staffers subsequently took the basic strategic air campaign concept and elaborated, refined, and expanded it to meet CENTCOM's needs. It fell to Horner and his planners to assemble the gigantic daily Air Tasking Order (ATO) that apportioned the air effort among the various services, spelling out the targets, the forces and weapons to be used against them, and integrating this into the schedule of a complete air offensive. (The target list eventually expanded from 84 to over 400.) In particular, all wished to avoid the Vietnam-era "route package" system of assigning targets and geographical areas to particular services. Air power, they believed, must be used in a unified, integrated manner, with all players "singing from the same sheet of music."[55]

Schwarzkopf and Yeosock eventually brought in a group of gifted young Army officers, the "Jedi Knights," most from the Army's Command and General Staff College at Ft. Leavenworth, for structuring the land operation. Horner and Glosson, in similar fashion, drew upon the abilities of selected air power experts to ensure that the plan utilized each and every appropriate air power system and capability to its best effect, and that air power received its due. For example, early in August, a few within the Air Force had proposed "let's wait and see" gradualist solutions, which would have had the effect of restricting CENTAF's air power to a wholly defensive and "support of ground forces" posture. Concerned, the Air Staff officers charged with responding to Schwarzkopf's request for *offensive* air options succeeded in presenting forceful counter-arguments during key briefings on the absolute necessity for a no-holds-barred strategic air campaign. They emphasized that strategic air attacks—not just "tacair" operations over the battle area—would be critical to any success land forces could expect to achieve on the battlefield itself.[56] The Checkmate team at the Pentagon proved especially useful, not only in the initial planning, but throughout the actual execution of the war. They furnished an intelligence-fusion function: keeping track of the latest multi-agency Washington information inputs, adding their own thoughts, making them available to Horner and Glosson, and providing a constant "sanity check" feedback ensuring that the plan and the campaign were the best possible.[57]

In the midst of this activity, an event occurred—the removal of Gen. Michael J. Dugan as chief of staff of the service—that distracted (however briefly) the Air Force from the task at hand. Dugan had succeeded the retiring Gen. Larry Welch as chief of staff in mid-August, after the crisis broke out. A charismatic fighter pilot who previously commanded the U.S. Air Forces in Europe (USAFE), Dugan was brilliant, outspoken, and a strong believer in openness with the media. Early in the planning phase, when the question of gradualism came up, Dugan left no doubt where he stood: "We are not looking at a gradual escalation," he emphasized. "We will attempt to be decisive."[58] During an inspection trip to Saudi Arabia, Dugan discussed with three journalists he had invited along from the Washington *Post,* Los Angeles *Times,* and the trade magazine *Aviation Week and Space Technology* what air power could accomplish in a war with Iraq, emphasizing striking Iraqi centers of gravity. Dugan's remarks were published widely, but most notably by the Washington *Post*, on Sunday, September 16. His comments addressed targeting issues and the Air Force's likely contribution to any war in the confident, grand, and somewhat inflammatory tradition of Billy Mitchell. Any criticism that his remarks compromised the security of potential target sets paled next to allegations that they revealed a "go it alone" attitude, an Air Force *über alles* thrown in the face of the other services. To jointness proponents and those skeptical of what air might accomplish, Dugan's remarks seemed singularly lacking in appreciation for partnership, inappropriate in the post–Goldwater-Nichols Defense Reorganization Act era.[59]

In fact, Dugan *was* a strong "jointness" proponent, having written only a little over a year before that "modern warfare is joint warfare . . . In the profession of arms, teamwork is fundamental to success."[60] Further, he had insisted that the plan be as "joint" as possible at all phases of air campaign planning, and tailored explicitly to meet Schwarzkopf's needs and wishes. On Monday, the Air Staff returned to the Pentagon wondering when the other shoe would drop. They were all too mindful that Defense Secretary Dick Cheney had sternly and publicly rebuked Larry Welch over a year before for the far less controversial action of going to the Hill advocating certain ballistic missile programs. In midmorning the word came down—Dugan was fired; no rebuke this time. In a press conference that afternoon, Cheney announced he had taken the action because the general had shown "poor judgment at a sensitive time," emphasized the necessity of a joint approach to solving the Gulf problem, and matter-of-factly announced the appointment of the distinguished Pacific Air Forces commander, Gen. Merrill A. "Tony" McPeak, as the next chief of staff.[61]

Though the removal of Dugan caused little public controversy, it stunned the service, unsettling many Air Staff members, who briefly wondered if it reflected an institutionalized Defense Department bias against the Air Force and worried (wrongly as it turned out) that Dugan's removal might be reflected in a campaign plan de-emphasizing air war in favor of a more traditional (and undoubtedly bloodier) ground war. The timing was terrible, for it came at the beginning of an annual ritual—a week of Air Force Association meetings in Washington. The whole tone of official presentations at the AFA conference had to be re-examined on short notice, and homages to jointness and the enduring strength of the Air Force hastily inserted. Fortunately, the vice chief of staff, General Loh (who had assumed the functions of acting chief until McPeak could win confirmation) skillfully shepherded the service onto the road to recovery. The Iraq crisis itself, of course, added its own acceleration to the healing process, for the magnitude of the tasks at hand demanded nothing less than the total concentration of the service and its people.

For his part, Mike Dugan left the Air Force he loved with a grace and elegance totally in keeping with his reputation, penning a note on his personal stationary that was subsequently copied and sent throughout the Pentagon:

> To the men and women of the Air Force—
>
> Your mission—providing airpower and spacepower to the nation—is essential and enduring. I bid you a fond farewell with my head high, my Mach up and my flags flying. Good luck, good hunting, and Godspeed to the greatest Air Force in the world.
>
> With warmest regards,
> Mike Dugan

The Iraqi Threat: A Third World Country with a First World Military

By early December, Horner, Glosson, Warden, and others had succeeded in making a strong case for air power as the decisive hammer of any war with Iraq, and Defense Secretary Cheney had become an ardent air supporter. The planners had structured an air campaign to support Schwarzkopf's theater objectives, recognizing that while Iraq might be a Third World nation economically, it was a First World nation militarily and certainly no "paper tiger."[62]

Iraq had a number of disturbing attributes, including:

- A robust, combat-tested army, air force, and navy, including:
  - —Over 950 combat aircraft, consisting of 200 support airplanes (including the home-built Adnan AWACS airplane), and 750 "shooters" including the Soviet-built MiG-21, -23, -25, -27, -29, Su-7, -20, -22, -24, -25, Tupolev Tu-16 and -22, Chinese H-6 and J-7, Czech L-39, and French Mirage F-1. They were armed with a wide range of weapons including French AM–39 Exocet antiship missiles, French AS-10, -11, -12, -14, -20, and -30 stand-off munitions (including the AS-30L laser-guided smart missile), French

Beluga bomblet dispensers, Soviet AA-6 and AA-7 air-to-air missiles, and French Magic and R-530 air-to-air missiles;

—7,000 antiaircraft guns;

—16,000 surface-to-air missiles, including Soviet-supplied SA-2, -3, -6, -7, -8, -9, -13, 14, -16, Franco-German Roland, and American I-Hawks captured from Kuwait;

—900,000 troops, organized in approximately 60 divisions including 8 Republican Guard divisions, but capable of fielding up to two million troops via conscription and mobilization—fully 75 percent of men between ages 18 and 34;[63]

—3,700 artillery pieces, as well as tactical rocket artillery;

—5,700 main battle tanks and approximately 3,000 tank transporters to guarantee rapid mobility;

—10,000 support vehicles, including 5,000 armored fighting vehicles;

—160 armed helicopters, including the Mil Mi-24 Hind gunship;

—43 naval surface combatants, including missile boats and hovercraft.

- Modern air fields with extensive shelter protection, consisting of 24 main operating bases and 30 dispersal bases.

- Excellent redundant command, control, and communications (C^3).

- Excellent "layered" air defenses consisting of a centralized air defense headquarters, sector centers, and numerous radar, SAM, flak, and fighter stations.

- Aggressive nuclear, chemical, and biological weapons development programs, and a demonstrated chemical warfare capability.

- Approximately 600 Scud-B missiles and improved Scud derivatives, the Al-Husayn and the Al-Abbas, capable of reaching Riyadh, Dhahran, and Tel Aviv, possibly with chemical- and biological-warfare warheads.

- A strong national industrial base for weapons and munitions manufacture, maintenance, and repair.

- A strong self-sufficient energy program involving petrochemical, nuclear, and electrical power generation.

- Good redundant road and rail networks.

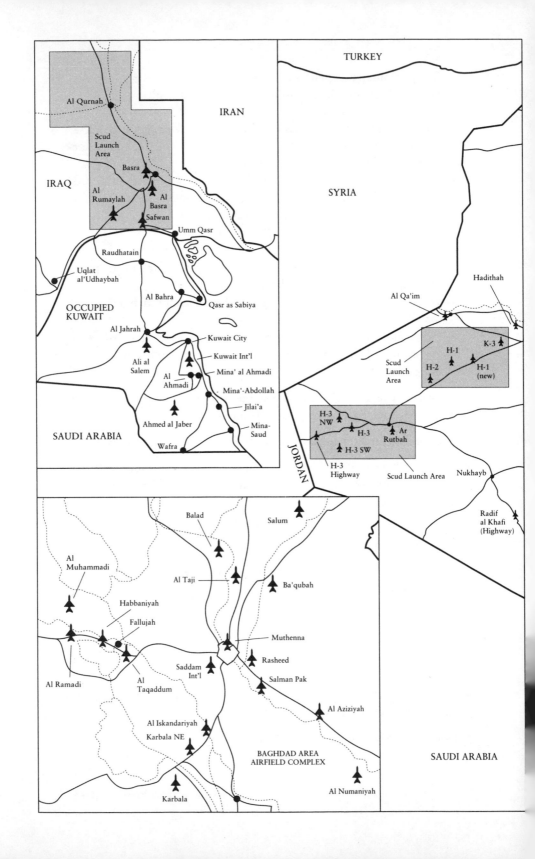

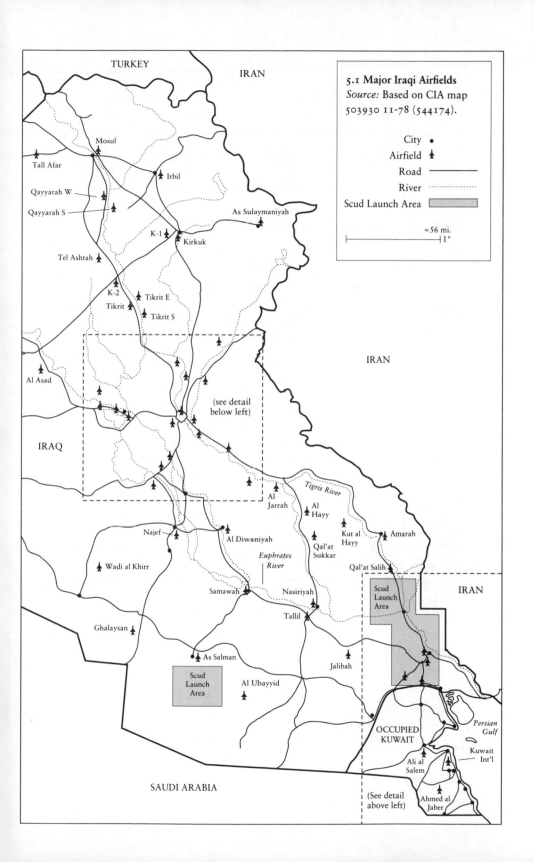

TURKEY

IRAN

Tall Afar

Mosul

Irbil

Qayyarah W

Qayyarah S

As Sulaymaniyah

K-1

Kirkuk

Tel Ashtah

K-2

Tikrit E

Tikrit

Tikrit S

Al Asad

IRAN

(see detail below left)

IRAQ

Al Jarrah

Tigris River

Al Hayy

Najef

Al Diwaniyah

Qal'at Sukkar

Kut al Hayy

Amarah

Wadi al Khirr

Euphrates River

Qal'at Salih

Samawah

Nasiriyah

Scud Launch Area

IRAN

Ghalaysan

Tallil

As Salman

Scud Launch Area

Al Ubayyid

Jalibah

OCCUPIED KUWAIT

Persian Gulf

Kuwait Int'l

Ali al Salem

SAUDI ARABIA

(See detail above left)

Ahmed al Jaber

5.1 Major Iraqi Airfields
Source: Based on CIA map
503930 11-78 (544174).

City   •
Airfield   ✈
Road   ———
River   ·········
Scud Launch Area

≈56 mi.
1"

Schwarzkopf and Powell appreciated these sources of Iraqi military strength, but two in particular bothered them, as befitted their status as ground warriors and as they made clear to Horner: *above all, take out the Iraqi tanks and artillery.* The airmen had complete faith that they could fulfill the ambitious goals of the campaign plan and, especially, Schwarzkopf and Powell's special charge. What was unknown, of course, was what price they would have to pay to achieve victory.

The Air Plan that Defeated Saddam Hussein

The air campaign plan had three key phases: (1) strategic attack; (2) Kuwaiti theater of operations air defense suppression; and (3) attack the Republican Guard and Iraq's army in Kuwait. There was no intention for the stages to be strictly "bordered" from one another; for example, missions could still be flown as needed against strategic targets right up to the last day of the war. Nevertheless, "windows" existed for each phase, so that they did, in a general sense, follow a sequential progression.[64]

Contrary to some accounts appearing after the war, there was never any explicit planning effort devoted to targeting Saddam Hussein personally. He was never "targeted" in the UN resolution, the U.S. national objectives, or the actual attack plans. Whether or not Saddam Hussein would be a legitimate target received a great deal of attention, much of it muddied by various speculative opinions on what does or does not constitute "assassination." In fact, over a year before the Gulf war, the Army's Office of the Judge Advocate General had issued a milestone Memorandum of Law on the subject of assassination, with the coordination and concurrence of a variety of other agencies, including the Department of State, the National Security Council, the CIA, and the Department of Justice, as well as the other legal branches of the Department of Defense and the military services. A reading of this memorandum—prepared by W. Hays Parks, the chief of the International Law Branch—leaves no doubt that the Iraqi leader would, indeed, have been a lawful target, had the national leadership chosen to do so. The following is a quote taken from the memo itself regarding the issue of whether civilians may be regarded as combatants, which renders them subject to lawful attack:

> Three points can be made in this respect. (a) Civilians who work within a military objective are at risk from attack during the times in which they are present within that objective, whether their injury or death is incidental to the attack of that military objective or results from their direct attack. Neither

would be assassination. (b) The substitution of a civilian in a position or billet that normally would be occupied by a member of the military will not make that position immune from attack. (c) Finally, one rule of thumb with regard to the likelihood that an individual may be subject to lawful attack is his (or her) immunity from military service if continued service in his (or her) civilian position is of greater value to a nation's war effort than that person's service in the military. A prime example would be civilian scientists occupying key positions in a weapons program regarded as vital to a nation's national security or war aims. Thus, more than 90% of the World War II Project Manhattan personnel were civilians, and their participation in the U.S. atomic weapons program was of such importance as to have made them liable to legitimate attack. Similarly, the [Allied raids] on the German rocket sites at Peenemünde regarded the death of scientists involved in research and development at that facility to have been as important as destruction of the missiles themselves. Attack of these individuals would not constitute assassination.[65]

Generally speaking, the strategic campaign followed Warden's concept of the Five Strategic Rings: isolate the leadership, degrade key production, disrupt the infrastructure via transportation attacks, "turn" the population and troops against the regime, and destroy Iraq's offensive and defensive military forces.[66] Desert Storm's strategic objectives included the seizing and retention of air superiority, the isolation and incapacitation of the Iraqi leadership, the destruction of Iraq's nuclear, biological, and chemical warfare capabilities, and the elimination of Iraq's offensive and defensive military capabilities. Planners estimated that this first phase would take approximately one week and inflict *strategic paralysis* upon Saddam Hussein's military machine: disrupting the connection of the command structure (the "head") from the military forces (the "fists" and "feet"). It would accomplish this by destroying internal control organizations (the "brain stem"), communications and electrical power (the "central nervous system"), and by targeting the transportation network and oil-refining capacity (the "circulatory system").

To do this was a daunting task, made more so by the lethality of Iraqi defenses, and the necessity of avoiding civilian casualties and destruction of the country's cultural, religious, and historic treasures. As a result, planners went over prospective targets in great detail, examining the attack axes to see if a wayward bomb could inflict civilian deaths or gratuitous destruction.[67] Targeting required establishing a series of DMPIs (pronounced "Dimpies")—Desired Mean Points of Impact—for any of the targets selected. A target might have multiple DMPIs, depending on

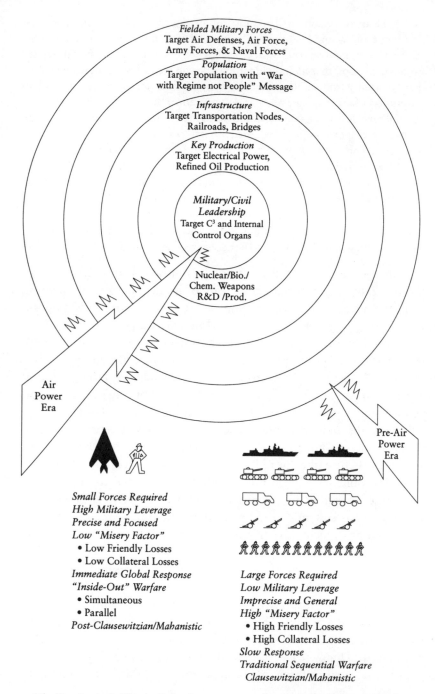

5.1 The Five Strategic Rings Only air power can strike across the spectrum of objectives unconstrained by traditional limitations.

how thoroughly planners wished to pound it. For example, a hardened command and control center might require six or even eight to be destroyed, but a hangar just one. Established procedure would have dictated striking each target with enough bombs on one attack to destroy it. Glosson's chief planner, Lt. Col. Dave Deptula, recognized that following this approach would quickly soak up available strike aircraft before all the critical targets could be struck. He reasoned that with precision-guided munitions (PGMs) a few bombs—even a single one—on each critical target would achieve a debilitating effect, allowing many more targets to be struck than otherwise possible if strikers adhered to conventional wisdom. As he put it to those who wanted to destroy each target one at a time, "If a 2,000-pound bomb hit the other end of this building [Royal Saudi Air Force Headquarters], do you *really* think business would go on as usual?" Stealth figured prominently in his thinking, for F-117s did not require the kind of "force packaging"—such as electronic warfare support, Wild Weasels, and air defense suppressors—which characterized conventional attackers, limiting the number of targets that could be struck and creating demands for support aircraft that might otherwise have been better used against multiple targets. With stealth, he could plan one strike across the entire country hitting the widest span of targets without running out of aircraft. Thus was born the concept of "simultaneity"—a result of technology, stealth, precision, and creative planning based on desired effects rather than a "cookbook" approach to target destruction.[68]

The greatest challenge was the seizing of air superiority, for that meant the destruction of the Iraqi air force's fighters and interceptors, suppression of SAM and AAA sites, and the jamming and destruction of Iraq's Franco-Soviet-British–based air defense network—the early warning and air surveillance radars, command and control facilities, communications and computer links, and electrical power supply. At H-hour on opening night, Iraq would be confronting the coalition with over 700 fighter aircraft, 7,000 antiaircraft guns, 7,000 radar-guided missiles, and 9,000 heat-seeking missiles.[69] To counter this integrated and hardened air defense network, the Allied coalition would have to mount a genuine air assault, using F-117A stealth attackers, Air Force and Navy cruise missiles, and special operations forces; EF-111A and EA-6B electronic warfare airplanes; F-4G radar-killers; F-15E, F/A-18A/C, F-111F, A-6E, and Tornado GR.1 strike aircraft; and F-15C air superiority fighters backed up by Tornado F.3, Saudi F-15A, and Navy F-14A fighters. Behind these would be tankers flying refueling tracks, and, of course, the omniscent E-3B AWACS complemented by Navy E-2Cs.

The second phase, suppression of enemy air defenses in the Kuwaiti theater of operations, was estimated to take only a day, for these defenses were neither as numerous nor as secure and redundant as those in Iraq. The third phase really had two related components: destruction of the Republican Guard, and destruction of the Iraqi army in Kuwait. In some respects, attacking the Republican Guard really constituted a strategic objective, for the Guard permeated the Hussein regime and served both as an instrument of internal control and as the most loyal and best-equipped offensive military force as well. Horner and Schwarzkopf had little desire to drive the Guard out of Kuwait; rather, they wanted to follow the classic military dictum of "find, fix, fight, and finish": locate the Guard, pin it in place, attack it, and destroy it. (Subsequently, as Horner related, "They obliged, surprisingly. We didn't think they would. General Schwarzkopf was very concerned about them decamping and going back to Baghdad or spreading out. Fortunately, they stayed nicely grouped up for us."[70] Ejecting the rest of the Iraqi army from Kuwait involved targeting the Army in the field, including its headquarters, troops, and—Schwarzkopf and Powell's pet interests—tanks and artillery. From the first day onward, B-52 strikes every three hours would hammer Iraqi forces. Other attacks would hit ammunition storage and fuel supplies, and deeper interdiction attacks would seek to sever resupply lines and communications into Kuwait, including railroads, bridges, and truck convoys. Bridge strikes were critical, for downed bridges could form bottlenecks. Iraq possessed fifty-four key bridges, forty-two of which were located between Baghdad and Basra. Planners were confident that smart munitions dropped from F-117s, F-15Es, F-111Fs, Tornado GR.1s, A-6Es and Jaguars would make short work of them, and this confidence subsequently proved justified. Overall, planners expected the third phase to take approximately three weeks.[71]

Thirty days after D-day (the launching of Desert Storm), Powell and Schwarzkopf hoped that they could begin G-day—the invasion and liberation of Kuwait. (In reality, the Gulf's worst flying weather in 14 years stretched this from 30 to 39 days.) Here the Air Force anticipated that JSTARS would work for the air-to-ground war as AWACS could for the air-to-air one. Originally, the experimental E-8A JSTARS had not been a player in Gulf planning, but following a highly successful demonstration of what it could do during a research deployment to Europe, Schwarzkopf ordered the two prototypes to the Gulf, and they subsequently arrived with teams of Ph.D. technicians to keep their complex systems functioning smoothly. In the war, planners also established "kill boxes," cubic blocks of space presided over by a forward air controller—either an OA-10A Thunderbolt II armed with marker rockets, or a F-16C/D "Killer Scout" (corresponding roughly to the Vietnam-era "Fast FAC"). If targets were spotted, the FAC/Scout could direct in strike flights of appropriate attack aircraft, such as A-10As or F-16C/D "Killer Bees." F-111Fs, F-15Es, and A-6Es would also strike at night, the Strike Eagles using their LANTIRN pods to improve their effectiveness, the F-111Fs operating with their Pave Tack sensor pods in a search mode, and the A-6Es using their TRAM multisensor, all looking for tanks and artillery. Marine A-6Es, F/A-18As, AV-8Bs, and AH-1Ws would support the operations of Marine ground forces, while the Navy would use its A-6Es, A-7Es, F/A-18A/Cs, and S-3Bs to go after Iraqi navy and other targets. The smaller coalition air forces would also play a role, such as the Free Kuwaiti Air Force's A-4KUs and Mirage F-1s that had escaped capture, the Saudis with Tornado GR.1s and Northrop F-5Es, the British with Tornado GR.1s and Jaguar GR.1As, the French with their own Jaguars, and the GCC nations with a range of their own attackers. Then, of course, so would the coalition ground forces, with their array of attack, scout, and troop transport helicopters.

All of this demanded tremendous coordination and support. The single ATO issued each day—a document the size of a telephone book—would coordinate the attacks of all Allied air assets in the Gulf, including all coalition air forces, special operations forces, naval and marine air, the Army's ATACMS (on occasion), and the cruise missiles; it did not cover Navy fleet air defense missions, or Army and Marine helicopter operations.[72] AWACS had the major responsibility for separating friends from foes, and preventing "blue on blue" fire, as well as no less lethal midair collisions. "It was like running a combination of Chicago, Atlanta, Washington, Denver, New York, and Los Angeles air traffic control, and doing so in the midst of a war," one AWACS crewman recalled.[73] Then there were the maintenance requirements; the coalition aircraft would have to maintain flight operations at "surge" levels, taxing the ability of maintainers to keep them in the air. Planners hoped to meet (and hopefully beat) peacetime mission capability rates, which, for the Air Force fighters involved in the Gulf, averaged just over 85 percent (i.e., 85 percent of the service's Gulf fighters were fully capable of flying combat at any one time. In fact, during the war, the average mission capability rate for the Air Force fighters involved was over 92 percent). Direct airlift support lines ran from the Gulf to Europe and the United States, and the various military services all created special task forces and crisis response teams to improve maintenance, resolve problems, and expedite delivery of key items to the Gulf air forces.[74]

On the Brink

Over the fall and into the winter of 1990–91, the coalition partners continued building up the strength of ground and air forces, even as the Iraqi dictator proved increasingly intractable. As the air and ground strength built up, the coalition forces gained familiarity with the terrain over which they would operate, and with each other. Intelligence collectors monitored Iraqi communications and signals, assessing potential threats and locating targets for electronic warriors and Wild Weasels. F-15 pilots honed their skills with dissimilar air combat training. Strike flights practiced tanking procedures and "packages" flew to the border before turning back for their bases. On the other side, Saddam Hussein's MiGs and Mirage fighters raced toward the Saudi borders, testing the reaction time of Allied interceptors, and turning back when illuminated by F-15 radars. Iraqi rocket forces testfired Scuds in a not-so-subtle signal of what Iraq might do (the Scud launches backfired, for they enabled refinement of Allied launch detection techniques). Troops dug in, and the first trickle of what would eventually become a veritable flood of mail to the Gulf arrived in Saudi Arabia. At the beginning of November, Allied ground strength stood at 243,000 troops, 150,000 of which were American.

Then, on November 8, the Bush administration announced plans to vastly increase coalition forces to provide for "an adequate offensive military option should that be necessary to achieve our common goals"; the other coalition partners immediately followed suit. Airlift operations intensified. When the VII Corps left for Saudi Arabia, the handwriting was on the wall. It could not be kept in Saudi Arabia indefinitely, which clearly implied the eventual use of force. Sending the VII Corps was, in its own way, like mobilization before the outbreak of the First World War, a situation not lost on one National Security Council senior staff member, who recollected later, "Nobody mentioned train schedules, but I got the point."[75] By the time of the ground operation, there were no fewer than 844,650 troops in the Gulf region representing sixteen coalition nations, 532,000 of which were American.[76]

On the eve of the war, coalition air strength stood at 2,614 aircraft; of these 1,990 were American, and of the American total, 450 were carrier-based (see Table 5.3).[77] There was still time for peace, but Saddam Hussein would have none of it; indeed, his rhetoric became even more violent. He would unleash the "mother of all battles," trigger a flood of American blood, and raise up mountains of skulls of Iraq's enemies, in words invoking the ancient brutality of Assyria and Nebuchadnezzar's Babylon.[78] Likely he was encouraged by what was happening in the United States. Dissent is the essence of a free society, and there were many thoughtful

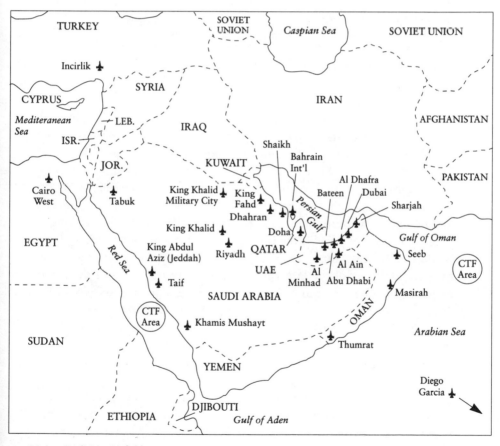

5.2 Major Coalition Airfields

Table 5.3. Coalition Air Strength on the Eve of War

Country	Fighter/ Attack	Tanker	Airlift	Other	Total	Percentage of Force
United States	1,323	285	175	207	1,990	76.1
Saudi Arabia	276	15	38	10	339	12.9
Great Britain	57	9	3	4	73	2.8
France	44	3	12	7	66	2.5
Kuwait	40	—	3	—	43	1.6
Canada	26	—	—	2	28	1.1
Bahrain	24	—	—	—	24	0.9
Qatar	20	—	—	—	20	0.8
UAE	20	—	—	—	20	0.8
Italy	8	—	—	—	8	0.3
New Zealand	—	—	3	—	3	0.1
Totals	1,838	312	234	230	2,614	99.9[a]

[a]Total does not equal 100 percent due to rounding.

critics of American involvement in the Gulf, from across the political spectrum. Unfortunately, most media attention focused on those who belittled the preparations with simplistic slogans such as "No Blood for Oil," and "Hell No, We Won't Go/We Won't Fight for Texaco." "Countries get invaded every day, and we don't send 500,000 troops," ran one criticism; true enough, but most invaders do not have nuclear, chemical, and biological warfare intentions; the self-proclaimed goal of making a "fire eat up half of Israel"; the fourth largest army in the world; and the world's sixth largest air force. With a relish that smacked of nostalgia for the good old days of the late 1960s and early 1970s, some of the more extreme protesters proclaimed that the coming war protests would be "bigger than Vietnam." The son of John Lennon released a new version of his father's Bolero-like antiwar song, "[All We Are Saying Is] Give Peace a Chance." In response, Checkmate's self-styled "Airpower Chorus" put up signs adorned with a B-52 that read "All we are saying is kick Saddam's ass."[79]

In a series of hearings before the Senate Armed Services Committee, a parade of witnesses—some thoughtful, but including others who had initiated and supervised the failed policies of the 1960s and 1970s, from Vietnam to Desert One—argued for a sanctions-only approach. They ignored the generally dismal record of sanctions in the past; by the best indicator, sanctions have worked only 40 times out of 115 post-1914 crises (a success rate of only 35 percent) and failed most spectacularly in 1941, where American sanctions actually stimulated the Japanese to attack Pearl Harbor.[80] Defense commentators cautioned that American tanks would suffocate from desert dust in their engines, sophisticated planes would break, Saddam's "simpler" approach to war would work better than Western "complexity"—all while mission availability rates in the Gulf continued to soar. Political scientists argued that the Arab nations would not fight if the conflict occurred during Ramadan (ignoring, of course, that the 1973 Arab-Israeli war—which the Arabs started—was a Ramadan war).

Arguments against air power were dusted off again. It was unreliable; advanced systems wouldn't work in the desert heat and dust; stealth could be defeated by multiple radars. Reporters confused the F-117 with the experimental B-2. On one Washington, D.C., news show, a leading journalist stated that the B-2 would fly in the Gulf; another commented that it would have to "do better than it did in Panama!"[81] Desert heat waves would distort the images seen by infrared and other electro-optical sensors so "smart" munitions would miss their targets. Bombing would only strengthen the will of Iraq to resist, dug-in troops could not be dislodged by bombing alone, et cetera. The coalition would fracture when Westerners inflicted massive civilian casualties upon the Iraqis, as (critics implied) air power must invariably do. (Suitably encouraged, Saddam Hussein took this advice to heart and parked his Scud launchers in the midst of residential areas.) Others feared for the treasures in Iraq that "imprecise" air power must necessarily destroy, curiously showing no apparent interest, appreciation, or anger for the large-scale museum-sacking and vandalism then occurring in Kuwait. (Their concern might have inspired the subsequent parking of MiGs next to historic sites and shrines.)[82]

On November 29, 1990, the United Nations passed Resolution 678, which authorized the use of force to expel Iraq from Kuwait if it did not withdraw on or by January 15. President George Bush, though not compelled to by the Constitution, sent a letter to the House and Senate requesting Congressional concurrence with the UN resolution. It was a risky, forthright, and courageous move. But before Congress could debate the issue, one last diplomatic maneuver had to play out. Secretary of State James Baker flew to Geneva, subsequently meeting Iraqi foreign minister Tariq 'Aziz without effect; the Iraqi envoy even refused to deliver a personal letter from Bush to Hussein. "Let us hope," Baker said pointedly afterward, "Iraq does not miscalculate again."[83]

The Congressional debate that followed was, for the most part, polite, reasoned, and enlightening. It could not have more dramatically highlighted the contrast between the assured, confident tone of 1980s-era decisionmakers and the pessimism of critics still stuck with a Vietnam mentality, who consistently painted a grim picture. Columnists opined that a land invasion would be costly in American lives.[84] Some senators predicted the war would turn from an air war to a ground war with perhaps tens of thousands of American casualties, and that the sound fabric of the country would be torn apart.[85] On January 12, Bush got his resolution on bipartisan votes of 250–183 in the House, and 52–47 in the Senate. The nation's political leadership was on board the administration's express.

The military was ready, both in the States and in the Gulf; airfields were stacked with airplanes (130 Air Force fighters at one base alone), and one logistics base had a perimeter 65 miles long, bespeaking the intensive buildup that had occurred. The strike forces had been briefed on the campaign plan, and the reaction of one F-16 pilot was to write in his diary:

> Got "The Plan" and my heart soared. I am so damn proud to be part of this! The guys that wrote this plan have put together an incredible air campaign. I was worried that when push came to shove, the right people weren't going to be in the right places where they'd be needed. I am not nearly as apprehensive as before.[86]

Right to the end, thoughtful commentators raised unsettling questions, made more disturbing by years of underestimating American military strength and abilities. Wrote Prof. Michael Walzer of Princeton's Institute for Advanced Study:

> There are a lot of good reasons to be afraid of fighting . . . Who can say how far the violence will extend? Modern military technology is massive and unpredictable in its effects: How many of the targets that we aim at will we manage to hit? How many homes, schools, hospitals will we hit without aiming at them? The U.S. Army and Air Force are pretty much untested: How effectively will they fight? A "quick and easy" war would be a war fought mainly through the air, but is that feasible? Would it even be tried? A ground attack that became bogged down, even for a month or two, might represent a "moral" victory for Saddam Hussein.[87]

On January 15, Saddam Hussein still had not budged from Kuwait, so George Bush signed a formal National Security Directive authorizing the execution of military action. Diplomacy done, the nation called on its military. Desert Shield transformed into Desert Storm; time had run out for Iraq.

six

The Breaking Storm

The United States relies on the Air Force and
the Air Force has never been the decisive
factor in the history of wars.
Saddam Hussein (1990)

Every war has its own particular defining moments when the nature of what is happening impresses itself on the combatants, and air wars are no different. It may come when armorers are loading bombs and missiles "in anger," or when the canopy closes and the crew chief realizes that perhaps the pilot and plane might not come back. To air crews, it may be when the landing gear retracts into the plane with a solid thunk, or when the first electronic warfare warning sounds, or they spot the sprinkling of flak and tracer lacing across a forbidding sky. Desert Storm certainly had its memorable moments; 3:00 A.M. January 17 was "showtime" over Iraq, and in the hours prior to that time final preparations had to be made so that the strike plan came together on time and in sequence.[1]

It began with transmission of the Air Tasking Order (ATO)—the massive document that spelled out details of planned strikes—throughout the joint forces via the Air Force's Computer-Aided Force Management System (CAFMS). Because the five Navy carriers on station (with a sixth about to arrive) could not use CAFMS, throughout the war a messenger had to hop a carrier delivery airplane every day to hand-deliver the ATO on a floppy computer diskette to the fleet for internal Navy reproduction

and dissemination. Once all players had the ATO, the myriad details inherent in military aviation combat operations now came into play. Aircraft were given final checks and "weaponized," and their pilots and
flight crews given final briefings. The fighter and attack pilots strapped
on G suits over their Nomex "green bag" flight suits, checked the condition of helmets, masks, hoses, and connections, and secured their survival
"beepers," sidearms, and knives. Then it was off to the ramp or deck to
preflight their aircraft, already meticulously inspected by their ground
crews and plane captains.

Air operations began at 6:36 A.M. on January 16, 1991, when the first
of seven B-52G Stratofortresses, popularly known as "Buffs," from the
Eighth Air Force left Barksdale AFB on a round-trip mission to Iraq.
Eight engines roaring, each "Buff" departed in a mist of spray, lifting off
like a ponderous bird into a rain-drenched predawn sky, disappearing
quickly into dense cloud. Breaking into the clear, facing a rising sun, the
aging B-52s—the most visible symbol of intercontinental air power—
began their long voyage. More than twelve hours remained before the
fury of Desert Storm fell upon Iraq, but the first mission was already
underway, in a true demonstration of Rice's *Global Reach—Global
Power* doctrine. The seven bombers carried AGM-86C cruise missiles,
specially modified versions of the Air Force's nuclear-tipped AGM-86B
air-launched cruise missile (ALCM), intended for eight high-value Iraqi
communications, power generation, and transmission facilities. These
"Charlie" models replaced the AGM-86B's nuclear warhead with a
1,000-pound conventional blast–fragmentation warhead, substituting
more accurate GPS satellite–based navigation for the nuclear model's terrain contour–matching guidance system. Repeatedly refueled on their
run to the launch tracks located within USCENTCOM's area of responsibility, the B-52 crews spent a total of two hours apiece hanging behind
a tanker. Morning gave way to midday, and finally, night, and still the
Stratofortresses made their way to war. As they closed on Iraq, ahead of
them, in and around the Gulf, other crews walked out into the night, to
risk their own lives aloft.[2]

The night was clear and moonless. In World War II, cities had dreaded
"Bombers' Moons," for attack aircraft in that primitive era needed as
much help with their navigation as they could get, and the moon's illu-
mination of ground features was very useful. But now, in the era of GPS
and sophisticated inertial navigation systems, such mattered not at all:
the darker the better. (Modern attack crews bragged, in fact, of "owning

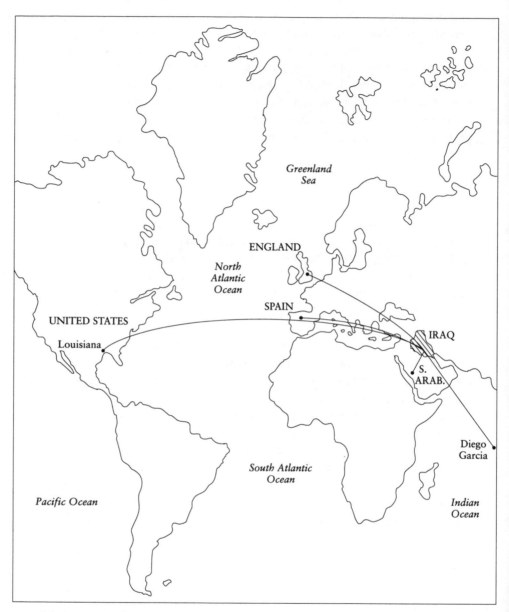

6.1 Global Reach, Global Power B-52G Stratofortresses attacked Iraq from bases as distant as the United States, Great Britain, Spain, and Diego Garcia.

the night.") Many events took place simultaneously beginning around midnight. One hundred sixty tankers—American KC-10s, KC-135s, and KC-130s; British Victors, Tristars, and VC10Ks; and Saudi KE-3Bs among them—took off and flew to multiple refueling tracks, staying out of range of Iraqi early warning radar. Deep in Saudi Arabia, at Khamis Mushait (dubbed "Tonopah East") near the Yemen border, ten soot-black F-117A stealth fighters from the 415th Tactical Fighter Squadron, loaded with laser-guided 2,000-pound bombs, taxied out, bobbing on their stalky landing gears. Briefly the F-117s "held" at the end of the runway while maintenance crews verified readiness for flight one more time with "last chance" checks. Then, at full power, they accelerated noisily down the runway and lifted into the sky like ominous black moths. It was 0022 Hours, January 17.[3]

At bases across Saudi Arabia and Allied Gulf nations, hundreds of strike, suppression, and support aircraft took off amid the thunder of afterburners, forming up, unlit and silent, moving toward the tankers and Iraq. Other B-52Gs, pregnant with bombs, flew toward Iraq from Diego Garcia. Operational security was challenging, and made more so at Dhahran, where a commercial pilot captaining a waiting jumbo jet from a coalition nation impulsively complained to the airport's tower controllers about a flock of RAF Tornadoes from 31 Squadron that suddenly cut ahead of him from a taxiway and took off into the dark, afterburners flaring. At sea, carriers in the Red Sea and lower Persian Gulf launched dozens of aircraft to protect the fleet and hit selected targets, as two cruisers and a battleship fired the first of 106 TLAMs (Tomahawk land attack missiles) launched against Iraq that day. Air Force and Navy cruise-missile launches held particular significance, for, unlike manned aircraft, the little missiles could not be recalled. Once these missiles left their launch canisters or fell away from their B-52 motherships, there was no turning back: the coalition was at war.[4]

In sum, the war opened with the full orchestration of Allied land-and-sea-based air power. There were electronic warfare jammers, the EF-111A Ravens and EA-6B Prowlers, and the lesser known standoff EC-130H Compass Call; HARM-firing F-4G Wild Weasels and F/A-18s, hunting for SAMs; F-117As and cruise missiles going to downtown Baghdad; F-15E Eagles, Tornadoes, F-111Fs, and A-6E Intruders, for strikes against key Iraqi airfields and Scud sites; stately eight-engine B-52G Stratofortresses (some of whose crews were younger than the planes they were flying) going after high-value targets; F-15C Eagles and a few F-14A + Tomcats for air superiority sweeps; and F-16C/D Fighting Falcons, Jaguars, and F/A-18A/C Hornets to suppress enemy air defenses and make the skies safer for more vulnerable attackers such as the B-52s. These were by no means all the types involved in the war. In the first four hours of the air war, nearly 400 Allied strike aircraft from the coalition stormed across Iraq, supported by hundreds of others over the Gulf region and over the fleet at sea. Altogether, in that first night, 668 aircraft attacked Iraq, 530 from the Air Force (79%), 90 from five Navy carriers and the Marine Corps (13%), 24 from Great Britain (4%), and 12 each from France and Saudi Arabia (2% each). In the first 24 hours, over 1,300 combat sorties were flown by American and coalition airmen.[5]

Out of the Dark

In the last hour before the attack opened, there was a deceptive calm along the Iraqi-Saudi border. Within Iraqi radar range, just behind the border, F-15Cs cruised along three combat air patrol tracks, appearing no different than they had on many previous nights. Behind them, three AWACS maintained station, their powerful radars looking deep into hostile territory. If what happened near the border seemed routine, the events occurring beyond Iraqi radar range were anything but. Opening honors belonged to three very special attackers: Task Force Normandy, an Air Force–Army team flying MH-53J Pave Low and AH-64 Apache helicopters; the 315th Tactical Fighter Squadron's F-117 stealth fighters; and the Navy's ship-launched TLAMs.

At 2:20 A.M., with H-hour still 40 minutes away, Task Force Normandy clattered unseen across the border from Saudi Arabia, as an Iraqi, spooked by the noise, fired an unaimed missile at them. Earlier, the force's helicopters had lifted off from Al Jouf, an outpost near the border. Task Force Normandy, consisting of three Pave Lows from the Air Force's First Special Operations Wing acting as navigational pathfinders for nine Army Apache gunships from the 1st Battalion of the 101st Aviation Brigade, had a small but important mission. Its targets were two Iraqi frontier early warning radar sites that might detect low-flying LANTIRN-equipped F-15E strike aircraft heading for Scud sites in Western Iraq up to 15 minutes before the Strike Eagles' designated time-over-target. It was important to destroy the sites simultaneously, not only so that the F-15Es could get in undetected, but so that no warning could reach Baghdad that hostilities had started. The helicopters, nearly invisible in their subdued camouflage, followed a circuitous route, flying a nap-of-the-earth profile, descending into wadis and hugging the desert floor; it was daunting, demanding work, requiring the highest standards of airmanship. The fuel-hungry Apaches, normally limited to two-hour endurance, had one of their rocket pods replaced by a large 230-gallon external fuel tank so they could make the flight. Thanks to GPS, FLIR, and night-vision goggles, the Air Force Pave Low crews had no difficulty navigating; their job done, they veered off, dropping chemical lights to mark the final navigational waypoint. The Apaches pressed on for an additional few miles, then acquired the sites in their FLIRs. At H-22—2:38 A.M. local time—the Apaches rocketed the sites with 27 Hellfire missiles and 100 Hydra unguided rockets, then hosed down the area with 4,000 rounds from their cannon. Task Force Normandy turned for home, dodging two heat-seeking SA-7 SAMs and small arms fire on its way out of the country. Twenty-five miles away, already over Iraq and skimming the earth at nearly the speed of sound, an ingressing LANTIRN-equipped F-15E crew saw one site explode in flames as the Eagle blew through the radar hole left by the special operations forces (SOF) crews. The Strike Eagle pilot later recalled, "We could see cars driving down the highways and [were] thinking 'that guy could stop and telephone somebody 150 miles away.'"[6]

The Eagle driver's reaction was justified, for, unfortunately, Task Force Normandy's incursion had not gone unnoticed; one Iraqi outpost made a frantic call to Baghdad. Thus, a few minutes after the Apaches blasted the sites, the skies over Saddam Hussein's capital city erupted with withering antiaircraft fire, interrupting evening news back in the United States, where it was approximately 6:45 P.M. East Coast time, January 16. Iraqi gunners and trackers at SAM sites had no idea where the incoming strikes were headed, what their targets were (although some, such as Scud sites, were obvious choices) and thus were like blindfolded boxers, lashing out with potentially lethal force at opponents they could not yet see. (Indeed, no airplanes or missiles were yet over Baghdad.)[7]

Well in advance of H-hour, having flown almost the length of the Arabian peninsula, the F-117 stealth fighters finished tanking, silently dropped off the booms, and then began their individual approaches into Iraq. By their nature, the stealth fighters were loners; each pilot had an individual mission plan tailored to his target and the threats that surrounded it. Effectively compressing the detection range of radars, stealth fighters could trace their way through a layered, redundant air defense network the way a commuter might step around pools of water on the

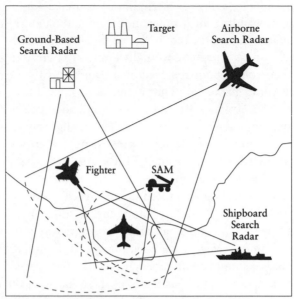

A: Detection Effectiveness against Conventional Aircraft

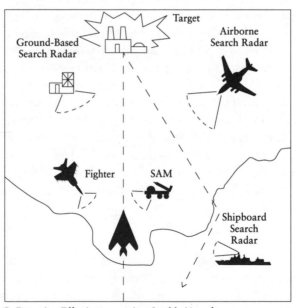

B: Detection Effectiveness against Stealth Aircraft

6.1 The Value of Stealth Stealth effectively reduces the detection ranges of radar.

way to work. For months they had practiced for this moment. Before the war, Congressman Dave McCurdy, an Air Force Reservist and chairman of the House Intelligence Committee, had met with the 37th Tactical Fighter Wing at Tonopah East and reviewed their plans. "They knew they'd pull it off," he recollected. "Their confidence was infectious."[8] Quietly, ominously, the F-117s passed into Iraqi airspace and headed for their targets across the country and in Baghdad: hardened air defense sites endangering nonstealthy attackers and critical command and control facilities. Baghdad had seven times the density of defenses as Hanoi had during Linebacker II, and defenses denser than the most heavily defended Eastern European target at the height of the Cold War. So dangerous was downtown Baghdad that the air campaign planners excluded all other attackers, except for F-117s and cruise missiles, from striking it. As they approached weapons release, the warning from the frontier reached Iraqi command posts, and tracer from automatic weapons, punctuated by heavier flak and an occasional unguided missile blasting heavenward, curtained the sky over Baghdad, like some menacing aurora borealis. Hoping only an unaimed "golden BB" could endanger them, the stealth pilots did their best to ignore the light show outside and concentrated on acquiring their targets and designating them for their smart bombs. The first to go—at nine minutes before H-hour—was the Nukhayb air defense operations center in southern Iraq that could endanger the coalition's nonstealthy strike packages. Other Nighthawks hit the centers at Al Taqaddum and Al Taji, as well as lesser air defense sites. But the most spectacular targets were those set for H-hour itself, in downtown Baghdad.

In one cockpit, as his F-117 cruised over Baghdad, a stealth pilot carefully kept the crosshairs of his laser designator on a telecommunications center the principal master attack planner had dubbed the "AT&T building." The weapons bay snapped open, disgorging a 2,000-pound laser-guided bomb, which sank away from the black arrowhead, streaming wisps of vapor off its fins as it maneuvered to pick up the "basket" and plunge at supersonic speed toward a little spot of laser light fixed unerringly on the top of the center. In Riyadh, Lieutenant General Horner and his "Black Hole" gang were waiting for CNN, the cable news station broadcasting via telephone from Baghdad, to go off the air. In Washington, planners and senior defense officials alike counted the minutes, fascinated at the irony of events about to unfold. If all went well, the first "BDA" (bomb damage assessment) would be inadvertently transmitted

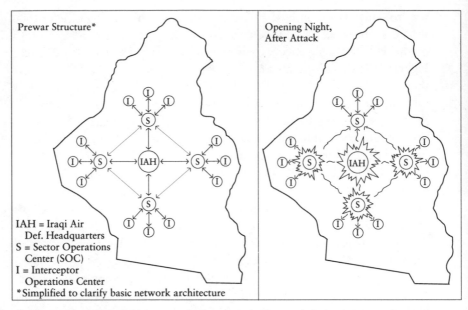

6.2 F-117 Disruption of the Iraqi Air Defense Network In a fashion analogous to a virus attacking a cell, F-117 Stealth fighters destroyed Iraq's air defense network, shattering its integrity and opening up the country to strikes by older, nonstealthy aircraft. Three of four SOCs were immediately destroyed, along with Iraqi air defense headquarters, while a fourth—which posed no immediate threat—was ignored until later in the war when it too was destroyed.

in "real time" directly to the people most responsible for executing the strike as well as to the world at large. In Baghdad, CNN correspondents Bernard Shaw and Peter Arnett were reporting the antiaircraft fire over the city to American audiences in a scene eerily recalling the central moment in Eugene Burdick and Harvey Wheeler's novel *Fail-Safe,* when Moscow is vaporized in a thermonuclear blast even as the American ambassador is describing the sight of bursting antiaircraft fire over the hotline.[9]

> **Shaw:** We have not heard any jet planes yet, Peter.
> **Arnett:** Now the sirens are sounding for the first time. The Iraqis have informed us—

Nothing but abrupt static. CNN's link went off the air. The U.S. Air Force had delivered the first Allied air weapon to strike into the heart of Saddam Hussein's city. In both the Black Hole and in the depths of the Pentagon, a wild cheer erupted.[10]

Shortly afterwards, at H + 6 minutes, the first Tomahawk slammed into the city, announcing its presence as had the F-117: with a shattering explosion. Fifty-three others followed. Unlike the F-117s, with their penetrating smart bombs, the TLAMs lacked the ability to attack hardened targets, for their warheads were too small and light. (For this reason, they were not used against Iraq's invariably hardened air defense sites, nor did they fly against enemy radars and SAMs, despite press statements to the contrary.) But they could be devastating on conventional structures. The tiny TLAMs had flown hundreds of miles after being ship-launched, rocketing away from their parent vessels as their wing and tail surfaces unfolded and deployed, their little jet engines firing up, and their rocket boosters eventually burning out, separating, falling into the sea as the Tomahawks whined their way toward a Kamikaze-like rendezvous in Baghdad. Across the sea, their gyroscopic inertial guidance system kept them on course. Then, crossing the Arabian desert at altitudes less than 100 feet, the pencil-like missiles bobbed and weaved their way onward, their TERCOM guidance systems mentally comparing the terrain below to stored images carefully prepared and installed in the missiles' memory. A few towns and roads came up, and soon Baghdad itself. Entering the city, the missiles literally "read" the city's map with a video camera, noting buildings, openings, boulevards, intersections, always mentally comparing the images against stored data.

Then came the end game—at nearly the speed of sound they sought out the precise coordinates of the target—a corner of a headquarters here, the side of a building there—before blowing themselves apart in violent eruptions. On the balcony of the Al-Rasheed Hotel (itself the site of a buried telecommunications switching center off-limits to Allied bombs because of the large number of foreign journalists who stayed there), a British cameraman gaped as a Tomahawk cruised past his window, fearlessly plunging into the Iraqi Ministry of Defense and severely damaging it. Other TLAMs disgorged bomblets that tumbled earthward and covered vast areas in storms of shrapnel. With every blast, the antiaircraft fire doubled or tripled, as gunners frantically tried to find a target. Following the TLAMs came the ALCMs, threading their way with GPS precision after having been air-launched from the Barksdale Buffs. The huge B-52s had arrived at their launch points "within fractions of a second" (as mission commander Lt. Col. Jay Beard recollected) of the planned time, fifteen hours after leaving Louisiana. Thirty-five ALCMs dropped away from their shackles, their tiny switchblade wings and tail surfaces deployed, and, as their small jet engines fired up, the little ALCMs streaked away in anger. As the missiles flew across the Arabian desert toward their targets, the huge Stratofortresses turned toward home, the longest portion of the flight still ahead of them as they bucked heavy headwinds. Postwar analysis indicated that thirty-one of the thirty-five ALCMs launched that night hit their targets, a success rate of nearly 89 percent.[11]

All over Iraq that night, young men from many nations and varied religions laid their lives on the line. Suited up, breathing hard, plugged into their aircraft with radio leads, oxygen hoses, and G-suit connections, strapped into their ejection seats, they fought solitary wars, peering through their HUDs and at the often frightening spectacle outside as they sought to impose by force what Saddam Hussein had refused to grant by reason. Aloft, a few Iraqi interceptors—F-1s, MiG-25s, and MiG-29s among them—blasted around, trying to intercept them. From below, long fingers of bright tracer weaved toward them. At a distance, coalition pilots could see dense flak over Baghdad from over 100 miles away. "It was an overwhelming amount," one Navy attack pilot reported,

> It spread over an enormous area of part of western Iraq. It looked like if you can imagine the fireworks display at Disneyworld, and you multiply Disneyworld by a hundred. It's just a continued sparkling effect of white flashes that range in height from the surface to 3,000–4,000 feet.[12]

Regrettably, Iraqi defenders destroyed a *Saratoga* F/A-18C and killed its pilot, the first coalition airman to die in combat. Across the border, safe themselves from Iraqi defenses, sophisticated EC-130H Compass Call electronic warfare aircraft jammed communications, hindering the effectiveness of Iraq's already crumbling integrated air defense network. SAMs raced off their launch rails and snaked upward, most fooled by electronic warfare standoff jamming or from pods on the strike aircraft themselves, although some came close enough to send air crews into violent breaks to escape their lethal path. Losses to Iraqi SAMs, fortunately, were a rarity—indeed, over the entire war, only about ten coalition aircraft fell to SAMs, against thousands of SAMs fired against them—although pilots knew how it could have been. One estimated that without electronic countermeasures, fully 50 percent of all strike aircraft would not have returned.[13]

F-4G Wild Weasels and Navy F/A-18 SAM-killers fought a merciless electronic war, identifying Iraqi radars, locking onto them, and shooting them with missiles, even as the sky around them filled with SAMs. Occasionally it was like old times: one Weasel crew dodged five SA-2s (the F-4's old Vietnam nemesis) while hunting down and destroying its controlling Fan Song radar. To deal with radars that weren't operating, coalition planners had air- and ground-launched drones that mimicked the radar signature of incoming strike airplanes. After launch, the little drones caused defenders to switch on their radars, giving radar-hunters something to shoot. At one point, following a shower of drones near Baghdad, over 200 HARM antiradar missiles were launched, homing on Iraqi radars. American strike airplanes relied on the straightforward HARM, but the British used the ALARM, a weird but highly effective weapon, eventually firing 123 of them from Tornadoes. ALARM was like a miniature Wild Weasel itself. The missile—so long it resembled a vaulter's pole with fins—possessed radar-finding sensors that enabled it to be fired autonomously from ingressing Tornadoes as a SAM self-protection weapon, three to a plane. Thus, it did not have to be fired from a "dedicated" special-purpose electronic warfare airplane.[14]

Britain had accelerated ALARM as the Gulf crisis built; firing trials over the U.S. Navy's China Lake test range proved very promising, and ALARM was rushed to the Middle East, being declared "operational" a mere 10 days after its arrival in theater. After launch, ALARM would home in on a radar and destroy it. But if it did not find a radar immediately, it could also loiter, climbing high over the countryside, and then deploying a parachute so that it could hang in the sky and "look" for offending radars as it descended slowly earthward. When it found them, its little microcircuitry would prioritize the targets against stored memory programmed by target planners. After correlating a specific signal to a desired target, the missile's control unit would order the 'chute to separate, and it would plunge earthward, almost straight down on the radar emitter, avoiding the classic "undershoot-overshoot" problems of traditional missiles.[15] Both HARM and ALARM were devastating. The Iraqis soon learned that turning on a radar was tantamount to suicide, and the mere threat of Weasels and other radar-hunters generally guaranteed that those Iraqi radars still active shut down fast. Occasional heat-seekers shot skyward, forcing strike aircraft into abrupt jinks and triggering long strings of defensive flares that popped out like fireworks behind them.

As the night wore on toward dawn, strike flights returned to their bases and their ships, even as others sortied to keep up the pressure. The Barksdale Buffs were almost out of the Mediterranean, the North Atlantic before them, pressing on to home, already having been aloft over 24 hours. Ahead of them were persistent headwinds exceeding 170 MPH—roughly twice as high as forecast—that forced additional refuelings, and added an additional six hours to the flight. Finally, over 35 hours after takeoff, all seven landed back in Louisiana, having flown over 14,000 miles. They had completed the longest combat mission—for both length and duration—in aviation history. In their wake they had left chaos.

Baghdad's offensive weapons and research and production sites—the known nuclear, biological, and chemical (NBC) weapons research, production, and storage centers—underwent repeated attacks to ensure that their products did not endanger the coalition; no less than 535 sorties by manned aircraft and TLAMs hammered thirty-one different NBC sites that first night and day.[16] The F-117As proved particularly devastating, for unlike the TLAM, they could destroy hardened targets. Laboratory, research, and production facilities staggered under stealth-dropped smart bombs; video subsequently showed blasts sending destructive ripples through buildings like some parody of waves crashing on a beach. Though constituting less than 2½ percent of all Allied fighter and attack aircraft in the Gulf, the F-117A attacked over 31 percent of strategic Iraqi targets struck on the first day of the war. Overall, during the entire Gulf air war, the stealth fighter flew only 2 percent of the combat sorties, but attacked 40 percent of Iraqi strategic targets—a measure of its leverage. The ominous F-117As eventually earned the nickname *Shaba*, or "Ghost" from admiring Saudis.[17]

Other strikes shattered communications and control centers, hammered storage and maintenance facilities, saturated air defense sites, and struck at Iraqi airfields. Unseen, an F-117 pilot cruised over Iraqi air force headquarters bordering Al Muthenna airfield, dropping a smart bomb down its ventilation shaft and blowing out the middle of the building. (The next day, narrating the strike video for reporters in Riyadh, Horner said pointedly, "This is my counterpart's headquarters in Baghdad," just before the bomb hit.) A massive strike force of nearly 100 airplanes targeted Iraqi air defense positions, with waves of F-16s, F-18s, and Jaguars attacking SAM sites and antiaircraft artillery. Diego's B-52G Stratofortresses skimmed the earth at less than 400 feet, stunning defenders with the shattering noise of eight thundering engines, before popping up to bombing altitude and unleashing dozens of bombs on their targets. They were far from alone in the night sky; one Buff copilot yelped, "Look at those guys!" as a pair of F-15Es raced *below* them at over 600 knots.

American F-111Fs, F-15Es, and A-6Es ranged over Iraqi airfields and Scud sites, as did Saudi Tornadoes. British Tornadoes attacked airfields and Scud sites with JP-233 munitions dispensers and cluster bombs. They struck low, fast, and hard—in the heroic tradition of their predecessors in Mosquitoes during the Second World War—on missions one pilot called "absolutely terrifying." One failed to return that first night, apparently from ground fire that set an engine ablaze and forced the crew to eject into a brutal captivity.[18]

Severed from its leadership, attacked where it lived, the Iraqi air force was largely preempted from fighting. Those few pilots that did go aloft did not fair well. The flight leader of four F-15s from the 1st Tactical Fighter Wing saw "solid streams of tracers" over Baghdad, arcing "like colored snakes," with "bombs going off everywhere." An AWACS warned him of an Iraqi Mirage F-1, which had just taken off and was closing on the four Eagles from astern. He broke hard, turned behind the Mirage, fired an AIM-7 Sparrow, and watched it track the Iraqi fighter, which disintegrated in a huge fireball—one of thirty-five Iraqi airplanes that eventually fell before American and Saudi fighters. Another F-15 flight leader shot down one of two low-flying F-1s with a Sparrow in a "look-down, shoot-down" attack; startled by the resulting explosion, the Mirage's wingman instinctively rolled inverted and dove into the desert floor.[19] Elsewhere that night, as Allied pilots watched, a MiG-29 wandered in front of another Fulcrum. The trailing MiG pilot probably had both his air-to-air radar and missile-firing triggers held down, for his MiG immediately loosed a missile that unerringly shot his comrade down. Whether startled, mortified, or just confused, the victor in this strange episode then flew his own Fulcrum into the ground. It was the IQAF's only certain air-to-air kill of the war, and an example of "red on red" fire as well. With runways cratered and many aircraft destroyed as ground crews readied them for flight, Iraqi commanders chose to keep their remaining planes sealed in bunkers, safe until they could be used at a moment of Iraq's own choosing. Thus, the Iraqi air force never really got into the air.[20]

By the time dawn broke the morning of January 17, Iraq was well on the way to losing the war, thanks to the coalition's strategic air campaign. That morning, a humane leader would have sued for peace, for all he could expect now would be the continued dismembering of the Iraqi infrastructure and its remaining military forces by virtually Olympian air power. The previous night's attacks separated Saddam Hussein and his leadership from each other and, more important, from their military forces. It drove his regime underground, where they no longer could control events or react to Allied initiatives. The most critical networks—Iraq's command, control, communications, and intelligence (C³I), integrated air defenses, and power-generating capacity—were in a shambles. Indeed, the major damage occurred in the first 10 minutes. Minutes after H-hour, the lights went out in Baghdad, and did not come on again until well after the ceasefire. Within a few more hours, communications—the microwave towers, telephone relay exchanges, cables, and land lines—had been transformed into rubble. Eventually, by the end of the second week, with even backup communications systems disrupted, Saddam Hussein was reduced to sending orders from Baghdad to Kuwait by messenger; the trip took at least 48 hours. The coalition air attack had imposed strategic paralysis upon the Hussein regime. Within an hour, the integrated air defense network had collapsed; SAM sites and interceptor airfields were no longer under centralized control. Radar sites were destroyed or intimidated. Sector control stations and air defense headquarters were blasted into rubble. Antiaircraft forces were operating on their own, without broader information or support. Within several hours, attacks had left key Iraqi airfields with cratered runways, taxiways, and ramps. Below, the Iraqi air force remained in its bunkers, soon to be its tombs. Known facilities for the research and manufacture of weapons of mass destruction had been destroyed or rendered unusable.

The Weather Factor

With the decisive first night of the air war behind them, USCENTAF planners and air crews settled down to fulfilling the remaining objectives of the air campaign. Joining in from the third day were aircraft from a Joint Task Force in Turkey—essentially a large composite wing of over 130 airplanes—that conducted both offensive and defensive air operations over northern Iraq. This task force consisted of 28 F-15Cs for air superiority operations; 46 F-16C, F-111E, and F-4 strike airplanes; 32 F-4G, F-16C, and EF-111A Wild Weasel and electronic warfare aircraft; and approximately 30 other support aircraft for AWACS, reconnaissance, tanking, and intelligence gathering.[21]

The weather over Iraq during Desert Storm was the worst in fourteen years, and twice as bad as the climatological history for the region would have suggested. The conditions, in fact, approximated a rainy European summer, and not the kind of blue-skies conditions one normally associates with desert warfare. Cloud cover exceeded 25 percent at 10,000 feet over central Iraq on 31 days of the 43-day war; it exceeded 50 percent on 21 of those days, and 75 percent on 9 days. Accompanying this cover were occasionally violent winds and heavy downpours that played havoc with targeting and bomb damage assessment. Eventually, about half of all sorties to Iraq were affected by weather, resulting in cancellations or diverts. The weather problem proved very serious, particularly because the coalition's rules of engagement (ROE) demanded visual identification of targets before weapons release.

This self-imposed constraint—a constraint not imposed by technology limitations, but rather as insurance against "collateral damage"—particularly hit the F-117s. During the Gulf war, F-117s flew 1,270 combat sorties and dropped 2,041 tons of bombs, 1,616 of which—79 percent—hit their targets, that is, fell within 10 feet of their aiming points. Weather severely impacted F-117 operations in the first two weeks of the war, although even late in the campaign, it posed problems: on February 25, for example, the weather was so bad that all F-117 missions were canceled. Generally speaking, weather improved in the middle of February. Over the first three weeks, the F-117 hit percentage had averaged 70 percent—seven out of ten bombs hit their aiming point. Thereafter, for the last three weeks, hit accuracy averaged 86 percent. On seven days, it exceeded 90 percent, the best performance coming on February 19, when, in a series of attacks against nuclear research, ammunition storage, biological warfare, and solid rocket propellant facilities, Nighthawk pilots scored with twenty-eight of thirty bombs—an impressive 93-percent success rate. Brief mention must be made on what constituted acceptable accuracy with the F-117. So great was planners' faith in the F-117's targeting system that, indeed, their instructions usually stipulated not merely hitting particular buildings or shelters, but a particular portion of a building or shelter—for example, a corner, a vent, or a door. In fact, if they hit the building, but not the particular spot, their sortie counted as a miss, not a hit. Nevertheless, despite this stringent requirement and the vagaries of weather, which forced some mission aborts, at least some of the F-117 pilots returned from the war with perfect bombing records—every bomb they had dropped during the war had scored a direct hit.[22]

The Great Scud Chase

Iraq's Scud missiles posed one of the air campaign's most serious challenges, for the Scud had the potential of dramatically affecting the conduct and outcome of the war; the weather situation made it worse. Although air attacks dramatically reduced the frequency of Scud launches, the mobile missiles proved particularly difficult to detect and were never fully suppressed. The anti-Scud campaign highlighted what will undoubtedly be a major research and development challenge in the 1990s, given the great proliferation of mobile ballistic missiles around the world: developing means of detecting and destroying mobile missile launchers before they can fire.[23]

The Soviet-designed Scud was a single-stage liquid-fuel rocket contemporaneous to the American Redstone of the early 1950s, although its limited accuracy and range made it more the Soviet equivalent of Hitler's infamous V-2. The Scud traded the V-2's spindle-like lines for a more readily produced cylindrical cross-section body capped by a conical warhead. In typical fashion, the Soviet Union exported Scuds widely to client states, including the original Scud-A, and a slightly larger long-range variant, the Scud-B. Iraq subsequently acknowledged purchasing 819 of the latter. The Scud-B could be fired from fixed sites, and was easy to transport and launch, using the MAZ-543 eight-wheel combined transporter, erector, and launcher (TEL). It could hit targets approximately 200 miles from its launch point, although not with any great accuracy.

The Scud-B served as Iraq's primary long-range missile. Easily fabricated, the Scud inspired a number of copies and derivatives. During the Iran-Iraq war, the Iraqi military had deployed two longer-range variants—the Al-Husayn, a slightly larger weapon, and the Al-Abbas, larger still, which used increased fuel capacity and reduced warhead size and weight to achieve ranges in excess of 400 miles. Further, Iraqi technicians produced large numbers of crude but serviceable TELs, using foreign-supplied tractor-trailers. These two missiles figured prominently in the Iran-Iraqi "battle of the cities," in which both Iran and Iraq used Scud variants to attack each other's population centers in purely terror attacks. In 1982, Iraq started using Scuds and Frogs—the latter a shorter-range missile—against Iranian forces and population centers. Then, in 1985, Iran rocketed Baghdad, launching Libyan-and Syrian-supplied Scuds from positions a mere 80 miles away. In 1987, Iraq began rocketing more distant Teheran, using its indigenously built Scud derivatives, eventually firing nearly 200. Psychologically, these strikes seemed to devastate Iranian morale. Thus, by the Gulf war, the Iraqi army had a skilled pool of rocket teams with experience in maintaining and firing fairly sophisticated long-range missiles, and no qualms about using them against civilian populations.[24]

The Scud-hunting campaign hinged on the accuracy of intelligence estimates relating to sources of production and supply, storage, location of Scud units and fixed launch sites, and numbers of mobile launchers. Unfortunately, the total number of Scud launchers that Iraq possessed was far higher than what prewar intelligence estimates had indicated. On the first night, F-15Es had struck at fixed Scud installations in western Iraq, in strategic attacks intended to remove the Scud threat to Israel. Other attackers hit sites aimed at Saudi Arabia, as well as Scud infrastructure targets—missile manufacture, storage, and fueling installations. The Scud infrastructure attacks were very successful. Although assessment later indicated that the fixed-base strikes had not been completely successful, they seem to have achieved their ends, as it was the mobile Scud missiles mounted on trailers and locally manufactured launchers and not the fixed sites that subsequently proved troublesome.[25] Intelligence services had estimated initially that Iraq had forty-eight launchers, then optimistically revised this downward to eighteen; thus, when the first night's strikes destroyed sixteen, General Schwarzkopf recollected, "We felt we had 'em."[26] Unfortunately, it wasn't true, as became obvious when Scuds started falling out of Israeli and Arabian skies. Intelligence eventually concluded the Iraqis might have as many as 15 battalions with 15 launchers apiece—a whopping total of 225, over twelve times as many launchers as estimated on the eve of the war. Further, the Iraqi rocket force had surveyed and prepared a number of launch sites within Iraq and Kuwait, so that they could fire their weapons with relative confidence that they would hit city-size targets in coalition nations and Israel.[27]

The Scud threat was a strategic one, not because of what it could achieve militarily, but because of its political implications. Indeed, like the V-2 itself, this inaccurate missile had only a gambler's chance of hitting a truly vital target. But precision was not necessarily required. If a Scud hit Israel, Saddam Hussein reasoned, historical experience indicated Israel would react violently, and the injection of "Zionist" forces into the war might shatter the coalition, for they would have to fly through Jordanian and perhaps Syrian and Saudi airspace to reach Iraqi targets. (Once Iraq did strike out at Israel, King Hussein of Jordan—no relation to Saddam, although he came perilously close to aligning his kingdom with Iraq during the war—proclaimed that Jordan would consider any violation of its airspace an act of aggression justifying retaliation. He remained silent about Scuds then rocketing over Jordanian heads as they sought out Israeli cities, impartially endangering Jews and Muslims alike.)

Subsequent events suggest tacit understandings were reached among the coalition members that the Arab partners would at least wait and see in the event of such an attack, and some even appear to have privately assured American officials that a "one-time" Israeli retaliatory strike would not necessarily endanger the coalition. After all, as much as they might dislike or even hate Israel, the coalition's Arab states clearly recognized the danger to regional stability posed by Saddam Hussein's regime. They realized if he attacked Israel, he would have, in any case, brought "Zionist" retaliation upon himself. Nevertheless, a forceful Israeli response was the last eventuality coalition leaders—particularly the United States—wanted. Reflecting on the possibility of Israeli intervention, Schwarzkopf later stated that "we could not have held [the coalition] all together . . . it would have made our task much, much more difficult."[28]

In the late afternoon of January 17, Iraqi rocket troops launched the first two Scuds fired at Israel; the missiles re-entered over the Jewish state, broke out of low cloud and rain, and plunged into the ocean, scant yards offshore. Then, early in the predawn darkness of January 18, Iraq's rocket forces launched more against Israel and Saudi Arabia. At 2:15 A.M., the first of seven Scuds fell around Tel Aviv, fortunately without causing serious damage or death. At 4:45 A.M., the first Scud fired at Saudi Arabia plunged into the atmosphere, on its way to Dhahran. In a dramatic intervention, a Mach 3+ Army Patriot PAC-2 missile intercepted it—the first combat use of an antimissile missile. Unfortunately, Israel had foregone the opportunity to acquire sufficient numbers of Patriot batteries to defend its territory, in part because the country already had a joint Israeli-American antitactical ballistic missile program, the Arrow, under development. Thus, additional Scuds caused numbers of injuries, serious destruction, and some—fortunately few—deaths. The firing of Scuds against Israeli population centers enraged the Israeli leadership, which had to be restrained from following their natural impulse to join the air attacks against Iraq, whatever the cost might have been to the coalition's sense of unity and purpose. (Indeed, the Israeli air force requested, and was refused, access to the IFF codes used by Allied aircraft operating over Iraq, necessary information if they were to send their F-16s deep into Iraq.) In return for Israeli forbearance, the United States rushed Patriot batteries to Israel, delivering thirty-two missiles in 17 hours (against a planned delivery schedule of twenty-two missiles in 18 hours). Thereafter, they intercepted a number of Scuds, although a controversy broke out over the amount of damage caused by fragmented

Scuds and Patriot wreckage falling to earth over Israel's cities. (The influence of Patriot on Scud casualties is discussed subsequently.) With a mix of constant U.S. urging and their own pragmatism, Israel's leadership remained out of the war. Thus, Saddam Hussein's attempts to fracture the coalition via an Israeli "wild card" failed, although he tried repeatedly to use his Scuds to force Israeli retaliation.[29]

The resulting Scud hunt triggered by these first firings was intense and ran throughout the war, ultimately involving 2,493 sorties, the greater number of which took place within the first three weeks of the war. Its goals involved targeting the missiles, their numerous TELs, and the Scud support infrastructure. Two sets of "Scud boxes"—a western set of Scud launch points near Ar Rutbah, Al Qa'im, and H-2 aimed toward Israel and south toward western Saudi Arabia, and an eastern set of launch points near Qal at Salih aimed south at Saudi Arabia and the other coalition states—constituted major coalition hunting grounds. But Scuds were found elsewhere as well; for example, early in the war, A-10s destroyed some TELs south of As Salman airfield in south central Iraq. As the war progressed, Scud teams operated along three major roads in western Iraq, hiding by day and shooting at night, earning the area the nickname "Scud Alley"; to help protect the teams from roving coalition attackers, the Iraqis, as much as possible, attempted to shield the launchers with SAMs. The anti-Scud air campaign involved a variety of aircraft, the Army's ATACMS tactical missile system, and, as well, courageous American and British SOFs on the ground deep behind enemy lines hunting them down and calling in air strikes. The air side primarily involved orbiting LANTIRN-equipped F-15E strike aircraft (sometimes cued by JSTARS as to the probable location of Scud TELs); Royal Air Force reconnaissance ("reccce") Tornadoes paired with strike Tornadoes in "look and shoot" teams; F-16C/D and A-10 road reconnaissance missions to detect TELs on the highways and under overpasses; and B-52G and F-117A strikes against Scud storage and production facilities. Early warning space systems proved critically important. Speaking after the war, Lt. Gen. Thomas S. Moorman, Jr., the commander of USAF Space Command, stated:

> Their full contribution remains sensitive, but the political, psychological, and military value of providing early warning was incalculable. These systems provided warning to threatened countries and served to contain the conflict. On the military side, these systems clearly enhanced the effectiveness of our missile defense.[30]

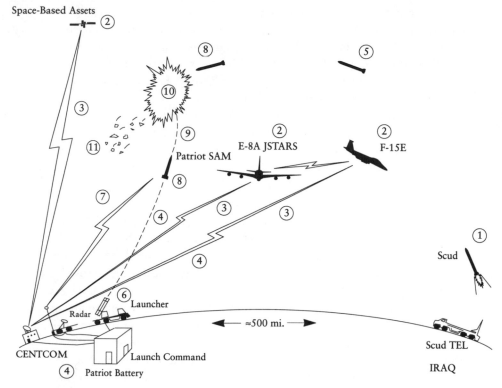

Space-Based Assets

Patriot SAM

E-8A JSTARS

F-15E

Scud

Scud TEL

IRAQ

≈500 mi.

Launcher

Radar

CENTCOM

Launch Command

Patriot Battery

SAUDI ARABIA

6.3 Scud Hunting: A Deadly Exercise in Integration   Provided a Scud was not destroyed before launch, a Scud firing triggered an intense defense effort: 1. A Scud is launched by a mobile transporter-erector-launcher. 2. The missile is detected during its boost phase by coalition aircraft, such as patrolling F-15E Strike Eagles, the E-8A JSTARS, or space-based assets. JSTARS and Eagle team to hunt TEL before it reaches shelter. 3. Launch warnings are sent to CENTCOM. 4. If appropriate aircraft are not aware of launch, CENTCOM passes information, triggering Scud hunt. Patriot SAM defenses are alerted to engage Scud. Civil defense is alerted so shelter warnings can be immediately issued. 5. During its ballistic coast near apogee, the Patriot battery search radar acquires and tracks the Scud as it moves at hypersonic velocities. 6. Patriot SAMs are launched to intercept (only one shown, for clarity). 7. Data-link between Patriot search radar, missile, and missile's own radar provide refined and sharpened guidance as terminal phase approaches. 8. Patriot SAM's own radar tracks Scud as range decreases. 9. With final updates, Patriot homes on Scud in end-game phase. 10. Patriot detonates, optimally destroying Scud warhead. 11. Scud-Patriot debris cloud descends to earth.

JSTARS used its side-looking radar to detect possible TELs, passing along the information via data link to ground stations for air and ground force commanders, to ATACMS, and to airborne F-15s. Sometimes, since launches took place at night, Strike Eagle and Tornado crews on orbiting anti-Scud patrols would actually see a launch, occasionally jinking hard in case it was a SAM. But then the missile would streak straight away, too fast for interception by air-to-air missiles, and the attackers would go low, attempting to find the launcher and destroy it. Under ideal circumstances, Iraqi Scud teams could fire a missile, drive away, and hide in a culvert, all within five minutes. Then, after letting the launcher cool some more (to reduce its infrared signature), they would drive off to some remote location to wait out the day, resuming firings the next night. In Basra, Iraqi forces took to hiding TELs in residential neighborhoods as well, also hiding them under highway overpasses. Thus likely culverts and hiding areas were routinely bombed to prevent their use by Scud firers. The intensive air campaign produced some gratifying video shots of Scud sites and desperately maneuvering TELs. When they were found, precision-guided weapons and occasional dumb bombs made short work of the Scuds and their launchers, peppering them with shrapnel (sometimes detonating their warheads, an added bonus), and transforming loaded ones into expanding fireballs. Overall, however, the mobile TELS and their missiles were never fully suppressed. Redoubled attacks against Scud infrastructure targets, including a missile production plant at Fallujah, ensured that Iraq could not increase its number of Scuds.

The air campaign had a demonstrable impact on Scud launches, which averaged five per day for the first 10 days of the war, and only one per day for the last 33 days. Further, the intensity of the air attacks increasingly forced the Scud teams to fire their missiles "on the run" from unprepared and unsurveyed sites, thus seriously degrading their chances of hitting population centers or militarily significant targets.[31] The "high point" of Iraq's rocket campaign came on day 9, when Iraqi rocketeers launched ten. Saddam Hussein did not fire his last Scud against Israel until February 25, when two plunged into the Negev Desert, one of which had a warhead filled with concrete ballast. Two days later, in one of those fateful moments that occur in war, an Air Force airman with a SOF observer team deep inside western Iraq spotted a force of approximately twenty Scuds "just as he was about to radio for a helicopter to extract him from what had seemed to prove a fruitless search."[32] In what may have been a last-minute bid by Saddam Hussein to involve Israel, his rocket forces had assembled the Scuds in an apparent attempt to swamp Israel's Patriot defenses with one massive strike. Such a strike might well have overcome the long-tried patience of Israel's conservative leadership, triggering Israeli intervention with possibly disastrous results on coalition unity. (Indeed, meeting the airman later, Secretary of Defense Dick Cheney reportedly said, "Thanks for keeping Israel out of the war.")[33] The airman called in A-10s sitting runway alert, which, in over six hours of afternoon and evening strikes, claimed all of the missiles in a boiling welter of Maverick and 30mm cannon fire. Sadly, three of the SOF troopers subsequently lost their lives, killed in the crash of a helicopter as they left Iraq.[34]

Dealing with missiles that *did* launch depended completely upon the success of the Mach 3 + Patriot surface-to-air missile at the "end game." The first challenge was speed: at an altitude of roughly 25 miles, as it closed on its target, an Al-Husayn had a typical velocity of Mach 8— over 5,300 MPH—posing a daunting closure challenge. Since the Scud did not incorporate any form of active guidance system, it could not be jammed or diverted. It had to be killed, by actual interception. But the basic nature of the Patriot—which, of course, had been originally developed as an antiaircraft missile—meant that its chances of completely destroying a Scud were small. When a Patriot did intercept a Scud, the Scud's own warhead sometimes tumbled out of the wreckage undamaged and fell earthward, exploding with violent force, accompanied by the dribbling Scud debris and the remains of the Patriot. For what it was—a modified antiaircraft missile—Patriot did well, earning the nickname "Scudbuster" and the affectionate respect of those it guarded. It had a profound and very valuable psychological impact as well; some Israelis living near an Army Patriot battery erected a sign reading, "Yankee, Stay Here!"

Very quickly, in fact, it became a veritable national symbol of the war effort: supporters of American policy in the Gulf wore T-shirts and carried banners that read, "Be a Patriot, not a Scud." The Patriot's radar determined when a Scud was re-entering in such a "threatening" manner as to endanger forces and facilities within range of the Patriot system. If it was not, the Patriot let it pass; numerous Scuds fired at Saudi Arabia, for example, exploded harmlessly in the vast desert or in the Persian Gulf. But whenever a Scud appeared likely to hit and cause death and damage, a Patriot battery would engage it. Normal engagement doctrine called for firing at least two missiles per target, a prudent means of maximizing the chances of a kill. Overall, Saddam Hussein's forces launched 93 Scuds, 42 fired at Israel, 48 at Saudi Arabia, and 3 fired at Bahrain. Patriot radars determined 47 of these threatening enough to warrant engaging with a total of 158 Patriots. Initial analysis suggested the missiles intercepted 45 Scuds, giving an engagement rate of nearly 96 percent, although later studies raised questions about how accurate this estimate had been.[35]

Patriot was a spectacular public and strategic success, conveying the image of indomitable high technology, and helping to keep Israel out of the war. But after the war, a debate broke out over its actual effectiveness. Some critics alleged that Patriot's limitations—short engagement range, for example—actually increased the material damage that occurred to Israeli targets, drawing upon trajectory and debris analysis to make their point. The reaction from Patriot supporters and, particularly, the Martin-Raytheon team that made it, can well be imagined. For this reason, it is worth examining the Patriot anti-Scud effort in some detail.[36]

Thanks to changes in the Scud's dynamic performance caused by Iraqi modifications to get longer range, as well as poor production quality control, many of the Scuds tended to break up when they re-entered, a problem, incidentally, that had plagued the V-2 during the Second World War. This was somewhat of a mixed blessing. The increased drag of the re-entering missile fragments reduced their range during the end game as they approached their target. But over a broad urban area, this made little difference. Further, it reduced the vulnerable size of the missile, lessening the likelihood of a Patriot's fragmenting warhead catastrophically impacting the Scud. Finally, the warhead now tended to maneuver as it re-entered; the twisted metal fragments acted as control surfaces. Thus the Patriot now had to deal with a spiraling, jinking, or wobbling re-entry vehicle, rather than the mathematically less demanding, straightforward interception of a body following a parabolic curve. And, in some cases, as the war demonstrated, the Patriot itself might veer off course and impact the ground. The single worst Scud hit of the war, however, was of an unengaged missile that approached Dhahran precisely at a time when the Patriot battery positioned to intercept it was down for computer maintenance. The warhead of this one missile killed 28 American soldiers and wounded 97 others housed in a barracks. This single event thus produced 25 percent of the deaths from enemy action and 25 percent of the wounded from enemy action that *all* American forces suffered in the entire war, and 36 percent of Army deaths from enemy action and 34 percent of Army wounded from enemy action in the war.[37]

Table 6.1 is a comparison of the results of Iraq's Scud campaign against the Allies and the Germans' V-2 campaign against London. These two missiles were generally similar in accuracy, range, and payload, although the longer-range Scud variants had a smaller warhead than either the basic Scud from which they evolved or the V-2 itself.[38] The numbers indicate that an individual V-2 and Scud destroyed or damaged a remarkably similar number of buildings and homes—238 (V-2) versus 224 (Scuds)—combining the effects of both direct blast destruction, and destruction or damage caused by falling debris. Where there is a dramatic difference, however, is in the number of personnel casualties: eighteen per V-2 versus eleven per Scud. Each V-2 that hit London wounded an average of thirteen people. Each Scud that hit Israel or Saudi Arabia wounded an average of ten people.

But the greatest disparity is in deaths per missile: five per V-2, only one per Scud. The ratio of wounded to killed is particularly interesting. The V-2 reaching a target area wounded three people for every one it killed; the less lethal Scud averaged ten wounded for every individual killed. The numbers indicate a small disparity between the material damage caused

Table 6.1. Comparison of Iraq's Scud campaign against the Allies and the Germans' V-2 campaign against London

	V-2	Scud
Number launched	1,190	93
Daily average	6	2
Number/percentage reaching target	517/43%	48/52%
Number engaged by defenses	(n/a)	47
Casualties		
Wounded	6,500	450
Killed	2,700	42
Combined killed/injured per missile	18	11
Wounded per missile	13	10
Killed per missile	5	1
Ratio of wounded to killed	3:1	10:1
Damaged/destroyed buildings/ homes	123,000	10,750
Damaged/destroyed buildings/ homes per missile	238	224

by individual V-2s and Scuds, a much greater disparity between the numbers of wounded caused by individual V-2s and Scuds, and, finally, an extremely large disparity between the numbers of killed caused by individual V-2s and Scuds. The effective early warning system detecting Scud launches enabled terminal area warning. However, though not so well known, similar warnings were often available from long-range radar tracking of V-2s during the Second World War as well. (Indeed, so precisely could British ballisticians predict the V-2's anticipated impact point from radar tracking that studies were undertaken on barrage-firing antiaircraft guns to detonate a V-2's incoming warhead. Anticipated casualty rates from unexploded antiaircraft shells falling to earth exceeded losses estimated from V-2 strikes, so such action was never undertaken.)[39]

Warning time alone thus cannot be considered responsible for the disparity in casualties. Likewise, the disparity of size between the V-2 and Scud warhead likewise cannot alone account for such a significant difference, nor can urban geography (like London, Tel Aviv and Riyadh are hardly "open" urban areas). Rather, Scud impacts, even of Scud warheads, generated lesser lethal force, despite the Scud re-entering at higher velocities (and thus greater energy) than the earlier V-2. This suggests the following: Patriot interceptions prevented high-velocity, high-energy, lethal impacts that characterized the earlier V-2. Therefore, while recognizing that resulting Scud debris (and Patriot debris, too) possessed great potential for widespread material destruction, it lacked the "P_k" (probability of kill) to generate large numbers of killed or wounded.

When it is recognized that over one-fifth of all Scud injuries and two-thirds of all deaths occurred from a single unintercepted missile—the Scud that fell on the Dhahran barracks—the magnitude of what Air Force Chief of Staff Gen. Merrill A. McPeak dubbed "the Great Scud Chase" and the Patriot end-game defenses accomplished is obvious. Given the number of casualties and damage that did occur in Israel and Saudi Arabia (and the historically high death and injury rates from Scud attacks in the earlier Iran-Iraq war and in Afghanistan, where Soviet forces fired them against Afghani towns and emcampments), one can surmise what the casualties and damage might have been like had Saddam Hussein's Scuds had free rein to reach their population targets. Without the air campaign and the Patriot, casualties could easily have run into the thousands—perhaps as many as 6,000 overall, including over 1,300 fatalities. The airmen and soldiers who prosecuted the anti-Scud campaign were peacekeepers, and there are numerous people of the many nationalities, creeds, and religions in the Gulf during the war who owe them their lives.

The Strategic Air Campaign: Decisive Accomplishment

Overall, the coalition air campaign accumulated a total of 109,876 sorties over the 43-day war, an average of 2,555 sorties per day. Of these, over 27,000 targeted Scuds, airfields, air defenses, electrical power, biological and chemical weapons, headquarters, intelligence assets, communications, the Iraqi army, and oil refining. Aerial tanking was crucial to producing these sortie figures. During Desert Storm, Air Force tankers exceeded even their Desert Shield support record, flying 15,434 sorties—nearly 60,000 flying hours—refueling 45,955 aircraft (20 percent of which were Navy or Marine airplanes), and off-loading 110.2 million gallons of aviation fuel. American airmen dropped 84,200 tons of munitions in the course of approximately 44,145 combat sorties, 67 percent of which were flown by the Air Force, 19 percent by the Marine Corps, and 14 percent by the Navy. Of the 84,200 tons, the Air Force dropped 72 percent, roughly 60,624 tons of both "smart" and "dumb" weapons. The Navy and Marine Corps shared the remaining 28 percent. The Air Force dropped 70 percent (53,964 tons) of the dumb bomb tonnage (76,800 tons total) expended in the war, the Marine Corps and the Navy roughly splitting the remaining 30 percent.[40]

Approximately 9 percent—7,400 tons—of the total tonnage expended by American forces was precision munitions. The Air Force dropped 90 percent (6,660 tons), the Marine Corps and the Navy accounting for the remaining 10 percent (740 tons), although a significant proportion of this—about a third—consisted of ship-and sub-launched TLAM cruise missiles. Roughly 30 percent of all Air Force precision tonnage was dropped by F-117s. Table 6.2 offers a percentage breakdown of the approximately 19,800 precision munitions American forces utilized in the war. Altogether, the precision munitions—particularly the laser-guided Paveway bombs—offered very high leverage, accomplishing approximately 75 percent of the damage inflicted upon Iraqi strategic and operational-level targets. Accuracy of smart bombs was such that successful strikes were the norm, not the exception. "To find yourself being blasé about zero CEP [circles inscribing bombing errors about aim points] accuracy is really astounding, but that's the way it was," one F-117 mission planner recollected.[41]

Although prewar campaign planning set generally sequential phases to the air war, giving the impression that the campaign would turn from "strategic" to "tactical" targets, and eventually (after G-day) to direct support of ground forces via close air support and battlefield air interdiction strikes, in fact the actual campaign as executed had considerable overlap; right to the end of the war, all phases of the air plan were still being flown simultaneously, though at varying levels of effort. The even greater force buildup that accompanied the second phase of the Desert Shield deployment also changed the strategic air campaign. Planners had initially anticipated that the "Phase I" strategic air campaign would sharply drop off by day 7 of the air campaign, from about 700 sorties per day to less than 100 per day. In fact, the added air assets enabled the coalition air forces to fly approximately 1,200 strategic sorties per day at the outset—almost twice as many as the planners initially had anticipated prior to war—and sorties never dropped to less than 200 per day over the first 35 days. Air defense suppression, the "Phase II" of the plan, likewise proved more extensive than in prewar plans. "Phase III" attacks against the Iraqi field army, instead of beginning about day 5 and building to about 1,200 sorties per day, started on day 1. After G-day, attacks against Iraqi forces reached nearly 1,700 sorties per day during the four-day ground operation at the end of the war.[42]

One can get some perspective on the scope of the Gulf air war by comparing it to some predecessors. Table 6.3 presents U.S. Air Service, U.S. Army Air Forces, and U.S. Air Force bomb tonnage statistics extracted from various wars, compared with Air Force tonnage dropped in the Gulf

Table 6.2. Precision Munitions Utilized by American Forces in Gulf War

Weapon	Percentage
Paveway bombs (GBU-10/12/16/24/27/28):	46.7%
Mavericks (AGM-65B/D/G)	27.8
Hellfires	13.7
HARMS	9.1
Tomahawks and AGM-86C	1.5
Misc. (Walleye, GBU-15, Skipper, SLAM)	1.1

war.[43] Viewed in this fashion, the Gulf war was not, as some of its critics alleged, an exercise in massive and unrestrained bombing unparalleled in previous air war history; neither the sortie rates nor the bomb tonnage statistics made it so.[44] The Air Force's tonnage expenditure in the Gulf war was only 11 percent of that expended against Japan (537,000 tons), less than 4 percent of that expended against Nazi Germany (1,613,000 tons), and less than 1 percent of the tonnage that the Air Force dropped in Southeast Asia. In measures of tonnage dropped per month, the Gulf air war ranked significantly below Vietnam, and very much below the Second World War. Yet it was more decisive overall in what it achieved than any of these previous wars.

What made it decisive was what the strategic air campaign managed to accomplish. One can comprehend what strategic air power achieved in the Gulf war by looking at five separate categories of effort: attacks on command and control, power generation, refined fuel and lubricants production, the transportation infrastructure, and the Iraqi air force.

First, the strategic air campaign struck forty-five key targets in the Baghdad area with F-117A–dropped precision-guided bombs or cruise missiles, which left the Hussein regime confused, and ignorant of what was happening above them. Yet the strategic air campaign did this without "carpet-bombing" Baghdad or inflicting massive civilian casualties as, say, the bomber raids on Berlin that forced Hitler underground had caused during the Second World War. Indeed, as was reported by one physician who visited Iraq after the war, the strategic air campaign hit with "neurosurgical precision."[45] The war revealed an interesting synergy between airlift and strike operations. Because of the leverage precision weapons offer, and the ease with which they are moved (the total precision munitions tonnage used in the war would have required only 450 C–141 airlift sorties to deliver) the airlifter in effect becomes the "first

Table 6.3. USAS/USAAF/USAF Bomb Tonnage Statistics for Five Conflicts

War	Tonnage	Length	Tonnage/Month
World War I	137.5	8.0 months	17.19
World War II	2,150,000.0	45.0 months	47,777.78
Korea	454,000.0	37.0 months	12,270.27
Vietnam/SE Asia	6,162,000.0	140.0 months	44,014.29
Gulf War	60,624.0	1.5 months	40,416.00

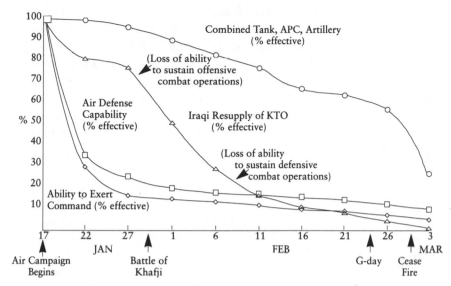

100
90
80
70
60
% 50
40
30
20
10

Combined Tank, APC, Artillery
(% effective)

(Loss of ability
to sustain offensive
combat operations)

Air Defense
Capability
(% effective)

Iraqi Resupply of KTO
(% effective)

(Loss of ability
to sustain defensive
combat operations)

Ability to Exert
Command (% effective)

17   22   27   1   6   11   16   21   26   3
       JAN   FEB   MAR

Air Campaign   Battle of   G-day   Cease
Begins   Khafji   Fire

6.4 Effectiveness of Iraqi Command Structure, Air Defense, Kuwaiti Theater of Operation Resupply, and Tank-APC-Artillery "Bottom Line": Air power shattered Hussein's military power well in advance of G-day. *Source:* CENTCOM/CENTAF/Checkmate statistics.

stage" of a "two-stage bomber." It carries the munitions around the globe and deposits them on an airfield. Then the munitions, in football terms, are "lateraled" to a strike airplane that carries the bomb over the "goal line." (The most telling example of this came late in the war, when two 4,700-pound GBU-28s arrived in the Gulf via a C-141, and, less than five hours later, were loaded on F-111Fs to go after a specially hardened command bunker; their bomb casings were still warm from the molten bomb mix poured in them back at Eglin AFB just hours before.)[46]

Second, the strategic air campaign shut down the Baghdad electrical power grid by attacking twenty-seven selected generation plants and transmission facilities across the country. The power strikes, which included cruise-missile attacks and a little over 200 manned aircraft sorties, were particularly significant, for to modern military forces—and Iraq's were very modern indeed—electrical power is a vital necessity. It cannot be stockpiled and thus, by targeting power generation, one shuts down so many other military facilities that large-scale bombing is unnecessary—one has achieved *passive,* as opposed to *active,* destruction. Again, the unprecedented accuracy of modern munitions meant that the coalition achieved maximum military effect with minimal force, minimal sorties, and minimal—in fact, no—friendly casualties. One airplane dropping two precision-guided bombs sufficed to destroy a single power-generating station's transformer yards. During World War II, in contrast, the Eighth Air Force found it took two full combat wings, a force of 108 B-17 bombers (flying in six combat "boxes" of eighteen aircraft each), dropping a total of 648 bombs (six 1,100-pound bombs per airplane) to guarantee a 96-percent chance of getting just two hits (the minimum necessary to disable a single power-generating plant for several months) on a single power-generating plant measuring 400 by 500 feet. Thus, by the time of the Gulf war, a single strike airplane carrying two "smart" bombs could function as effectively as 108 World War II B-17 bombers carrying 648 bombs and crewed by 1,080 airmen. Further, for the number of bomber sorties in World War II required to disable just two power stations, the coalition disabled the transformer capacity of every targeted power generation facility in Iraq.[47]

Third, the strategic air campaign targeted fuel and lubricants—the lifeblood of any military machine. Iraq was a major petroleum and electrical power exporter, with one of the most modern petroleum extraction, cracking, and distillation industries in the world. Before the war, it already possessed fifty times more reserve oil, per person, than the United States; after seizing Kuwait's oil assets, Saddam Hussein's government controlled more than 10 percent of the world's oil production capacity and 20 percent of the world's known oil reserves. The oil campaign was as decisive as it had been in World War II, but in a shorter time, with greater effectiveness, and with incomparably fewer losses. Further, it only targeted Iraq's militarily significant refined product production, and not its crude oil production facilities; there was no desire to impose greater hardship on Iraq than necessary. In the Second World War, American bombers dropped 185,841 tons of bombs during 50,000 sorties against 69 Nazi refineries (an average of nearly 2,700 tons of bombs and 725 sorties per refinery), cutting refined petroleum production by 60 percent. Of this total bomb tonnage, only 15 percent—approximately 27,876 tons, an average of only 404 tons per refinery—actually hit within the target area. In contrast, in the Gulf war, strike aircraft flying slightly over 500 sorties precisely dropped 1,200 tons of bombs on 28 Iraqi oil facilities (an average of only 43 tons and 18 sorties per facility), effectively ending refined petroleum production.

Thus, for less than half the tonnage dropped on a single German refinery during the Second World War, Allied strike aircraft destroyed all of the Iraqi facilities targeted for attack, a clear indication of the greater precision and destructiveness of modern air attack. (It should be noted that the Iraqi refineries were at least as large as and more sophisticated than German ones had been.) Therefore, for only 2.5 percent of the sorties as would have been required in World War II, and for only 1.5 percent of the bombs that would have been necessary in that earlier conflict, the Gulf attackers shut down Iraq's refined petroleum production. Within three days of the commencement of the oil campaign, Iraqi refined oil production was only 50 percent of its prewar level; within five days, it was at 10 percent, and five days later it was at zero.[48]

Fourth, the strategic air campaign achieved clearcut interdiction of Iraqi transport into the Kuwaiti theater of operations. This was the first clearcut case of air interdiction in military aviation history. At the start of the war, there were fifty-four key railroad and highway bridges vital to the supply of Iraqi forces in Kuwait, most on roads running southeast from Baghdad into Basra and Kuwait. At the end of the war, forty-one of the fifty-four were dropped (others had not been targeted for various reasons), and thirty-two pontoon bridges hastily built to offset the Allied air attacks had been destroyed as well. It had taken only 450 bomb-dropping sorties to accomplish this. As a result, the flow of supplies and some key communications between Iraq and Kuwait were totally disrupted. By the third week of the war, transport south from Baghdad was so badly damaged that the amount of supplies getting to Basra—the major transshipment point for the Iraqi army in Iraq—was far below the amount necessary to maintain any sort of meaningful combat effectiveness. Historically, bridges have been profoundly difficult targets that have quickly become flak traps for attacking aircraft. The precision-guided bomb, either a laser-guided or electro-optical-guided weapon, dramatically revised that relationship. Now, strike aircraft such as the F-15E, Tornado, Jaguar, and F-117 could achieve virtual "one bomb, one hit" results.[49]

Fifth, the strategic air campaign destroyed the Iraqi air force, preventing it from coming to the aid of the Hussein regime and its fielded forces in Iraq. As mentioned previously, the Iraqi air force played little role in the war, for two reasons. First, Saddam Hussein evidently believed that the coalition could not sustain its air effort beyond four or five days, and then the Iraqis could come out of their shelters and fight. Second, it was the smartest thing they could do, for when they did venture out, they ran into a veritable buzz-saw of eager Eagle, Tomcat, and Hornet pilots ready to do battle. During the immediate prewar period, the first two weeks of January, the Iraqi air force had averaged approximately fifty-five "shooter" sorties per day, and another forty or so sorties by support aircraft. On the first night of the war, the IQAF flew about twenty-five "shooter" sorties and ninety or so support ones. For the first week, Iraqi fighter sorties averaged about thirty per day, but they quickly found that Allied fighters—and pilots—were better. For example, on January 17, two Navy F/A-18s approaching H-3 airfield in western Iraq with four 2,000-pound bombs apiece received a warning of two MiG-21s coming head-on. With hardly a pause, the Hornet drivers switched from air-to-ground radar viewing to air-to-air mode, locked up the MiGs, and shot both down with an AIM-9 and AIM-7 apiece. They then switched back to air-to-ground radar mode, pressed on, and accurately bombed their target from an altitude of 18,850 feet, something that would have been unthinkable in any previous air war. Altogether, sixteen Iraqi fighters fell before F-15s and F-18s—fourteen to Eagles and two to Hornets—during that first week. Very quickly, the Iraqis decided not to fight, and it showed. For example, frustrated Navy Tomcat crews watched their radars as MiGs consistently fell back 40 to 50 miles beyond oncoming coalition strike packages, and the commander of the Air Force's 1st Tactical Fighter Wing, Col. John McBroom, remarked, "If somebody were going after my homeland, I'd [fight] a little harder."[50]

Coalition air leaders were initially uncertain of their success in so effectively shutting down Saddam Hussein's air force; accordingly, they feared a possible "Air Tet" that Iraq might spring for maximum destructive and propaganda effect. Historically, there was a disturbing precedent: the New Year's 1945 attack by the battered remnants of the Luftwaffe against Allied air bases in Western Europe, which came as a great shock and destroyed a number of Allied aircraft, demonstrating that no air force is down and out until it is planted in the ground. Thus, on January 23, day 7 of the war, the coalition began an active program of "shelter busting." If the IQAF would not fight, it would be bombed in place. The airfield strikes were more complex than might have been imagined, and not just because of air defenses. Iraq's many fields were large, with redundant hangar and taxiway facilities. Tallil airfield, for example, covered 9,000 acres, twice the size of London's Heathrow Airport, and only slightly smaller than Washington's expansive Dulles Airport.[51] Allied strike aircraft carrying hardened laser-guided bombs began striking Iraqi shelters, which had been patterned on Warsaw Pact models designed to withstand the rigors of nuclear attack. The impact was immediate. On day 9, January 25, the IQAF appeared to "stand down," to take stock of what was happening to it. Then, the next day, it "flushed" to Iran. Why the IQAF fled to Iran is not precisely known; was it a prearranged deal? Was it an act of defiance to Saddam—a recognition that the war was lost and an effort to try to salvage a useful force out of the disaster that had hit Iraq? The answer may never be fully known. In any case, Iraqi fighters and support aircraft fled for the border (leading to a popular joke that Iraqi fighters had a bumper sticker reading, "If you can read this, you're on your way to Iran"). More than 120 left, trying desperately to evade the probing eye of AWACS and the F-15's powerful air-to-air radar. Some ran out of fuel and crashed over Iranian territory. Others fell before Air Force F-15 barrier patrols (the last on February 7), raising total coalition fighter-vs.-fighter victories by the end of the war to 35, with no friendly losses.[52] Meanwhile, back in Iraq, over 200 aircraft were destroyed on Iraqi airfields, and hardened 2,000-pound bombs devastated Iraq's supposedly impregnable shelters and the aircraft within many of them. Eventually day and night air strikes destroyed or seriously damaged 375 shelters out of a total of 594. One night, F-117s launched a particularly effective series of attacks and were rewarded by seeing fireballs blasting out of shelter doors after they had been penetrated by hardened bombs. In sum, then, the Iraqi air force died ignominiously.[53]

All success in war is, unfortunately, accompanied by loss, and each loss is tragic and profound; sadly, the Gulf war was no exception. But what was different about this war was the remarkably low loss rate of Air Force and coalition aircraft. Optimists predicted losing one-half of 1 percent of all sorties (150 aircraft over a 30,000 sortie campaign, a .005 loss rate) with roughly a quarter of all shot-down air crews killed, a quarter captured, and half rescued or able to return to friendly territory. Thoughtful pessimists estimated losses at 2 percent (which the Israelis had suffered in their spectacularly successful campaign of 1967). The Air Force Studies and Analysis Agency estimated 4 percent. Dire pessimists—and there were some—forecast losses as high as 10 percent, equivalent to the casualties experienced by RAF Bomber Command and the Eighth Air Force during the worst days of 1943. In October, while briefing President Bush, Brigadier General Glosson had estimated the coalition would lose no more than eighty (more likely around fifty) aircraft; in fact, it lost forty-two. Two days before the war, Lieutenant General Horner had remarked to Glosson that he anticipated losses of thirty-nine Air Force airplanes (and possibly one hundred overall to the coalition). Given the number of combat sorties that CENTAF flew, this would have generated a loss rate per combat sortie of .00132 (slightly more than one-tenth of one percent) for the Air Force. In actuality, the Air Force lost fourteen aircraft in the war, giving an overall Air Force loss rate in Desert Storm of .00047—one-twentieth of 1 percent—per CENTAF combat sortie, which was unprecedented in military aviation history.[54] For the record, Table 6.4 is a historical summary of USAS/USAAF/USAF aircraft combat losses and combat sortie rates for five conflicts: World War I, World War II (European theater), Korea, Vietnam (South and North), and the Gulf.[55]

Key to the success of the air campaign was maintenance; from the suppliers to the line crews sweating under the desert sun, the coalition's maintainers worked miracles, enabling ever-higher sortie rates as the war progressed—essentially, a constant surge. As a result, wartime mission capability rates actually exceeded peacetime rates. Table 6.5 lists peacetime and wartime mission capability rates for selected Air Force aircraft in the Gulf war (generally similar ones existed for Navy and Marine aircraft as well).[56] These rates validated the Department of Defense's investment in high-technology, high-leverage systems, refuting prewar critics who suggested that such policy had resulted in the acquisition of overly complex and unreliable systems that could not be maintained in the operational intensity of actual war.

The Strategic Air Campaign as the Public Saw It

In sharp contrast to Saddam Hussein's endangering of civilian populations in Israel, Saudi Arabia, and the Gulf states stood the precision of the coalition's air attacks and the lengths to which coalition planners and air crews went to minimize any chance of civilian casualties. As news

Table 6.4. USAS/USAAF/USAF American Aircraft Combat Losses and Combat Sortie Rates for Five Conflicts

War	Combat Sorties	Losses	Losses/Sortie	Percentage
World War I	28,000	289	.010	1.0%
World War II	1,746,568	18,369	.010	1.0
Korea	341,269	605	.0017	0.17
Vietnam/SE Asia	1,992,000	1,606	.00081	0.081
Gulf War	29,393	14	.00047	0.047

Table 6.5. USAF Peacetime and Wartime Mission Capability Rates
(in percent)

Aircraft	Peacetime	Gulf War
A-10	90.4	95.5
C-5	69.0	78.0
C-130	78.0	84.0
C-141	80.0	86.0
F-4G	83.7	88.7
F-15C/D	85.1	93.7
F-15E	80.4	95.5
F-16	90.2	95.4
F-117	81.6	85.8
KC-10	95.0	95.0
KC-135	86.0	89.0

and, in particular, video accounts of the air war over Iraq reached the rest of the world, a remarkable transformation in popular attitudes toward air power took place. The skepticism, doubts, and outright pessimism that had characterized previous judgments were at once swept away. Pictures of bombs threading their way down ventilator ports, elevator shafts, and bunker doors demonstrated more eloquently than any amount of written analysis how effectively and devastatingly air warfare could strike.[57]

The precision and damage limitation particularly impressed reporters in Baghdad and those who visited the city afterward. Michael Kelly, a freelance writer reporting for the *New Republic,* was in Baghdad during the initial F-117 and TLAM attacks. On the morning after the first night's strikes, he watched smoke pouring from the Ministry of Defense, which had taken a TLAM hit, and saw, in quick succession, two more TLAMs leave it "a burning rubble." But, he noted, "the hospital next to it, though, was untouched, and so were the homes crowded around it."[58] It was this aspect of modern air power that seemed to stun observers—that attackers could strike targets deep within urban areas without causing the kind of wracking devastation that had characterized the city raids— even the "precise" ones—of the Second World War. Another aspect was the seeming omnipotence of the attackers. Kelly recalled that attackers would remain unseen: "Generally you knew that they had come only when the bombs fell and the big yellow-red bursts ballooned up over the stricken target. Then they were gone, leaving the Iraqi guns firing crazily and hopelessly in the air for another forty-five minutes or more."[59]

As a result, when a "victory" occurred, the locals went wild. Reporters outside the Al-Rasheed Hotel saw a Tomahawk missile explode in flight, due to lucky antiaircraft fire or premature detonation, and rain debris over the hotel, demolishing its conference center. "It is pathetically indicative of the shape of things," Kelly wrote later,

> that from this minor stroke of relative luck the Iraqis claimed a great victory. Shortly after the explosion Iraqi soldiers brought into the hotel bomb shelter pieces of the blown-apart missile. Hoisting the debris high, they declared it to be the earthly remains of a fighter-bomber, shot down by the great Iraqi gunners. The women in the shelter stopped their weeping and let loose with a high-pitched keening of false triumph.[60]

In April, writer Milton Viorst arrived in postwar Iraq as a reporter for the *New Yorker,* a journal whose best-known previous foray in war reportage had been John Hersey's *Hiroshima,* an account of the aftermath of a very different bombing. Viorst found "papers moved around the city only by messenger."[61] He traveled widely, driving from Amman, Jordan. During the war, he discovered, Jordanian drivers routinely charged $18,000 for a one-way trip to Baghdad, so effective was coalition air power. Wreckage still littered the road where Scud-hunters had had their way with Iraqi transports. Baghdad, he found, was not a blitzed city; in contrast, "the streets we drove through on the way to the Al-Rasheed looked very much as they had during my visits last year and the year before."[62] The war, he found, "does not seem to have created much hardship in Baghdad," In contrast, the damage was extraordinarily precise:

> Oddly, it seemed, there was no Second World War–style urban destruction, despite the tons of explosives that had fallen. Instead, with meticulous care— one might almost call it artistry—American aircraft had taken out telecommunications facilities, transportation links, key government offices, and, most painful of all, electrical generating plants . . . The central post office, in downtown Baghdad, was struck with such exquisite accuracy that three of its four brick walls remained standing but the interior was transformed into a maze of twisted girders and piles of debris.[63]

Only when Viorst went to southern Iraq, where the Shiites and forces loyal to the Iraqi government had battled it out after the war did he find the kind of damage he had expected to find from coalition air attack in

Baghdad; here it came from civil war. Mentally he contrasted "how few scars the allied bombing had left on Baghdad," with the civil war between Iraqis:

> The devastation here was in fact comparable to the levelling of cities in the Second World War . . . It seemed that no neighborhood had been spared . . . The wreckage suggested block-by-block, if not house-by-house, resistance, and many casualties.[64]

In every war mistakes happen, and bombs or missiles stray off course, killing civilians. But whereas such casualties had been numerous in previous wars, in Iraq they appeared remarkably low. Well into the war, the Hussein government was claiming that only a total of forty-one Iraqis had lost their lives to coalition air strikes, a preposterously small figure by the standards of previous wars. Then, on February 13, an F-117 strike on the Al Firdos command, control, and communications bunker (which, unknown to strike planners, also doubled as a shelter) killed a hundred or more Iraqi civilians. This tragedy caused such negative publicity that the senior military leadership in Washington severely curtailed bombing in downtown Baghdad after February 16. (At least some of the other damage in the city attributed to "air attacks" had, in fact, come from errant Iraqi antiaircraft fire and descending SAMs).[65] Allied attempts to minimize civilian casualties were evident to the Iraqis themselves; Iraqi soldiers repeatedly sought shelter in civilian areas, knowing they would not be hit.[66] Viorst discovered they were appreciated as well:

> I found Iraqis, on the whole, remarkably tolerant of the allied bombs that had destroyed homes or killed civilians. *They referred to them as "mistakes"— conceding, in effect, that American pilots had occasionally missed their aim but had not deliberately sought out civilian targets.* I also heard Iraqis speak with appreciation of the decent treatment their sons and brothers who were taken prisoner had received at American hands [emphasis added].[67]

Kelly and Viorst were by no means the only reporters to make such discoveries. CNN's Peter Arnett remarked that "after the first few days the Iraqis were not afraid of our bombs. They knew we were only going after military targets."[68] New York peace activist Erika Monk visited Baghdad immediately after hostilities, in the wake of a UN team that had concluded Iraq had been devastated to a "pre-industrial" level.[69] Instead, she found "a city whose homes and offices were almost entirely intact, where electricity was coming back on and the water was running." She concluded it was "post-industrial enough for us to be caught in a lot of traffic jams."[70]

Later, interviewed on National Public Radio, she reported that "the smart bombs had functioned"; she had seen "communication centers which had been sheared away, down to the bones." The evidence of such precise bombing left some of her activist colleagues "very disturbed"—because the use of smart bombs "doesn't produce the kinds of images that mobilize peace movements."[71] Joost R. Hiltermann, a reporter for the counterculture magazine *Mother Jones,* reported, "What struck me the most, however, was how little damage allied air raids had actually caused to civilian areas, relative to the amount of bombs said to have been dropped. Especially in Baghdad, the bombing was eerily precise."[72] New York *Times* reporter Paul Lewis wrote that in downtown Baghdad,

> The post office tower on Rashid Street, the Saddam Hussein conference center, the tall ministry of military industries building, the ministries of justice and local government and many telephone exchanges are all still standing with life going on busily around them. Only from close up is it apparent that they are gutted shells, their innards either collapsed or trying to burst through the windows.[73]

When such results had been predicted a few months before, believers of the conventional wisdom that air power could not do its job without necessarily inflicting massive destruction and death dismissed them as preposterous fantasies.[74] Now, the effectiveness and precision of coalition air strikes convincingly demonstrated that such results were not fanciful but, rather, the objective reality of modern war.

Seven

Air Power and the Conclusion of the Gulf War

Air power is the decisive arm so far, and I

expect it will be the decisive arm into the end

of the campaign, even if ground forces and

amphibious forces are added to the equation

. . . If anything, I expect air power to be even

more decisive in the days and weeks ahead.

Gen. Colin L. Powell (1991)

The preceding judgment, which Chairman of the Joint Chiefs General Powell expressed before the Senate Armed Services Committee on February 21, 1991, during defense appropriations testimony, neatly summarizes the role that air power played in the Gulf war. From the first night of the air campaign, the Allied coalition directed air attacks against the Iraqi army, both in Kuwait and in Iraq. After the war, Air Force Chief of Staff Gen. Merrill McPeak stated that "there was no time from day one on, that the Iraqi ground forces were not under heavy air attack."[1] Such attacks reflected the strategic goals of air campaign planners, as well as Powell's and Schwarzkopf's wishes that Iraqi tank and artillery strength be reduced as much as possible.

One of the major challenges confronting Allied attackers was ensuring that significant numbers of Iraqi tanks and artillery were destroyed so that when G-day (the onset of ground operations to reoccupy Kuwait) came, coalition ground forces would face minimal resistance and suffer minimal casualties. Four problems were inextricably bound up within that challenge: locating the tanks, mechanized vehicles, and artillery; discriminating between real targets and decoys; successfully attacking the real targets; and getting reliable bomb damage assessment that could give General Schwarzkopf accurate information on which to base his subsequent actions.

The first part of the problem was by no means an easy one. Iraq's ground forces were superb combat engineers, adept at digging in, camouflaging, and hiding forces and weapons. Initially reflecting the legacy of Soviet-style doctrine emphasizing such operations, Iraq's military recognized it as a vital necessity during the long Iran-Iraq war. Locating vehicles in the open was obviously not as difficult as locating ones buried in defensive positions. Various overhead systems, including the E-8A JSTARS and the Lockheed TR-1 and U-2R possessed optical and electronic sensors that could "image" a tank or artillery piece against its background. Dug-in tanks and artillery were a different matter, and made more complex by Iraq's heavy investment in decoy technology. Before the war, Iraq had contracted with an Italian company for delivery of thousands of dummy tanks, artillery, and even aircraft. Unlike the famous "rubber tanks" of World War II (which were, in their time, remarkably effective), modern decoys not only visually looked like the real thing, but could in many cases mimic the infrared and even radar signature of a genuine item, forcing intelligence analysts to employ sophisticated cross-checks to ensure that a target was genuine. Such checking procedures generally worked, although occasional decoy bombing occurred. Once targets were identified, successfully attacking them meant attempting to achieve maximum results for minimal risk. Antiaircraft fire, particularly over Kuwait, was always dense enough to warrant attackers dropping from medium altitudes, rather than from low altitude right over the targets. In World War II or Korea, and even as late as the 1973 Arab-Israeli war, such situations greatly hindered the effectiveness of ground attackers. But now, in the era of precision-guided weapons coupled with sophisticated target location, tracking, and designation systems, this problem disappeared.

The Antiarmor and Artillery Campaign: Smart Weapons, Questionable Intelligence

During the Gulf war, smart weapons reigned supreme against tank, artillery, and mechanized vehicle targets. After the war, Horner, the wartime Joint Force Air Component commander for the coalition, recalled that one Iraqi officer, a prisoner of war, stated during interrogation that "during the Iran War, my tank was my friend because I could sleep in it and know I was safe . . . During this war my tank became my enemy . . . none of my troops would get near a tank at night because they just kept blowing up."[2] Swing-wing F-111F "Aardvarks" dropping laser-guided bombs were particularly successful. Carrying the Pave Tack targeting pod, F-111Fs would cruise over Iraqi lines, using the swiveling FLIR pod to sweep-search back and forth across the ground, a technique they had refined before the war on training flights, spotting tanks and armored vehicles of the VII Corps. Twilight and night attacks proved particularly devastating, for the differential cooling rate of metal vehicles and equipment against a desert background produced a heat pulse well above the ambient infrared background. With a tank or vehicle located, the F-111F weapons system operator would designate it with a laser, then drop a 500-pound GBU-12 Paveway laser-guided bomb. Using these tactics, the F-111F became an outstanding antiarmor airplane. At the height of the air-to-ground air war, Aardvarks actually had an armor destruction rate per sortie seven times higher than that of the A-10 Warthog. In the last days before G-day, F-111Fs achieved up to 150 armor kills per night; in one concentrated period of attacks over a single target area, F-111Fs destroyed 77 armored vehicles and tanks belonging to the Iraqi 52nd Armored Division. Overall, F-111Fs were credited with 1,500 verified kills of Iraqi tanks and armored vehicles throughout the conflict. Other strike airplanes were also very effective using laser-guided bombs; on several occasions, two-ships of LANTIRN-equipped F-15Es destroyed sixteen tanks with an expenditure of sixteen GBU-12 bombs.[3]

The GBU-12, ideally sized for destroying Iraqi vehicles, constituted nearly 50 percent of all smart bombs dropped by American forces, but the Maverick missile also played a major role in the destruction of Iraq's mechanized forces, artillery, and fortified positions. During the war, the Air Force fired over 99 percent of the nearly 5,500 Mavericks American airmen employed in the war, from F-4Gs, F-16s, and, primarily, from A-10s. Two-thirds of these were AGM-65D imaging infrared (IIR) versions of the missile, 30 percent were TV-guided AGM-65Bs, and 3 percent were larger warhead IIR AGM-65Gs. (The Marines fired the remaining Mavericks used in the Gulf, the laser-guided AGM-65E.) When used against tanks, the $70,000 AGM-65D IIR missile routinely destroyed $1.5 million T-72 tanks in virtual "one missile, one tank" exchanges, an example of the high leverage and cost-effectiveness of smart weapons on the modern battlefield.[4]

Accuracy of intelligence estimates was the single most controversial issue during the entire air campaign, particularly bomb damage assessment. Was, in fact, the air campaign achieving the levels of destruction that planners had hoped and that videotapes seemed to indicate? This question possessed far more than academic interest, for the lives of coalition ground forces depended upon the answer. After the war, in a series of well-publicized comments, including testimony before the Senate Armed Services Committee, Norman Schwarzkopf was characteristically blunt in his assessment of the intelligence side of the war:

> There were so many disagreements within the intelligence community that by the time you got done reading many of the intelligence estimates you received, no matter what happened, they would have been right. And that's not helpful to the guy in the field.[5]

Arguments between intelligence practitioners and users of their information are as old as warfare itself, and were certainly not unexpected and unanticipated by decisionmakers in the Gulf war.[6] But they resulted in great controversy and, indeed, occasional friction and some real bitterness between the intelligence community (with its natural tendency toward conservative damage estimates and the close-holding of information) and air campaign planners who were more inclined to believe damage estimates from the firsthand evidence of pilots and videotape, and who believed in getting intelligence data into the hands of the war fighters who needed it to survive and win. Both sides clearly had some justification to their arguments, but in wartime combat needs come first. In the end, CENTAF planners relied far more upon timely "back channel" aircrew-supplied and bomb-camera video data—supported by their own analysis and "sanity checks" furnished from Checkmate in the Pentagon—than upon the often outdated "caveated, disagreed with, footnoted, and watered-down" reports (as Schwarzkopf dubbed them) from stateside intelligence agencies and organizations that inched along formalized command (and staff) channels. The two differing approaches triggered well-publicized disagreements over the numbers of tanks, armored vehicles, and artillery put out of action.

At any given time, CENTAF's planners were running three wars; one was the *execution war* (what's being done today); another was the *ATO war* (what will happen tomorrow); the third was the *planning war* (what will happen the day after tomorrow). Accurate intelligence was vital to all of these. On the eve of G-day, CENTAF's planners estimated (and

CENTCOM concurred) that air attack had destroyed approximately 40 percent of Iraqi tanks, 40 percent of Iraqi artillery, and one-third of Iraqi armored vehicles in the Kuwaiti theater of operations (KTO). The intelligence community estimated that losses were no greater than 20 to 30 percent, and some analysts declared them as low as 15 percent; US-CENTCOM in general and CENTAF in particular were accused of exaggerating the effectiveness of the air campaign. In fact, CENTAF's estimates *were* in error—they were *conservative:* the actual losses to the Iraqis by the eve of G-day were much higher—on the order of 60 percent of tanks, 60 percent of artillery, and 40 percent of armored vehicles. (Eventually, by the end of the war, Iraq had lost over 90 percent of its tanks, 90 percent of its artillery, and nearly 50 percent of its other armored vehicles in the KTO.) Nothing could more dramatically indicate the serious discrepancies that afflicted intelligence as this, for—had Schwarzkopf not believed his air campaigners—he might have unnecessarily prolonged the air campaign, revisited destroyed targets, and endangered unnecessarily the lives of his air crews. Several classic examples exist of intelligence underestimation of Iraqi losses, each of which might have resulted in unnecessary follow-up air strikes that could have produced lost aircraft and captured or killed air crews. Three suffice, from the shelter-busting campaign, the bridge-dropping interdiction effort, and the tank-plinking effort.[7]

When strike aircraft hit hardened aircraft shelters with penetrating laser-guided bombs, the shelters often contained the resulting explosion, and, in at least some cases, even the shelter doors held up from inside. Oftentimes the strike video from the airplane would show a bomb hitting a shelter, the shelter shaking violently from within, and a hot jet of black smoke lancing back out of the penetration hole—a clear indication that something unpleasant had happened inside. But a following reconnaissance overflight, often hours after a strike, would show what appeared to be an intact or slightly nicked shelter with perhaps a small hole in its roof. Intelligence assessors would consider the shelter partially damaged at best, or perhaps not damaged at all. In fact, as planners discovered when they inspected Iraqi airfields after the war, the penetrating bombs typically cut through the roof and buried themselves tens of feet under the floor before detonating and literally blasting any airplanes within against the roof of the shelter itself.[8]

During the interdiction campaign, strike aircraft destroyed a rail bridge on the Baghdad-Basra rail line. Further along, another bridge was left standing, since the cut rail line reduced any significance it might have possessed. But bomb damage assessors judged the line only 50-percent destroyed, for only one of the two bridges was down—despite the fact that the only way a train could have reached Basra or Baghdad would have been if the destroyed bridge were completely rebuilt.[9]

Tanks are typically quite heavy—the Soviet-designed T-72 favored by the Iraqi army weighed over 40 tons. Often a bomb, missile, or cannon round destroying one would leave but a small entry hole, although it would completely destroy the interior and typically detonate fuel and stored ammunition. After the tank "brewed up" and the fires burned out, it would often not look too badly damaged, if at all, from a distance. Thus, imaging reconnaissance systems often could not reliably indicate whether in fact a tank had been destroyed. In one case, intelligence reported a targeted tank as completely functional before sharp-eyed analysts operating out of Checkmate noted that the turret had shifted nearly a foot out of position. In other cases, where a bomb or missile caused such a catastrophic secondary explosion as to tear it apart, remnants of the tank, such as its turret and chassis, would be blown out of its dug-in position. As Horner recalled with some bemusement after the war, "The picture-takers would come by, and they'd take a picture, and then they'd go and they'd say, 'See, that revetment you hit was empty.' And in fact the tank had been killed."[10] Once again, strike video, showing the results of a Maverick, GBU-12, or Hellfire hitting a tank, proved the most useful means of assessing true destruction.

The Targeting Priorities Controversy

The intelligence problem nearly had a profoundly damaging impact upon the air campaign, for the unfounded allegations that air was not destroying as much as it (in fact) was caused some ground commanders to press for more sorties devoted to destroying Iraqi ground units. Traditionally, ground force commanders are far more concerned with the battle immediately in front of them than they are on threats and forces deeper behind enemy lines; this is a dangerous fixation, for in at least two well-known cases—the fall of France in 1940, and Kasserine in 1943—it contributed to notable defeats. It had been the Army's intent with their AirLand Battle doctrine to address this short-sighted perspective on land combat, but in the midst of Desert Storm, it resurfaced. Commanders repeatedly nominated targets directly in front of their positions for air attack, threatening to reduce the theater-wide impact of the carefully structured air campaign that had established targeting priorities based on Schwarzkopf's overall *theater* needs, rather than the individual *tactical* needs perceived by any one subordinate ground commander.[11]

In shifting the weight of the air campaign into the KTO, Schwarzkopf sought to reduce the strength of the Iraqi army throughout the KTO, while at the same time facilitating the task of coalition ground forces charged with responsibility for the reoccupation of Kuwait. To do this, he directed that USARCENT, MARCENT, and the Arab allies in the coalition each put together a prioritized target list. They would then send it to the deputy USCENTCOM commander, Lt. Gen. Calvin A. H. Waller, who would combine the multiple lists, establishing a single prioritized

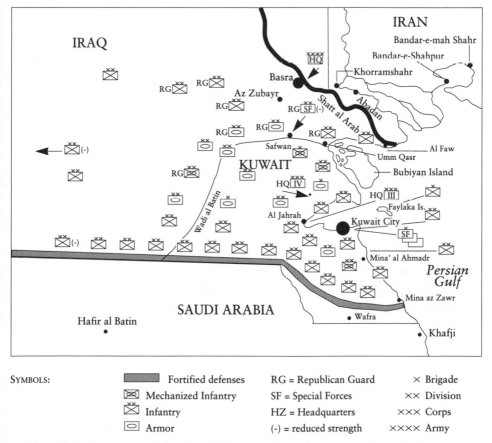

SYMBOLS:

	Fortified defenses	RG = Republican Guard	× Brigade
⊠	Mechanized Infantry	SF = Special Forces	×× Division
⊠	Infantry	HZ = Headquarters	××× Corps
⊡	Armor	(-) = reduced strength	×××× Army

7.1 **Disposition of Iraqi Forces in the Kuwaiti Theater of Operations**   *Source:* DoD Interim Report to Congress, 1991.

listing Schwarzkopf would approve prior to its delivery to the JFACC: Lieutenant General Horner, the Joint Force Air Component commander. Horner's planning staff, under Brig. Gen. Buster Glosson, would then allocate the requisite air assets for attack. In practice, this method of targeting distribution unfortunately encouraged a potentially dangerous "fair share" mentality among the ground force commanders, rather than a desire to achieve theater-level objectives.

Amazingly, despite a distribution of targets made by an Army deputy Cinc (Waller) using lists provided by ground force commanders, and approved overall by an Army theater Cinc (Schwarzkopf himself), ground commanders *still* complained that they weren't getting sufficient air support! They continued to demand unnecessary targeting of Iraqi forces and positions directly in front of their sectors. Schwarzkopf, tasked with responsibility for the entire theater, thus often had to take time away from other critical matters to redirect misplaced targeting priorities established by the ground commanders, based on his larger view of the theater and appreciation of the strategic situation, rather than just individual "local" conditions. In this, generals Horner and Glosson played critical roles, for, as airmen, they took a much broader view of the battlefield than individual corps or division commanders, and could furnish Schwarzkopf with the kind of overall guidance necessary to ensure that the air campaign worked as profitably as possible.[12]

Magnifying the problem were inaccurate assessments of the damage being inflicted upon Iraqi forces and Republican Guard units. USARCENT evaluators, biased toward the A-10 as the only Air Force aircraft that could contribute to "their" war, generally ignored bomb damage assessment from other strike aircraft, such as the B-52, F-111, and F-16; accordingly, their estimates of what had been destroyed differed markedly from CENTAF's. The confused information and assessments intelligence agencies relayed from the United States exacerbated this, and encouraged them in their belief that air was not seriously damaging the capabilities of the Iraqi military. In fact, many Iraqi divisions were suffering severely under Allied air attack (as prisoner interrogations were already revealing) and over time, the effective strength of these Iraqi divisions was sinking to about the 50-percent combat strength level, via deaths, wounding, desertions, and surrenders.[13]

At that point, a military unit—even a remarkably resilient and motivated one—is so damaged as to be essentially unusable; thus, there was no real point in bombing them below the 50-percent combat effective level. Yet that is precisely what the additional air strikes called for by ground commanders would have done: risked aircraft and crews on "revisit" missions of but marginal value, while taking away available air power from deeper attacks against more distant units that, in fact, would pose a far more serious danger to Allied forces once the ground operation began. Fortunately, Schwarzkopf recognized the danger of overbombing the frontline Iraqi forces even if some of his commanders did not. In mid-February, still over a week away from the launching of the ground operation, Schwarzkopf issued guidance directing that Iraqi units not be bombed below the 50-percent strength level. He at least was convinced of the success of the air campaign, and his timely action prevented unnecessary wasted sorties, although some inevitably occurred. In particular, he recognized the profound limitations of intelligence, remarking at one point that guidelines for assessing damage were so stringent that a vehicle would have to be on its back "like a dead cockroach" before evaluators would score it destroyed. As a solution, he emphasized relying upon pilot reports and strike-camera video instead—precisely what the Black Hole was doing at Buster Glosson's direction.[14]

Destroying the Battlefield

To understand what air power enabled the land operation to accomplish, it is worth examining what it was intended to do, via the air campaign's "Phase III" attacks. The air campaigners had targeted Iraq's fielded military forces with a view to reducing their effective combat strength, cutting off their supplies, and destroying their command and control. To the ground forces, these strikes constituted "preparing the battlefield"; but planners saw it differently. "We are not *preparing* the battlefield,'" Lt. Col. David Deptula declared emphatically, "we are *destroying* it."[15]

And so coalition airmen were. Air Force, Navy, and Marine aviators targeted Iraqi forces and equipment in around-the-clock strikes. Coalition European and Arab airmen risked their lives on sorties throughout the Iraqi theater of operations, attacking defensive positions and emplaced weapons. More than 35,000 coalition attack sorties pounded Iraqi troops, including 5,600 directed against the Republican Guard.[16] Every day, all day, and every night, all night, a constant parade of "shooters," from modified trainers like the British Aerospace Hawk and old warhorses such as the A-4 and B-52 to high-tech F-15Es and stealth fighters, entered Iraqi and Kuwaiti airspace. That their efforts were appreciated within Kuwait was evident to some airman, who overflew letters spelling out "FREE KUWAIT," hastily (and covertly) laid out by Kuwaiti patriots.

No airplane—not even the F-117 or the Navy's glamorous F-14s—received more attention during the war than the ugly A-10, the least sophisticated strike airplane that operated in the Gulf. From the outset, it was seen as the "Army jet," the plane that had been foisted on the Air Force against its wishes. In fact, the Air Force *was* less than wildly enthusiastic about the A-10, not because of its mission—close air support and battlefield air attack—but because of legitimate and serious questions about its survivability in the face of modern and dense ground-to-air threats. Historically, the fighter-bomber had always proven a more survivable airplane than the special-purpose battlefield attacker. Indications from recent wars—notably the Afghanistan conflict, where Soviet A-10 equivalents, the Su-25 Frogfoot, had proven very vulnerable to Stinger missiles—hinted that the slow A-10 might have difficulty surviving the modern battlefield, despite its imaginative redundant and rugged design. Then a rumor sprang up: the Air Force had not wanted the A-10 in the Gulf at all until Schwarzkopf himself had personally intervened! Such was not true (as is the case with most rumors), but it added to the air of expectation; would the Gulf war be the war where the A-10 proved its worth and enduring value?

The answer was a strong yes for the first, but a disturbing no for the second, as well. Flown with rare courage, dedication, and fierce loyalty—as befitted men who saw themselves the heirs of the P-47 tradition from the Second World War—the A-10 demonstrated its versatility and value in a variety of missions, but also its grave vulnerability to gun and missile systems. One A-10 pilot wrote to a friend:

> I haven't had a day off since the shooting started. I have, as of [February 10], dropped 17 tons of Mk-82 [500-pound conventional bombs], 6 tons of Rockeye anti-tank CBU [cluster bomb units]; fired 14 Maverick missiles, and shot 3,400 rounds of 30mm party mix at various tanks, APC's, and artillery sites in Iraq and Kuwait. The A-10 is doing things no one ever anticipated, including deep strike/interdiction on mobile Scud launchers, Wild Weasel duty, armed recce, escort, air-to-air, cargo (mail delivery) and of course, SAR [search and rescue]. *I'll be honest—70–80 miles behind enemy lines is no place for the Hog, but so far we've done o.k.* They tell me this builds character. We can't wait for the ground war to start so we can begin doing Close Air Support [emphasis added].[17]

Throughout the war, the 144 A-10s in the Gulf flew almost 8,100 sorties, primarily in attacks against frontline infantry positions. Also used against Scuds, and much more profitably on armed road reconnaissance missions, the A-10 proved devastatingly effective when it did attack ground targets, in part because its pilots used binoculars to assist in identifying targets, an aspect of the "down and dirty" A-10 war not shared by other fixed-wing aircraft. Due to the low-altitude ground-to-air threat and the greater precision necessary to hit targets from higher altitudes, its principal weapon proved to be the Maverick missile, rather than its much-touted huge 30mm GAU-8 rotary cannon. Altogether, A-10s fired 4,800 Mavericks, over 87 percent of all Mavericks fired in the war. At one point, two A-10 pilots destroyed twenty-three tanks in six sorties. But overall, its successes—Warthog drivers claimed approximately 1,000 tanks, 2,000 other vehicles, 1,200 artillery pieces, and two helicopters shot down by the cannon—came at the price of numerous damaged aircraft. Emergency Aircraft Battle Damage Repair (ABDR) teams kept A-10s in the air with jury-rigged parts (including, in one case, a wooden broomstick cut to replace a damaged flight control system push-rod), but others were too badly damaged to be simply patched up. Five A-10s fell to enemy fire, and a sixth was so badly damaged as to be unrepairable.[18]

While the A-10's rugged structure saved many pilots, others were not so lucky. Two were shot down on one mission: after his comrade was downed, a Warthog driver unselfishly returned into the target area to help organize a search attempt; tragically, he, too, fell victim to groundfire. CENTAF commander Horner, recognizing that the loss rate of the A-10 was inching up, confirming prewar Air Force estimates as to its vulnerability in the face of intensive defenses, prudently downscaled Warthog operations. Overall, 4 percent of the A-10 force in the Gulf had fallen to Iraqi air defenses (equivalent to the loss rate for the much smaller force of F-15E Strike Eagles, which lost two of forty-eight airplanes, and roughly equivalent to that of the Navy's A-6Es), but there can be little doubt that the losses would have increased greatly had A-10s continued their intensive low-altitude attacks. The battlefield attack role in higher threat areas would be fulfilled by the F-16, which had the speed and agility to better survive the intensive threat environment that had endangered the feisty Warthogs.[19]

The 249-large F-16 force generated more sorties—nearly 13,500—than any other strike aircraft in the Gulf war, covering an array of targets ranging from Scuds to production facilities through battlefield emplacements and dug-in armor and artillery. The "Electric Jet" flew primarily as a bomb-dropper, preferably with two Mk.-84 2,000-pound bombs, but also carrying other munitions such as the Mk.-20 Rockeye cluster munition and the more deadly CBU-87 Combined Effects Munition (CEM). F-16 pilots also fired approximately 450 Mavericks, claiming upward of 360 armored vehicles. One Air National Guard squadron operating F-16As in the CAS role relied upon a 30mm gun pod carried under the plane's belly, though with no great success. While the F-16 demonstrated great versatility, it also highlighted the advantages of precision weapons over "dumb bombs," and emphasized the importance of targeting and navigation advances such as LANTIRN. Although LANTIRN was intended for the so-called Block 40 model of the F-16, in the Iraqi war F-16s were not able to self-designate for their bombs, for they lacked LANTIRN targeting pods. Targeting pods were unavailable—there were only twenty-five in the Gulf, and they were urgently needed by the F-15Es. Indeed, even LANTIRN navigation pods were in short supply, and only seventy-two of the F-16 fleet eventually carried them. As a result, F-16s had to rely on "buddy lasing" from F-111Fs or F-15Es, in much the same fashion that British Tornadoes had to rely on buddy lasing from older Buccaneers.[20]

Although the F-16 had excellent "dumb" bombing accuracy at lower altitudes, the intense antiaircraft environment confronting F-16 pilots forced them to drop at higher altitudes, with slant ranges on the order of 17,000 to 20,000 feet. Under these conditions, accuracy degraded significantly. CEPs—circles inscribing bombing errors about aim points— went from a peacetime low-altitude figure of about 30 feet to a wartime medium-altitude one of approximately 200 feet. This reflected the accumulated effects of greater distance on bombing accuracy (for example, the size of a sight "pipper" itself relative to the target picture tends to limit accuracy from higher altitudes), but also training practices that had emphasized low-altitude release. Above all, it demonstrated the limitations of dumb bombs, no matter how precise the navigational positioning of attack aircraft: the future, clearly, belonged to precision-guided weapons. Although their small size—as with the Navy/Marine F/A-18— forced constant reliance on external fuel tanks, extensive tanker support, and limited the offensive payload, the range-limited F-16s nevertheless did yeoman work, literally swarming over the battle area and earning the nickname "killer bees." Killer scouts—F-16s configured as controllers and target-markers—marked targets and directed attack aircraft hitting targets within individual 15- by 15-mile "kill box" grids laid out across the KTO in a fashion analogous with the tactics employed by "Fast FACs" during Vietnam.[21]

The experiences of one F-16 squadron, the "Werewolves" of the 69th Tactical Fighter Squadron, were typical of F-16 units in the Gulf. The Werewolves deployed twenty-four Fighting Falcons from Moody AFB, Georgia, on January 5, arriving at Al Minhad Air Base in the United Arab Emirates (UAE) on January 8. Between then and the beginning of the war, they conducted in-theater training, emphasizing medium-altitude weapon drops, and checked out twenty-nine pilots in the squadron on LANTIRN navigation pods. A week after the war broke out, they shifted operations to King Fahd Airfield. Through the end of the war, the Werewolves maintained a 96-percent in-commission rate, flying 1,509 day and night sorties, an average of 1.46 per plane per day; sorties averaged 3.6 flight hours. During the first week, they attacked nuclear plants, Scud production and rocket fuel plants, power plants, airfields, and SAM sites. By night they hit Republican Guards, airfields, supply lines, and stood Scud alert. Then, for the rest of the war—a full month—they lived up to their name, flying their entire schedule by night with the primary mission of destroying Scuds. Unlike daytime strikes, which had emphasized large strike packages, nighttime strikes used two-ship tactics, supported by JSTARS and GPS positioning. Together, the synergy of JSTARS and GPS made for "a deadly team"; F-16s could be positioned to best effect to score "first pass" kills against targets, and GPS (which served as their primary aid to navigation) provided the Werewolves with easier target acquisition and more defensive lookout time. Night and bad weather provided no sanctuary; during all-night attacks against Basra highway, the Werewolves flew forty-eight sorties in 15 hours.[22]

Air Force air was not, of course, the only form of air power playing in the Gulf war prior to G-day. In accordance with the ATO, Navy, Marine, and Allied strike airplanes operated over the KTO, taking a constant toll of Iraqi forces, and the various armies' own organic air arms participated in the steady attrition of Saddam Hussein's military strength. Tornadoes of Britain's Royal Air Force and the Royal Saudi Air Force were particularly active, as were British, French, and Arab Jaguars, Mirages, and Skyhawks.

At first, as part of the strategic air campaign, British and Saudi Tornadoes had gone after Iraqi airfields. RAF Tornadoes used JP-233 runway denial munitions, with other Tornadoes suppressing antiaircraft sites with 1,000-pound bombs to screen the runway attackers. In four days, British Tornadoes had closed eight Iraqi airfields and "markedly reduced" operations at other fields.[23] On one airfield strike, a Saudi crew laid down a pattern of bombs so tight that theater commander Schwarzkopf remarked it looked like the bombs had been dropped from a pickup truck.[24] Unfortunately, the successes coalition airmen had came at the loss of eight Tornadoes: six RAF, one Saudi, and one Italian. The British losses—13 percent of the total number of Tornado strike aircraft (approximately forty-six) then serving with the RAF in the Gulf—attracted great press attention, for the losses were disproportionate to those of other attackers. Subsequent analysis of individual losses failed to reveal any one consistent single factor, although all were at low or medium altitudes where, of course, Iraqi antiaircraft fire was most dense. Some may have come from control system failures (a seventh British Tornado was, in fact, lost in a noncombat flying accident due to control failure); or the crew becoming distracted and flying into the ground; or from premature detonation of their own bombs; or from the fact that, for the nearly six months prior to the war, Germany refused to rescind a ban on NATO low-flying practice.[25] Tragically, one Tornado crew setting up a laser-bomb drop missed an urgent SAM warning (perhaps because of too much background chatter from other aircraft), and continued straight and level until the plane was destroyed by two simultaneous SAM hits.[26]

There is something very touching about the British Tornado losses, for the RAF crews, on average, were younger than other coalition airmen, and they took to the war with the same vigorous spirit as had their predecessors who all too often perished during "Bloody April" 1917, or over the Ruhr in 1943, or in any of the numerous postwar "small wars" the RAF found itself fighting, from Africa and Asia to the South Atlantic. At once cheeky and courageous, they adorned their Tornadoes, resplendent in desert pink, with slogans such as "Snoopy Airways" and "Hello Kuwait G'Bye Iraq," as well as some fetching damsels, and launched off on lonely strikes into murderous flak. Overall, Tornado losses in the Gulf war recall those first encountered with the immature F-111A when it entered service in Vietnam, and should be regarded in the same way. Much was learned from that bitter experience that subsequently made later F-111As effective and fearsome strike airplanes, although the losses forever tarnished the reputation of the Aardvark. The Gulf war was the Tornado's baptism in combat, and while it is to be earnestly hoped that neither it—nor any other combat aircraft—will ever fly in anger again, there can be little doubt that it will evolve into an even more formidable and effective attacker, much as the F-111A eventually led to the devastating F-111F.

As the attention of the air campaign increasingly shifted to the KTO, Tornado operations turned toward interdiction strikes at medium altitudes. Here, at first, the Tornado suffered from its lack of a self-designation system. Like so many other coalition strike airplanes, the Tornado had to rely upon buddy lasing from older Buccaneer strike aircraft hastily flown out to the Gulf and equipped with Pave Spike designators. Before the Buccaneers arrived, the Tornadoes contented themselves with dumb-bomb strikes on airfields and supply dumps, but once the Buccaneers were in theater, laser-guided bomb (LGB) strikes predominated. The Tornado-Buccaneer teams worked on the antibridge campaign in the Tigris and Euphrates valley and, as the bridges collapsed out of the target set, returned to hitting shelters and dumps. Not quite a week before G-day, Tornadoes in the Gulf received the first self-designating thermal-imaging laser designators, freeing up the Buccaneers to do strike work on their own, and, of course, vastly increasing the effectiveness of the Tornadoes themselves. One late-war airfield strike against Shaibah resulted in twenty LGBs hitting ten individual aiming points that "put paid to the last possibility that the Iraqi Air Force [could appear] over the battlefield." Overall, Tornado strike and recce aircraft flew 27 percent (1,670 sorties) of the RAF's approximately 6,100 Gulf sorties.[27]

British and French Jaguar pilots undertook their own series of strikes, in an airplane rapidly nearing the end of its service life. The twin-engine Jaguar, designed for the low-altitude battlefield attack role, had seen some combat in its previous existence, with French forces against Qaddafi's Libyans in Chad. Now, in the Gulf, it assumed a new lease on life, although as a mid-altitude attacker. French Jaguars went into Kuwait from the first night, striking airfields and other targets at low altitude with both smart and dumb bombs. During these strikes, four Jaguars were hit by missiles and flak, although in each case the pilot (including one with a head wound) returned to base safely. One of the Jaguars, having taken two SA-7 hits, got back home, but was fit only for scrapping. Prudently, subsequent attacks used higher approaches above the densest antiaircraft fire. French airmen flew a total of approximately 2,400 sorties during the war, and their accuracy on strike missions was commendable, particularly when using AS-30L laser-guided missiles; video repeatedly showed the deadly AS-30Ls destroying bunkers, bridges, and shelters. Before the war, CENTAF planners requested that France ground its small number of Mirage F-1s in the Gulf, lest they be mistaken for Iraqi ones and shot down; the French concurred. In late January, however, with the Iraqi Mirage threat eliminated, air campaign planners cleared the French (and GCC air forces) to operate their own Mirage F-1 recce fighter-bombers on strikes in Kuwait and Iraq. From that point on, the French seasoned their Jaguar operations with Mirage ones.[28]

British Jaguar pilots complemented the activities of their Tornado brethren by flying over 600 daylight combat sorties against antiaircraft sites, dumps, roads, and—totally unexpectedly before the war—Iraqi naval forces. Jaguars proved particularly valuable in the latter role during the battle of Khafji, firing pods of CRV-7 air-to-ground unguided rockets (which coupled high velocity with an extremely flat trajectory), which sank or damaged fifteen vessels attempting to assist Iraqi ground forces in their cross-border fight. Thus they contributed significantly to the sea war against Iraq's navy, a war in which combined American, British, and coalition naval aviation and surface forces quickly and utterly destroyed Iraq's naval combatants. (The naval campaign culminated in the so-called Bubiyan Turkey Shoot, when air strikes and surface actions on January 30 devastated Iraqi naval vessels attempting to cross the Persian Gulf to internment in Iran.) Next, they added American CBU-87 cluster bombs to their repertoire, for attacks on antiship Silkworm missile sites endangering friendly naval units in the Gulf, SAM sites, and antiaircraft positions along the Kuwaiti coast. Overall, Jaguars flew only 10 percent of all RAF sorties, making contributions far out of proportion to the actual number of sorties involved.[29]

Kuwait's airmen, more passionately and personally committed to freeing Kuwait from Iraqi occupation, went to war in the most anachronistic of the Gulf's warplanes, the shapely Douglas A-4 Skyhawk, a design that dated from the early 1950s. It was the Skyhawk's sixth war since the 1960s, and, as operations over Vietnam, the Middle East, and Falklands had already indicated, the versatile little "Scooter" was showing its age, clearly being more vulnerable to flak and SAMs than most of its successors. Right off, Kuwait lost an A-4 from flak during a first-day strike against Kuwaiti targets. Subsequently, like other strikers, the Kuwaiti A-4s switched from low to medium altitudes to avoid ever-present Iraqi ground fire; since they were limited to carrying only dumb ordnance, this somewhat degraded their accuracy. These new tactics, plus not a little luck, prevented further A-4 losses, for Kuwaiti airmen were bold and impassioned, and often pressed home their attacks with commendable if often alarming zeal. The F-1 grounding bothered Kuwait's tiny F-1 force, and, as might be imagined, they welcomed the CENTAF decision late in January to permit Mirage operations alongside their Skyhawk comrades. Thereafter, Skyhawks and F-1s were common sights over the Kuwaiti-Saudi border, as Kuwait's airmen fought to ensure the freedom of their relatives, some of whom, regrettably, had already died at the hands of Iraqi occupation forces.[30]

The effect of all of these attacks was a veritable firestorm of munitions raining down upon Iraqi forces. It inflicted operational paralysis upon the Iraqi soldiers in the KTO, immobilizing them, preventing them from fighting, breaking their will, and reducing many units to a rabble waiting to surrender. Previous attacks on Iraqi communications had so decimated Iraq's command and control structure that, as Saudi general Turki Bin Nasir commented to reporters, it was unlikely that Saddam Hussein knew how much his forces were actually being hurt.[31] The destruction in Iraqi armored and infantry divisions was severe. Each armored division averaged approximately 250 main battle tanks, 175 armored personnel carriers, and 75 artillery pieces, although even infantry divisions possessed substantial numbers of tanks, mechanized vehicles, and artillery. Repeated air attacks reduced the military effectiveness of these formations from a mid-January level of 100 percent or nearly so to mid-February average levels of less than 50 percent for units along the Kuwait-Saudi border (the "tactical" echelon), roughly 70 percent for second-echelon forces further back (the "operational" echelon), and approximately 80 percent for "theater" echelon forces (primarily Republican Guard), located deeper in Iraq, or clustered along the Iraqi-Kuwaiti border near Basra. After the war, Horner remarked that the success of precision weapon attacks against Iraqi armor enabled him to establish targeting quotas "like an insurance salesman," he recalled.

> I said, "All right, guys, we've got a quota." And I set the quota originally at a hundred tanks a night. And they started exceeding it and I bumped it up to 150. I wouldn't go to 200 because I didn't want guys doing crazy things. But it became very productive . . . The pilots called it tank-plinking. Now the tankers don't like to hear you say that. General Schwarzkopf asked that I not call it tank-plinking, and so I told the troops "General Schwarzkopf does not want you to call it tank-plinking," and that way I ensured that it will forever be known as tank-plinking.[32]

Precision strikes were critical for targeting Iraq's military equipment, but area strikes against Iraqi troop formations were equally important, both for inflicting casualties and inducing surrenders. Here the aging Boeing B-52G Stratofortresses proved particularly devastating. Sometimes "Buff" strikes had a serendipitous result benefiting other attackers. In one case, a Saudi Tornado crew passing over Iraqi forces after bombing Republican Guard tanks saw the ground ahead of them light up with small arms fire. High above them, illuminated by moonlight, were the massive contrails of a cell of three eight-engine Buffs—a sight possessing a breathtaking if deadly beauty. Suddenly, where there had been a hurricane of small arms fire was instead a huge rectangle of massive explosions as the Stratofortresses each unloaded their cargo of bombs. As the shockwaves and blasts dissipated, the Tornado crew flew on, unmolested by any ground fire at all.[33]

Overall, the Stratofortress flew 1,624 sorties in the Gulf war—some from bases in the continental United States (in a true example of global reach and global power), others from Great Britain, Spain, and the Middle East, and from Diego Garcia—and dropped 25,700 tons of munitions, approximately 30 percent of all U.S. bombs. Altogether, 74 of the nation's 122 B-52Gs, nearly 61 percent, were dedicated to Gulf bombing missions. From the end of the first day onward, they were bombing Republican Guard positions every three hours. Despite the intensity of Iraq's antiaircraft and missile defenses (which forced special attention by coalition air defense suppression forces to protect the gargantuan Buffs), only one was lost, and that to a noncombat accident while returning to Diego Garcia. The B-52G's bomb tonnage alone was 42 percent of that dropped by the Air Force overall, and over twice that dropped by all six of the carrier-based air wings in the Gulf war. As had been true in the Vietnam War, prisoner interrogations revealed that the B-52 was the weapon ground forces feared most. Between 20 and 40 percent of Iraqi troops attacked from the air deserted their units prior to G-day, and B-52 strikes appear to have played the major role in forcing their decision. A captured Iraqi general "said he couldn't walk to the latrine without wondering if a B-52 would bomb him."[34] One troop commander, interrogated after the war, stated he surrendered because of B-52 strikes. "But your position was *never* attacked by B-52s," the interrogator exclaimed. "That is true," he stated, "but I saw one that *had* been attacked."[35]

From the First World War onward, air strikes against military formations have always generated profound psychological effects, and the Gulf war was no different. One deliberate demonstration pointedly hinted at what air power could do. The crew of a Lockheed MC-130E Combat Talon special operations airplane (a modified version of the ubiquitous Hercules transport) dropped a massive 15,000-pound BLU-82 bomb in the midst of barren desert near Iraqi positions. The bomb, looking like some sort of misshapen and ominous egg, detonated in an awesome and thunderous explosion that momentarily lit up the entire front, reputedly causing some British witnesses to think the United States had dropped a nuclear device on Kuwait. A following leaflet drop advertising more such bombs directly on Iraqi positions caused mass defections, including virtually the entire staff of an Iraqi battalion. In sum, delivered by long-range bombers, shorter-range fighters and attack aircraft, and specialized attackers such as the MC-130E, air power was decisive in cracking Iraqi morale. An Iraqi division commander put it bluntly. "Why did your men give up?" his interrogator asked. "You know," he replied sullenly. "I don't know. Why?" the interrogator persisted. "It was the *airplanes!*" he responded.[36]

Khafji: Saddam Hussein Lashes Out

Much as coalition air planners worried that Saddam Hussein might husband his air force for an "Air Tet" that might have profound psychological and political impact even if its actual military impact was small, coalition ground planners remained alert to the possibility of a "Ground Tet," too—an attempt to preempt the careful Allied ground preparations by an Iraqi thrust against coalition forces. Such concern was well founded, for Hussein's military did exactly that on January 29, when they launched the battle of Khafji. The attack came at an interesting time in the war. It coincided with Schwarzkopf's declaring air supremacy over Iraq and Kuwait, and with a telling nationwide survey by the Washington *Post* that found 85 percent of Americans had "a great deal" or "quite a lot" of confidence in the American military, a two-decade high, twice as high as confidence in public schools, and approximately three times higher than confidence in newspapers, large corporations, organized labor, and the U.S. Congress. An Iraqi success, even if it were just a perceived one, however, could send confidence tumbling.[37]

Saddam Hussein's motivations in striking at Saudi Arabia remain unclear. Was it because he wished to inflict heavy casualties even if he lost, thus scoring a propaganda coup and perhaps triggering a desire within the coalition to cut a deal? Or was it because he wished to entangle the coalition forces in ground combat, retreat back toward the Kuwaiti border, and hope that the coalition forces would pursue him until they were entangled in his formidable defensive positions? (Such a move might disrupt completely the war plans of the Allies, for if Saddam could take the initiative, he could determine the unfolding of events, although not necessarily their outcome.) Or was it borne of the frustration of continually absorbing Allied air strikes, and not being able to do anything about them? By the end of January, the Iraqi air force had ceased to exist as an effective force, the Iraqi navy was virtually under water or hounded to Iran, and the Iraqi army was substituting for live-fire targets found at the National Training Center, or the Fallon and Nellis ranges. Any and all of these factors could—and probably did—play a role. In any case, as naval analyst Norman Friedman has perceptively written, "Saddam Hussein could not passively accept the destruction of his country by air attack."[38]

In retrospect, Saddam Hussein appears to have begun his buildup for a probe into Saudi Arabia a week earlier, on January 22. Unfortunately for Iraqi forces, that day, an E-8A JSTARS, under the command of Col. George Muellner, a distinguished fighter and test pilot, happened to be orbiting over Saudi territory, its moving target indicator and side-looking radar system looking deep into the KTO, laying bare the battle area. An experimental airplane, the JSTARS was anything but "user friendly"; it had, as Muellner recalled subsequently "four very highly paid Ph.D.s from the contractor keeping its software going." But what it could furnish was remarkable. During its 14-hour missions, the JSTARS could locate targets as small as individual vehicles, and then direct strike airplanes to them, increasing sortie productivity. This meant that with so many targets available, properly cued attack aircraft would run out of weapons before they ran out of fuel, rather than wasting fuel searching and having to return with or jettison unused weapons. "With JSTARS," Muellner recalled, "fighters went 'bingo [empty] ammo,' not 'bingo fuel.'" Further, it furnished such precise guidance to attackers that they located their designated targets on 90 percent of their initial passes, thus minimizing exposure over the battlefield and potential losses from having to make multiple passes to acquire a target. During its orbits on this particular mission, the crew detected an Iraqi armored division's assembly area, and a sixty-vehicle convoy ominously moving toward Kuwait. In one of the most dramatic examples of how battlefield intelligence coupled with responsive targeting and the lethality of strike airplanes synergistically transforms modern warfare, the JSTARS crew vectored two A-10s and an AC-130 gunship onto the convoy. Between them, the two Warthogs and the AC–130 destroyed fifty-eight of the seventy-one vehicles—82 percent of the available targets.[39]

On January 29, the actual battle for Khafji itself began. The attack opened with three brigades of Iraqi mechanized forces supported by an offshore landing force; the brigades cut across the Kuwait-Saudi border, one following the main coast road that ran down to Dhahran through the abandoned town of Khafji, and the others further west, hoping to hook left and link up once they were within Saudi territory. Upon entering Saudi territory, they stumbled across lightly armed U.S. Marine forces, as well as Saudi and Qatari troops, and were immediately engaged. On the ground, coalition troops fought doggedly and well. Marines and Saudi National Guardsmen stood firm, destroying Iraqi armored vehicles with TOW missiles; Qatari tankers, operating twenty-four French-built tanks, likewise took a heavy toll of Iraqi tanks. In the air, American and coalition airmen struck at the Iraqi forces. B-52Gs attacked Iraqi assault forces massing behind the front. Marine AH-1W Cobra gunships and AV-8B Harrier II jets, together with A-10s and AC-130s, attacked the encroaching Iraqis with cannon and guided missiles, destroying at least sixty vehicles. Two-seat Marine F/A-18Ds, acting as "Fast FACs" and crewed by airmen with night-vision goggles, marked targets with white phosphorous rockets, including a column of Iraqi armored forces subsequently devastated by A-6Es carrying Rockeye antiarmor munitions.[40]

Fighting continued for two days, with the offshore Iraqi reinforcements falling victim to Jaguars, British and American helicopters, and A-6s. Although Saddam Hussein's forces had gone to ground in Khafji, Saudi and Qatari troops quickly routed them (despite occasionally stubborn resistance), supported by Marine and Air Force air attacks. Iraq's offensive, utterly shattered, collapsed; over 200 vehicles in all had been destroyed or disabled. Saddam Hussein's surviving soldiers wisely surrendered. Tragically, the victory came at the price of two attention-getting losses: first, a special operations force AC-130 gunship on a night support mission was shot down after dawn by an Iraqi missile, with the loss of all fourteen crewmen (the greatest single personnel loss of the air campaign, and the second-highest contributor to overall American combat losses in the war), and second, the deaths of seven Marines killed in a light armored vehicle hit by a Maverick missile fired from an A-10.[41]

The Khafji battle resulted in a dramatic refocusing of media emphasis, indicating that had Allied losses been higher, and those of Iraq less so, it might have resulted in the kind of misinterpretation and misplaced emphasis that had characterized the Tet offensive over two decades before. Previously, media treatment emphasized smart weapons, the high-tech nature of the war, and the Scud campaign. Now, media accounts suggested, such had been merely ephemeral: with Khafji, the "real" war had begun—one of great uncertainty, but which would likely produce numerous casualties. That Iraq was able to lash out in such fashion immediately resulted in editorial writers and columnists questioning how much the Iraqi forces had actually been hurt by the two-week-old air campaign. Herb Block encapsulated this thought with an editorial cartoon showing Saddam Hussein in front of the "Baghdad Butcher" shop, balloons proclaiming "Open" and "Welcome," and a sign in the window proclaiming "Grand Opening of Our Ground War Hamburger Counter," as if he were calling the tune to which the Allied coalition would have to dance.[42]

What drew particular attention, however, was less the willingness of Iraq to fight than the discovery that seven Marines had been killed by "friendly fire," a term made memorable—indeed, infamous—by C. D. B. Bryan's sobering book of the same title about an episode from the Vietnam War.[43] Such losses always are particularly tragic. Although subsequent investigation revealed a Maverick missile had "lost" its target-lock at launch, headed off course, and unfortunately "acquired" the Marine vehicle immediately afterward, the tragedy reopened a nearly 50-year debate over how air and ground forces could work together to minimize such episodes, echoing the furor that erupted in the midst of 1944, when a misplaced air strike had killed Army Gen. Lesley J. McNair during Operation Cobra.[44] In fact, two other incidents of friendly fire occurred at Khafji, one involving Marine ground forces that fired on each other, killing four Leathernecks, and then, on February 2, a Marine A-6E bombed a Marine howitzer position, killing another Marine. After Khafji, these incidents continued. In mid-February, Army troops fired on each other, resulting in some woundings. Then, on February 17, an Apache helicopter gunship fired Hellfire missiles on some suspected Iraqi vehicles, instead destroying two Army armored personnel carriers and killing several soldiers. Numerous other incidents followed, particularly during the ground operation, when forces plunged head-long into Iraq and Kuwait and fought in often confusing engagements.[45]

The incidents of air-to-ground friendly fire stimulated an immediate rush program to develop technical means of identifying friendly vehicles and forces from above. As a result of this multiservice activity, evaluators examined sixty different ideas, with test models of proposed equipment being evaluated at the Yuma Proving Ground. By late February, 15,000 simple infrared beacons termed "Bud lights" were delivered to the Gulf, together with 190 more-sophisticated blinking Anti-Fratricide Identification Device (AFID) IR lights developed by the Defense Advanced Research Projects Agency and known more familiarly as "DARPA lights." They complemented identifying symbols painted on vehicles and proved very useful. Unfortunately, they did not arrive in time to prevent some very serious incidents, including multiple friendly fire exchanges in the heat of battle between Army mechanized vehicles, and a misidentification that resulted in two A-10s attacking a British armored force, destroying two personnel carriers and killing a number of British soldiers. Friendly fire, from the air and (especially) on the ground, is clearly a subject demanding intensive work to prevent such episodes in the future.[46]

The battle of Khafji was an important engagement for reasons that went beyond American casualties and friendly fire. Saddam Hussein had tried and failed to engage coalition forces in a bloody, prolonged war. If he and his generals hoped to grasp onto the Allies and then drag them into a larger and more costly engagement, they failed. As coalition ground forces fought valiantly and to good effect against the Iraqis, coalition air power broke the back of the assault, transforming troop carriers and tanks into blackened hulks. Khafji was not a totally clearcut case of a victory through air power, but it came very close—close enough for the point to be argued with vigor. But more than this, it signaled refreshing thought on the relative merits of air and land warfare in the "decisive" phase of battle. Norman Schwarzkopf clearly and commendably appreciated that there was nothing to be gained by prematurely coming to grips on the ground with Saddam Hussein's forces. Instead of directing that ground units pursue and close with Iraqi forces, a traditional approach that could had led to serious and unnecessary casualties, Schwarzkopf wisely let air do the follow-up.

Toward G-day

In the weeks prior to G-day, preparations went forward for the reoccupation of Kuwait. Over three months before, in early November, Schwarzkopf had decided on his basic strategy, blending the classic elements of an Army planning concept known as the METT-T: Mission, Enemy, Terrain, Troops Available, and Time. He had recognized early on that Saddam Hussein was so busy "stuffing forces into a bag called Kuwait" (as Schwarzkopf subsequently characterized it) that the Iraqi dictator was ignoring his vulnerable flanks. On November 10, Schwarzkopf met with his combat commanders and sketched out what became known as his "Hail Mary" play. First would come a rapid relocation of forces into the west. Then, on G-day, these forces would begin driving north into Iraq, the onset of the fourth phase of Desert Storm, effectively cutting all contact between the eastern and western portions of the country, and hooking back eastward to prevent the Iraqi forces in Kuwait from retreating. It was a breathtaking gambit, on a par with MacArthur's bold invasion at Inchon, with which it shared a colossal audacity—a driving, roundhouse punch on a gigantic scale into the solar plexus of the enemy. Then, Schwarzkopf hoped, the Allied coalition could fight a veritable battle of Cannae (one of his favorite examples from military history), annihilating Iraq's military power.

He had no desire to risk the lives of the Marines or Navy with a foolish assault on the fortified eastern coast of Kuwait, or repeating history in the area of the Shatt al-Arab, which Iraq had fought over throughout the 1980s, and which had been the scene of often frustrating riverine operations during the First World War, including the disastrous defeat of a British army at Kut-al-Amara.[47] Rather, instead, his was to be a war of decisive movement. After developing his strategy, Schwarzkopf understandably worried that Hussein would redeploy to cover his flanks, particularly after mid-November, when the size of coalition forces increased dramatically. "Opsec"—operational security—was a significant concern, for if media sources learned of the maneuver, it was likely they would mention it.[48] Once the air war started, Schwarzkopf was relieved—any opportunity Saddam Hussein may have possessed to redeploy his forces along the Saudi-Iraqi frontier had passed. "The day we executed the air campaign," Schwarzkopf recollected subsequently, "I said, 'We gotcha!' "[49] Air would fix Saddam Hussein in place, destroy his ability to fight, and leave him with no militarily significant options. Joint Chiefs chairman Colin Powell put it bluntly in a Washington press conference on January 23, a week into the war: "Our strategy to go after this army is very, very simple. First we're going to cut it off, and then we're going to kill it."[50]

With the ground operation only a matter of time, decisionmakers debated when the offensive should be launched. The hidden subtext, of course, was really the question of air power's effectiveness: had it reached the point where it could do no more, where ground action was the only alternative for decisive result? The answers depended on one's service orientation and view of history. Horner and Glosson did not think so, and recommended deferring to air power. But some ground commanders, eager to launch an offensive and show what their forces could do, argued that only ground forces had ever inflicted decisive defeat. Others who were more dispassionate—particularly Norman Schwarzkopf—recognized the danger of triggering a ground offensive too soon. In their eagerness to do their part, proponents of ground action could unnecessarily risk the lives of their troops. (The troops themselves, as correspondents routinely reported, were more than willing to let air pound away as long as it took.)

Back in the United States, the issue increasingly dominated thought within the planning staffs of the Pentagon, and was expressed openly in the Congress and the news media.[51] At the White House, within the National Security Council, Brent Scowcroft and his deputy Robert Gates grappled with the question, amid advice and suggestions proffered by the NSC staff. On February 5, in part because of this growing debate, President Bush held a press conference to announce he was sending Secretary of Defense Cheney and Colin Powell to Riyadh to assess the state of the war. Although both Bush and Scowcroft were former military pilots, if they had any predisposition favoring air power above other forms of military projection, it certainly didn't show. But Bush did have great faith in Gen. Merrill McPeak. He had gotten to know the tall, spare officer well (an opportunity denied the short-term Mike Dugan) and he greatly respected his judgment. McPeak had particularly impressed Bush before the war, during a meeting at Camp David, when he forcefully made the case for air power during a strategy session. Bush, afterward, had asked Scowcroft his reading of McPeak's views, and the national security advisor had concurred in them. The subsequent successes of the air campaign confirmed Bush's confidence in McPeak, though he remained reluctant to accept wholeheartedly the dominance of air power. Thus, responding to a reporter's question at the February press conference, Bush confessed he was "somewhat skeptical" that air could win on its own.[52]

After a briefing in Checkmate on the current status of the air campaign, Cheney departed for the Mideast, accompanied by Powell. Later that week, Cheney and Powell listened while Schwarzkopf and his commanders argued the air-or-ground question while at USCENTCOM headquarters. The evidence Horner and Glosson presented convincingly demonstrated that the success of the air campaign against Saddam Hussein's army could no longer be questioned; it certainly had not passed the point of diminishing return. Cheney and Powell returned to Washington late on Sunday, February 10, and the secretary received additional update information from Checkmate. The two men then briefed the president for an hour the next morning. Bush, now reassured that air was more than doing its job, then met with reporters, stating that the air campaign had been "very, very effective," and that the United States would continue to rely upon it "for a while."[53]

All in all, it had been an important week; it was the final significant instance in Desert Shield–Desert Storm in which an incorrect decision could have been reached with regard to air power. Had decisionmakers concluded the air campaign had done as much as it could, it would have resulted in a premature launching of the ground offensive, with much greater casualties. Further proof that air had proven itself beyond doubt came over a week after Bush's remarks, when JCS chairman Powell, in unusually candid and strong language, testified before Congress on February 21 that air power would likely "be the decisive arm into the end of the campaign, even if ground forces and amphibious forces are added to the equation."[54] Such a candid admission indicated how far respect for air power had come since August 1990.

In the weeks prior to G-day, the air arms of the coalition armies had joined with their air force and naval aviation brethren in pounding away at the Iraqis. In anticipation of the close air support missions that would have to be flown, Air Force A-10s trained with AH-64 Apaches, refamiliarizing both with joint air attack team (JAAT) tactics. The menacing-looking AH-64s worked out with little OH-58D Kiowa Warrior scouts, the scouts finding and designating targets with their mast-mounted sights (which gave them the appearance of teed golf balls buzzing through the air) for the lethal gunships. Marine AH-1W Cobras practiced in concert with Harrier IIs and F/A-18s acting as FACs, in accordance with established Marine Corps doctrine; plans to rely on older Vietnam-era OV-10D FACs were abandoned after two OV-10s fell to Iraqi antiaircraft fire. Troop helicopters and theater airlift assets, already heavily tasked, prepared for the explosion of activity that would accompany an invasion of Kuwait. These air support systems went to war well in advance of the onset of G-day, inserting special operations forces into Iraqi-controlled territory for a variety of secretive missions, and undertaking their own strike missions against Iraqi forces deployed across from Allied ones. For example, on February 20, four days before G-day, an Apache-Kiowa team attacked a bunker complex miles inside Iraqi territory. More than 400 Iraqis surrendered—a sign of how badly their morale had deteriorated under constant air attack—and the scout-attack helicopters called in CH-47 Chinooks to haul them out—an example of a "deep capture" ferry operation unprecedented in previous military history. In another case, Harriers attacked a convoy of twenty-five trucks in southern Kuwait, leaving it rocked by secondary explosions and burning fuel.[55]

As the air campaign pounded Iraq, Schwarzkopf directed the redeployment of American and attached foreign forces to the far west, beginning his Hail Mary maneuver. It was an extraordinary logistical effort; Allied air crews marveled at the columns of trucks and vehicles they saw heading west into the Saudi desert. Two whole Corps—the XVIII Airborne and the VII Armored, totaling 200,000 troops, involving 65,000 American and coalition vehicles—moved 250 and 150 miles, respectively, across the desert on the Trans-Arabian Pipeline highway called the Tapline Road. In any one minute, every hour, eighteen trucks would pass a given spot. (In historic terms, it far surpassed the famed "Red Ball Express" of World War II and the emergency redeployment of Lt. Gen. George Patton's Third Army against the flank of Nazi forces during the Battle of the Bulge.) The Abrams tank and Bradley fighting vehicle, two systems targeted by some critics for alleged "unreliability," experienced no difficulties during the move; the 3rd Armored Division, for example, moved approximately 125 miles at night, and not a single one of its 300 tanks broke down. The C-130 theater transports were vital to the Army's move. During the westward shift, they flew almost 1,200 missions, delivering 14,000 people and over 9,000 tons of equipment; at the height of the airlift, C-130s flew with 10-minute separation between planes, a surge rate that required some airlift units to fly at twice their programmed wartime utilization rate. The Army's airlift needs resulted in establishment of Logistics Base Charlie—a selected strip along the Tapline Road measuring a mile long. C-130s flew hundreds of sorties into this base furnishing fuel and general cargo to the Army's XVIII Corps.

To cover the move west, the Marine Corps maintained a highly visible east coast presence, and the "necessity" of an amphibious invasion was broadly hinted. Then, three MC-130s, supported by Navy E-2C radio jammers and EA-6B radar jammers, dropped three massive BLU-82s on the western edge of Faylaka Island on the night of February 16. This "BLUes brothers" strike, complementing near-continuous shelling by the battleship USS *Wisconsin,* further encouraged Iraqi beliefs that the coalition planned a coastal invasion. From its position in Kuwait, Iraq continued to look east and south, well away from the west. More berms went up, more oil-filled fire trenches were dug, more minefields were laid (on land and sea). Meantime, the coalition forces spread out. On the eve of G-day, the Iraqi forces in the KTO—43 divisions, 142 brigades—were confronted, from east to west, by Saudi-Qatari-UAE-Omani-Bahraini-Kuwaiti forces; Marine divisions and an Army brigade; and a coalition Arab force of Saudis, Syrians, Egyptians, and Kuwaitis. Then, further west along the Saudi-Iraqi border, came the VII Corps and British forces, and, in the far west, the XVIII Corps and French troops.[56]

The exact composition of these forces is listed in Table 7.1. Islamic forces were under the command of Lt. Gen. Khalid bin Sultan (and thus were not part per se of the USCENTCOM structure); non-Islamic forces were commanded by Schwarzkopf and did, of course, come under the USCENTCOM aegis.[57]

After all the destruction he had experienced, after all the fighting that had already occurred, Saddam Hussein still had a chance at salvaging something out of his misadventure in the Gulf. On February 21, the Soviet Union floated a last-minute peace offer that smacked more of an attempt to help an old client state rather than a serious attempt to resolve the Gulf war.[58] It came at a bad time—the United States had managed to weld together both national and world opinion, UN forces were in place, Schwarzkopf was ready to launch his ground offensive, and Saddam Hussein had shown absolutely no willingness to comply with UN sanctions and to leave Kuwait. Though publicly expressing appreciation for the Soviets' interest in seeing a peaceful solution to the Gulf war, many administration officials were privately irritated and, indeed, angered. "A lot of people," one recollected tellingly (if inelegantly), "were [upset]."[59] President Bush responded to the Soviet plan with an ultimatum of his own: Iraq had until mid-day Saturday, February 23, to begin an "immediate and unconditional withdrawal" from Kuwait.[60] But Saddam Hussein refused to budge, again proving that he was his own troops' worst enemy. So the last deadline came and went. Hussein's previous intractability had resulted in the destruction of Iraq's command and control, its infrastructure, its air force and navy, and much of its offensive striking power. Now

Table 7.1. Coalition Ground Force Structure on Eve of G-day

Formation	Units
Joint Forces Command—East	Task Force Omar
	10th Infantry Brigade (Saudi)
	UAE Motorized Infantry Battalion
	Omani Motorized Infantry Battalion
	Task Force Othman
	8th Mechanized Infantry Brigade (Saudi)
	Bahraini Infantry Company
	Kuwaiti Al-Fatah Brigade
	Task Force Abu Bakr
	2nd Saudi N.G. Motorized Infantry Brigade
	Qatari Mechanized Battalion
I Marine Expeditionary Force	1st Marine Division
	2nd Marine Division
	1st (Tiger) Brigade, 2nd Armored Division (USA)
Joint Forces Command—North	3rd Egyptian Mechanized Division
	4th Egyptian Armored Division
	9th Syrian Armored Division
	Egyptian Ranger Regiment
	45th Syrian Commando Regiment
	20th Mechanized Brigade (Saudi)
	Kuwaiti Shaheed Brigade
	Kuwaiti Al-Tahrir Brigade
	4th Saudi Armored Brigade
VII Corps	1st Infantry Division
	1st Cavalry Division
	1st Armored Division
	3rd Armored Division
	1st British Armored Division
	2nd Armored Cavalry Regiment
	11th Aviation Brigade
XVIII Corps	82nd Airborne Division
	101st Airborne Division (Air Assault)
	24th Mechanized Infantry Division
	6th French Armored Division (light)
	3rd Armored Cavalry Regiment
	12th Aviation Brigade
	18th Aviation Brigade

Air Power and the Conclusion of the Gulf War   229

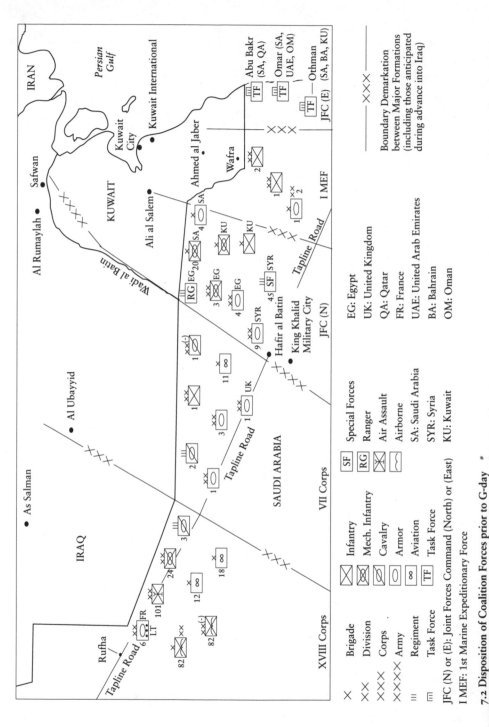

7.2 Disposition of Coalition Forces prior to G-day

that intractability would lead to its logical result: the destruction of an entire army.

By this time, Kuwait resembled a Dante-inspired vision of Hell. Saddam Hussein's troops had begun torching its oil fields, igniting pipelines and well-heads, and sending billowing orange flames and dense black smoke skyward. This was but their latest environmental atrocity, for earlier, on January 25, Iraq had deliberately fouled the Persian Gulf with a massive oil spill from a tanker terminal. (Two days later, on January 27, F-111Fs launching GBU-15 guided bombs managed to destroy the oil manifolding from storage tanks to the terminal, drastically cutting the oil flow, but not before so much had already spilled that the ecological system of the Gulf region was severely damaged.) Now, the oil fires posed new threats; many of the wells emitted great quantities of poisonous gases so that they endangered anyone who ventured near them. Further, other wells had failed to ignite, forming vast pools of raw crude, covering hundreds of acres and, in addition to destroying the desert's fragile eco-system, creating potential fire traps for anyone caught in them. So great was the smoke from burning oil well-heads—eventually over 700 would be torched—that it severely limited visibility in the KTO and into Saudi Arabia as winds blew it around. For fliers, it often meant abruptly and repeatedly transitioning from clear to instrument-flying conditions. One Marine helicopter pilot was so startled by his transition from bright light to utter darkness that, for a moment, he thought he had died. On another occasion, four AH-1W Cobras and eight CH-46 Sea Knights were suddenly enveloped by shifting smoke, and "had to break in a dozen different directions," fortunately without colliding.[61] The weather likewise was miserable, with routine oil-thickened overcasts; occasional cold, drenching downpours turning the surface of the desert to a thick, viscous mud that vehicles churned up; obscuring fogs that settled into wadis and depressions; howling *shamals* that blasted grit across people and equipment alike, endangering sophisticated optical systems and permeating clothing; and, overall, the pervasive stench of black-splattering oil-laden rain, settling like an evil grimy mist on all it touched.

Desert Roundup

The fourth phase of Desert Storm opened at 4:00 A.M. local time, February 24. Over the previous several days, a series of artillery and air strikes had destroyed much of the Iraqi artillery that had survived the weeks of air attack, and helicopter attack teams had decimated Iraqi command posts, air defense sites, and gun positions with Hellfire missiles and by calling in Copperhead artillery fire. Thus, when the invasion actually began, it went quickly. The First Marine Expeditionary Force (I MEF) began the assault at 4:00, breaching Iraqi defenses and driving toward Ahmad Al-Jabir airfield. Fixing attacks prevented Iraqi forces from maneuvering, and when they did so, they were pounded unceasingly by air, artillery, and tank fire. Masses of Iraqi soldiers ("ridden down by bombing," as one British spokesman described them) began surrendering, fearful at first, and then running toward Allied troops in great rushes, clutching surrender leaflets or anything white. They were starving; air had cut their supplies of food and water to nothing, and most were infested with lice, covered with sores, sick, demoralized or in shock from the constant scream of jets and blast of bombs. Some welcomed the coalition forces with almost as much fervor as the Kuwaitis. British Corporal Rex Butt came across an Iraqi officer (leading nearly 200 troops) who "was pleading with us to help, because they were scared stiff of the planes. Every time a plane came over they were terrified."[62] Over 8,000 prisoners were in custody by day's end; over 78,000 more would be eventually picked up. The VII and XVIII Corps advanced rapidly as well. At 4:00, the 6th French Armored Division moved out, accompanied by a brigade from the 82nd Airborne Division, advancing across the line toward As Salman airfield. At 8 A.M., a brigade of the 101st Airborne Division air-assaulted deep into Iraq, riding Chinooks and Blackhawks covered by helicopter gunships, seizing a section of Iraqi real estate and carving out Cobra, a forward operating base. These forces, too, encountered large numbers of surrendering Iraqis. Corporal Thomas Smith of the 82nd Airborne recalled that "they were really malnourished . . . [They] were just as well equipped. But they had no will, and they were so scared because they had been bombed for six weeks."[63]

By mid-day, the Franco-American force had seized As Salman. The westernmost coalition forces were now poised to threaten the entire Tigris and Euphrates valley—and the operation was less than eight hours old. At 8:00, Joint Forces Command–East had also leapt off, conducting a difficult breaching operation without delay, then moving north into Kuwait, where large numbers of Iraqis surrendering threatened their pace of advance. In the very far west, the 24th Mechanized Infantry began an end-run north that eventually sent it hooking around over 250 miles, ending up 27 miles west of Basra, a charge of epic proportions, faster than the Germans into Russia in 1941, faster than Patton across France in 1944, or the Soviets into Manchuria in 1945. When Iraqi resistance showed itself, on-call Air Force air strikes by F-16s and A-10s, Apache-Kiowa attack teams, MLRS rocket launchers, and artillery battered and shattered it; like other coalition forces, the 24th could hardly keep up with the prisoners that surrendered to it. It overran two airfields—Jalibah and Tallil—though discipline broke down somewhat, as soldiers shot up intact Soviet MiG-29s, MiG-27s, and Frogfoots, with no thought to how much more worthwhile it would have been to retain them for subsequent analysis.[64]

The cutting edge of the ground attack was air power. Through all of this action, air power proved critical. GPS position updates offered Army ground forces unprecedented knowledge of their location, enabling them to maneuver and to direct artillery fire with remarkable precision. C-130 airlifters supplied advancing coalition land forces with air-drops of food, water, and ammunition, and evacuated wounded and nonbattle casualties, as well as over 600 wounded Iraqi prisoners requiring immediate medical attention. Air strikes continued the devastation of Iraq's remaining military forces. On the first day of the invasion, the E-8A JSTARS detected a blocking force of Iraqis forming to confront the 3rd Egyptian Mechanized Division, moving north and held up by extensive fire trenches. The Egyptians prudently formed defensive positions, and the JSTARS directed devastating air strikes against the Iraqis, breaking up their anticipated counterattack. Helicopter gunships came into their own. TOW-firing British Army Lynx helicopters blasted tanks and mechanized vehicles. French army attack helicopter pilots, firing wire-guided HOT-2 antitank missiles from Gazelle helicopters, scored 127 hits against Iraqi targets for an expenditure of 180 missiles—a success rate of 70 percent. The Gazelle teams followed a French army doctrine known as the "Iron Fist": large formations of up to twenty-five machines would fly repeated sorties against enemy ground forces. Other Gazelles carrying Mistral air-to-air missiles to protect the formation from enemy aircraft or helicopters escorted the antitank choppers, and search-and-rescue Puma helicopters conveniently followed behind. (On occasion, the Gazelle Mistral-carriers would also cover American Kiowas seeking targets for the Apaches.) But even these successes paled next to those of the U.S. Army's helicopter crews. Kiowa-Apache teams—and sometimes Kiowa-Cobra ones—claimed as many as twenty tanks destroyed per mission. Apache crews from the 4th Battalion of the 229th Aviation Brigade destroyed approximately fifty Iraqi tanks during a single encounter. Again, engagements between helicopters firing precision-guided Hellfire missiles and armored vehicles were characterized by virtual "one missile—one kill" exchanges. Analysis of one Apache unit revealed that it expended 107 Hellfires, achieving 102 hits, a rate of better than 95 percent.[65]

The entire panoply of coalition attack aviation forces operated over the Kuwaiti theater. Air attacks had set the stage for the rout of the Iraqis, and on the second day of the ground operation it began, even as Allied ground forces raced across Iraq and Kuwait, far ahead of schedule. On the night of February 25, tipped by intelligence reports from Kuwaiti resistance of an impending Iraqi evacuation from Kuwait City, Brig. Gen. Buster Glosson ordered JSTARS to watch road traffic for any sign of Iraqi withdrawal. Shortly afterwards, orbiting on its racetrack search pattern, JSTARS detected hundreds of vehicles moving toward the Iraqi frontier. The Iraqi III Corps, desperately trying to escape the rapid advance of the I MEF and Joint Forces Command–East, had lost cohesion, become enmeshed with Iraqi occupation forces in Kuwait City, and then, with a panic palpable even on radar, had begun blindly driving toward Basra, heading for a causeway that formed a fatal bottleneck. They had every kind of vehicle imaginable: tanks, armored personnel carriers, school buses, trucks, delivery vans, ambulances, "confiscated" Mercedes, many stacked high with looted goods—televisions, radios, refrigerators, clothes, jewelry, computers, anything that had caught their fancy. So dense was the road traffic, that the individual radar "hits," which looked like little crosses superimposed on a map readout on the JSTARS moving target display, merged into thick lines, becoming themselves a roadmap of desperation.

It was imperative that these forces not be allowed to retire so that they could regroup and threaten coalition ground forces; air power had to intervene despite truly appalling weather conditions. Glosson diverted standing anti-Scud patrols, and then scrambled twelve Strike Eagles, whose crews had been roused from well-deserved sleep after already having flown once that night against other targets. The Strike Eagles began hammering the road congestion, triggering a level of destruction from air attack rarely seen before. The first had been the Wadi el Far'a, in Palestine, in 1918. Then Guadalajara, on the road to Madrid, during the Spanish Civil War, in 1937. In 1944, Falaise added its own grim legacy with its *Coulour de la Mort,* the "Corridor of Death." Mitla Pass, in 1967, witnessed the destruction of Egypt's armored forces. But none was more complete, more total, as what was about to happen on a stretch of road soon to be known as the "Highway of Death."[66]

Coming unseen out of the dark, relying on the LANTIRN pods to turn night into day, flying under miserable weather, the twelve F-15E crews hit these targets repeatedly. Other strikers, including Navy and Marine aircraft, continued the attacks by day. In better weather, the next morning, they attacked along the Kuwait City–Basra road, and then others that had jammed up as well. One pilot compared the jam to the road into Daytona Beach on spring break. When the jams became too great, many Iraqis simply fled away from the road, into the desert. To do otherwise, to stay with their vehicles, to fire back (as some did, with guns and missiles), was to risk death by bomb blast or incineration. Strike video showed this, from the perspective of the aircraft; racing toward vehicles like predatory sharks, the Iraqis running away into the desert, and then the blossoming of cannon, rocket, and bomb hits up and down the road, blowing vehicles in half, blasting them off the road entirely, or melting them in their own fuel-fed conflagrations. Some Iraqis did not run, a decision of utter folly.

The results taxed the ability of reporters traveling the road to describe it. Reporter P. J. O'Rourke, visiting the road four days later, noted:

> The wreckage was still smoldering four days later . . . most of the transport had been stolen, stolen in a perfectly indiscriminate frenzy of theft that left the ground covered with an improbably mixture of school buses, delivery vans, sports coupes, station wagons, tank trucks, luxury sedans, fire engines, civilian ambulances and tractor trailers . . . It looked like a bad holiday traffic jam in the States except charred and blown up, as though everybody in hell had tried to go the Hamptons on the same weekend . . . The killing field here was littered not so much with corpses as with TVs, VCRs, Seiko watches, cartons of cigarettes, box lots of shampoo and hair conditioner, cameras, videotapes, and household appliances . . . What we had here was the My Lai of consumer goods.[67]

Michael Kelly noted that:

> For a fifty- or sixty-mile stretch from just north of Jahra to the Iraqi border, the road was littered with exploded and roasted vehicles, charred and blown-up bodies . . . [It] was thick with the wreckage of tanks, armored personnel carriers, 155-mm. howitzers, and supply trucks . . .
> The heat of the blasts had inspired secondary explosions in the ammunition. The fires had been fierce enough in some cases to melt windshield glass

into globs of silicone that dripped and hardened on the black metal skeletons of the dashboards . . .

Most of the destruction had been visited on clusters of ten to fifteen vehicles. But those who had driven alone, or even off the road and into the desert, had been hunted down too. Of the several hundred wrecks I saw, not one had crashed in panic; all bore the marks of having been bombed or shot.[68]

Nothing could have more dramatically illustrated just how total air power's victory over the Iraqis had been than this. They had not been shattered by massive tank duels in the tradition of El Alamein or Kursk (the war had no such decisive land battle), or by the methodical advance of infantry across ground. Rather, as one Army officer put it, "The Air Force just blew the —— out of both roads."[69] In truth, it had been the combination of American air power—Air Force, Navy, Marine, and Army—that had turned the roads out of Kuwait into Iraq into horrifying testaments to the destructiveness of air attack. But away from Kuwait City, whose citizens had barbarically suffered at the hands of the very soldiers who now wandered the desert or lay in shattered and burned clumps with their vehicles, air had been no less destructive. The Iraqi army had died at the hands of coalition land- and sea-based attack helicopters, fighters and bombers, strike airplanes, rocket artillery, and naval gunfire directed via drone targeting airplanes. Saddam Hussein had styled himself the heir of Nebuchadnezzar and Hammurabi, but, in truth, he was a modern-day Sennacherib. Like that earlier Assyrian, his cohorts, too, had "come down like the wolf on the fold," and Lord Byron's words were never more chilling than when applied to the Iraqi army that had occupied Kuwait:

> Like the leaves of the forest when Summer is green,
> That host with their banners at sunset were seen,
> Like the leaves of the forest when Autumn hath blown,
> That host on the morrow lay withered and strown.[70]

On the morning of February 24, Schwarzkopf recollected after the war, he expected that the ground operation would take three weeks. Instead, it took 100 hours, before President Bush announced a ceasefire. At the end of G + 2, the coalition had taken over 30,000 prisoners. Twenty-six of Iraq's forty-two divisions in the KTO had been destroyed or, in the laconic words of the military, "rendered combat ineffective"; the remainder—every one—would suffer the same fate over the next day and a half, for there was no way home to Iraq from Kuwait. On the third and fourth days, G + 3 and G + 4, all coalition forces advanced ahead of schedule, straddling Highway 8 between Baghdad and Basra, and consolidating their hold on the Tigris and Euphrates valley. The road to Baghdad was open, but true to its stated objectives, coalition forces did not move toward the Iraqi capital.

Sporadic ground combat occurred as coalition forces hemmed in the trapped Iraqis. In one case, the VII Corps took on the remnants of three Republican Guard divisions, the Hammurabi, Medina, and Tawakalna, as they vainly sought safety. While the vast majority of Iraqis surrendered willingly and almost joyously, these hard-core Baathists did not; like lumbering rhinos, they lowered their heads and blindly charged straight-on. So they resisted and died, as Abrams and Bradleys ripped their tanks and mechanized vehicles apart with high-energy depleted uranium rounds or TOW missiles. At Medina Ridge, Abrams tanks from the 2nd Brigade of the 1st Armored Division outranged and destroyed about 100 tanks and 30 personnel carriers in a 45-minute fight as the Iraqis desperately sought to get away. In contrast, only 3 Abrams (0.162% of 1,847) and 5 Bradleys (0.297% of 1,682) were damaged by enemy fire during *all* of Desert Storm. It was not all one-sided and bloodless for the United States; engagements were sharp and characterized by high-volume tank and automatic weapons fire that occasionally killed and wounded American soldiers and airmen, fortunately in small numbers. Most distressingly, numerous cases of "friendly" ground fire claimed victims, as tanks fired on tanks and on mechanized vehicles, often in conditions of poor visibility and bad weather.[71]

The ground casualties suffered in the Gulf war should be compared to those experienced in previous American conflicts (see Table 7.2). Fortunately, a data base on loss rates has been assembled by military analyst Trevor N. Dupuy, and relevant parameters are presented here, coupled with data from the Department of Defense for the Gulf war. The measure used is U.S. Army casualties (killed and wounded) per day as a percentage of theater strength, reflecting only combat losses.[72] American soldiers had rarely come into direct combat with Iraqis, and when they did so, the weapon of choice was overwhelmingly an air one—a plane, a helicopter, a missile. The vast majority thus never once had to fire their personal weapons at an enemy. The reason was air power, which dramatically reduced the risk to coalition ground forces from the enemy, shattering potential resistance.

Offensive operations against Iraq ceased at midnight on G + 4, February 28. In the postwar settling out, a number of matters came to light,

Table 7.2. Army Casualties Suffered in the Gulf War Compared to Army Casualties in Previous American Conflicts

War	Strength	Casualties	Casualties/Day (as a Percentage of Theater Strength)
Civil War	400,000	387,200	0.07
Spanish American War	50,000	1,872	0.02
World War I	990,000	261,657	0.45
World War II	1,500,000	800,735	0.05
Korean War	220,000	97,241	0.04
Vietnam War	240,000	127,405	0.03
Gulf War	530,000	366	0.0016

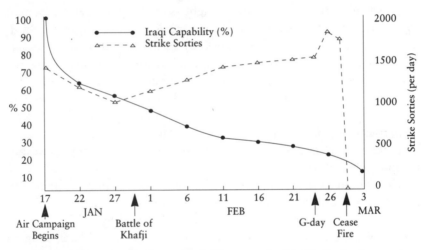

7.1 **Decline of Overall Iraqi Military Capabilities versus Coalition Strike Sorties**
Source: CENTCOM/CENTAF/Checkmate statistics.

triggering greater or lesser controversies, many that will require years before they are fully resolved. Air attack had inflicted far more damage upon Saddam Hussein's military forces than had been initially expected, highlighting pervasive weaknesses in bomb damage assessment and intelligence. Further emphasizing those weaknesses was the discovery, after the war, that Saddam Hussein's nuclear establishment and intentions were far more extensive than had at first been suspected.

Any doubts about the duplicity of the Hussein regime were ended by postwar discoveries. Iraq denied it had a biological-warfare research program—then the UN forced an admission that it was processing anthrax for weapons use. Iraq denied it had a nuclear weapons program—then the UN forced an admission that it had, in fact, processed weapons-grade uranium. Iraq denied that it was developing a so-called super gun—then UN inspectors were shown it, and components for others as well. What the coalition had known about, it had targeted. And what it had targeted, it had generally destroyed. But it had not known the full extent of his willingness to invest in nuclear weaponry, and some sites—such as the uranium enrichment equipment manufacturing facility at Furat—remained undetected until revealed after the war, thanks to a defector and persistent UN follow-up.

The war left unanswered many questions about the future of the Middle East—but every war leaves its share of unsettled matters and open questions. It could not be expected that this would be any different, nor should the Gulf war be held to different historical standards than previous conflicts. As for the UN, it had never looked better. No longer an ineffective hostage of the Cold War, the United Nations was, to the contrary, robust, respected, and confident, poised (many thought) on the verge of a renaissance. In the weeks ahead, the UN asserted its influence over the Gulf region with an assurance and authority that, given its long years of impotence, was truly remarkable. Quickly, coalition prisoners returned to the States; over time, stories emerged indicating (not surprisingly) that Saddam Hussein's jailers were fully as inhumane as the North Vietnamese and North Koreans had been to their prisoners in earlier wars. The graphic account of atrocities in Kuwait demonstrated that being Muslim was no protection, either. A brutal civil war broke out in Iraq, as Shia and Kurdish minorities grappled with the weakened Hussein regime, triggering an intense debate over the decision to terminate the war and what America's postwar obligations might now be in the region.

Nothing could change one fact: the coalition had triumphed in an outstanding feat of arms, a victory that, in its swiftness, decisiveness, and scope, came from the wise and appropriate application of air power by courageous men and women, assisted by their comrades on the ground and at sea. A meeting on March 3 between Iraqi and coalition leaders, at Safwan airfield in southern Iraq, made the magnitude of triumph manifest. Present were Schwarzkopf, Khalid bin Sultan, other coalition commanders, and two Iraqi generals and their senior staff: Lt. Gen. Sultan Hashim Ahmad Al-Jabburi, the vice chief of staff of the Iraqi army, and the Iraqi III Corps commander, Maj. Gen. Mohammed Al-Dughastani.

The Iraqis arrived in American vehicles, passed along a parade-ground line-up of American equipment and stoic soldiers, were taken aside and checked for arms, and then escorted to meet the coalition delegation. While not contemptuous or humiliating, the tone and climate were stiff and formal, echoing another morning nearly a half-century before, when the beaten military leaders of the Third Reich met with another Allied coalition at Rheims. As required, Al-Jabburi furnished details on the number of coalition prisoners held by Iraq, and then asked for the same from the coalition. Schwarzkopf informed him that the coalition held more than 58,000, but that counting was far from complete. (It would eventually rise to over 86,000.) Al-Jabburi, in disbelief, turned to Al-Dughastani and asked if it could be true; the III Corps commander replied that he didn't know, but it could be. Then Schwarzkopf proposed that a mutually agreed-upon line be established between Iraqi and coalition forces to prevent incidents, and showed them a possible location. The Iraqis concurred, but Al-Jabburi wanted to know why the line was behind their troops. Schwarzkopf remarked that it was, in fact, the forward line of American forces. Stunned again, Al-Jabburi again looked to his III Corps commander for confirmation; again Al-Dughastani replied that it was possible, but that he did not know. "Following this," the Department of Defense interim report to Congress on the conduct of the war laconically concludes, "the Iraqi attitude was noticeably more subdued."[73]

Eight

Questions, Answers, and Conjectures

Gulf Lesson One is the value of air power.
President George Bush (1991)

The air campaign was decisive.
Secretary of Defense Dick Cheney
(1991)

*The Iraqi military machine folded
under the pressure of Allied smart
bombs and air power.*
Harry Smith, CBS (1991)

As happens with all wars, the conclusion of the Gulf war has led to an intense interest in understanding how it came about, how it was prosecuted, and why it turned out as it did. Not surprisingly, much of this discussion hinges on its implications for future war.

There are a number of questions that the war has raised that suggest both ways in which it is being viewed, and issues that need to be considered. Columnists representing various viewpoints have battled it out in newspapers and journals. Each service, to a greater or lesser extent, has prepared "lessons learned" documents for public consumption, and more private classified studies within the service. The Department of Defense issued an interim report on the conduct of the war to the Congress, with a more detailed report to follow. Private organizations such as defense think tanks and study groups—bodies as diverse as Greenpeace, the Rand Corporation, the Hudson Institute, and the Center for Strategic and International Studies—have gone to great lengths to study and analyze the war, often reaching differing conclusions representing diverging views.

The following, then, is a brief examination of just some of the questions and issues raised by the war, together with the author's answers (and some conjectures). We begin with two general ones.

What Worked

Any successful war is the product of multiple factors that combine to generate success. The short answer to this question is "people, leadership, training, technology, and doctrine." On balance, the American forces in the Gulf were better trained and better motivated than their predecessors in any war since the Second World War, and the same held true for the "Weekend Warriors." (When the crisis came, as one officer recalled of National Guard and Reserve forces, "we had no shortage of volunteers.") Their leaders were veterans of Vietnam who had no desire to repeat that sorry experience, and the national government's leaders, from all parties and political viewpoints, were equally committed to the notion of "No More Vietnams." They had excellent equipment, and maintained it well. Their training had been realistic, against identifiable potential foes and weapons, and consistent with the doctrinal underpinnings of the various services. Thus, the Air Force, Navy, Army, and Marine Corps, with relative minor exceptions, fought as they trained.

The technology the services employed was reliable, adaptable, maintainable, and appropriate for the tasks at hand. Some systems proved extraordinarily valuable, in most cases not unexpectedly, but in some cases (notably the Patriot) to degrees their developers little imagined. Particularly significant were the F-117A, GPS, JSTARS, AWACS, and Patriot. The frustrations that accompanied American introductions to war in earlier conflicts—for example, the discovery that Japanese and German fighters were superior to American ones at the beginning of World War II, or the shock of encountering T-34 tanks in the opening phase of the Korean War, or the disastrous introduction of the M-16 rifle into combat in Vietnam—were unknown in this war.

The weapons development process did not stop even in the midst of the war. Air Force Systems Command (AFSC), for example, monitored weapons deployed to the Gulf to prevent any problems that might come up from inhibiting their use. In one case, sand erosion of LANTIRN pods during Desert Shield forced AFSC to develop and rush a lens-recoating

Air Power and the Gulf War

Iraq: A Third World Country with a First World Military

Overwhelming Iraqi military power made Saddam Hussein's invasion of Kuwait possible. Iraq's aerospace forces were particularly robust.

Possessing low military value but enormous strategic significance, Iraq's Scud missiles could reach deep into Saudi Arabia and Israel, potentially inflicting serious civilian casualties and possibly shattering the Allied coalition.

While much of Iraq's air force consisted of Vietnam-era MiG-21 Fishbed interceptors *(top)*, the service also possessed large numbers of the more modern Mirage F-1, the swing-wing air superiority MiG-23 Flogger *(middle)*, and other strike aircraft, as well as the massive MiG-25 Foxbat, a near-Mach 3 + interceptor with "look-down, shoot-down" radar and missile capabilities *(bottom)*.

Iraqi airmen also flew the impressive MiG-29 Fulcrum, a highly agile and thoroughly modern fighter.

Responding to the Crisis

To protect Saudi Arabia, an international coalition sent air, land, and sea forces to the Gulf region. F-15C Eagle fighters from the Air Force's Tactical Air Command reached Saudi Arabia after a 15-hour, 8,000-mile nonstop flight made possible by air refueling.

Top: Transports such as the Lockheed C-5B Galaxy, air-refueled en route, ferried over 17 million ton-miles of supplies per day into the Gulf region, much of this directly from the continental United States. *Right:* At the height of Desert Shield, sixty-five aircraft per day delivered up to 8,000 troops a day to sixteen different airfields in the Gulf region.

Top: The venerable Lockheed C-130 Hercules was the mainstay of "theater" airlift, often operating in daunting sand and dust conditions across the Arabian peninsula, with both American and coalition air forces. *Middle:* Over the five months of Desert Shield, coalition air strength in the Gulf region built to over 2,600 aircraft, approximately 450 of which were at sea. Here is Task Force 155, commanded by Rear Adm. Riley D. Mixson, operating in the Red Sea. Eventually, six carrier battle groups participated in Desert Storm. *Bottom:* Various nations contributed to coalition air strength. Here is a multinational formation led by a French Mirage F-1, flanked by a Qatari Mirage F-1 and an American F-16 Fighting Falcon, and a Qatari Dassault Alphajet and Canadian F/A-18 Hornet. Because both Iraq and coalition states operated the Mirage, F-1 operations were restricted until the Iraqi air force was eliminated as a threat, to prevent "blue on blue" encounters.

Planning the War

Author of "the clearest expression of air power thought since the days of Mitchell and Seversky," Col. John A. Warden III headed "Checkmate," whose staff brainstormed possible responses to Hussein's aggression. (Photo courtesy of Col. John A. Warden III.)

As theater commander, General Schwarzkopf bore overall responsibility for war planning and military operations. He proved a shrewd and resourceful general who, like Dwight Eisenhower before him, had faith that his air commanders knew how to best employ air power.

In early August 1990, Checkmate's planners created "Instant Thunder," a strategic air campaign concept briefed extensively to the senior defense leadership and USCENTCOM "Cinc" Gen. H. Norman Schwarzkopf.

General Michael Dugan *(right)*, Air Force chief of staff, ensured that the service's response to the crisis was rapid and effective. He is shown at Riyadh with Lt. Gen. Charles Horner, the CENTAF and JFACC commander. After making highly publicized pronouncements on the role of air power in the Gulf crisis, Dugan was replaced as chief of staff by . . .

Gen. Merrill A. "Tony" McPeak, whose confident briefings on what air could accomplish should war come particularly impressed Pres. George Bush and his national security advisor, Brent Scowcroft. Here he is shown *(left)* with Col. John A. Warden III *(center)* and Secretary of the Air Force Donald B. Rice *(right)*. (Photo courtesy of Col. John A. Warden III.)

Horner entrusted overall responsibility for air war planning to Brig. Gen. Buster C. Glosson. Feisty, imaginative, and energetic, Glosson assembled a multiservice planning staff that worked out of the "Black Hole" in Saudi air force headquarters.

"We are not *preparing* the battlefield, we are *destroying* it!": Lt. Col. David "Zatar" Deptula, assigned to the Black Hole from the Secretary of the Air Force's Staff Group, played a key role in targeting the "vital centers" of Iraq's military machine.

The Storm Breaks

On January 15, Black Hole air campaign planners briefed Gen. Norman Schwarzkopf on the opening air attack plan. Shown *(left to right)* are Brig. Gen. Buster Glosson, Schwarzkopf, and briefer Lt. Col. David A. Deptula. (Photo courtesy of Lt. Col. David A. Deptula.)

As Desert Storm opened, Boeing E-3B Airborne Warning and Control aircraft furnished early warning of potential Iraqi air threats, controlled Allied fighters and strike aircraft, and "deconflicted" air operations.

Top: Task Force Normandy, nine modified Army AH–64 Apache gunships, guided by three Air Force MH–53J Pave Low pathfinders *(background)* opened Desert Storm by striking at two small radar sites on the western Iraqi-Saudi border. *Middle:* Flown by the 37th Tactical Fighter Wing's "Bad Boys of Baghdad," the F-117A stealth fighter was the only coalition weapon capable of hitting hardened targets in extremely high threat areas. The F-117A constituted less than 2.5 percent of all coalition strike aircraft, but struck 31 percent of strategic air targets attacked on the first day. *Bottom:* Supporting aircraft operations were attacks by unmanned cruise missiles launched from ships, submarines, and B-52 bombers (which, in the longest raid in aviation history, had flown nonstop from Louisiana to strike at Iraq). Here a Navy BGM-109 Tomahawk launches from the battleship USS *Missouri* on the first day of Desert Storm.

Top: Coalition fighters harried the Iraqi air force out of the air. Particularly effective were the Air Force's F-15C Eagles, using a mix of Sidewinder and Sparrow air-to-air missiles. The Iraqi air force opted to remain in its shelters—and then, when the shelters were hit, "flushed" to Iran. *Bottom:* Conventional strike aircraft relied on electronic warfare jammers such as the Grumman–General Dynamics EF–111A Raven firing electrons to achieve "soft kills" against Iraq's air defenses.

Top: Air Force F-4G Phantom II "Wild Weasels" launching AGM-88 HARM antiradar missiles, scored "hard kills" against Iraqi radar sites, demoralizing defenders and forcing individual Iraqi radars to shut down. *Middle:* Other HARM-toters included the Navy-Marine F/A-18 Hornet. Here a HARM-loaded F/A-18C of Marine Fighter Attack Squadron 232 taxies out for takeoff from Shaik Isa Air Base, Bahrain, while another bomb-loaded Hornet from VMFA-314 accelerates for takeoff. *Bottom:* In addition to attacking Iraqi airfields and strategic targets, some Royal Air Force Tornado G.R. Mk. 1 strike airplanes carried ALARM antiradar missiles to suppress Iraq's air defenses. ALARM was a little "Wild Weasel" itself, for it could hunt for radars on its own as it flew. (Photo courtesy of British Aerospace, Ltd.)

With their air defense network shattered, Iraqi forces were devastated by powerful air attacks. Heavily reinforced aircraft shelters proved no protection against penetrating smart bombs.

Top: For the first time in military aviation history, attackers achieved clear-cut inter-diction. Air strikes prevented Iraqi forces from replacing and distributing supplies from stockpiles. *Bottom:* Against fielded military forces, air-launched precision weapons proved devastating. Here is one victim, a tank with its turret blown completely out of it.

Throughout Desert Storm, coalition airmen and commanders relied on a variety of so-phisticated means to increase their understanding and efficiency. Space-based systems, lofted by boosters such as this Titan III, furnished precise navigation, accurate weather analysis, intercontinental and theater communications, and early warning, among other services.

Top: Lockheed's TR-1A, a 1970s descendant of the famed U-2 of the 1950s, ranged far and wide on diverse intelligence-gathering missions. *Middle:* The aging Vietnam-era McDonnell-Douglas RF-4C Phantom II furnished reconnaissance information on the disposition of Iraqi troops and Scuds. *Bottom:* Filled with sensors and operators, Boeing RC-135 *Rivet Joint* aircraft provided vital intelligence information.

Top: Other important aircraft included the EC-130E, a modified Hercules transport operated by the 193rd Special Operations Squadron and configured to conduct sophisticated electronic combat operations against Iraqi forces. *Right:* Nowhere was intelligence more important than in the anti-Scud campaign. Cued by various sensors, Patriot surface-to-air missiles engaged Scuds that did launch in dramatic encounters witnessed around the world. (Photo courtesy of Raytheon Company.)

The coalition dropped warning leaflets encouraging Iraqi forces to abandon their equipment, desert, and surrender.

Top: Troops that ignored leaflets—such as the one that read simply, "Don't sleep in your tank"—did so at their peril. F-111F "Aardvarks," equipped with belly-mounted Pave Tack sensor turrets and carrying laser-guided bombs, scored up to 150 armor kills per night. *Middle:* Here an A-7E Corsair II from the *Kennedy*'s Attack Squadron 72 is shown heading to its target with a load of eight 500-pound "dumb" bombs. *Bottom:* With 249 aircraft in theater, the ubiquitous General Dynamics F-16 Fighting Falcon was the war's most numerous attacker. Here *Night Stalker,* an F-16C belonging to the 17th Tactical Fighter Squadron, is prepared for a night mission from Al Dafra Air Base in the United Arab Emirates.

Top: Boeing B-52G Stratofortresses of the 1708th Bombardment Wing (Provisional) are shown sharing the ramp at Jeddah with Royal Saudi Air Force C-130 Hercules transports. The Stratofortress, the most widely recognized international symbol of air power, was the most feared Gulf attacker, as revealed in prisoner reports. From Day 1 of the campaign, B-52 cells struck every three hours, dropping nearly 50 percent of all dumb bombs unloaded by Air Force aircraft. *Middle:* The undeniably ugly Fairchild A-10A "Warthog" flew strike, combat search-and-rescue, close air support, and even Wild Weasel ("Wart Weasel") missions. Rising loss and damage rates from low altitude Iraqi air defenses confirmed prewar Air Force expectations of its vulnerability and caused CENTAF to relegate it to less-threatening areas. *Bottom:* The Anglo-French SEPECAT Jaguar fighter-bomber flew battlefield interdiction missions and anti-shipping sorties. Here a British G.R. Mk. 1A is shown carrying two AIM-9L Sidewinder air-to-air missiles on overwing pylons. During the course of the war, one was fired at an Iraqi armored vehicle by an eager pilot seeking to suppress ground fire. (Photo courtesy of British Aerospace, Ltd.)

Top: Striking out of the night, sensor-laden Lockheed AC-130H Spectre gunships devastated Iraqi attackers at Khafji with their battery of 20mm, 40mm, and 105mm cannon. Unfortunately, the gunship's vulnerability to defenses when seen was tragically confirmed when one was shot down off the Kuwaiti coast, with the loss of all fourteen crewmen. *Bottom:* At sea, coalition helicopters such as the British Westland Lynx H.A.S. Mk. 3 joined with aircraft to prevent the Iraqi navy from taking part in the war or fleeing to Iran. The Sea Skua missile (shown here) proved deadly against patrol boats, landing craft, and minelayers. In one case, fourteen of fifteen Sea Skuas struck their targets, a success rate of over 93 percent. (Photo courtesy of British Aerospace, Ltd.)

As the air campaign unfolded into February, General Schwarzkopf and his senior staff
met in Riyadh with Secretary of Defense Dick Cheney and Chairman of the Joint
Chiefs of Staff Gen. Colin Powell for final briefings and discussions to fix the date of
the ground operation. The meeting coincided with public debate over the efficacy of
air attack, the reliability of bomb damage assessment intelligence estimates, and the
merits of continuing the air campaign versus starting a ground war.

Cartoonist Chris Britt of the *Houston Post* caught the essence of this debate (*left*) as
did cartoonist Ed Stein of the *Rocky Mountain News* (*right*). (Used with permissions
of Chris Britt and Ed Stein.)

Top: During the westward positioning of forces, C-130s flew extensive supply missions. Once the ground operation started, the pace of support flights became even more urgent. Here two are shown over one of Hussein's most distasteful legacies: a burning Kuwaiti oil well. *Bottom:* During the ground operation, helicopter gunships provided punishing fire support for racing coalition columns. Here is the business end of an Apache, showing its sensors, the pilot and gunner positions, the chain-gun cannon, and the pylon-mounted Hellfire missiles.

Top: Aerospatiale Gazelles of the *Armée de terre* destroyed numerous Iraqi vehicles and positions with HOT missiles as Franco-American forces stormed north to As Salman. *Bottom:* Troop helicopters proved invaluable for rapid mobility, prisoner removal, and casualty evacuation. Here a French Army Puma hovers before three American CH-47D Chinooks.

Top: As the Iraqis fell back, advancing coalition forces overran damaged and abandoned equipment. Here, at Talil airfield, soldiers inspect an abandoned Soviet-built Mil Mi-24 Hind gunship. *Bottom:* Inside a shattered, hardened aircraft shelter at Talil airfield, troops discovered this destroyed Sukhoi Su-25 Frogfoot ground attack aircraft. (Photo courtesy of Lt. Col. David A. Deptula.)

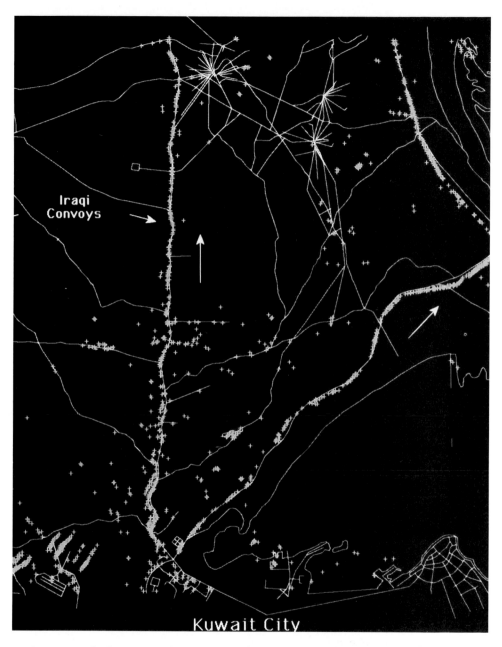

On the evening of February 25, the side-looking radar of an orbiting Boeing E-8A JSTARS detected the Iraqi III Corps retreating in gigantic convoys toward Basra. Scope operators could see a road map of Kuwait simply by looking at the multiple radar "hits" on thousands of individual vehicles. (Photo courtesy of United Technologies Norden Systems.)

The JSTARS sighting triggered waves of air attacks that left Kuwait strewn with smoking wreckage. Here, two days later, is a small stretch of what became known as the "Highway of Death" (though, mercifully, most Iraqis were able to flee into the desert, where they awaited capture while their vehicles burned). In this one photograph are more than 200 destroyed vehicles.

Top: Losers: Iraqi generals Mohammed Al-Dughastani and Hashim Al-Jabburi meet with generals Schwarzkopf and Khalid bin Sultan at Safwan airfield on March 3 to end the Gulf war. *Right:* "New Kids on the Block": Air campaign planners visit Talil airfield after the war to see their handiwork. (Photo courtesy of Lt. Col. David A. Deptula.)

Top: Quickly—in marked contrast to other wars—coalition POWs returned home. Here arriving at Andrews Air Force Base is an understandably exuberant group of Air Force, Navy, and Marine airmen: *(left to right)* captains William Andrews, Harry Roberts, and Richard Storr; lieutenants Jeffrey Zaun, Lawrence Slade, and Robert Wetzel; captains Michael Berryman and Russell Sanborn; and Lt. Robert Sweet. *Bottom:* Greeting America's returning prisoners and Desert Storm veterans were thousands of Americans, whose flags spoke more strongly than any words.

Winners (I): The key to victory was the skill and teamwork of the coalition forces. From all backgrounds and races, the young Americans of Desert Storm—like these armorers loading a Sidewinder onto its launch rail—validated the notion of the all-volunteer force.

Top: Winners (II): Sophisticated technology consistently demonstrated its leverage and power in the Gulf war. The F-117A stealth fighter best exemplified the new revolution in aerospace power made possible by advanced technology. (Photo by Richard P. Hallion.) *Bottom:* Winners (III): The biggest winners of the Gulf air war were the ground forces. Air power obviated any need for a punishing land war and confounded "experts" who had predicted thousands of American casualties. Had the air power option not been available, casualties undoubtedly would have been higher. With air, there were many more scenes like this one.

process to the Gulf; the process enabled LANTIRN to play a major role in Desert Storm. The command developed a new 4,700-pound penetrating smart bomb, the GBU-28, in 17 days. After one validating test drop at the Tonopah Range in Nevada (where the test round plunged so deep into the earth that it could not be found), Eglin's armament staff made up others, and flew them via a "dedicated" C-141 to the Gulf. Less than five hours after arriving in-country, the two bombs were slung under F-111Fs and on their way. Naval Air Systems Command had similar successes, as did the coalition partners. Great Britain greatly improved the effectiveness of its Tornado and Jaguar strike aircraft. For example, developers qualified the Jaguar to use AIM-9L Sidewinders on overwing pylons, and the high-velocity Canadian CRV-7 air-to-ground rocket; qualified the Tornado to carry and use a thermal-imaging and laser designation pod, then supported the Tornado designation teams sent to the Gulf; qualified the Tornado to carry an advanced infrared reconnaissance system that proved its value in the anti-Scud campaign; accelerated development trials so that Tornado could carry the ALARM antiradar missile; added radar-absorbing tiles and coating to significantly reduce the Tornado's radar cross section; and cleared RAF troop-transport helicopters to carry guns and flare dispensers. In sum, the coalition's research, development, test, and evaluation process had produced weapons that worked for warriors who knew how to use them.[1]

The doctrinal underpinnings of the war were sound and appropriate. The Air Force operated in a manner consistent with thinking embodied within AFM 1-1, the Army with FM 100-5. Having said this, it is important to note that doctrine always has to be tailored to the nature of a particular conflict. Therefore, some of the strongly NATO-versus-Warsaw Pact structural elements contained in both of these—and, for that matter, in the Navy's approach to sea warfare—had to be adjusted accordingly. Air Force planning benefited greatly from the thought of Col. John A. Warden III, and reflected that thought in its targeting emphasis. Above all, the war reaffirmed the importance of gaining and holding air superiority: with air superiority, a military force can undertake the "Hail Mary" play; without air superiority, it is stuck in a traffic jam outside Kuwait City along the Highway of Death. The Army's AirLand Battle doctrine spelled out many of the elements that the Army sought to use in this war—elements they would have used had not air power so devastated the Iraqi military that the ground war, in effect, became overshadowed by the roundup of prisoners. The Army's air defense forces, using the Patriot missile, played a major role in preventing a widening of the war to include Israel.

The Navy performed well in its traditional role of protecting the seas and blockading enemy coasts. It used appropriate elements of naval warfare—coastal patrols, maritime aviation, shore bombardment—to achieve locally valuable results. Examples of these include embargo enforcement, attacking offshore Iraqi positions, destroying the Iraqi navy, and bombarding Iraqi forces in Kuwait with battleship fire support missions. What could not be as successful were deeper operations against Iraq itself, as will be discussed more fully subsequently in response to other questions.

The Marine Corps never had an opportunity to try its hand at an amphibious operation, although the threat of just such an assault pinned down large numbers of Iraqi troops—approximately ten divisions. On the ground and in the air, the Marines proved formidable opponents, first at Khafji, and subsequently during the rest of the war—worthy heirs of a military tradition dating to the founding of the country. During the drive into Kuwait, the Marines advanced rapidly and to good effect, thanks to Marine attack helicopters and aircraft roaming over Kuwait. Marine air attacks on Iraqi forces fleeing Kuwait City, coupled with those of other services, shattered any chance for an orderly withdrawal into Iraq.

What Didn't Work

At the top of the list of disappointments is intelligence information interpretation, timeliness, and distribution, despite the availability of imaging systems and technology (such as the TR-1 and other more sensitive resources) that consistently furnished excellent raw data. In fact, the Gulf war nearly fulfilled Clausewitz's dismal dictum:

> Many intelligence reports in war are contradictory; even more are false, and most are uncertain . . . In short, most intelligence is false, and the effect of fear is to multiply lies and inaccuracies. As a rule most men would rather believe bad news than good, and rather tend to exaggerate the bad news.[2]

Schwarzkopf complained bitterly about intelligence shortfalls in postwar testimony to Congress (as discussed previously). The danger always existed that incorrect assessments would unnecessarily prolong the war and boost the resulting risk to American and coalition forces.

Dissent rocked the intelligence community itself, triggering often contentious and, indeed, acrimonious meetings between key players. While numerous individuals within all of the national intelligence organizations—for example, the CIA, DIA, NSA, and military intelligence services—performed brilliantly and to good effect when consulted outside the constraints of their institutions, the *institutionalized* intelligence process—the systematic acquisition, analysis, and distribution of intelligence—was far less satisfactory. Analysts persistently underestimated the level of destruction being inflicted upon Iraq's military machine and overqualified their assessments, and dissemination of intelligence products likewise proved cumbersome. Intelligence estimates were hopelessly conservative when treating Iraqi armor and artillery destruction, and untimely target assessments forced CENTAF planners to rely on strike video as their primary source of bomb damage assessment. Additionally, the intelligence community could not furnish reliable information on the number and location of Iraq's Scud launchers, forcing an intensive anti-Scud campaign that seriously reduced the number of Scud firings, but never totally ended them.

Several solutions offer themselves: first, intelligence must be tightly integrated with operations, and the "operators" themselves can help ensure this by making certain that the intelligence community receives accurate planning materials in a timely fashion to help facilitate their work. Other remedies include training in bomb damage assessment for intelligence analysts; the inculcation of an "ego risk-free" approach to analysis, so that analysts and agencies will not be so fearful of appearing "wrong" that they produce bland analysis of little use; and the development of better real-time intelligence acquisition platforms and systems, data-linked directly to planning cells. JSTARS, for example, consistently furnished high quality real-time high-value information directly to air and ground commanders, and then passed it to strike aircraft. (As Col. George Muellner, the Desert Storm JSTARS commander, noted subsequently, "There is no substitute for responsive targeting and intelligence on the battlefield."[3]

As mentioned, intelligence weaknesses hurt the quest for Scuds. The anti-Scud campaign confirmed that the mobile ballistic missile is a difficult target to locate and destroy. Even with the coalition's best efforts, the Scud threat was never fully eradicated, although it was reduced significantly. As with "tactical" aircraft, "tactical" ballistic missiles have profoundly strategic implications. For example, Scud attacks, sans aggressive countermeasures and the Patriot missile, could have resulted in Israel entering the war, with unknown but certainly ominous implications for coalition unity. Further, it was a "first-generation" ballistic missile, without means of deploying defensive countermeasures, maneuvering, or reducing its radar cross section. Nevertheless, it was the classic military example of the "low cost" threat forcing a "high cost" and very complicated defense—a 1950s missile that could not be confronted until the 1990s.

Even before the Gulf war, "tactical" ballistic missiles had proliferated around the world; they are easy to build, easy to hide, and easy to use. Therefore, far greater attention must be paid to refining locating technologies, and developing rapid-response antimissile defense—perhaps using air- or ground-launched hypersonic missiles, space-based assets, and, certainly, advanced versions of systems such as JSTARS. While the future of the Strategic Defense Initiative (SDI) is unclear, there are aspects of research work within it that are potentially suited to confronting both the strategic and the theater ballistic missile problem.[4] As the antiship cruise missile first attracted international attention in the wake of the 1967 Arab-Israeli war, so now has the ballistic missile, thanks to its use in this one. Clearly this attention will spur continued antiballistic missile research, and, perhaps, the eventual modification or repeal of the long-standing but increasingly anachronistic Anti-Ballistic Missile (ABM) Treaty.

One disappointment was combat search and rescue (CSAR). CSAR in peacetime is one of the first defense items to feel the budget axe, but in wartime one can never have enough. In the Gulf war, CSAR fell under the control of Special Operations Command Central Command (SOC-CENT), with all U.S. CSAR forces placed under the management of Air Force Special Operations Command Central. While the CSAR forces operated with their traditional reputation for bravery, dedication, and willingness to take chances to rescue downed air crew, there were simply too few aircraft available to meet the requirements of both combat search-and-rescue and special operations needs. In many cases, downed air crew were so deep within enemy territory, or immediately surrounded by hostile forces, that rescue was impossible. in any case, only three of sixty-four downed air crew—roughly 5 percent—were actually picked up: an extraordinary daytime rescue of a Navy pilot from deep in Iraq by an Air Force Pave Low cued by an AWACS and escorted by two "Sandy" A-10s that strafed an interfering Iraqi truck; an Air Force pilot plucked in daytime from the Gulf by a Navy SH–60; and an Air Force pilot rescued at night by two Army SOF Blackhawks, one of which had to evade an Iraqi heat-seeking missile. Indeed, only a total of seven CSAR missions were actually launched; one of these, tragically, resulted in the loss of the rescue helicopter, several of its crew, and the imprisonment of survivors, including a badly injured woman physician. The development of sophisticated night-vision systems and advanced navigation equipment and techniques enabled two of these three saves to occur. But the need remains for fast, responsive, and survivable CSAR systems, perhaps "decoupled" from other SOF missions that often generate competing demands for their use.

One shocking failure was the number of friendly fire incidents that claimed American and coalition lives. The statistics on the incidents indicate that of the 615 total American battle casualties in the Gulf war— 148 dead and 467 wounded—35 were killed and 73 wounded by friendly fire, a total of 108, representing 18 percent of all U.S. battle casualties, and 24 percent of all deaths. No Army personnel were killed by Air Force air attack, although two were wounded when a HARM missile, fired from an F-4G at an Iraqi radar, homed instead on an Army counter-battery radar after the Iraqi one hastily shut down. Two Army soldiers were killed and six wounded by Army helicopter gunships. Air Force A-10s killed seven Marines, possibly an eighth, and wounded three, and possibly two others; a sailor serving with the Marines was also wounded by an A-10. A-10s struck a British column with Maverick missiles, killing and wounding a number of troops. A Marine A-6E mistakenly bombed a Marine unit, killing one Marine and wounding two others.

But despite the highly publicized incidents of air attack on friendly forces—attacks predicted before the war, in fact—the greatest number of incidents, and with greater losses, occurred during ground combat—a problem that the vast majority of military commentators had not foreseen. Land force–vs.–land force incidents were over twice as numerous as air-vs.-land incidents (2.14:1), the worst being a single engagement on February 27 that left 6 dead and 25 wounded; 58 American soldiers were wounded and 24 killed by ground fratricide, while 15 others were wounded and 11 died from air attacks. Army-vs.-Army fire claimed 21 killed and 63 wounded, 22 percent of all Army personnel killed in action, and 18 percent of all Army personnel wounded in action. Of these 21, 1 was an Abrams tank crewman, 15 were Bradley fighting vehicle crewmen, 1 was a M-113 crewman, and 4 were infantry. Seven Abrams tanks were hit by friendly fire—70 percent of all Abrams damaged from combat in the war—and 20 Bradleys were hit from friendly fire—80 percent of all Bradleys damaged in combat. Altogether, 27 of the 35 Army tanks and personnel carriers destroyed or damaged in the war were damaged by friendly fire—a figure of 77 percent. With the exception of 2 Bradleys destroyed by an Apache helicopter, all of these were victims of ground-vs.-ground fire.[5] These incidents were not limited to American forces. One British commentator referred dryly to British incidents by noting that "the good news is the Challenger's [a British tank] Chobham armour stands up to tank fire; the bad news is the Challenger gun can't pierce Chobham armour."

With the bulk of attention in "friendly fire" prevention having gone to preventing air-to-ground fratricide, the Gulf war illustrated that an equal amount of attention must be devoted to preventing ground-to-ground fratricide as well. Both forms of attack must be addressed, and vastly improved means of recognition employed. The tragic loss of a nation's soldiers—individuals who have volunteered to put their lives on the line against skilled and resourceful enemies—at the hands of their comrades is unacceptable, inexcusable, and, indeed, outrageous.

Points of Contention

There are a number of more specific opinions and charges that have surfaced since the Gulf war, and it is worth examining some of them, as they reflect current interests and interpretations of the war.

Did stealth prove its value? After the war, defense critics (mostly "low-tech" supporters) noted that while stealth worked, so did everything else.[6] They suggested that the use of stealth aircraft was unnecessary (and, by extension, therefore, stealth aircraft are unnecessary), since all other aircraft systems—the F-111's, and F-15E's, for example—had high survival rates. In fact, all other aircraft survived only after (and because) the stealth fighters—the F-117As—had destroyed Iraq's air defense headquarters, sector air defense centers, and key air defense infrastructure targets. After the war, an unfounded myth grew up: that Iraq's air defenses had been adroitly crippled by a computer virus planted by American intelligence in equipment that the Hussein regime had acquired from abroad. In fact, such was not the case: on opening night, Iraq's integrated air defenses were fully up and functional, shut down and taken apart only by the courage and skills of the stealth pilots themselves, and the jammers and shooters who followed. Stealth achieved precisely what it was intended to. It sneaked into the densest of air defense environments, confronted radars it had been intended to confound, defeated them, proved unengagable, destroyed its targets, and stole away into the night. As President Bush put it in a speech at the Air Force Academy after the war, "The F-117 proved itself by doing more, doing it better, doing it for less, and targeting soldiers, not civilians. It . . . carried a revolution in warfare on its wings."[7]

With this war, stealth technology—under development, off and on, for the last three decades—came of age. The F-117 first entered service in 1983, over seven years before it went to war. Since that time, and for the foreseeable future—at least to the year 2000, in fact—there is no equivalent system elsewhere in the world. This itself is remarkable by the standards of twentieth-century military technology, for previous weapons have stimulated the introduction of rival systems of near-identical or superior performance in at most a few years, if not months. (Consider, for example, the introduction of steam turbine propulsion, the submarine, the tank, the fighter airplane, radar, the jet engine, the atomic bomb, the sweptwing, the hydrogen bomb, earth satellites, and manned spacecraft.) Critics often allege that some new or improved system will render stealth "visible." In fact, proponents have never said that stealth is *invisible*— only that it is so difficult to detect and track that engagement would be unlikely. (Similar allegations of vulnerability have been made repeatedly against submarines, which are the only comparable military system that approximates the stealth airplane, and yet, nearly 80 years after their introduction in combat, the submarine continues to confound easy detection.)

During the Gulf war, many telling examples of the value of stealth occurred: on one attack against one airfield, four A-6Es and four Tornadoes striking the airfield were protected by four F-4G Wild Weasels, five EA-6B radar jammers, and twenty-one F/A-18C Hornets carrying radar-homing missiles. This package of thirty-eight aircraft (and sixty-five men) was needed to ensure that eight aircraft could hit one target with a good expectation of survival, a ratio of support aircraft to strike aircraft of almost 5 to 1, and an aircraft-to-target ratio of 38 to 1. At the same time, twenty-one F-117s were striking thirty-seven targets, by themselves.[8] In another example, eight F-117s with eight pilots hitting sixteen different aimpoints could accomplish the same at much less risk than a strike package composed of sixty nonstealthy aircraft—thirty-two F-16 bomb-droppers, sixteen F-15 escorts, four EF-111 jammers, and eight F-4 Wild Weasels—crewed by seventy-two air crew.[9] Stealth represents a genuine revolution in warfare and, like the submarine, aircraft making use of it will prove very difficult to defeat—the ideal attribute for a high-leverage weapon.

Could cruise-missile attacks have substituted for manned aircraft? Some defense critics suggest that cruise missiles make manned strike aircraft superfluous. Again, this is an argument offered largely by "cheaper, simpler" advocates; occasionally it is coupled with antistealth arguments as well. Without doubt, cruise missiles contributed greatly to the success of the air campaign. They destroyed vital targets of great military and political significance, and did so without endangering a human operator. But although they acted as "force multipliers" for manned aircraft (freeing up these more useful systems for many other tasks), their success should not be misinterpreted as suggesting that manned aircraft are unnecessary. They had commendable accuracy, though they lacked the fine precision of a laser-guided bomb dropped with a craftsman's eye. (The F-117 was about ten times more accurate than the TLAM, thanks to the benefits of "man-in-the-loop" weapons control, and carried four times the payload.) Unlike the F-117s, the TLAM cruise missiles were unable to strike hardened targets, and they also proved vulnerable to being shot down. Further, being incapable of interpreting what they were seeing with the flexibility of a human mind, they could not adjust or compensate for the images they saw that contained blasted or ruined buildings from previous strikes in correlating those images against stored memory. Thus, previous damage from earlier raids could cause the terminal guidance system of later missiles to misread their internal "map," possibly sending the missile off course during its terminal phase. (This was particularly true for missiles launched after the first wave of TLAM strikes. The addition of GPS-based navigation should greatly enhance the already impressive accuracy of these small but very dangerous weapons, and offset this particular problem.) Furthermore, cruise missiles cannot provide the feedback so necessary in planning follow-on attacks as do piloted aircraft.

The economic argument that cruise missiles are cheaper than manned aircraft, and therefore that they have a tremendous cost benefit, is, unfortunately, specious. Since one is throwing away a sophisticated miniature airplane every time a cruise missile is launched, the cost benefits are illusory, unless manned aircraft loss rates are so high—literally on the order of 50 percent—that planners have no other option. Each TLAM costs approximately $1.2 million, to deliver a 1,000-pound warhead against "soft" targets. (In contrast, a 2,000-pound laser-guided hardened pene-trating bomb costs approximately $73,000.) Just to deliver the same ton-nage as dropped in the Gulf war by the F-117 (approximately 2,000 tons, worth $146 million) would require the expenditure of $4.8 billion dollars worth of TLAMs. This same price would buy 112 F-117s, which can be used repeatedly (potentially thousands of times for each airframe) to carry vastly cheaper laser-guided bombs that can strike with greater ac-curacy.[10] And the mission planner can, of course, operate the manned aircraft—F-117s, in this example—with much greater flexibility: for ex-ample, as a "show of force," something that cannot be done with a mis-sile. To deliver all the smart-weapon tonnage expended by the United States—approximately 7,400 tons—would have required nearly $18 bil-lion worth of TLAMs.[11]

Cruise missiles should be used where one fears to use a manned air-plane, where manned strikes may be politically unacceptable, or on tar-gets that do not require the precision strike that manned systems can of-fer, or because they have some inherent value—a special weapon or certain capability—that is needed. They are difficult (but not impossible) to defend against, and this is another strong point in their favor. For this reason they are a welcome and powerful weapon in the national arsenal. But nothing is to be gained by overemphasizing their significance at the expense of other equally or even more significant systems—particularly stealth ones. In sum, then, the argument for cruise missiles should not be an "either/or" one—either we have them, or we have manned airplanes. Both have attributes and strengths that make them useful to national de-fense, and, when used together, they generate a tremendous synergistic effect that challenges the abilities of a defender to defeat them. Both are needed now and in the foreseeable future.

Was the ground war decisive? There are a number of individuals who have suggested that the Gulf experience confirmed that wars cannot be won by air power alone. Many of these critics use the old argument that air cannot hold and occupy territory, therefore it is not decisive in land warfare, and thus it could not "win" the Gulf war. In short, they suggest that what air power couldn't destroy in 39 days, the ground campaign crushed utterly in 4 days. Several responses suggest themselves, all some-what abrupt: First, the judgments of George Bush, Colin Powell, and Dick Cheney quoted previously in this work, all of which leave no doubt that in their view, at least, air power was the decisive force in the war. Second, the following questions: Where was there ever a decisive battle?

Where was the Iraqi Gettysburg? Or El Alamein? Or Kursk? And, had the coalition *lost* every ground action it fought, would Iraq have "won" the war?[12]

Many analysts have claimed that the Gulf war was won by employing the tenets of AirLand Battle, a reference to the doctrine espoused in the Army's FM 100-5 manual. They mistakenly credit the appearance of *elements* of AirLand Battle for the decisive application of the *entire* doctrine. In reality, the neutralizing of Iraqi ground opposition meant that AirLand Battle, with its notions of two well-led top-of-the-line forces maneuvering and fighting in accordance with broad strategic and tactical objectives, of attacking aggressively advancing robust and combative follow-on forces, and intense and bitterly contested air-armor duels, could not really occur. What the Army planned, however, was undeniably brilliant—a bold masterstroke of an assault that will be studied in military academies for generations. And those elements of AirLand Battle that could be applied—antiarmor helicopter operations, deep insertion of forces and striking into the enemy rear areas—proved sound. Army helicopter crews contributed significantly to the success of the air war, by attacking enemy forces, inserting troops, conducting special operations, and undertaking extensive supply operations. Indeed, both on the ground and in the air, the Army's logistics support effort was nothing short of incredible. However, the war did not—indeed could not—constitute AirLand Battle: paraphrasing General Bosquet at Balaclava, "C'est magnifique, mais ce n'est pas la guerre [aero-terrestre]."

The Gulf war was a case of conflict interruption: it takes two to fight, and in this case, the war was held, but the other side couldn't come— thanks to air power. When asked in early March 1991 why the war went as it did, Dick Cheney replied:

> The reason the . . . Iraqi forces collapsed as rapidly as they did, I think, was because of the campaign we mounted against them. This was a force that was very successful against Iran. A force that had fought an eight-year battle with Iran; it was well-equipped with Soviet equipment. It was not a backward force by any means. *It was crushed, I think, by the air campaign, and the way in which we went about the [air] campaign meant that when we finally did have to move our ground forces in, and we sort of kicked in the door, they collapsed fairly rapidly* [emphasis added].[13]

Asked again about this on the first anniversary of Saddam Hussein's invasion of Kuwait, Cheney responded even more bluntly: "They [the Iraqis] didn't fight back *because the air war turned out to be absolutely devastating*" (emphasis added).[14] Sporadic ground action did occur, in which American ground forces acquitted themselves courageously and professionally sometimes, sadly, at the cost of their lives; undoubtedly, had the full extent of AirLand Battle been required, the Army could have furnished it. But such was not the case. The ground war could not be decisive in the way that earlier ground wars had been.

Air power can hold territory by denying an enemy the ability to seize it, and by denying an enemy the use of his forces. And it can seize territory by controlling access to that territory and movement across it. It did both in the Gulf war. Further, air power has become pervasive, even for armies themselves: in the Gulf war, troops went into battle by air, were supplied and supported by air, and were defended and bolstered by air attacks against enemy formations. And that air power saved their lives: as Army Lt. Col. E. W. Chamberlain stated bluntly, surveying his unit's advance across the Euphrates Valley, "If we had not had the effectiveness of the air campaign, we'd have lost a lot of guys fighting our way into this valley. [The] Air Force did a hell of a job hitting the right targets on the ground."[15] Thanks to air, the ground "offensive" resembled less a *blitzkrieg* than the Oklahoma land rush. The results of this war can hold no comfort for armored vehicle advocates, for air attack rendered all categories of armored fighting vehicles superfluous—they were no protection to their occupants whatsoever, no matter how thick their armor. In sum, air power produces the conditions conducive to both defeat and victory—by destroying enemy points of resistance, communication, leadership, morale, and means of supply, among others. Put another way, presuming that, for the moment, air power did not exist in this century, and the coalition forces had gone to war against Iraq: would the rate of advance have been the same? Would the casualty rates have been the same? Would the degree of destruction of the Iraqi forces, the Iraqi infrastructure, and Iraq's command and control have been the same? The answer is clearly *no*.

There is likewise the matter of the three-dimensionality of modern war. Two-dimensional forces have to grapple with the traditional problems of surface maneuver—typified in this war by the "Hail Mary" ground operation, or the maneuvers of a fleet at sea. Air warfare turns a flank from above, unconstrained by terrain or natural barrier (in somewhat analogous fashion, submarines endanger naval surface forces from below, from their own 3-D striking environment). *Only air power, how-*

ever, can strike anywhere in the world, anytime, hitting multiple targets in a way that an army advancing along a front or a fleet steaming at sea cannot. And while it was true in previous conflicts that the partnership of air and surface action together ensured victory—for example, the best means of ensuring that interdiction really worked was by forcing an enemy into intensive ground warfare at the same time that the air campaign was hitting interdiction targets—such is not necessarily true today. The combination of *lethality* of modern air weapons, coupled with the *freedom of maneuver, range, precision,* and *sustainability* of air attack, has revolutionized war. As a result, the principal value of armies today is in occupying territory (when it is required); the value of navies is in controlling sea lanes and preserving coastal access. In the air power era, neither armies nor navies can be considered the *primary* instrument of securing victory in war.

Could carrier-based air power have done more than it did? As Air Force Chief of Staff Gen. Merrill A. McPeak stated after the war, naval aviation "made a tremendous contribution" to the Gulf war. "We were," he concluded, "delighted to have worked as a partner with them."[16] During the war, land- and sea-based air power forces worked well and harmoniously together. Navy P-3 Orions and Royal Air Force Nimrods watched the waters and enforced the embargo, Air Force and British tankers refueled Navy strike airplanes, Navy E-2C Hawkeyes assisted Air Force and Saudi AWACS aircraft in maintaining airspace management, Navy EA-6Bs worked well with EF-111s to target and defeat Iraqi air defense radars, and Navy planners participated in the Black Hole operation at Riyadh.

Unfortunately, some naval proponents charged after the war that naval aviation could have been used more significantly, but the CENTAF staff had been unwilling to do so. Others argued that naval aviation had performed spectacularly, but that better Air Force public relations had distorted the Navy's contribution. Both charges were untrue. The air campaign was structured on the basis of making the most effective use of force, regardless of its source; as one JFACC planner stated, "It's a war; we're not trying to make budget decisions, we're trying to defeat someone." Allegations of unfair news coverage denied reality, for, by quantitative measure of "spots," the media actually furnished far greater coverage of the Navy than any land-based air force. In the Black Hole in Riyadh, this earned CNN two nicknames: "Carrier News Network" and "Continuous Naval News."[17]

During the war, the Navy flew over 18,100 fixed-wing aircraft sorties from six carriers operating around the Arabian peninsula. Table 8.1 shows the mission percentages for the various kinds of sorties flown from these carriers.[18]

Carriers in Desert Storm had an average air wing strength of seventy-five airplanes. Depending on the makeup of the individual carrier air wing, these could include F-14s for fleet air defense and strike escort, F/A-18s for strike and strike escort, A-6s and A-7s for strike, KA-6 and KS-3 tankers, EA-6 and E-2 electronic warfare airplanes, SH-3 helicopters for search and rescue, S-3s for antisubmarine patrol and some strike missions, and C-2s for logistical support. The category of sorties most likely to hurt the Iraqi regime were what the Navy called "theater-strike" sorties. The average number of theater-strike sorties that a carrier launched in the war was only 18.82 per day—equivalent, say, to launching only one or up to two squadrons of Navy A-6Es.[19] This represented approximately 24 percent of a carrier's daily total of fixed-wing sorties. Throughout the war, the Navy's six carriers launched a grand total of 4,855 theater-strike sorties.

Since an aircraft carrier has to essentially bring its own mini–air force with it—as the above composition indicates, virtually every conceivable mission, from tanking to air transport to electronic warfare is included in a single carrier air wing—the amount of aircraft it has available for any *particular* mission is small. (The only way a carrier could deliver decisive striking power would be if it were much larger—an obvious impractical-

Table 8.1. Apportionment of Carrier-based Naval Aviation Sorties in the Gulf War

Mission Type	Percentage of Total Sorties Flown
Offensive counter air	8
Defensive counter air	20
Theater strike	27
Maritime strike	6
SEAD/electronic warfare	8
Aerial refueling	15
Combat support	9
General support	5
Miscellaneous	2

ity.) The overwhelming concern for the Navy—as for the Air Force—is maintaining control of the skies. Thus, fleet air defense predominates; for a carrier, that means launching fighters and E-2s, together with tanking support, for protection of the surface forces. On any particular day in the Gulf war, roughly 30 percent of a carrier's air operations were devoted strictly to fleet air defense duties, although in the more dangerous Persian Gulf this rose to 50 percent.[20] Because a carrier's hangar deck is small— even with the gargantuan fleet carriers of the present day—the need to have adequate fighters for fleet defense, large early warning aircraft, and tankers, means that the space available for "strikers" is strictly limited. Smaller numbers can be carried, which translates into fewer sorties per deck per day. For example, in the first two weeks of Desert Storm—arguably the most critical weeks of the war—the Navy's six carriers averaged only 10.87 theater-strike sorties per deck per day. Rounding this, and presuming that each airplane carried an average of four 2,000-pound bombs, means that each day, for the first two weeks, each carrier was only able to launch 44 tons of high explosives aimed at key targets in Iraq.[21]

With the preponderance of land bases, it made perfect sense that land-based air was the predominant force element. This was not a coastal conflict: carriers simply could not be positioned to perform to the same levels of "target servicing" that they had in Korea and Vietnam. Distance and the constricted waters of the Persian Gulf produced serious challenges, handicapping the Navy's response. The service rightly had a fear of operating carriers within the Persian Gulf, and although they did so briefly (at the mouth of the Gulf), their fears proved justified: two naval vessels—one an assault helicopter and V/STOL fighter carrier, the other a sophisticated AEGIS-class cruiser—were mined and seriously damaged.[22] Complicating this was the need for the Navy to devote so much of its attention to fleet air defense, and the limitations the service had in not being equipped to receive the daily ATO electronically, as could the land-based forces. As noted earlier, whereas the ATO could move from computer to computer for the coalition forces involved in the war, it had to go via S-3 courier from Riyadh to the fleet, and then be transmitted by an internal Navy communications system.[23]

After the war, Rear Adm. Riley D. Mixson, the commander of Carrier Group Two in the Red Sea during the Gulf war, addressed two serious problems that afflicted the Navy in the Gulf war—an inability to provide enough tanker resources to support strike operations, and a serious shortage of laser-guided bomb kits to convert "dumb" Mk-80 family bombs into smart weapons. Had Air Force tankers not been available, two-thirds of the Navy's strike sorties would have had to been canceled; in such a situation, he wrote, "the Navy is becoming hostage to Air Force land-based tanking for sustained power-projection warfare beyond 200 nautical miles from the battle force."[24] Worse, when the coalition went to war, the Navy lacked sufficient numbers of LGB kits to give their strike aircraft large-scale precision-strike capabilities, and lacked any sort of penetrating weapon like the I-2000 used by the Air Force. The Red Sea carrier group, he recollected, "started the war with only 112 Mk-82 500 lb. bomb kits, 124 Mk-83 1,000 lb. kits, and 258 Mk-84 2,000 lb. kits—and that was all we were going to get. The day the war ended I had 7 Mk-82 kits and 30 Mk-83 kits left."[25]

Such problems were not missed by naval aviators in the Gulf. One Hornet squadron's air crew recollected that they had watched smart-bomb strikes:

> with incredulous amazement at a capability that only a select few knew existed but all wished the Navy had possessed . . . The pilots outwardly applauded the Air Force for the overwhelming success of their missions and then retreated to the privacy of their own ready rooms, whispered, rolled their eyes in disbelief, and shrugged their shoulders as they measured the full impact of the rebroadcast that they had just witnessed. The priorities in naval aviation seemingly missed a generation of weapons' employment and development. The strike-fighter pilots realized, then, that they would fight the Gulf War with the tactics of the nineties, in a front-line aircraft procured during the eighties, utilizing air-to-ground weapons designed, in some cases, as long ago as the fifties.[26]

Captain Steven U. Ramsdell, a naval observer sent to the Gulf in the midst of the war, wrote a surprisingly frank and disturbing report based on numerous interviews of personnel involved in strike planning and campaign execution. While the Navy's air crews added luster to the service's traditional record of courage in war, he found the service itself lacked an appreciation for the *operational* level of warfare (as distinct from the tactical and strategic levels of war), which prevented the service from planning and waging an effective naval air campaign. "The Navy did not bring to Desert Storm any system for planning and directing air campaigns," he stated,

> because the Navy does not possess such a system. The Navy does not even possess a system to plan the integrated employment of aircraft from more than

a single carrier, let alone plan and execute an air campaign involving several carriers. After the first preplanned strikes, multiple carrier strikes were not attempted because they were too hard to organize given the pace of the war . . . Several senior officers expressed reservations about the Navy's involvement in an air campaign centrally directed by a Joint Force Air Component Commander (JFACC) . . . They were concerned that independent Navy operations were threatened by that participation because the carriers' missions were tasked by the JFACC using the Air Force Air Tasking Order (ATO) system. But the Navy has no alternative to the ATO system. Without it, the campaign would have been planned and directed manually. Sortie rates would have been far lower and strike deconfliction much less certain.[27]

To cope with the war's strike planning challenges, Navy planners prudently formed strike cells within each carrier, combining representation from the ship's staff, air wing, and ship's company, and markedly improving subsequent performance. The Navy's larger problem, however, was focus: senior staff had envisioned not a strategic air campaign against Iraq but, rather,

[a campaign] which would have begun by attacking air defenses along the coast and moved inland as the air defenses were "rolled back." Strategic targets such as the Iraqi nuclear, biological, and chemical forces, the central command and control facilities, Scud missiles, and so on would have waited until the campaign got to them . . . this conceptual approach was held consistently by numerous officers . . . The source of the trouble is that the concept of conducting campaigns and the process of implementing an approach to war in which tactical decisions are driven primarily by strategic objectives have not been within the field of view of our leaders in the fleet.[28]

In conclusion, he wrote:

Many of the senior officers I spoke to pointed out that Desert Storm was not well suited to carrier operations. In their view the CV's [carriers] are suited to one-time raids similar to the Libyan action of 1986, but not to sustained campaigning. This opinion is widely held in the fleet. It ignores the use of the carriers in both Korea and Vietnam and the fact that our huge investment in carriers cannot be justified by such limited usefulness. In fact, the implication of this attitude is that carriers are little more than political instruments, not real war fighters.[29]

During the Gulf war, the U.S. Navy—particularly its surface forces—did many things very well, and the problems that naval aviation encountered in the war should not diminish that perception of significant accomplishment. As the interim report of a study group from the Center for Strategic and International Studies stated, "The lessons derived from the war suggest neither that carrier aviation is perfect nor that it should be abandoned."[30] Nevertheless, as former Deputy Undersecretary of Defense Dov S. Zakheim has written, "Desert Storm did not directly demonstrate the centrality of naval aviation."[31]

Did Goldwater-Nichols make victory possible? Commentators have singled out the Goldwater-Nichols Defense Reorganization Act of 1986 for special mention as one of the key factors that made victory in the Gulf possible. Goldwater-Nichols was born of noble desires—to create a clear line of command and genuine "jointness" within the American military, ending the often frustrating and difficult task of dealing with multiple commands and command relationships, and to end the sometimes myopic tendency of the military services when selecting and developing new weapon systems. Culturally, it codified movements well underway within the military services after Desert One and Beirut. It gave theater commanders and other Cincs some authority—such as control over selection of subordinate commanders—that they had previously lacked. It had the practical effect of making the chairman of the Joint Chiefs of Staff the principal advisor to the secretary of defense—the senior military member of the national chain of command. No longer would the Joint Chiefs vote on matters during their meetings in the exclusive JCS conference room, the famed "Tank." Instead, they would offer advice to the chairman who, alone, would make the decisions—and their advice was no longer subject to the control of the civilian service secretaries. Gone was the climate of strained deference that led to a forced collegiality emphasizing not cutting any service's "pet rocks." Such reorganization had the effect of streamlining the chain of command. In retrospect, the lesson of what happens when there is no clearcut chain of command—for example, Desert One, or, later, Beirut—offers a strong argument for the kind of changes that Goldwater-Nichols sought. Implementation began under JCS chairman Adm. William Crowe, but it was Gen. Colin Powell who greatly accelerated and expanded the process after he succeeded Crowe as chairman.

Though Goldwater-Nichols undoubtedly changed the defense process within the Pentagon, any beneficial impact it may have had upon Desert Storm is much more difficult to discern. Instances where planners or other officials might have consulted it before undertaking some critical action are difficult to imagine. In his exercise of command, Schwarzkopf acted no differently than many theater commanders before him in the pre–Goldwater-Nichols era. Indeed, his behavior, authority, and relationship with subordinate organizations and individuals recalled Dwight Eisenhower or Douglas MacArthur in 1943–45. His trusting relationship with Horner echoed MacArthur's with George Kenney in the Pacific, or Eisenhower and Tedder in Europe. For his part, Horner, as JFACC, acted little differently from the various joint force air commanders in the Solomons campaign during World War II. Certainly, Goldwater-Nichols made no impact on the technology, force structure, or operating doctrines employed in the Gulf war. All the systems that performed so well in the war—the F-117, Abrams tank, Patriot, and the cruise missile, for example—were conceived, developed, and fielded in the pre–Goldwater-Nichols era. Likewise, the doctrines under which American forces fought in the Gulf were products of the pre–Goldwater-Nichols period. Undoubtedly, command in the Gulf war worked better than in, say, Vietnam—but one cannot say (in post hoc, ergo propter hoc fashion) that since this war was fought *after* Goldwater-Nichols, it was a success *because of* Goldwater-Nichols. Rather, it was a success—as is every successful war—because common sense governed the relationships among key players of all services.

In reflecting upon what Goldwater-Nichols meant to Desert Storm, some held that the act eliminated the necessity of assigning tasks for parochial reasons.[32] In fact, throughout Desert Storm, "fair sharing" of roles among the services in the interest of "jointness" continually came up—whether it be diversion of Air Force tankers to assist Navy strike sorties (at the dilution of the land-based air effort) or in initial desires for a nonstrategic air campaign exclusively structured "in support of" the ground forces. (True jointness, of course, is the use of the *most effective* force—regardless of source—for each situation.) Such a tendency raises a caution for the future, as does the remarkable sweep of powers embodied in the chairman of the Joint Chiefs of Staff. As a result of Goldwater-Nichols, the chairman wields extraordinary autonomous authority. It is, as Prof. Eliot A. Cohen has noted, unsettling to imagine a George McClellan with the same powers the chairman commanded in the Gulf war.[33] Their abuse could easily lead to a situation in which a future chairman did not effectively make use of the military forces available to him. On the enduring value and merit of Goldwater-Nichols, one must reluctantly conclude that the jury is still out.

The View from the Kremlin

In the weeks after the Gulf war, some of the most perceptive analytical commentary came from individuals who, under different and far more unpleasant circumstances, may have been unwilling recipients of American military attention—the Soviet military.[34] This commentary took on even greater significance several months later, after the failed hard-line attempt to overthrow Gorbachev, the subsequent removal of Defense Minister Marshal Dmitriy Yazov for his part in the coup, his replacement in the immediate wake of the coup attempt by Gen. Mikhail Moiseyev, and Moiseyev's virtually immediate discrediting and replacement by Air Force chief Col. Gen. (subsequently Marshal) Yevgeniy Shaposhnikov.

In previous wars—such as the Arab-Israeli conflicts, and, notably, after the Bekaa Valley fighting—there were strident claims that Soviet systems had performed well or even brilliantly against the technology of the West. Such claims were notably lacking after the Gulf war. *Krasnaya Zvesda* (Red Star), the house organ of the Soviet Ministry of Defense, the government paper *Izvestiya* (News), and the Communist Party paper *Pravda* (Truth) ran a series of articles over several weeks that took an ever-increasing pessimistic tone. Early claims that the coalition's successes stemmed in large measure from deficiencies in Iraqi training and organization were replaced by thoughtful examinations of the implications of the Gulf war to future conflict.

The evolution of Soviet thought regarding the Gulf can be traced with examples drawn roughly at one-month intervals from the Soviet media. Lieutenant General V. Gorbachev, faculty chief at the Voroshilov General Staff Academy, wrote bluntly less than a week into the war that "the outcome of the war has been determined by the fact that the coalition forces seized the initiative and won air superiority from the outset. Hussein has lost his chance."[35] Colonel Aleksandr Tsalko, a defense reformist Soviet Army officer who also served as a deputy to the Supreme Soviet of the USSR, noted that the "crushing" defeat of the Iraqi army called into question the doctrine of the Soviet army. After the Gulf war, the notion of seeking to achieve victory through the clashing of large-scale ground forces was, Taslko stated, "sheer madness."[36]

Subsequently, in an influential interview, General-Lieutenant of Aviation Anatoliy Malyukov stated that "the war in the Persian Gulf provided a textbook example of what air supremacy means both for the country that gained it, and for the country ceding it." Further, in response to a question of whether the war constituted an application of the U.S. Army's AirLand Battle doctrine, he went on,

> I think not. Classic "AirLand Battle" it wasn't. Why? The fact is that from this war's very beginning—and here we are forced to remember [Air Force General Michael] Dugan—evidently it was planned as an air war, in order to exhaust the enemy by means of air strikes, to disorganize the control system, to destroy the air defense system, to weaken the striking power of the ground forces. One may sooner speak of classical—according to target selection—air offensive operations. These aims were achieved. On the whole, this was the first time we saw a war like this, in which aviation practically bore by itself all fundamental missions.[37]

Commentator Gennadiy Vasilyev addressed more technical issues a month later when he stated:

> The Gulf war was a triumph for state-of-the-art weapons packed with electronics, such as the "all-seeing bombs" and the Patriot missile interceptors. At the same time, it called the effectiveness of tanks into question, particularly in the situation in which the Iraqi armored troops found themselves—deprived of air cover or intelligence data from space.[38]

All of these conclusions were, of course, correct. Their implications were profound, for, to varying degrees, these articles implied that Soviet weapons development had resulted in weapons that were not adequate to meet the real needs of modern combat—precisely the same charge that American defense critics had been making for years about the U.S. weapons that had destroyed Iraq's military machine! When the war began, Chief of the General Staff Moiseyev created an operations group to assess the Gulf war and its implications; Defense Minister Yazov subsequently announced a conference to examine the war and its implications, admitting (with notable understatement) that the war "requires a review of attitudes toward both tactical air defense and the country's air defense network. I think we have weak points in our air defense. They need to be examined."[39]

Ominously, Defense Minister Yazov stated in a speech in late March that the Gulf war warned of "the danger of complacency and abstract pacifism," a pointed reference to the growing ties between the United States and the Gorbachev regime; for his part, Moiseyev raised the spectre of a reinvigorated NATO confronting an ally-less Soviet Union, and the former Warsaw Pact chief of staff, Gen. Vladimir Lobov, asserted that the Gulf war had acted as a huge operational test and evaluation exercise, the results of which would pose even greater danger for the Soviet Union.[40] It may never be known precisely what role the coalition's victory in Desert Storm played in stimulating the lashing-out of hard-line fervor that manifested itself in the abortive coup against Gorbachev, but there can be little question that it did play a role. Air Vice Marshal R. A. "Tony" Mason, RAF (ret.), during a June visit to the Soviet Union, found that "resentment at the overwhelming allied success was frequently ill-concealed."[41] In the coup that followed, the mass of the Soviet military threw in their lot with the citizens of Moscow. The reform-minded air force chief, Shaposhnikov, even contemplated bombing the coup leaders in the Kremlin into submission, although he himself would be in the building: "The bombers will fly," he said, "and nothing will be left of us."[42] Fortunately, it did not come to that, and the coup collapsed. The future of what was once the Soviet Union is uncertain, but the changes that have occurred to date can be seen only as most encouraging.

Toward the Future

Writing in 1945, the noted British military analyst Maj. Gen. J. F. C. Fuller stated that "the barbarism of any period pales before the barbarism of today . . . From the javelin and the arrow to the Superfortress and the rocket-bomb, the very power to destroy, first slowly and then at terrific speed, has intoxicated man."[43] As a means of illustrating his dismal point, he compared the destruction of Madgeburg during the Thirty Years War, and the subsequent massacre of its 30,000 inhabitants, with the destruction of Hamburg in 1943 by RAF Bomber Command.[44] In the years after the Second World War, it was the images of bombed cities that haunted air power—the postwar photographs of Berlin and Tokyo rubble, the blasted ruin of Hiroshima and Nagasaki. It had taken the massive application of destructive force with unprecedented ferocity to eliminate the military strength of Nazi Germany and Imperial Japan, at a cost of hundreds of thousands of civilian lives. It was the anticipation of even greater levels of destruction by atomic and nuclear bombing that compelled the disarmament movement from the 1950s through the 1980s. But the reality was vastly different. At the end of the Gulf war, the ability of Iraq to threaten its neighbors was no less incapacitated than that of Japan and Germany in 1945, but Baghdad was intact. Its civilian population was virtually untouched directly by the war. Humane values had, in fact, prevailed.

What made this possible, ironically, were changes in the general attributes of weaponry, characteristics first alluded to by Fuller himself in 1945: *range of action, striking power, accuracy of aim, volume of fire, and portability.*[45] Indeed, one of them—the revolution in precision, Fuller's "accuracy of aim," per se—made the Gulf war more humane than previous conflicts and has, in fact, made up for the notable lack of success in trying to regulate air power employment in warfare via international agreement.[46] In 1943, after a raid on Pilsen, Bomber Command planners were delighted to find that 95 percent of the bombs had hit within three miles of the aiming point.[47] In 1991, approximately 85 percent of smart bombs hit within 10 feet of their aiming points. The difference is the difference between the axe and the scalpel. Fuller perceived that throughout military history these five values had led to ever more deadly and effective weapons, and that of the five, the dominant characteristic—"the characteristic which dominates the fight"—was range. "The weapon of superior reach or range," Fuller perceptively wrote, "should be looked upon as the fulcrum of combined tactics. Thus, should a group of fighters be armed with bows, spears and swords, it is around the arrow that tactics should be shaped; if with cannon, muskets and pikes, then around the cannon; and if with aircraft, artillery and rifles, then around the airplane."[48]

Experience has proven the validity of Fuller's perceptions. Today, air power is the dominant form of military power. Does this mean that all future wars will be won solely by air power? Not at all. But what it does mean is that air power has clearly proven its ability not merely to be *decisive* in war—after all, it had demonstrated decisiveness in the Second World War and, to a degree, as early as the First World War—but to be the *determinant of victory* in war.

The success of the Gulf air campaign has generated greater appreciation for "simultaneity" rather than "sequentiality" in striking at strategic targets, or what Col. John A. Warden III has subsequently called "Parallel Warfare." Indeed, this was one of the first lessons that Soviet observers drew from studying the results of the war.[49] Further, modern air power is so versatile that the traditional distinction between "strategic" and "tactical" air warfare has been permanently blurred; as a result, in September 1991, Air Force Secretary Donald B. Rice and Chief of Staff Gen. Merrill A. McPeak announced the restructuring of operational air commands into an *Air Combat Command* (consisting of fighters, bombers, recce aircraft, C³ platforms, some airlifters and tankers, and intercontinental ballistic missiles) and an *Air Mobility Command* (consisting of the majority of airlift and tanker assets). Both represent responses to the unpredictable national security environment, and the increasingly CONUS (Continental United States)-based nature of military forces. Air Combat Command affords the Air Force a means of furnishing integrated employment of air power, acting as an independent force provider to joint commander-in-chiefs in some contingencies, and as a force augmenter for forward-deployed theater air forces in others. Air Mobility Command's integration of lift and tanker assets enhances rapid response and the Air Force's ability to operate with other services and nations better enables the Air Force to supply global mobility and reach.[50]

But if the future of long-range land-based air power was bright in the wake of Desert Storm, that of sea-based power was much less so. Much of the debate about how well naval aviation functioned in the war really centered on a larger and more explosive issue: how effectively do carriers project power? The Gulf war results, unfortunately, suggested that the answer was "not very well." In response, naval proponents argued marginal issues, such as claiming that carriers exert visible "presence" that land-based air power does not, ignoring that carriers typically operate miles off hostile shores, far from prying eyes. They did not address the carrier's serious limitations—a small number of strike airplanes, marginal resources for conducting sustained operations, the tremendous built-in cost of an entire carrier battlegroup needed to support the operations of only a few aircraft, the serious dependency that carrier aircraft have upon land-based aerial tankers, and the often-ignored great dependency of carrier battlegroups upon foreign bases. Above all, they did not address the central issue—that while the carrier has always been an important element of *sea control,* it has been far less successful as an element of *long-range power projection.* One naval enthusiast could only state lamely that "sea power tends to act invisibly but powerfully," to which land-based air power supporters could respond, "Yes, but land-based air power can act both visibly and invisibly, and always *very* powerfully."[51]

The war illustrated that the time is long overdue to reassess the role of the aircraft carrier in long-range strikes against deeply located land targets, and to rethink to what degree large, expensive, and manpower-intensive carrier battle groups are needed. Finally, there are two revolutions that must be embraced if carrier-based naval aviation is to continue to have a viable future: those of precision weapons, and stealth. It is ironic, because the Navy contributed greatly to the former, which is also the most easily remedied. But the stealth revolution is one that so far has passed the Navy by. Its initial participation—with the A-12 program— ended when Secretary of Defense Dick Cheney canceled the A-12 in early 1991 because of basic unsuitabilities. The continuing viability and need for naval aviation will depend on how well the Navy assesses its future in warfare, and pursues both precision weapons and the A-12's successor.

There are several inferences and speculations one can draw from the use of air power in the Gulf. First, so precisely destructive is modern air attack that one can achieve selective nuclear effects by conventional attack. For example, Iraq's hardened command, communications, and control nodes were precisely destroyed by small tonnages of smart bombs, achieving the same effects that might have been achieved only with nuclear weapons that would have also killed thousands (or more) of civilians. Aircraft shelters designed to withstand nuclear blast overpressures succumbed to smart bombs that lanced them and blew them up from within. And no matter how deep one went, smart-bomb technology— typified by the "design to mission" GBU-28—literally could follow. One implication is that, in the future, the atomic and nuclear weapon will increasingly be seen as the weapon of the barbarian. Nations that have them will be under a moral compulsion to remove them from their inventories, and nations that desire them will be diligently monitored by the world community—the reinvigorated post–Cold War United Nations. The experience of Iraq—which maintained a vigorous and dynamic atomic weapons research program under conditions of secrecy many thought impossible prior to the war—is a most sobering and instructive one, and hopefully will stimulate far closer scrutiny of similar rogue states in the future.

Another implication is that no society, no matter how developed, is immune from the kind of destruction that afflicted Iraq once it lost control of the skies, and attack aircraft carrying precision weapons were free to hammer it. If Washington, D.C., were subjected to the very same attacks that hit Iraq in the first 24 hours of the air campaign, the equivalent damage would have been the destruction of the White House; the Pentagon; the Capitol; the Blair House (part of the White House Complex); the Executive Office Building; FBI Headquarters; CIA Headquarters; Defense Intelligence Agency Headquarters; National Security Agency Headquarters; Bolling and Andrews air force bases; the Navy Yard and Navy Annex; the Naval Air Test Center at Patuxent River, Maryland; the Federal Communications Center; forts Belvior, McNair, Myer, and Meade; Camp David; Quantico Marine Corps base; Suitland Federal Center; Sprint, MCI, and AT&T regional centers; and all significant power plants and fuel storage facilities. One postwar analysis indicated that *every* developed nation has within it a remarkably similar number of key targets (about 500) and aiming points (about 3,000). The concentration of these targets is such as to render these nations vulnerable to the same paralytic destruction that visited Iraq. But even the United States is not immune to some serious aspects of this—imagine, for example, the near-simultaneous severing of all major bridges in the United States, and the impact it would have upon national transportation: recovery would take literally years. Such is the power of modern precision conventional air attack.[52]

Blending the Gulf war experience, previous military history, and the collapse of the Soviet Union offers another intriguing prospect. Simply put, the United States is the last remaining superpower. (As one NSC staffer put it, "When some nation dials 911, guess whose phone rings?") Other nations may have economic advantages, but the measure of international power is still the ability to project force. When the Gulf states needed assistance, for example, they did not turn to Germany and Japan, however financially powerful these two countries were: they turned to the United States, which subsequently employed roughly 35 percent of its military power to resolve the crisis. As dominant land power characterized a *Pax Romana,* and dominant sea power a *Pax Britannica,* dominant air power is the characteristic of modern America. This does not imply, as some would fear, a mindless policy of global interventionism, nor does it imply a millennium of untroubled peace. But it does imply that, for the future, conflicts around the world will be small ones, and aggressors who dare to threaten the vital interests of the United States and its friends will risk their own destruction amid a hurricane of air attack. It is entirely fitting that this century, which began with epochal flights by two American brothers that transformed the world, closes with the United States the projector of global air power.

Today the fighters and bombers are home, the ejection seats are safed, the wheels are chocked, the weapons are back in storage. In the Gulf, the skies are clear of MiGs, flak, and SAMs, the detritus of war is slowly being cleared from the desert floor, Kuwaiti wells no longer belch flame and toxic gas, and the Gulf itself is slowly recovering. The only flying now is that for training and vigilance, the ever-present "ready for next time" one prays won't come. Those charged with responsibility for maintaining the watch take comfort in the confidence and experience they acquired in the Gulf war, in the confirmation of expectations that it offered. For, in truth, the outcome of the Gulf war held little surprise for airmen. Conditioned by 75 years of previous air power history, they knew what to expect. Indeed, it was intuitively obvious. What was surprising was the degree to which people who *should* have known better *were* surprised. But after all, as one sage has written, history is "mainly a matter of people rediscovering the obvious by tripping over it."[53]

Abbreviations

ABM	Antiballistic missile
AFB	Air Force Base
AFV	Armored fighting vehicle
ALARM	Air-launched antiradar missile
ALCM	Air-launched cruise missile
ALFA	AirLand Forces Application
APC	Armored personnel carrier
ATACMS	Army Tactical Missile System
ATBM	Antitactical ballistic missile
ATO	Air Tasking Order
AWACS	Airborne Warning and Control System
BAI	Battlefield air interdiction
CAS	Close air support
DARPA	Defense Advanced Research Projects Agency
DoD	Department of Defense
ECM	Electronic countermeasures
FAC	Forward air controller
FLIR	Forward-looking infrared

FOFA	Follow-on Forces Attack
GCC	Gulf Cooperation Council
GLCM	Ground-launched cruise missile
GPS	Global Positioning System
HARM	High-speed antiradiation missile
HOTAS	Hands on throttle and stick
HUD	Heads-up display
ICBM	Intercontinental ballistic missile
IFF	Identification Friend or Foe
IIR	Imaging infrared system
IQAF	Iraqi Air Force
JAAT	Joint air attack team operations
JCS	Joint Chiefs of Staff
JSTARS	Joint Surveillance Target Attack Radar System
LANTIRN	Low Altitude Navigation and Targeting Infrared for Night
LGB	Laser-guided bomb
MAC	Military Airlift Command
MLRS	Multiple Launch Rocket System
NASA	National Aeronautics and Space Administration
NATO	North Atlantic Treaty Organization
NSC	National Security Council
PGM	Precision-guided munition
RAF	Royal Air Force
RCS	Radar cross section
SAC	Strategic Air Command
SAM	Surface-to-air missile
SAR	Search-and-rescue
SDI	Strategic Defense Initiative
SLAM	Standoff land attack missile
SOF	Special operations forces
SPO	System Program Office
TAC	Tactical Air Command
TEL	Transporter-erector-launcher
TERCOM	Terrain contour matching
TLAM	Tomahawk land attack missile
TOW	Tube-launched, optically tracked, wire-guided
TRADOC	Training and Doctrine Command
TRAM	Target Recognition Attack Multisensor

TVM	Track via missile
UAV	Unmanned air vehicles
UN	United Nations
USAAF	U.S. Army Air Forces
USAF	U.S. Air Force
USARCENT	U.S. Army Forces Central Command
USCENTAF	U.S. Central Command Air Forces
USCENTCOM	U.S. Central Command
USSR	Union of Soviet Socialist Republics
V/STOL	Vertical and short takeoff and landing

Defense Technologies of the Post-Vietnam Era: A Selective Perspective

In our days wars are not won by mere

enthusiasm, but by technical superiority.

Vladimir I. Lenin (1918)

Lenin's statement implicitly recognizes that while it is true that leadership, training, motivation, and doctrine are generally more significant to the functioning of a military force than the quality of the weapons it possesses, it is nevertheless important to note that few good armies equipped with inferior weapons do very well. (Witness, for example, the Polish cavalry versus Nazi tanks in 1939, or the United States in the Philippines in 1941–42.) One of the major reasons that American and NATO service chiefs in the 1980s could confront with greater confidence a Warsaw Pact threat—one that a mere decade before had their predecessors privately fearing NATO could not survive—was because profound advances in aerospace technology had generated new weapons and systems offsetting the numerically superior Warsaw Pact forces. Further, as the 1980s progressed, results from both test centers and conflicts around the world offered solid evidence that this new technology worked very well indeed, an ominous portent for the Pact and other Soviet-style forces. The air warfare technology used in the Gulf war ranged from aircraft to sophisticated missiles and bombs, from the radical to the mundane, and it enabled fulfillment of all the traditional missions of air warfare, and a few new ones as well, including: air superiority; battlefield air support; long-range strike (including strikes by cruise missiles); heavy bombardment; air defense; airlift, search and rescue, and special operations; reconnaissance and battlefield observation (including observation by drone aircraft); electronic warfare; airborne command and control; aerial tanking; and antishipping and maritime patrol. One could write separate volumes on each of these topics. Therefore, the following appendices should be considered but a selective introduction to some of the ones the author believes were the most significant and innovative.

They offer just a glimpse at some of the relevant technologies and systems developed in the 1970s and 1980s and then utilized against Saddam Hussein's aggression. Many others existed, some quite sensitive, and others that merely fell beyond the scope and intent of this work. It was fashionable after Vietnam to decry reliance on high technology to solve problems and confront challenges, for it was perceived to have "failed" in Vietnam. Faith in it was held to be peculiarly "American," and to some—such as social commentators Lewis Mumford, Herbert Marcuse, and Jacques Ellul—inherently arrogant, bad, or even evil.[1] And if these were the most strident of technology's critics, there were others, such as E. F. Schumacher, who argued with only a little more moderation for a return to "appropriate" technology, a vision encapsulated in the touchingly naive expression, "Small Is Beautiful."[2]

There certainly were problems enough with technology in the 1980s. As the tragic loss of the space shuttle *Challenger,* the horrible accident at Chernobyl, and the grounding of the *Exxon Valdez* clearly showed, technology is never forgiving of weakness, miscalculation, and bad decision-making. But it has its place, and it is well again to reflect on the truth of Lenin's statement, uttered at the end of the first great mechanized war at the beginning of the twentieth century. At the beginning of the last decade of that century, during his State of the Union address on January 29, 1991, Pres. George Bush offered his own perspective on technology, even as combat still raged in the Gulf. "The quality of American technology," he said, "thanks to the American worker, has enabled us to deal successfully with difficult military conditions and help minimize precious loss of life. We have given our men and women the very best. And they deserve it."

Appendix A **Air Superiority Technology**

The design of fighter aircraft traditionally has been the form of aerospace technology where the latest state-of-the-art reigns supreme. Two fighter-pilot adages say it all: "A second-best fighter is like a second-best hand in poker," and "When you lose air superiority, you *lose*." In "leader-follower" fashion, technology first used on high-performance fighters is then passed down to bombers, and on to transports, and eventually into the commercial sector. (Examples from the past would be the turbojet engine and the sweptwing, and, from the present, the transfer of computer-dependent electronic "fly by wire" flight control systems from fighters to bombers and now to air transports and airliners.) Some of this has been noted previously, but the relationship of advances in technology, coupled with notions of combat employment, needs to be explored so as to present the context in which air superiority operations occurred in the Gulf air war, particularly fighter-related aerospace technology and the advent of energy maneuverability theory.

Electronic Advances in Radars and Flight Controls

A number of changes in technology encouraged the development of advanced fighter aircraft. Among these were the increasing power and sophistication of airborne radars (thanks to the microminiaturization revolution), the development of stability augmentation systems that promised to make high-performance aircraft more controllable and predictable, and major advances in turbojet engine design. These synergistically led to fighters that had remarkably different—and safer—handling qualities than their predecessors: virtually none of the fighters developed prior to the F-14 could ever get through the flight test process today without undergoing drastic improvement to their handling qualities, including such "greats" as the P-51, F-86, and F-4. Radar advances promised such features as multiple target track-while-scan, and look-down, shoot-down. (As early as 1964, the YF-12A Blackbird experimental interceptor demonstrated the latter, undertaking successful head-on look-down shoot-downs of drone JQB-47 bombers; on one, the YF-12A, cruising above 80,000 feet at Mach 3.2, blasted a Stratojet flying at 1,500 feet 120 miles away with a single XAIM-47 missile, the immediate predecessor of the Navy's AIM-54 Phoenix. The two planes had a combined closure of Mach 4.)[1]

Increasing sophistication of stability augmentation systems and the advent of the small digital airborne computer (a spinoff from the space program) promised to make possible the era of the "electric airplane." A flight control system could be "fly-by-wire," ensuring quicker control response, greater redundancy and tolerance to battle damage (a problem with aircraft having conventional hydraulic control systems, which would "bleed" when hit). Further, if a computer could take over the moment-to-moment monitoring and maintaining of an aircraft's attitude, then planes could be designed to be deliberately unstable, further enhancing their agility and maneuverability. Enhanced cockpit and instrumentation design promised to revolutionize the way a pilot flew a plane; no longer would he have to scan back and forth from the instrument panel to the outside, changing concentration and focus. Now, technology could give him the ability to control an airplane without removing his hands from the throttle and stick, and could furnish him with all the information he needed to do his job in combat by presenting it on a sophisticated electro-optical "heads-up display" (HUD). The emergence of the lightweight afterburning turbofan jet engine, coupled with refined aircraft design (a product of ever-increasing ground test capabilities, particularly wind-tunnel prediction techniques) promised to generate combat thrust-to-weight ratios for advanced fighters in excess of 1. This meant, essentially, that new fighters could accelerate straight up, and transition quickly from high- to low-energy states and back again, making energy maneuverability a reality.

Engine Technology

By the late 1960s, a technology base existed in materials and fabrication processes to produce smaller and lighter jet engines having thrust-to-weight ratios on the order of 10 to 1, as compared to the "normal" 4 to 1 standard of engines then in service. These powerful new engines, typified by the Pratt & Whitney F100, which powered both the F-15 and F-16, and the General Electric F404, which powered the F/A-18, were "pulled" along in their development by the need for new high-performance fighters. The F100, for example, existed only because of the F-X (F-15) program. Developing it was not easy; one engineer referred to the F100 effort as "a constant struggle of man against nature."[2] One caught fire and disintegrated during testing at the Arnold Engine Development Center, seriously damaging its test cell, due to a rubbing problem between components. Then early production engines exhibited serious stall stagnation difficulties. Eventually, with rigorous management, thorough testing, and insightful fixes, such problems were worked out.[3] To keep proper perspective, however, it is important to note that such difficulties were well within the historical experience of jet engine design. For example, in the 1940s, the General Electric J33 and Allison J35 experienced numerous teething troubles, as did the General Electric J79 and Westinghouse J46 of the 1950s, and the TF30 of the 1960s. But, with the exception of the truly appalling J46, all were refined into reliable power plants that exhibited standards by which other engines were measured. Not for nothing have engines traditionally been considered the "long pole in the tent" of fighter development, although that dubious distinction increasingly belongs now to avionics. As aerospace manager, analyst, and executive Norman R. Augustine has stated, in reference to many of the systems that worked well in the Gulf but which were characterized by occasionally difficult development,

> "Tough it Out . . . It is difficult to do things that have never been done before—that is what research and development is all about. Sometimes almost

as much perseverance is required in the laboratory as on the battlefield. Military R & D [research and development], like war, is not for the faint of heart."[4]

Energy Maneuverability and Its Design Impact

Two obvious and simplistic means of placing the advanced fighter aircraft of the 1970s and 1980s in relation to their predecessors and contemporaries involve comparing thrust-to-weight ratios and wing loadings. Thrust-to-weight ratios nearing or in excess of 1 ("unity") clearly indicate an aircraft's ability to take advantage of energy maneuverability, and a wing loading as low as possible, consistent with strength requirements, is highly desirable for maneuvering. A combined high thrust-to-weight ratio and reasonably low wing loading offers one measure of good fighter design (see Appendix Table 1).[5] However, a more significant measure of relative fighter performance is that of *energy maneuverability*.

The energy maneuverability concept is inextricably linked to Maj. (later Col.) John Boyd, a graduate engineer, fighter pilot, and fighter tac-

Appendix Table 1.   Historical Trends in Fighter Thrust-to-Weight Ratios and Wing Loading

Aircraft Type	Thrust/Weight Ratio	Wing Loading (lbs./sq. ft.)
F-86F	0.39	48.5
MiG-15bis	0.54	49.6
MiG-17F	0.63	48.4
F-100D	0.57	77.2
MiG-19S	0.85	62.3
Mirage IIIC	0.46	79.3
MiG-21MF	0.80	73.0
F-4E	0.61	109.4
MiG-23MF	0.66	95.0
Mirage F-1	0.66	89.3
F-14A	0.73	101.4
F-15A	1.07	73.1
F-16A	1.04	75.9
F/A-18A	0.88	90.4

tics instructor, although some aspects of it—for example, trading air-speed for altitude and vice versa—had been around since the Western Front of World War I. Boyd looked to tradeoffs of speed, thrust, weight, and drag loadings to achieve enhanced maneuverability, in which the critical parameter was specific excess power. High specific excess power could give a fighter the ability to outzoom and outmaneuver a heavier, less energy-efficient opponent.[6] Since the speed of an aircraft generates kinetic energy, and since an aircraft using gravity to assist it in diving (thereby gaining increased kinetic energy) benefits from operating at a great height, altitude can be considered a measure of potential energy. Thus, the combination of speed and altitude can indicate the total energy state of an aircraft at any particular moment in flight.[7] Thrust increases energy state and drag decreases it; the rate of change in energy state is termed *specific excess power* (P_s). Under flying conditions where $P_s = 0$, (the so-called "limiting curve"), the high-thrust-to-weight fighters of the 1970s—particularly the F-15 and F-16—had an ability to attain and hold higher sustained g turns than their predecessors.

The first indications that a revolutionary discontinuity had arrived in fighter development came with the initial flight tests of the F-15 and F-16, which established standards for agility, maneuverability, power, and control that had simply not existed with previous airplanes. The development of the heads-up display meant that a pilot was now free to engage the enemy without having to look back and forth between the outside "arena" and the cockpit (thus improving his critical situational awareness), and the grouping of essential controls on the traditional stick and throttle meant that a pilot could fly and fight HOTAS (hands-on-throttle-and-stick), using basically two controls: the stick (for pitch rate and roll rate, with other controls governing radar operation, weapons selection, and weapons firing) and the throttle (for acceleration and deceleration, the latter aided by having the aerodynamic speed brake control also on the throttle). So laden with controls have sticks become that, indeed, they often resemble some sort of bizarre saxophone. But their principle use remains flight-path control. By pulling back or pushing on the stick, a fighter pilot controlled pitch rate in order to hold or change angle of attack (AOA) and thus establish a certain desired turn rate. He moved the stick from side to side to control roll rate in order to hold or change bank angle and thus change the plane of maneuver. Finally, he moved a throttle forward or backward to hold or change a certain amount of thrust, and thereby add or subtract acceleration; by deploying a speed brake, he could decelerate even more quickly. The combination of maneuverability (the ability to change speed and the direction of flight path) and controllability (the ability to change aircraft attitude and thrust) produced agility.[8]

The Quest for Agility

Agility is of vital importance in dogfighting: being able to move out of opponents' weapons envelopes and moving them into yours. If a fighter (say, an F-16) encountered multiple "bogies" (for example, two MiG-23s), the ability to point the aircraft quickly, continue to point, and accelerate quickly could enable its pilot to position himself for a quick kill against one opponent while denying that opponent the opportunity to launch against him, and then offer the opportunity to engage and kill the second MiG, or disengage to "extend" and regain speed for maneuver, or to pursue fleeing targets. Critical to doing this was the ability for a fighter to attain high angles of attack ("High AOA," or "High Alpha"), for high AOA could give a fighter a better chance to take a "snap shot" at an enemy fighter, reverse a turn to point at an enemy, achieve better positioning for a missile or gun shot at an opponent, or undertake a defensive maneuver such as a high AOA barrel roll that could force an enemy to overshoot. Unlike the Century series, the new super-fighters had superlative high AOA performance, although achieving this required careful tailoring of their configurations and control systems, coupled with extensive and sometimes hazardous flight testing at Edwards and "Pax River." So significant were these new changes in air superiority aircraft that they gave rise to a special field of study called "agility metrics," the effort to find both qualitative and quantifiable "measures of merit" that could be used for the design of subsequent fighters.[9]

Early in their flight tests and service life, all of the new fighters—the F-14, F-15, F-16, and F/A-18—demonstrated their mastery over less-capable opponents in mock air combats. The F-4, for example, was an easy "kill," and smaller, more agile opponents (such as the A-4—a MiG-17 surrogate—and the F-5, which played MiG-21) fared only somewhat better. Given the new air-to-air missiles they would fire, their new and more sophisticated radars, the linkage with airborne warning and control aircraft, and such niceties as much better visibility than previous fighters, the new super-fighters promised to be devastatingly effective in combat.

That promise was hinted at over the Gulf of Sidra in 1981; demonstrated incompletely in two small air wars in 1982 (the Falklands war and fighting over the Bekaa Valley in Lebanon) and over Libya in 1986; and confirmed by the Gulf war of 1991.

Battlefield Attack Technology

One of the major advances in air warfare since 1945 has been the remarkable improvement in bombing precision. Since World War II, the accuracy of bombing has increased phenomenally, even when using "dumb" bombs, thanks to improved navigation technologies, better aerodynamic design of the bombs themselves, improved weapons-release computing systems, and improved cockpit displays. The number of bombs required to hit a target is a function of the average bomb miss distance (termed the CEP, for "Circular Error Probable"), target size, and weapon effectiveness. The CEP is the radial distance from a target inscribing an imaginary circle with an area large enough so that 50 percent of the bombs dropped will fall within it. The improvement in bombing accuracy can be illustrated by looking at a single case—trying to hit (with a hit probability of 90 percent) a target measuring 60 by 100 feet, using 2,000-pound *unguided* bombs from medium altitudes. Appendix Table 2 presents by war the number of unguided bombs needed (and the average CEP) required to destroy that target.[1]

Thus, on the eve of the Gulf war, small formations of strike aircraft

Appendix Table 2. Historical Trends in Bombing Accuracy

War	Number of Bombs	Number of Aircraft	CEP (in feet)
World War II	9,070	3,024	3,300
Korean War	1,100	550	1,000
Vietnam War	176	44	400
Fall 1990	30	8	200

Note: Conditions: Dropping 2,000-pound unguided bombs against a 60 × 100-foot target.

could achieve the same destructive results with unguided bombs that had taken hundreds and even thousands of aircraft in World War II. (Guided bombs had even greater accuracies, demonstrating CEPs within six feet during the Linebacker campaign; in both Vietnam and Desert Storm, it was usually a case of "one target, one smart bomb.") This accuracy, coupled with the better payloads of tactical aircraft, had profound implications for future tactical air attack. Defense analyst Seymour J. Deitchman hinted of this with a table comparing an actual case of World War II tactical air attack capability with a theoretical equivalent effort in 1983 (although he also argued that the realities of future war—including "fog and friction" issues, air defenses, and the like—would prevent the "unequivocal impact on modern land warfare" that the numbers suggested) (see Appendix Table 3).[2] Ironically, of course, air power in the Gulf war *did* achieve the very kind of "unequivocal impact" Deitchman and other analysts (with justified caution) found so difficult to predict a few short years before.

As with air superiority, there was more to tactical CAS/BAI warfare than merely developing a new attack airplane or helicopter. Instead, one had to devote considerable thought to the circumstances under which a new aircraft might be utilized, and then develop it as a total, integrated system, linked to particular weapons or technologies, such as the Maverick, Hellfire, or JSTARS. Three special battlefield ground attack aircraft used in the Gulf war exemplify this: the Fairchild A-10A Thunderbolt II, the McDonnell-Douglas AH-64A Apache gunship, and the McDonnell-Douglas AV-8B Harrier II.

Appendix Table 3. Tactical Air Attack: World War II versus a 1983 Theoretical Model

Category	World War II	1983
Number of aircraft	2,500	100
Sorties per day per aircraft	0.61	1 to 3
Average bomb load	2 × 500-lb. bombs	8 to 18 × 500-lb. bombs or 3 to 6 precision-guided munitions (PGMs)
Tank equivalents damaged or destroyed by force, per day	60 to 70	300–800, using PGMs
Sorties required to destroy a bridge over a minor river	20 to 30	1 (using PGMs)

The A-10A Thunderbolt II ("Warthog") and the Maverick Missile

When conceived in 1966, planners hoped that the A-10 (then known as the A-X) would be a low-cost alternative to reopening the Douglas A-1 Skyraider production line, and they emphasized the kind of protection and payload requirements needed for counterinsurgency warfare in South Vietnam. As the war in Vietnam wound down, the mission of the A-X changed into one of Warsaw Pact–tank killer, and the centerpiece— quite literally—of the airplane became a huge 30mm multibarrel Gatling-like cannon (with an ammunition drum the size of a Volkswagen Beetle) firing depleted uranium armor-piercing rounds to destroy Soviet main battle tanks. Unlike previous cannons, added awkwardly under the wings or fuselage of an airplane, the winning A-10 was literally built around the cannon, and even had an offset nose landing gear to accommodate the long barrels. Eventually, Fairchild's A-10 won the A-X contract in an aerial fly-off against Northrop's A-9.

Designed to be resistant to direct 23mm cannon hits, the A-10 emphasized battle damage tolerance and survivability, with podded engines high enough to use the horizontal tail as shielding from upward-looking heat-seeking missiles, a rugged structure, and an armored "bathtub" for the pilot, and the ability—proven in the Gulf war—to return to base with great sections of its wing and tail surfaces shot away, like its famous predecessor, the P-47 of World War II. The A-10 experienced serious engine problems during flight testing caused by gun exhaust gas ingestion.

On one flight, an A-10 flamed out both engines during a trial gunnery run at Edwards, forcing the test pilot to eject; he suffered severe injuries, though he recovered to fly again. Gun exhaust gas ignition created comet-like fireballs around the nose of test airplanes, spoiling aiming and, of course, offering an unacceptable clue as to where the A-10 was. The gun design itself promoted jams and potentially hazardous scattering of explosive powder through the airplane. All of these problems took time to work out, but the A-10 nevertheless entered service quickly, taking only five years to go from its first test flight (in May 1972) to achieving operational status with the Tactical Air Command (in 1977). Extraordinarily agile, the 400 MPH A-10 could easily devastate tanks, but it suffered from a severe lack of speed, and in the 1980s critics doubted—with good reason—its survivability in the face of intensive flak and missile fire.[3]

Though it could carry a wide range of weapons on eleven hardpoints for ground support missions, the A-10 relied primarily on three: the Maverick missile, the laser-guided bomb, and its 30mm cannon. The laser-guided bomb will be discussed subsequently, and the cannon has already been mentioned. The Maverick dated to 1964, when the Air Force established a tactical missile office to examine the service's needs for various air-to-ground missiles. In 1966, Hughes and North American were selected to prepare definition studies for a medium-size tactical television-guided missile. Hughes won in 1968 with a missile that drew on the proven aerodynamic configuration of the Falcon, coupled with TV guidance, and a 125-pound warhead. Flight testing began the next year, and the new missile, designated the AGM-65 Maverick, entered TAC service in 1973, being delivered to Israel during the 1973 Arab-Israeli war. Subsequently, a laser-guided version of the Maverick entered service with the Marine Corps. The most significant model, however, was the AGM-65D, an imaging infrared (IIR) version of the Maverick that became the principal weapon used by the A-10 against Iraqi tanks. The IIR Maverick produced a TV-like picture on a cockpit display, but its IIR guidance gave it much greater accuracy in bad weather, haze, and smoke conditions than the earlier TV system. The IIR Maverick entered development in 1976, first flew in 1980, and entered service in 1986.[4]

The AH-64 Apache Gunship and the Hellfire Missile

The Vietnam performance of armed helicopter gunships left no doubt as to their value for battlefield air support. After the war, the Army and Marine Corps continued to refine the basic Cobra gunship, eventually generating the TOW-armed AH-1S (Army) and the twin-engine AH-1W (Marine Corps). Disappointment with the experimental Lockheed AH-56 Cheyenne gunship—a complex but spectacular-performing machine that had numerous development problems but tremendous potential—led the Army to cancel the Cheyenne program in 1972 and replace it with a competition for a less sophisticated, smaller, and more agile gunship. Hughes won a competitive fly-off against a Bell design with its twin-engine AH-64 in 1976. (Eventually, Hughes merged with McDonnell-Douglas, by whose manufacturer's name the Apache is referred to presently.) As with the GAU-8/A-10, the Apache had its own designated special weapon—the laser-guided Hellfire antitank missile. The Hellfire, mandated for the AH-64 program by Department of Defense directive in 1976, carried a shaped-charge warhead and had an anticipated 98-percent kill rate against targets out to a range of five miles, unlike the TOW family, which generally had seriously degraded performance beyond 1.5 miles. Unhampered by the wire-guidance limitations of the TOW, an Apache crew could fire a Hellfire from out of sight of a target, and the Hellfire would home on the laser spot of a designator carried by a scout helicopter, or by an infantryman on the ground. (In contrast, a TOW-firing Cobra had to remain in line-of-sight of the target after firing a TOW, steadily hovering for approximately two seconds after the TOW launched so that the missile could "capture" the target. Then the Cobra's crew could rock back and forth in a gentle "jink" while the TOW homed in—which could take over 20 seconds—all the while staring down Soviet main battle tanks and ZSU-23-4 mobile flak.)[5]

The AH-64 typically carries eight Hellfires (for tanks), 2.75-inch unguided rockets in two pods of nineteen each (for area suppressive fire), and a 30mm cannon capable of traversing, elevating, and depressing over a wide range (for suppressing air defenses such as the SA-9 and the ZSU-23-4, and attacking lightly armed vehicles). The Apache offers significantly greater combat potential than the Cobra, in part because it has greater speed, survivability (thanks to a rugged structure and extensive use of Dupont-developed Kevlar armor), twin-engine power, range, and better avionics. It has a laser rangefinder-designator and spot-tracker; comprehensive electronic and missile countermeasures (including passive radar warning, an infrared jammer, a radar jammer, and a chaff-flare dispenser); sophisticated communications; and multiple sighting systems, including direct-view magnified optics, a forward-looking infrared (FLIR) having four different fields of view that gives the Apache crew superb night vision or vision through smoke, and a magnified low-light-level television (LLLTV) for daytime target acquisition. Additionally, the crew has individual helmet-mounted sights which, when placed over the right eye, display selected symbology and video. After surviving two serious attempts to kill it—one by the Congress in 1978 and another by members of the Department of Defense in 1981, who suggested making do with a gunship version of the UH-60 Blackhawk—the Apache entered production in 1983. Delivery to Army combat brigades commenced in February 1986, and it saw its first combat in Panama in 1989. With a maximum speed of 184 MPH, the Apache is no world-beater, but over the battlefield, particularly if operating in joint air attack teams with Kiowa scouts and Air Force A-10s—it can easily be a tank's worst nightmare, as the Iraqis found to their misfortune.[6]

The AV-8B Harrier II

The Marine Corps' McDonnell-Douglas AV-8B Harrier II took a completely different approach to battlefield air support, offering the speed and payload advantages of a tactical jet fighter with the helicopter's ability to take off and land vertically. The Harrier II, an American derivative of the proven Harrier V/STOL jump-jet that had performed so well in the Falklands, bore a marked resemblance to its earlier cousin, but, in fact, the newer airplane represented a considerable departure from the original Harrier. The new aircraft (dubbed "AV-16" because its designers wanted it to be twice as good as the AV-8A, the American production model of the original Harrier) featured an extensively redesigned structure making use of new graphite epoxy composite materials. These made it a lighter, stronger, stiffer airplane. The wing design itself was new, a low-drag high-lift "supercritical" design to improve the Harrier's aerodynamic performance. The AV-8B featured a more powerful vectored-thrust engine, and the latest avionics technology, such as a HUD, digital electronic engine controls, fly-by-wire flap controls, HOTAS, and sophisticated weapons controls including laser targeting and tracking. Pilots flying the new Harrier II found that it had approximately half the pilot workload requirements of the earlier AV-8A. In perhaps the finest complement to their American cousins, the Royal Air Force agreed to acquire the Harrier II for its own service.

The Harrier II completed its first test flight in 1978, and the first production models were delivered in 1983. It entered widespread service with the Corps following lengthy flight testing to resolve some engine-inlet "matching" anomalies. The Harrier family (and the Harrier II was no exception) have always had to fight their image as quirky, fuel-guzzling freaks, and this issue (as well as cost questions) led to various attempts in Congress to terminate or drastically trim the program. In fact, the Harrier was ideally suited to the Marine Corps' traditional need for forward-base tactical aircraft in austere conditions in support of Marine amphibious forces. While both the Navy and the Air Force rejected the Harrier in favor of more conventional aircraft, the Marines cultivated the design as particularly valuable for the kind of landing and support operations the Corps had always undertaken. The Harrier II, with fighter agility, a new 25mm Gatling cannon, and the ability to drop or fire a variety of weapons, including laser-guided bombs, Maverick and AIM-9L Sidewinder missiles, "dumb" bombs, cluster bomb units such as the Vietnam-era Rockeye, rocket pods, and gun pods, promised to deliver the same quality and kind of air support that had been available to the Corps with the earlier Douglas A-4 Skyhawk, but faster and more accurately. The Harrier II delivered on that promise during the Gulf war.[7]

Appendix C Strike Warfare Technology

Technology systems for strike missions improved markedly in the 1970s and 1980s, typified by continued refinement of the Vietnam-era Grumman A-6 and General Dynamics F-111, the introduction of the Anglo-French SEPECAT Jaguar and Anglo-German-Italian Panavia Tornado, the refinement of the McDonnell-Douglas F-15 into the F-15E, the development of the Lockheed F-117 stealth fighter, and the introduction of special weapons and equipment such as the laser-guided bomb, GPS satellite-derived position information, and the LANTIRN navigation and targeting system, which will be treated separately.

Aircraft Upgrades and New Starts

Improving the subsonic A-6 and supersonic F-111 required upgrading their offensive avionics and targeting capabilities; well in advance of the Gulf war both added systems to make them much more potent all-weather day-and-night attackers. The A-6E received the TRAM (Target Recognition Attack Multisensor) chin-turreted electro-optical sensor package in 1974, which incorporated a laser designator and rangefinder, and an infrared sensor. (In the early 1980s, the Navy upgraded A-6s to carry Harpoon antiship missiles as well.) The F-111F (the only version of this controversial airplane to actually meet the performance specification requirements laid down for the initial F-111A) received Pave Tack, a turreted sensor system housed in the Aardvark's weapons bay that could acquire, track, and then designate targets for infrared, laser, or electro-optically guided weapons. Both the A-6 and the F-111 updated their bombing and navigation systems with digital electronic equipment, and both added receivers for the Global Positioning System (GPS) satellite navigation system. The A-6E and the F-111F flew in the Gulf war, with the F-111F demonstrating extraordinary versatility as a strike aircraft and—surprisingly—as a battlefield "tank plinker." (Presciently, in 1975, then-Air Force Chief of Staff Gen. David C. Jones characterized the F-111 as the "best all-weather tactical airplane we have," emphasizing that it should be thought of as more than a deep-strike airplane; it was an ideal machine for battlefield interdiction as well.[1]) The Navy had initially planned to follow the A-6E with a new A-6F having more power and state-of-the-art avionics, but the service canceled it in the mid–1980s in favor of the General Dynamics–McDonnell–Douglas A-12 Avenger II stealth aircraft. Thus, the collapse of the A-12 program in 1991 (a week before Desert Storm) has left the Navy with a very serious deficiency in its strike forces that can only be addressed by development of a suitable modern—and stealthy—attack airplane.

In the late 1960s, Great Britain and France devoted increasing attention to developing dual-role fighter and attack aircraft. The best examples of these were the British Aerospace Harrier, the Anglo-French Jaguar (an aging but still potent attacker at the time of the Gulf war), and the later Anglo-German-Italian Tornado. Variants of all three served in the Gulf war. The Jaguar and Tornado flew with several coalition air forces, and both proved very useful. The single-seat Jaguar, designed for low-altitude battlefield air attack and air interdiction, underwent continuous refinement from the time of its first flight in 1968, and, by the time of the Gulf war, could carry a variety of precision-guided munitions such as the laser-guided Aerospatiale AS-30L, as well as "dumb" bombs. The multi-national twin-engine two-seat Tornado, which first flew in 1974, had started out as the MRCA: Multi-Role Combat Aircraft. (British wags dubbed it the "Must Replace Canberra Again," a reference to an aging bomber.) It constituted a veritable European F-111, even to having swingwings, and it came in two models: a long-range strike and recon-naissance variant, and an interceptor variant intended for air defense. Tornado strike aircraft could carry a wide range of munitions, ranging from standard NATO unguided and guided bombs, to the JP-233 runway attack munitions dispenser and ALARM, a specialized antiradar missile. The Tornado's introduction to combat in the Gulf war was initially dis-appointing; it suffered high losses and also initially lacked the ability to do its own laser target designating, requiring it to rely on older Bucca-neers hastily flown in from Great Britain to "lase" targets. Changed tac-tics and the Buccaneer teaming greatly improved its effectiveness toward the end of the war.

The F-15E Strike Eagle

The most capable conventional attacker used in the Gulf war was the McDonnell-Douglas F-15E Strike Eagle. The Strike Eagle's success as a deep interdictor, tank hunter, and Scud-buster is ironic, given that when the F-15 was under development, proponents felt so seriously about the Eagle's air superiority mission that they hung a huge banner in the F-15 system program office (SPO) at Wright-Patterson AFB reading, "Not a pound for air to ground!"[2] Advocates could not justify such a statement historically, for with the limited exception of a few special-purpose inter-ceptors, virtually all "air superiority" fighters have eventually been called upon to attack ground targets. Their intent, of course, reflected a deep-seated and absolutely justified belief that a fighter, first and foremost, must be able to achieve victory in air combat.

The Strike Eagle effort began in the late 1970s as an effort to identify a successor to the F-111 for night and adverse-weather deep strike. In Oc-tober 1982, the Office of the Secretary of Defense directed that the Air Force conduct a comparative demonstration of the F-15 and F-16 to de-termine which had greater potential as a dual-role air-to-ground and air-to-air fighter. McDonnell-Douglas had modified the first F-15B as a "de-rivative fighter," equipping it with a new radar, advanced displays in the rear cockpit, and (most visibly) outfitting it with large "conformal" fuel tanks that hugged the flanks of the Eagle, giving it the appearance of an F-15 on steroids. For their part, the General Dynamics team had stretched the basic F-16 and given it a "cranked arrow" delta wing, re-naming it the F-16XL. The fly-off ended in February 1984, and if the

F-16XL was the prettier of the two (indeed, General Dynamics engineers dubbed the Strike Eagle as the "Wart-Eagle Strike-Pig"), the F-15 was clearly the better airplane. It had excellent range, tremendous growth potential, twin-engine power and reliability, and a second crewman—a desirable feature for a strike airplane.[3]

The production F-15E Strike Eagle did not make its first flight until December 1986, and it did not enter TAC's operational inventory until 1990, a few months prior to the war. The F-15E differed from previous Eagles in a number of ways, though, surprisingly, it retained generally similar handling qualities and flight performance. It incorporated a greatly strengthened structure to accommodate its predilection for low-altitude high-speed flight, "glass cockpit" multipurpose displays (three in front, four in back), wide-field-of-view HUDs, LANTIRN navigation and targeting pods (the nav pod consisting of a FLIR sensor and a terrain-following radar, and the targeting pod having a high-resolution FLIR, a missile boresight correlator, and a laser designator and ranger), a digital electronic flight control augmentation system, conformal fuel tanks (which also permitted so-called tangential low-drag weapon carriage, the bombs or missiles snuggling on the rounded corners of the tanks); an advanced inertial navigation system, and a strengthened landing gear permitting the plane to operate to 81,000-pounds gross takeoff weight (compared to 68,000 pounds maximum for the F-15C air superiority fighter), including 24,500 pounds of weapons ranging from air-to-air missiles to laser-guided bombs, cluster munitions, and conventional "dumb" bombs.

The real "heart" of the F-15E was a new Hughes synthetic aperture radar that had a high resolution map feature that could easily distinguish buildings, roads, or even individual vehicles and aircraft on the ground from dozens of miles away. (The radar attained this accuracy by "synthetically" generating an image equivalent to that produced by a radar having a "real" antenna as long as 2,000 feet; by looking at a particular target—say, for example, an airfield—for a specified length of time, the necessary "aperture" would be created to generate resolutions measured in feet.) Above all else, the F-15E was a true electronic airplane; while the F-15A had 60,000 lines of computer software code for its avionics, the avionics-intensive F-15E had 2.4 million. In sum, the F-15E, at the time of the Gulf war, was the most sophisticated and advanced conventional strike fighter in the world, with capabilities far beyond those of older aircraft and even contemporaries such as the Tornado.[4]

The F-117A Stealth Fighter

The word *conventional* does not apply to the most dramatic and effective strike aircraft developed in the late 1970s and 1980s: the Lockheed F-117A "stealth" fighter. The development of the F-117 is shrouded in secrecy, and for good reasons. What is now known as fact is even more intriguing than what was speculated upon from that moment, in 1980, when Carter administration spokesmen blew the lid off stealth research at a public news conference. In fact, the origins of stealth predate both the Carter presidency and the Vietnam War; for example, in the late 1950s, Lockheed took special pains to reduce the radar signature of the Blackbird strategic reconnaissance aircraft, and during Vietnam, Ryan reconnaissance drones covered with radar-absorbing "blankets" and inlet screens routinely flew over the North. The experience of Vietnam and the 1973 Arab-Israeli war constituted powerful stimuli for stealth research. In both those conflicts, radar detection and radar-guided weapons took a high toll of attackers. Within private industry and the federal government, a number of engineers and airmen determined that ideal future strike aircraft systems could feature dramatically reduced radar cross sections (RCS). (RCS is the apparent size of an aircraft as it appears to search and fire control radars, and has absolutely no relationship to the actual physical cross section of an airplane.) Reducing RCS can be accomplished in any number of ways, the chief ones being by careful shaping and use of radar absorbent materials and coatings.

Gradually, the potentiality of dramatically negating the very value of air defense networks—their comprehensive radar coverage—became apparent. If aerospace technology could generate a "stealth" airplane that had such a low signature as to be difficult to spot and track until so close to an enemy as to be impossible to engage, the tremendous investment in radar technology made by the Soviets since the Second World War would be negated at once. Stealth would have the effect of reducing the detecting radius of radars and the lethal "cone" of surface-to-air weapons, so that a stealthy attacker could thread around and through defenses on its way to its target. In November 1978, the Air Force contracted with Lockheed to develop such an airplane. The result was the single-seat twin-engine F-117, designed to attack vital targets deep in enemy territory in the face of extensive radar threats. The F-117 had approximately the same dimensions as the F-15 fighter, and a maximum gross weight of 52,500 pounds. It first flew on June 18, 1981, and achieved operational status with the

TAC in October 1983, merely 28 months later. With the introduction of the F-117 into service, the United States literally possessed the ability to strike with impunity deep into the most densely defended target areas conceivable—something never before possible in the history of air warfare.[5]

The F-117 incorporated a so-called faceted design approach of angular surfaces coupled with a sharply swept planform and a "Vee" tail to help reduce its radar return. In fact, the F-117 was the first airplane in aviation history designed primarily to meet radar signature requirements rather than aerodynamic ones. Not surprisingly, in an attempt to reduce risk, Lockheed incorporated off-the-shelf components wherever possible. The engines came from the F-18 program, and cockpit components came from both the F-16 and F-18. It utilized existing navigation and attack systems, computers and electronics, and a modified F-16 fly-by-wire flight control system. It also featured a so-called two-dimensional exhaust system to reduce the plane's infrared signature, and the engine inlets had grids to prevent a radar return from the engine face.

Flight testing proceeded generally smoothly, although Lockheed found it had to increase the size of the Vee tail; later, a more serious problem appeared when, during a test flight, a fin experienced aerodynamic flutter and disintegrated. The pilot managed to land the plane safely, and Lockheed again had to redesign the fin structure. Contrary to press reports and the allegations of critics, at no time was the airplane *ever* known as the "Wobbly Goblin"; in fact, it had generally pleasant flying characteristics throughout its "envelope." Perhaps more surprising was the cost of the program. Rumored by critics to be so expensive that the flyaway cost of individual aircraft was measured in the hundreds of millions of dollars, the actual flyaway cost per aircraft turned out to be $42,600,000, comparable to far less exotic aircraft, such as the F-15E. Lockheed produced a total of 59 "stealth fighters," the last entering service in July 1990, a month before Saddam Hussein invaded Kuwait. Its subsequent service during the Gulf war was nothing short of spectacular, and led to calls for further production of this exotic airplane.

Appendix D Missile Technology

In the years after Vietnam and the 1973 Arab-Israeli war, the United States and Western European nations made major investments in advanced "smart" weapons that minimized the need for piloted aircraft to risk themselves in target areas having dense defenses. Some of the most notable of these, used subsequently in the Gulf war, were the Harpoon/SLAM (for Standoff Land Attack Missile) family, the AGM-86C, Tomahawk land attack cruise missile, the MLRS/ATACMs tactical battlefield missile system, and the Patriot air defense missile. None of these could have been built earlier than the late 1960s, for all depended upon the electronic revolution for their guidance, control, "memories," and targeting. Once again, each of these had faced bitter criticism for being "wasteful," "inaccurate," "useless," and "destabilizing," and it took the test of combat to finally demonstrate convincingly that not only did they work, they worked well.

Cruise Missiles

The McDonnell-Douglas Harpoon was an important predecessor to the genuine cruise missile. This all-weather, over-the-horizon, specialized antiship missile could be fired from submarines, surface ships, and coastal launchers on land, or air-launched (the AGM-84D variant) from a wide range of aircraft, eventually including the Air Force's own B-52 (when modified for employment on sea control and surveillance missions). Inspired both by internal McDonnell-Douglas studies in the mid-1960s for antiship missiles and by the sinking of an Israeli destroyer by an Egyptian Styx antiship missile after the 1967 Arab-Israeli war, the jet-powered Harpoon used a small digital computer for guidance and control, relying upon a radar altimeter and attitude reference system to fly a sea-hugging profile, and an on-board radar to search out and destroy enemy vessels. Ship-launched versions had a range in excess of 70 miles, air-launched ones in excess of 120 miles; both carried a 500-pound warhead. The Navy launched the Harpoon effort in 1969; it made its first flight in 1972, and entered operational service in 1977—remarkably quickly, given the technical challenges of developing this kind of system. First used in the 1986 campaign against Qaddafi, it served again in the Gulf war. In the mid-1980s, McDonnell-Douglas designed a specialized land-attack version of the Harpoon for use by carrier-based aircraft against high-value land targets and ships in port. The new missile, the AGM-84E SLAM, used the same 500-pound warhead and propulsion as the Harpoon, but had different guidance and control, consisting of an inertial navigation system using Global Positioning System (GPS) updates for midcourse guidance, a data-link system adopted from the earlier Walleye missile program for terminal "man-in-the-loop" aimpoint control, and a imaging infrared (IIR) seeker adopted from the Maverick program. SLAM, the newest weapon in the Navy's inventory at the time the Gulf war broke out, made its combat debut against Iraq when an A-6E fired two against an Iraqi hydroelectric plant, with GPS and an accompanying A-7E controlling them into the target during the final phase of the attack.[1]

The General Dynamics BGM-109 Tomahawk Land Attack Missile (TLAM) was a seagoing cousin of the land-based Ground-launched Cruise Missile (GLCM) deployed to Europe in the early 1980s to offset the Soviet SS-20 threat, and subsequently withdrawn and destroyed as a result of U.S.-Soviet negotiations. The cruise missile concept dated to the First World War, and the first practical weapon of this sort was the infamous German V-1 "buzz-bomb" of World War II. Throughout the 1950s, the various military services had promoted development of cruise missiles to attack targets at long range; while many of these successfully flew, they had doubtful overall reliability and accuracy. At the end of the 1960s, however, the microelectronic revolution gave the promise of developing small weapons that could be launched from ships, submarines, and land transporters, or air-dropped from bombers. Out of this came the American joint USAF-Navy cruise missile program of the 1970s.[2]

Cruise missile proponents had to fight the established manned aircraft communities within both the Navy and Air Force, and their efforts met with success in the early 1970s. At that time, Congress directed that Air Force studies on armed air-launched bomber decoys and Navy interest in submarine-launched missiles (either derivatives of the Harpoon antiship missile or a special-purpose longer-range weapon) be focused toward developing offensive weapons and given greater priority. This activity generated a technology-sharing arrangement between the two services; the Air Force shared engine and fuel advances, and the Navy shared a guidance system called TERCOM—for Terrain Contour Matching. With TERCOM, a cruise missile would constantly compare terrain it flew over with stored memory of what it should be seeing at this point in its flight, and would correct its course accordingly to make the images "fit." Eventually, following tests of a small air-launched cruise missile (ALCM), the Air Force contracted for a larger model, the Boeing AGM-86B ALCM, and deployed it on B-52 bombers starting in December 1982. In June 1986, under extreme security conditions, the Air Force modified a small number of ALCM-Bs as conventional weapons, equipped with a 1,000-pound blast/fragmentation high-explosive warhead, and using GPS navigation in place of the nuclear model's TERCOM system. This new model, the AGM-86C, entered service with the Strategic Air Command in January 1988, and thirty-five of them were subsequently fired at high-value Iraqi communications and power generation targets during the first night of Desert Storm.[3]

The Carter administration generally favored the cruise missile program, and used it as a rationale for killing the Air Force's B-1A bomber program in 1977. Interestingly, many peace activists lobbied hard for the pro-cruise position, seeing it as a means of attacking the B-1A (afterwards, they planned to take on cruise itself.)[4] Their efforts were for naught, however, and both the Air Force's AGM-86 and GLCM, and the Navy's Tomahawk program went forward. There were four versions of the Tomahawk: the TASM (a Tomahawk anti-ship missile), TLAM-C (a conventionally armed land-attack missile), TLAM-D (another conventional derivative carrying bomblet submunitions), and the TLAM-N (a nuclear-armed land-attack missile). The TLAM-C/D used updates of its inertial guidance system with a digital scene matching correlation during the final "terminal guidance" phase of its flight. Looking like a long torpedo with folding wings and tail surfaces, the 700-mile-range TLAM-C/D used a small turbojet engine to power it during its flight, and a rocket booster to accelerate it for launch. The TLAM-C/D first flew in early 1977, and entered service with the fleet in November 1983. During Desert Storm, 288 TLAMs were fired at Iraq, 276 from ships and 12 from submarines.[5]

Battlefield Rocket Artillery

At first glance, battlefield rocket artillery, typified by the Army's Multiple Launch Rocket System (MLRS) and the Army Tactical Missile System (ATACMS) may not seem to be high-tech aerospace weapons. In fact, they constituted important elements of modern battlefield air power. Both represented the latest products of a long heritage of battlefield rocketry dating to the Russian *Katyusha* and Nazi *Nebelwurfer* of the Second World War, and, for that matter, back to the Hale and Congreve rockets of the nineteenth century, which themselves drew on an older rocketry tradition dating to India and China.[6] After the Second World War, the U.S. Army invested extensively in rocket technology, seeing rockets as the natural extension of tube artillery; for example, the Army secured the services of the Nazi rocketeers from Peenemünde virtually *in toto,* using them to help create a whole family of guided missiles, and losing them to NASA when Congress created that agency after Sputnik. The first American satellite, Explorer I, rose into space on the tip of an Army-developed missile, as did America's first suborbital astronaut, Alan Shepard; Apollo itself flew on a booster first conceptualized in Army studies. So enthusiastic was the Army about rockets, in fact, that it actually undertook studies of transporting squad and platoon-size formations behind enemy lines using derivatives of short-range ballistic missiles.[7]

Out of all of this interest came a family of Army missile and rocket systems intended to furnish American forces with the kind of battlefield support they might need if confronting a major war in Europe or Korea. In the early 1970s, reflecting changes in Army doctrine, the service initiated studies for a new battlefield rocket support system called the GSRS: General Support Rocket System. The Army envisioned using GSRS for a variety of missions, including suppressing enemy air defenses, artillery counterfire, and deploying scatterable mines. In time, the service determined that such a system should have the mobility advantages of a tracked vehicle, and selected a derivative of the Bradley AFV (armored fighting vehicle) then under development to be its launcher-transporter. The solid-fuel rockets—twelve per vehicle, in two "boxes" of six—would have a range over 18 miles, and be large weapons, each measuring nearly 13 feet in length and weighing 600 pounds at launch. In September 1977, the Army began development of the system, and in 1979 redesignated it the MLRS. Manufactured by the Vought Missiles and Advanced Programs Division, the MLRS first entered Army service in 1983, subsequently deploying to NATO and Korea. During the Gulf war, Army MLRS units fired "at least" 10,000 rockets at a variety of Iraqi targets (including artillery, command and control, and air defense forces) with results officially termed "outstanding." (British units fired huge numbers themselves, and the combined total of all MLRS firings reached 17,000 rounds.)[8]

ATACMS had different origins, related directly to the notion of Air-Land Battle. With a range more than 60 miles, ATACMS would use a maneuvering ballistic missile with a variety of warheads capable of striking targets in the deep battle area beyond the reach of cannon or the Army's previous standard long-range tactical missile, the MGM-52 Lance. ATACMS related to another and more ambitious joint Air Force–Army program, JTACMS (for Joint Tactical Missile System), which was one of the famous "31 Initiatives." JTACMS was a much more classified and sophisticated weapon study effort that eventually spawned a tri-service missile still under development at the time of the Gulf war. Both ATACMS and JTACMS were offshoots of a 1970s Defense Advanced Research Projects Agency (DARPA) study effort called "Assault Breaker," which examined a variety of technologies and potential means of confronting massive Soviet-style armored and mechanized forces operating against U.S. and Allied forces. ATACMS could use the MLRS launcher-transporter, although its hefty diameter (two feet as opposed to nine inches) limited the MLRS to carrying just two of the larger weapons. Each missile would deliver a 70-percent greater payload than the older Lance, with three times the accuracy of the earlier missile. In March 1986, Vought won a contract to build the ATACMS, and the system entered the Army's operational inventory just before the Gulf war. In January 1991, in response to an urgent request, the Army sent 105 ATACMS missiles to the Gulf for use against Scud and SAM sites, rocket batteries, and logistics centers. Each ATACMS carried 944 M-74 submunition bomblets. Considered a "precious asset," ATACMS was used sparingly but with great effect; analysis indicated that the thirty-three missiles fired destroyed or rendered inoperable all of their targets.[9]

The Patriot Surface-to-Air Missile

The most attention-getting missile of the war was, of course, the Patriot surface-to-air missile. Ostensibly, the Raytheon MIM-104 Patriot was merely an antiaircraft missile, the latest in a long series of Army SAMs, intended to replace the earlier Nike Hercules and the Hawk in Army service. In fact, the Patriot was also capable—at least in a limited sense—of destroying incoming tactical ballistic missiles as well as supersonic attack aircraft, and it had always been envisioned as such a dual-role weapon.

Patriot's roots dated to 1946, when the Army first considered how to defend against an incoming ballistic missile.[10] At that time, Gen. Dwight D. Eisenhower summarized the problem as "hitting a bullet with another bullet." Very quickly, Army study efforts branched to examine pure-ICBM interception systems like the Nike-Zeus, Sentinel, and Safeguard (in short, the kind of comprehensive ICBM-killers outlawed by the 1972 ABM treaty) on one hand, and sophisticated antiaircraft missiles having at least some ability to intercept tactical ballistic missiles. This led to a succession of studies—notably Project PLATO, and the Field Army Ballistic Missile Defense System (FABMDS)—that culminated in the Army Air Defense System for the 1970s (AADS-70s), subsequently redesignated SAM-D (for Surface-to-Air Missile Development) in 1964. In 1967, the Army awarded development contracts to Raytheon. Two key challenges were its "phased array" radar (essentially an electrically "steered" antenna that did not require an actual rotating dish) and its seeker. Of the two, the seeker was the most difficult, but here Raytheon had an edge: a remarkable guidance proposal for a "track via missile" (TVM) seeker by engineer Donald Banks. Banks had originally been thinking of antitank radar-guided missiles when he conceptualized TVM; now it was applied to the SAM-D. TVM essentially involved using the radar return from a target to update the missile's guidance directly, without having to wait for the return to reach the ground radar and then have corrective signals sent to the missile. Instead, the missile would constantly narrow its margin of error as it approached the target, relying more and more on its own receiver until finally, in the last seconds of an intercept, the missile would essentially be functioning in an autonomous mode.[11]

SAM-D faced numerous critics as well as its serious technical challenges. In the early 1970s, Congressional critics attacked it as violating the spirit of the ABM treaty and being technologically questionable. Senator George McGovern judged it a "complicated system of marginal utility," and Sen. Birch Bayh tried unsuccessfully to strip its funding. Flight testing began in February 1975 and, in August 1976, the Pentagon cleared the missile for full-scale engineering development. That same year, the two-hundredth anniversary of the signing of the Declaration of Independence, SAM-D became the "Patriot" because, in the words of one project official, "We knew in the Bicentennial year, nobody—not even Congress—would kill a patriot."[12] Before the Bicentennial, the Army had decided to emphasize development of the antiaircraft aspects of the Patriot, because this requirement alone was a daunting one. The Army itself increasingly ignored the antiballistic missile option though, as a "just-in-case" hedge, the service continued to pursue an optional improved dual-purpose nonnuclear warhead at a low level of interest. As the 1970s made way for the 1980s, Patriot—now justified as strictly an antiaircraft missile—largely dropped off the Congressional radar screen, replaced by more controversial programs like SDI and the B-2. In September 1980, it entered low-rate production, reached its first air defense battalion in May 1982, completed operational testing in 1984, and eventually joined Army air defense forces in Europe in 1985.[13]

Meantime, the idea of using Patriot to destroy ballistic missiles just would not die. Giving the Patriot an ability to engage not only airplanes but TBMs gained support when the Soviets deployed new families of missiles accurate enough to target NATO's airfields and air defense systems with conventional (i.e., nonnuclear) weapons, and the Iraqis and Iranians attacked each other's cities with ballistic missiles in the Iran-Iraq war. In the early 1980s, with Department of Defense approval, the Army began an upgrade program for the Patriot called the Patriot Pre-Planned Product Improvement (P³I, or "P Cubed I"). This program itself had two phases. The first, known as PAC-1 (for Patriot ATBM Capability, Level-1) mandated software changes enabling the Patriot to engage and destroy short-range ballistic missiles. The more ambitious PAC-2 required not only software changes, but changes to the missile's warhead and fuzing.

Little doubt existed even among program proponents that the Patriot was a compromise antiballistic missile system; so-called hit to kill (i.e., collider) weapons such as were being explored by the SDI program had a better chance of destroying an incoming warhead, rather than the Patriot's explosive fragmenting warhead, which was perfectly fine for destroying airplanes. These technical criticisms, coupled with teething problems in the Patriot's operational testing, and a resurgence of Congressional criticism over the Army decision to pursue ATBM missions for the missile, threatened to kill the program once and for all. Key Congressmen fought it, including two in Raytheon's own home state of Massachusetts: Sen. Edward "Ted" Kennedy (who argued that it violated the ABM treaty) and Rep. Chester Atkins. At this point, one individual worked constantly and persuasively to ensure that it went ahead: Sen. J. Danforth Quayle, later elected vice-president of the United States. Quayle held hearings on tactical missile defense, requested the first Congressional studies on the issue, and pressed for support of both the Patriot upgrade program and the joint American-Israeli Arrow long-range antiballistic missile interceptor. His efforts met with success; Patriot PAC-1 and PAC-2 went ahead. In 1986, a PAC-1 Patriot intercepted a Lance missile; then, in November 1987, in two consecutive tests, more-capable PAC-2 Patriots destroyed other test missiles (including a Patriot simulating a Soviet SS-23).[14]

Once Saddam Hussein invaded Kuwait and the Desert Shield forces buildup began, the Army accelerated PAC-2 development. On the day of the invasion, only three Scud-capable Patriots were in existence; quickly, working around the clock and ignoring weekends and holidays, Martin-Marietta assembled seventeen others, sending one to White Sands Missile Range for what proved to be a successful flight test. Four weeks after his invasion, the first PAC-2 Patriots arrived in Saudi Arabia. On January 18, 1991, in the night skies over Dhahran, Saudi Arabia, 45 years of persistence paid off. For the first time in the history of warfare, a surface-to-air missile intercepted an incoming ballistic missile "in anger": the bullet *had* hit another bullet.[15]

Appendix E The "Smart" Bomb

Laser- and electro-optically guided "smart" bombs were, of course, one of the most dramatic weapons used in the Gulf war. Pictures of bombs flying through bunker doors, elevator shafts, and hitting individual tanks stunned viewers.[1] What the vast majority of viewers did not realize, of course, was that the smart bomb was not a new weapon, but rather one that had appeared in Vietnam and been constantly refined since. Here is the great irony of "smart bomb" history—heralded as a weapon of the Gulf war, it actually demonstrated almost equally impressive performance nearly 20 years before in a conflict a third of a world away—and its antecedents, indeed, stretched to crude predecessors in the Second World War.[2]

The challenge of attacking North Vietnamese bridges led directly to smart bomb development. (Ironically, difficulties dropping North Korean bridges led the Navy to develop the first mass-produced air-to-ground guided missile, the Bullpup.) Since bombs are basically ballistic-drop weapons—that is, they follow a mathematically predictable course once they are released—a guided bomb would have to have some sort of aerodynamic control surfaces and sophisticated guidance system to effectively change it into a high-speed homing weapon that could seek out a target. In the early 1950s, largely at the instigation of Gen. Gordon Saville, the Air Force examined technologies necessary for producing guided bombs under the "Zero CEP" study effort. As early as 1958, a study group of the National Academy of Sciences recommended looking to the new technology of lasers (for light amplification by stimulated emission of radiation) for weapon guidance. As Air Force interest in developing precision conventional munitions increased with the onset of Vietnam, the potentiality of laser guidance became increasingly apparent within the weapons community. The Air Force maintained a small weapons research staff at Eglin AFB, Florida, and this group received reports from Vietnam indicating that the Bullpup, when used on Vietnamese bridges, tended either to bounce off or break up, without doing too much damage. Worse, it required a pilot to steer it into the bridge using a small hand controller in his cockpit, and thus made the attacking plane very vulnerable to anti-aircraft fire.[3]

In 1965, thanks to Col. Joseph Short and Weldon Wood of Texas Instruments, the Air Force launched a laser-guided bomb (LGB) development effort called Paveway. Very quickly feasibility studies determined that the best technical approach combined modular guidance units and stabilizing fins with range-extending winglets that could be added to existing weapons such as the Mk. 117 750-pound and Mk. 84 2,000-pound bombs. In 1967, the Navy placed its own electro-optically guided smart bomb in service, the AGM-62 Walleye, which used a television guidance system so that a crew could steer it to a point where they could lock it onto the target and then turn away. Walleye was an impressive weapon, but its warhead—450 pounds—was still too small to do a decent job on a bridge. The next year, the first Air Force LGBs went to Vietnam for operational testing. The results were mixed, in part because of the newness of the weapon, inexperience of the operators (particularly the laser designators, firing a small laser "gun" at the target from the backseat of an F-4, and then holding the spot of laser light on the target for up to thirty seconds), and difficulty in finding appropriate targets (a bombing halt was in progress).

Yet more than half those dropped scored direct hits—far more impressive than conventional bombs—and analysts concluded that 2,000-pound LGBs could consistently hit within 20 feet of an aiming point, a revolutionary breakthrough in accuracy. Back at Eglin, developers refined the concept, and created a family of modular components to convert conventional dumb bombs into smart ones called Paveway I. The Mk. 84-based 2,000-pound GBU-10 LGB was ideal for bridge busting, and the smaller Mk. 82-based 500-pound GBU-12 LGB perfect for trucks and vehicles. To get away from the vulnerability of operating two aircraft in high-threat areas, one a designator, one a dropper (although the British did just that in the Gulf war, with the Buccaneer designating for the Tornado), the Air Force developed Pave Knife, a laser designator boresighted to a television set so that a F-4 crew could "self-designate" a target, keep maneuvering if necessary, and drop an LGB on it. For more permissive environments, there was Pave Nail, a laser designator developed for OV-10 FACs to use when working with strike aircraft dropping LGBs. Both systems were in place for Linebacker I and II.[4]

The performance of the LGB in the 1972 North Vietnamese invasion of South Vietnam and the subsequent Linebacker campaigns was impressive. The 2,000-pound Mk. 84s demonstrated accuracies within six feet of their aiming point when used against bridges and other targets. In one notable case, an OV-10 illuminated a Communist tank overrunning a Special Forces camp and an F-4 destroyed it with a direct hit by an LGB without injuring or killing any of the friendly defenders. In another case, three LGBs destroyed three artillery pieces and five trucks. Another time, two F-4s using the older "buddy" designation system destroyed two tanks with two bombs in three minutes.[5]

Developing even more sophisticated and capable LGBs in the post-Vietnam years assumed a high priority, for they offered the kind of desirable "one bomb, one kill" potential that post-Vietnam air-to-air missiles were reaching toward themselves. The next major advance came with the introduction of the GBU-16 Paveway II in the early 1970s. Unlike Paveway I, the Paveway II had folding wings so that more could be carried by strike aircraft, structural improvements, and improved guidance ability; it eventually went into service with over thirty nations, and a variant based on a British 1,000-pound bomb design served with the British in the Falklands, and later in the Gulf war. Incredibly, given the potential and value of the LGB, Congressional cutbacks in the fiscal year 1974 budget request forced the Air Force to scrounge money from other programs to keep the Paveway program going. Developmental testing of the Paveway II went smoothly, and in 1976, Texas Instruments received a contract to manufacture nearly 7,800 kits to convert conventional bombs in the Paveway II configuration; TI delivered all the kits by the end of the next year. (The U.S. Navy subsequently developed a powered variant of the Paveway II, using a solid-fuel rocket booster from the Shrike anti-radar missile, and designated it the Skipper II; it gave Navy strike airplanes improved standoff range when attacking heavily defended vessels, and was first used in combat in 1988, sinking an Iranian frigate in the Persian Gulf.[6]

Good as Paveway II was, it still required a strike aircraft to bomb from medium altitudes, where a plane might be vulnerable to dense Warsaw Pact–type air defenses, or above cloud. Thus, in 1976, the Air Force issued a requirements statement for a new low-level LGB. Out of this came the GBU-24 Paveway III, a very different standoff weapon that, if not "brilliant," was at least "intelligent." It demanded on-board autopilot stabilization so that the bomb could "cruise" toward its target, a scanning seeker to find the spot of laser light illuminating the target, and the ability to be dropped outside the target "basket," and then maneuver itself inside it. Initial testing went smoothly, with but one failure in thirty-one drops, but operational testing of the Paveway III using the 500-pound Mk. 82 bomb shape revealed serious control sensitivity problems—problems that Paveway III using the heavier 2,000-pound Mk. 84 shape did not have. Paveway III eventually completed follow-on testing and evaluation in March 1986, demonstrating forty-four successful drops out of forty-seven attempts, a success rate of almost 94 percent. The Paveway III kit could be fitted to either the Mk. 84 conventional 2,000-pound bomb, or, with some software changes to its control system, the BLU-109 2,000-pound hard target earth penetrator bomb. Carried by F-15Es, F-111s, and F-16s, the GBU-24 would not get its chance to demonstrate what it could do in combat until the Gulf war. An advanced derivative, the GBU-27, was carried to the F-117s. During the war, the Air Force and Texas Instruments developed the massive 4,700-pound GBU-28 hardened penetrator using Paveway III guidance coupled to a new bomb shape based upon discarded cannon barrels. Altogether, approximately 9,000 Paveway II and III bombs were dropped in the Gulf war, constituting approximately 47 percent of all the precision-guided munitions used by American forces.[7]

Although the best known and generally most useful of the smart bombs, LGBs were not the only such weapons. The Air Force had earlier used an electro-optically guided bomb in Southeast Asia (the GBU-8), though it did not achieve the same kind of precision as did the LGB. One of the major Air Force development efforts of the 1970s was the GBU-15. A cruciform-wing glide bomb built around the proven Mk. 84 or hardened BLU-109 bomb shapes, the GBU-15 offered greater standoff range than a conventional LGB, ideal for attacking heavily defended targets, air defense systems, or ships. Unlike the LGB, the GBU-15 utilized either television guidance (the GBU-15[V]1/B model) or a Maverick-like imaging infrared (IIR) system (the GBU-15[V]2/B model). In the direct attack mode, the GBU-15 locked onto the target before being released from the launch aircraft, and thus flew an essentially line-of-sight approach to it. In the indirect attack mode, a weapons system officer in a F-111 or F-15E could fly the weapon into the target using guidance updates transmitted via a data link to the bomb, or he could lock the seeker onto the target after launch. Further, it could attack in weather conditions preventing laser-weapon attacks, for the bomb could "break out" under the overcast, and then acquire a target on its viewing system. Begun in 1974, the TV GBU-15 took nearly a decade to enter service, and the IIR version did not enter service until 1987. As with the Navy's Skipper program, the Air Force developed a rocket-boosted version of the GBU-15, the AGM-130, to achieve even greater standoff. But it experienced developmental difficulties (one Air Force general stated, "If ever there was a snake-bit development program, this is it") and was not available for service in the Gulf.[8] A large and, indeed, awkward-appearing weapon, the GBU-15 helped stem the flow of Iraqi oil into the Persian Gulf after Saddam Hussein launched his campaign of eco-terrorism. GBU-15s also hit mine entrances, chemical plants, missile sites, bridges, bunkers, building complexes, and command facilities. Altogether, seventy-nine of eighty TV and IIR versions of the GBU-15 dropped in the Gulf war hit their aiming points, a success rate of over 98 percent.[9]

Battlefield Information and Control

It is already a truism to state that modern warfare is invariably electronic in nature, with demanding information requirements. In particular, communications and air traffic control were critical functions. Information and control systems developed by the U.S. military in the years prior to the Gulf war ranged from the mundane (secure facsimile communications machines) to the exotic (AWACS, JSTARS, and orbiting satellites), and to the somewhat odd (battlefield drones). But all had impacts offering dramatic proof that modern warfare is as dependent upon electrons and information as it is upon petroleum and metal. The following are selected information and control technology systems that subsequently proved of extraordinary value in the Gulf war.

The Tactical Digital Facsimile

The Tactical Digital Facsimile (TDF) machine example is a case in point. In the late 1980s, the Air Force ordered development of a new fax machine capable of operating at temperatures up to 125°F and in conditions of blowing sand. Critics lampooned the device, stating (as one story argued) that "most Air Force commanders operate from bases where grueling conditions are rare." The next year, the TDF was in place in Saudi Arabia, and operating in tents in—guess what!—conditions of 125°F and blowing sand, while other commercially available fax machines were literally melting or grinding their innards to metallic powder. During the opening weeks of the Desert Shield deployment, it furnished the *only* secure means of updating target folders—the actual information and images on terrain, routes, headings, and threats—short of having a flying courier service between the United States and the Gulf. An after-action report concluded that "the TDF was today's telephone to the modern battlefield commander."[1]

The E-3 Sentry AWACS

One of the major coalition resources employed in the Gulf war was the Boeing E-3B Sentry Airborne Warning and Control System (AWACS), used both by the United States and Saudi Arabia. Intended to furnish long-range detection and surveillance of aircraft, AWACS began in 1961 as the latest in a long line of airborne early warning radar observation aircraft dating back to the Second World War. But where most of these had been intended to look out over the oceans for incoming threats, AWACS was intended to function over a land environment, and in a much more closely integrated fashion with friendly aircraft. It would serve as a force multiplier, to enable interceptor and fighter assets to be best applied against incoming air threats. Extensive studies followed before, in 1970, Boeing received a contract to modify a jet transport as a testbed. (The next year, in 1971, during the Indo-Pakistani war, a Tupolev Tu-114 Moss Soviet AWACS-style system—but a great deal more primitive—apparently assisted the Indian air force during their attacks upon Pakistani forces, demonstrating [if even in an immature way] the value of such systems to air campaign operations.)[2]

Boeing's AWACS testbed first flew in 1972, and by the end of the year, following competitive evaluations of various radars, Westinghouse won the contract to develop the airborne radar, which perched, flying saucer–like, on the back of the transport. Boeing delivered the first production E-3A Sentry in mid–1977, and TAC declared AWACS operational in September of that year. Subsequently, the E-3B succeeded the E-3A in production, featuring a more advanced Westinghouse radar. Sales to NATO, Great Britain, France, and Saudi Arabia followed. AWACS maintained a constant surveillance of the Persian Gulf during the Iran-Iraq war, and participated in the fight against drug smuggling over the Gulf of Mexico as well. Enhancing its effectiveness were the Have Quick secure voice communications system, the Joint Tactical Information Display System (J-TIDS), Mark XV Identification Friend or Foe (IFF) radar, and the Navstar GPS positioning system. With a crew of over twenty, AWACS could furnish timely information and warnings to airborne fighter and strike aircraft, though it was not, in the Soviet fashion, an airborne "command" post. When Desert Storm broke out, AWACS flew constantly, controlling over 3,000 Allied sorties per day, detecting threats, and pairing targets with strike aircraft.[3]

The E-8A JSTARS: Toward the "God's Eye View" of Battle

JSTARS promised to do for land warfare what AWACS did for air warfare. Subject of one of the "31 Initiatives" between the Air Force and the Army (though it had been under consideration for some time prior to their release), Writing in September 1989, retired Army general William E. DePuy stated unequivocally that JSTARS

> is to the Army what the AWACS is to the Air Force itself. By locating and tracking the movement of enemy ground forces, JSTARS provides the real-time information required by corps, division, and brigade commanders to maneuver their forces and target the enemy. It is therefore at the heart of Army tactical operations. *It is not just nice to have—it is indispensable* [emphasis added].[4]

Its lineage included two significant previous programs, the Army's standoff target acquisition system (SOTAS) and the Air Force's Pave Mover effort. Both of these had sought to take advantage of developments in radar technology to produce side-looking radars capable of spotting individual vehicles on the ground. SOTAS, a helicopter-based system, actually saw limited service in Europe. The Pave Mover technology demonstration program, part of the previously mentioned DARPA Assault Breaker effort, consisted of a multimode radar mounted on a F-111 that could detect both stopped and moving vehicles. Flight tests at Holloman Air Force Base in 1981 through 1983 were highly encouraging, and led to the termination of both SOTAS and Pave Mover in favor of a new program, JSTARS, begun in May 1982. For a brief time, supporters argued whether the carrying platform should be an Army OV-1D observation airplane, an Air Force TR-1 (an advanced U-2 derivative), or a larger airplane. In 1984, at the time the two services issued the "31 Initiatives," the Army and the Air Force agreed to using a derivative of the Boeing 707 commercial airliner. After detailed proposal evaluations, the Air Force announced in September 1985 that a Grumman-Norden team would develop the JSTARS aircraft system. JSTARS was intended to identify targets and provide "real-time" surveillance and attack management, particularly in striking deep targets such as second-echelon Warsaw Pact–type forces. Controllers in the JSTARS could data-link targeting information to tactical airplanes, missiles, and ground stations, and direct strikes on targets by airplanes, cruise missiles, tactical missiles such as the ATACMS, and battlefield rocketry and artillery. It would use a fixed side-looking airborne radar (SLAR) mounted in a long "canoe" under the fuselage of the modified Boeing 707. It had its share of critics, one of whom stated, in August 1986, that JSTARS should be deferred, and the United States should "stop plunging a lot of money into promising but unproven, longer-range technologies."[5]

But JSTARS continued on, with the Air Force funding development of a 24-foot Norden phased array (i.e., an electronically "steered") radar, and the Army procuring the companion AN/TSQ-132 Ground Station Module (GSM). The first prototype E-8A JSTARS aircraft flew in December 1988, with the second following in August 1989. In 1990, the system went to Europe for an extensive six-week series of developmental test and evaluation trials totaling twenty-five missions and over 110 flight test hours, working with Army ground forces. (In one case, it passed positioning and targeting data to Army attack helicopters, enabling them to "attack" a simulated assault.) Then Hussein invaded Kuwait. Initially, JSTARS was considered too immature to deploy to the Gulf; the planned JSTARS initial operational capability date was still six years in the future. Then, in mid-December, after seeing what it could do, CENTCOM's Gen. H. Norman Schwarzkopf requested it. After three weeks of intensive work, the two E-8As arrived in Saudi Arabia where they performed with consistently excellent and often spectacular results.[6]

Battlefield Drones

The most unprepossessing intelligence and control systems of the Gulf war were undoubtedly the so-called Unmanned Air Vehicles (UAVs) and drones operated for battlefield intelligence and targeting information.

(Other drones were used for a variety of classified purposes, and their contributions cannot yet be discussed.) Indeed, they would not have looked out of place at any model airplane meet in the country, but they were fully functioning miniature airplanes with sophisticated sensors. Interest in small UAVs (called Remotely Piloted Vehicles—RPVs—in the 1970s) directly stemmed from the success the Israelis had while using them over the Bekaa Valley in 1982, from the limitations of battleship gunfire control, and from Air Force trials of small "fearless" drones against radar emitting targets at the Utah Test and Training Range (UTTR) outside Hill AFB in the late 1970s and early 1980s. In 1983, Defense Secretary Caspar Weinberger had received a briefing on Israeli drone work, including seeing video taken of him during a recent trip to visit American troops in Beirut from a small UAV. Impressed, he directed the Joint Chiefs to rapidly implement UAV research and development programs. A major goad for this activity was the surprising problems with securing reliable targeting information for battleship shore bombardment gunfire. When the Sixth Fleet attempted to support the multinational peacekeeping force in Beirut with fire support missions by the battleship *New Jersey*, the inability to accurately target small military facilities without the risk of causing widespread civilian casualties from errant shells severely curtailed the potential usefulness of the ship. UAV targeting could overcome this problem. A good rule of UAV development is that if one is more concerned about getting a drone back than in it doing its job, it is probably too complex. Such complexities and concerns helped kill the Army's Aquila, an ambitious RPV program of the early 1980s. In contrast, systems such as the Marine Pointer and Navy Pioneer could furnish real-time information, particularly battlefield video, and if lost, were so cheap as to be easily replaced. The Pointer, manufactured by AeroVironment, Inc., was a nine-pound hand-launched UAV. The larger and more capable Pioneer, an Israeli-developed system produced by AAI for the Navy, had a five-hour endurance and a range of 100 nautical miles. It entered service in 1985, and by the time of the Gulf war had flown over 2,550 flights (a total of over 5,200 flight hours) with a mission availability rate (i.e., "ready to go" rate) in excess of 85 percent. During the war, the Navy launched Pioneers from refurbished battleships to provide day and night gunfire correction spotting. The Pioneer did not have the vulnerability that an artillery spotting airplane might have, although there was one case where Iraqi troops spotted an errant Pioneer and, fearing that 16-inch shells would follow, promptly tried to surrender to it![7]

Appendix G Space-based Systems, LANTIRN, and Pave Low

The sensitivities attending space-based systems for military operations preclude more than the most general discussion of what systems were available for use in the Gulf war. Their undoubted significance compelled the authors of an Air Force survey to conclude, "Desert Storm was America's first comprehensive space-supported war."[1]

Satellite Systems for Navigation, Weather, and Communications

Three of the most significant available for use were the Navstar Global Positioning System (Navstar GPS), the Defense Meteorological Support Program (DMSP), and the Defense Satellite Communications System (DSCS). Navstar, a system relied upon both by military and civilian users, consists of a satellite "constellation" orbiting nearly 11,000 miles above the earth which broadcasts to receivers carried by aircraft, vehicles, ships, or, for that matter, individuals. (In fact, more than 10,000 handheld receivers called "Sluggers"—for SLGR, small lightweight GPS receiver—were sent to the Gulf during the Desert Shield buildup.) Users can determine their position within 60 feet (in contrast, previous ground-based systems often had a built-in error of as much as eight miles). The development of small lightweight atomic clocks capable of being orbited enabled Navstar to transmit precise time data accurate to plus or minus one second in 300,000 years, thus making its accuracy possible. As a concept, Navstar dated to a joint Air Force–Aerospace Corporation study in 1964; the first research and development satellite flew in 1978. A victim of almost continuous funding cutbacks by Congress and the Department of Defense itself, Navstar only possessed sixteen of its planned eighteen satellites at the time of the Gulf war. It was nevertheless able to provide American forces with the positioning information necessary to provide accurate guidance of air, land, and naval forces.[2]

Not quite so dramatic, DMSP and DSCS were likewise two workhorse systems. DMSP was an orbital meteorological system designed to furnish high resolution near-real-time weather information. With weather in the Gulf war the worst in fourteen years, DMSP played a critical role in supporting mission planning, as well as being the first system to spot Saddam Hussein's use of eco-terrorism in the Gulf. Admiral Alfred Thayer Mahan once remarked that "communications dominate war," and to that end DSCS was created as a Department of Defense secure communications system using orbiting satellites. A complex system that required years of refinement and testing, DSCS entered full-scale development in 1977, and the first developmental flight took place in 1982. During the Gulf war, more than 100 ground terminals in the combat theater met the communications needs of tactical commanders.[3]

LANTIRN: Attack Out of the Night

Two aircraft systems need to be mentioned: LANTIRN and Pave Low III. Both represented the creative application of high-technology electronics to give military aircraft new and previously unattainable performance and safety. LANTIRN (for Low Altitude Navigation Targeting Infrared for Night) promised to provide pilots with the ability to undertake low-altitude high-speed night attacks. Night attack, and low-level attack at night in particular, has always been one of the most hazardous and unproductive forms of air attack. For that reason, air forces have generally stood down at night, which, of course, allows an enemy relative freedom of movement. In 1983, asked "what is the greatest weakness in Tac Air?"

then-TAC commander Gen. Wilbur Creech responded, "Our greatest weakness is our inability to fight at night."[4]

LANTIRN, developers hoped, could change all that. LANTIRN had a Marconi wide field-of-view HUD, a Martin-Marietta navigation pod housing a terrain-following radar and a wide field-of-view forward-looking infrared (FLIR) system, and a Martin-Marietta targeting pod having a high-resolution FLIR, a missile boresight correlator, and a laser ranging and designation system. All this was very high risk technology, and the targeting pod subsequently encountered serious development flight testing difficulties that delayed it considerably. The first LANTIRN test aircraft, a modified F-16B, flew in July 1984 at Edwards AFB. Despite problems with the targeting pod, developers were generally pleased, for success with the navigation pod indicated that a tactical fighter could be expected to operate safely at night using daytime attack tactics. (One cannot speak highly enough of the test crews who often flew this immature system on very high risk test flights involving low-level supersonic flights at night across the mountains and deserts of California.) To save the LANTIRN program from a delay or outright cancellation, Air Force Systems Command's leadership insisted that Martin-Marietta improve its management and production facilities, and assume increased responsibilities for the quality of the final product. To their credit, Martin-Marietta's management did their best, resolving LANTIRN's early technical difficulties. LANTIRN performed well in the Gulf war, literally completing its operational test and evaluation while employed by F-15Es hunting Scuds, tanks, airfields, and the like.[5]

Pave Low: Enhancing Special Operations Capabilities

Like LANTIRN, Pave Low was largely a night flying system, but with a difference: it had been developed in response to needs from the Air Force search-and-rescue (SAR) community, and, in a broader sense, was an effort to give the HH-53 family of helicopters an ability to perform combat SAR missions at night or in adverse weather. In many respects, combat SAR is a lot like aerial reconnaissance; in wartime, one can never have enough, in peacetime it is virtually impossible to fully fund. In 1967, in the midst of the Vietnam War, Pacific Air Force identified a requirement for night combat rescue; downed airmen were having to be left overnight or abandoned because helicopters could not rescue them in the dark or in bad weather and forboding terrain. This concern triggered the Limited

Night Recovery System (LNRS) program begun the next year. LNRS envisioned modifying eight of the large HH-53s to have a low-light-level television (LLLTV), other vision devices, and control system changes to ease pilot workload as the crew approached a downed airman and went into hover. LNRS proved anything but easy to accomplish, and quickly slipped behind schedule; after three years of research and development and only six successful test flights out of twenty-six attempts, work on LNRS was suspended.

Meantime, a more ambitious program had been started by the Air Force, Pave Star, which was intended to provide worldwide night-rescue capabilities to Air Force helicopters. Pave Star grew so greatly in cost that after a mere two years of work the service canceled it in mid-1970, three months before LNRS collapsed. Pave Star gave way to a smaller program called Pave Imp, and from the wreckage of all these programs sprang an operational requirement to evaluate a forward-looking radar for SAR helicopters. This radar, a spinoff of the Army's Cheyenne gunship effort, underwent extensive testing aboard a HH-53 testbed in the late summer and fall of 1972.[6]

By this time America's involvement in Vietnam was nearing an end, but the night SAR requirement still had not been fulfilled. Accordingly, while Sikorsky evaluated the forward-looking radar on their HH-53 in 1972, Military Airlift Command—the parent command for the Aerospace Rescue and Recovery Service—launched Pave Low II: an effort to develop an "integrated" system to undertake night-adverse weather low-level combat SAR, including rescue in hostile territory and mountainous terrain. Program goals emphasized precise navigation, terrain avoidance, and improving the ability of a helicopter to locate and hold a hover over the person needing rescue. In February 1974, this crystallized in an effort to build an actual flying prototype, Pave Low III. The Air Force entrusted program responsibilities to veterans of the service's AC-130 Gunship program office at Wright-Patterson AFB, Ohio, under the creative and dynamic leadership of Col. Ronald W. Terry. To succeed where so many predecessors had failed was no mean challenge; Terry's group scrounged equipment from the Gunship program—such as an airborne digital computer and a FLIR—and coupled it with systems from other efforts as well, such as a radar and map display from the A-7D attack aircraft and an inertial navigation platform from the Boeing SRAM missile system. They modified a HH-53 "in house" with the new equipment, and began flight testing in 1975, eventually evaluating the Pave Low III system in West

Virginia's hill country, the mountains around Kirtland AFB, New Mexico, and on to jungle testing in the Panama Canal Zone. In brief, this "on the cheap" effort succeeded where more extensively funded industry ventures had failed miserably; Pave Low III's prototype development cost the Air Force almost $3 million, only one-fourth of what the lowest commercial estimate for the prototype had been.[7]

With the system, a pilot could fly at low level and high speed (for a helicopter) using a terrain following/terrain avoidance (TF/TA) radar, augmented by a FLIR, referencing his flight to a projected map display. A central avionics computer integrated all of this information, and inputs from the helicopter's inertial and doppler navigation systems as well. Encouraged by the results of the demonstrator program, the Air Force ordered nine HH-53Cs modified as night SAR helicopters and redesignated MH-53H. All nine MH-53H Pave Low III helicopters arrived at Hurlburt Field, Florida, for special operations duties in 1979–80, and not using them was one of the major weaknesses in the tragic Iranian hostage rescue debacle. Eventually, in response to a subsequent Congressionally mandated requirement to upgrade Air Force H-53 helicopters to improve the technical capabilities of Air Force and Army special operating forces, Sikorsky modified the thirty-one remaining HH-53 and CH-53 helicopters in the Air Force's inventory to MH-53J Pave Low III Enhanced standard in 1987. This included adding machine guns, advanced ECM protection, digital avionics, and GPS receivers. Fittingly, on the first night of the Gulf air war, Air Force MH-53Js acted as pathfinders for Army Apache gunships sent to attack two small Iraqi radars. Nearly a quarter-century had passed from the time—and war—when the Air Force first framed its requirements for what became Pave Low III.[8]

Notes

Chapter 1. An Uncertain Legacy

1. R. A. Mason, "The Air War in the Gulf," *Survival* 33, no. 3 (May–June 1991): 211–29.

2. For a thoughtful examination of the air power case, see Eliot A. Cohen, "The Unsheltering Sky," *New Republic* 204, no. 6 (Feb. 11, 1991): 23–25.

3. Jean Heller, "Air Power: Brutal, but Not Enough?" *St. Petersburg Times,* January 12, 1991.

4. Joel Achenbach, "The Experts in Retreat," *Washington Post,* February 28, 1991.

5. Edward Mann, "Desert Storm No Textbook for AirLand Battle," *Army Times,* September 30, 1991.

6. John J. Fialka and Andy Pasztor, "Grim Calculus: If Mideast War Erupts, Air Power Will Hold Key to U.S. Casualties," *New York Times,* November 15, 1990.

7. See, for example, Harry G. Summers, Jr., "It Was a Lot of Hot Air," *Washington Times,* September 20, 1990.

8. Quoted in "On the Record," *National Review* (April 1, 1991): 8.

9. Ibid. See also William J. Perry, "Desert Storm and Deterrence" *Foreign Af-*

fairs 70, no. 4 (Fall 1991): 77. For several examples of reformist arguments, see Kosta Tsipis, "A Question of Quality: U.S. Military R&D," in *Review of U.S. Military Research and Development,* ed. Kosta Tsipis and Penny Janeway (Washington, D.C.: Pergamon-Brassey's, 1984), esp. 20–32; Kosta Tsipis, "Scientists and Weapons Procurement," in *Kosta Tsipis on the Arms Race,* ed. Kenneth W. Thompson, vol. 3 of the W. Alton Jones Foundation Series on Arms Control (New York: University Press of America, 1987), 185–89; Dina Rasor, *The Pentagon Underground* (New York: Times Books, 1985); Richard A. Gabriel, *Military Incompetence: Why the American Military Doesn't Win* (New York: Hill and Wang, 1985); and James Fallows, *National Defense* (New York: Random House, 1981). Forrest E. Waller, Jr.'s "Paradox and False Economy: Military Reform and High Technology" (*Air University Review* 34, no. 4 [May–June 1983]: 11–23) is a good examination of the reform movement, its goals, and impact. For a refreshing explication of the fallacies of reformist thought (and, particularly, their tendency to substitute ridicule for rationality), see Fred Reed, "Let's Reform the Military Reformers," *Washington Post,* October 11, 1987. Finally, for two generally useful and rational examinations of defense matters, see Maurice A. Mallin, *Tanks, Fighters and Ships: U.S. Conventional Force Planning since World War II* (Washington, D.C.: Brassey's, 1990); and Edward N. Luttwak, *The Pentagon and the Art of War: The Question of Military Reform* (New York: Simon and Schuster and the Institute for Contemporary Studies, 1985).

    10. Norman R. Augustine, "How We Almost Lost the Technological War," *Wall Street Journal,* June 14, 1991.

    11. Andrew G. B. Vallance, "The Conceptual Structure of Air Power," in *Air Power: Collected Essays on Doctrine,* ed. Vallance (London: Her Majesty's Stationery Office, 1990), 1.

    12. Appreciation for what the First World War in the air meant to future aviation is growing. For example, see Lee Kennett, *The First Air War, 1914–1918* (New York: Free Press, 1991), and Richard P. Hallion, *Rise of the Fighter Aircraft, 1914–1918* (Baltimore: Nautical and Aviation Publishing Co., 1984).

    13. F. E. Humphreys, "The Wright Flyer and Its Possible Uses in War," *Journal of the United States Artillery* 33, no. 2 (March–April 1910): 145–46.

    14. Douglas H. Robinson, *The Zeppelin in Combat* (London: G. T. Foulis and Co., 1961).

    15. K. N. Finne, *Igor Sikorsky: The Russian Years,* ed. Carl J. Bobrow and Von Hardesty (Washington, D.C.: Smithsonian Institution Press, 1987); Raymond H. Fredette, *The Sky on Fire: The First Battle of Britain, 1917–1918* (Washington, D.C.: Smithsonian Institution Press, 1991).

    16. For Soviet reaction to the collapse of their integrated air defenses, see Gabriel Schoenfeld, "The Loser of the Gulf War Is . . . the Soviet Military," *Wall Street Journal,* March 19, 1991. A more detailed examination can be found in

Mary C. FitzGerald, *The Soviet Image of Future War: "Through the Prism of the Persian Gulf,"* Report HI–4145 (Washington, D.C.: Hudson Institute, 1991).

17. Giulio Douhet, *The Command of the Air* (Washington, D.C.: Office of Air Force History, 1983). For two excellent summaries of the major thinking of air power spokesmen, see David MacIssac, "Voices from the Central Blue: The Air Power Theorists," in *Makers of Modern Strategy: From Machiavelli to the Nuclear Age,* ed. Peter Paret, in collaboration with Gordon A. Craig and Felix Gilbert (Princeton: Princeton University Press, 1986), 624–76; and Barry D. Watts, *The Foundations of U.S. Air Doctrine: The Problem of Friction in War* (Maxwell AFB, Ala.: Air University Press, 1984). James L. Stokesbury, *A Short History of Airpower* (New York: William Morrow, 1986) is a useful survey. I have also benefited from discussions with Lee Kennett.

18. See R. A. Mason, "The British Dimension," in *Air Power and Warfare: The Proceedings of the Eighth Military History Symposium, USAF Academy, 18– 20 October 1978,* ed. Alfred F. Hurley and Robert C. Ehrhart (Washington, D.C.: Office of Air Force History, 1979), 22–35, esp. 32; Andrew Boyle's impressive *Trenchard: Man of Vision* (New York: W. W. Norton, 1962); and Alfred F. Hurley's *Billy Mitchell: Crusader for Air Power* (Bloomington: Indiana University Press, 1975).

19. William Mitchell, *Skyways* (Philadelphia: J. B. Lippincott, 1930), 253.

20. Herman Kahn, *On Thermonuclear War: Three Lectures and Several Suggestions* (Princeton: Princeton University Press, 1961), 376.

21. Surprisingly, the air war in Spain generally has not received the attention it deserves. One particularly useful account is Raymond L. Proctor's *Hitler's Luftwaffe in the Spanish Civil War* (Westport, Conn: Greenwood Press, 1983).

22. The bombing campaign has been the subject of innumerable works, many of which are extremely partisan (both pro and con) in nature. The following are recommended exceptions: Lee Kennett, *A History of Strategic Bombing* (New York: Charles Scribner's Sons, 1982); David MacIssac, *Strategic Bombing in World War II: The Story of the United States Strategic Bombing Survey* (New York: Garland Publishing, 1976); and Max Hastings, *Bomber Command* (New York: Dial Press, 1979).

23. James Lea Cate, "Development of United States Air Doctrine, 1917–41," paper presented at the annual meeting of the Mississippi Valley Historical Association, Columbus, Ohio, April 24, 1947, reprinted in *The Impact of Air Power: National Security and World Politics,* ed. Eugene M. Emme (New York: D. Van Nostrand, 1959), 190. Emme's book is one of enduring and extraordinary value to air power and aerospace historians.

24. See Haywood W. Hansell, Jr.'s fascinating personal perspective, *The Strategic Air War Against Germany and Japan: A Memoir* (Washington, D.C.: Office of Air Force History, 1986), 15.

25. Cate, "Development of United States Air Doctrine," 191.

26. From USAAF, *AAF Bombing Accuracy Report #2* (Eighth Air Force: Operational Research Section, 1945), Chart 2, "Distribution of Effort and Results." I thank Tami Davis Biddle and W. Hays Parks for making this information available to me. Approximately 22 percent of all visually dropped bombs hit within 1,000 feet of their aim point, while only 2 percent of bombs dropped using blind navigational techniques or radar bombing fell within 1,000 feet of their target. The overall base statistics for this time period were 140,807 tons dropped, of which 9,700 tons hit within 1,000 feet of their aim point. Of the total, 33,821 tons were dropped visually, of which 7,544 were judged to have fallen within 1,000 feet of the aim point. See also Albert Speer, *Inside the Third Reich* (New York: Avon, 1971), 445.

27. Cohen, "Unsheltering Sky," 24. For a most useful summary of AAF strategic air power thought and the conduct of the European and Pacific bombing campaigns, see Hansell, *Strategic Air War.*

28. Both quoted in James Lea Cate and Wesley Frank Craven, "Victory," in *The Army Air Forces in World War II:* Vol. 5, *The Pacific: Matterhorn to Nagasaki, June 1944 to August 1945,* ed. Craven and Cate (Chicago: University of Chicago Press, 1953), 756.

29. USSBS, *Summary Reports* (European and Pacific Theaters) (rpt.: Maxwell AFB, Ala.: Air University Press, 1987), 37.

30. Ibid., 110, 111.

31. F. M. Sallagar, *Operation "Strangle" (Italy, Spring 1944): A Case Study of Tactical Air Interdiction,* Rand Report R-851-PR (Santa Monica: Rand Corporation, 1972); Eduard Mark, "A New Look at Operation Strangle," *Military Affairs* 52, no. 4 (Oct. 1988); and Price T. Bingham, "Ground Maneuver and Air Interdiction in the Operational Art," *Parameters: The U.S. Army War College Quarterly* 19, no. 1 (March 1989), offer useful and differing perspectives on this issue.

32. There are a series of excellent essays treating the application of tactical air power in Benjamin Franklin Cooling, ed., *Case Studies in the Development of Close Air Support* (Washington, D.C.: Office of Air Force History, 1991). See also my *Strike From the Sky: The History of Battlefield Air Attack, 1911–1945* (Washington, D.C.: Smithsonian Institution Press, 1989).

33. Ferdinand Miksche, *Attack: A Study of Blitzkrieg Tactics* (New York: Random House, 1942), 73.

34. Pierre Cot, *Triumph of Treason* (New York: Ziff-Davis, 1944), 274.

35. B. H. Liddell Hart, ed., with the assistance of Lucie-Maria Rommel, Manfred Rommel, and General Fritz Bayerlein, *The Rommel Papers* (New York: Harcourt, Brace, 1953), 285–86.

36. Friedrich Ruge, *Rommel in Normandy: Reminiscences by Friedrich Ruge* (San Rafael, Calif.: Presidio Press, 1979), 187.

37. John S. D. Eisenhower, *Strictly Personal* (Garden City, N.Y.: Doubleday, 1974), 72.

38. FM 100-20, *Command and Employment of Air Power* (Washington, D.C.: U.S. War Department, July 21, 1943). This was reissued by Gen. Michael Dugan shortly after he succeeded retiring Gen. Larry Welch as Air Force chief of staff in the late summer of 1990.

39. The single best source on the creation of the USAF is Herman Wolk's *Planning and Organizing the Postwar Air Force, 1943–1947* (Washington, D.C.: Office of Air Force History, 1984); see also Perry McCoy Smith, *The Air Force Plans for Peace, 1943–1945* (Baltimore: Johns Hopkins Press, 1970). De Seversky's most influential work was his *Victory Through Air Power* (New York: Simon and Schuster, 1942), which was made into a nationally distributed film by Walt Disney. For Arnold's views, see his "Air Power and the Future," reprinted in *American Military Thought,* ed. Walter Millis (New York: Bobbs-Merrill Co., 1966), 445–59.

40. Quoted in *Impact of Air Power,* ed. Emme, 300.

41. Dennis M. Drew, "The American Airpower Doctrine Dilemma," in *Air Power,* ed. Vallance, 63.

42. Theodore von Kármán, *Where We Stand: A Report Prepared for the AAF Scientific Advisory Group, August 1945* (Wright Field, Ohio: HQ Air Materiel Command, 1946), esp. iv, 8, 38.

43. I have explored some of these issues in two essays: "Girding for War: Perspectives on Research, Development, Acquisition, and the Decisionmaking Environment of the 1980s," *Air University Review* 37, no. 6 (Sept.–Oct. 1986); and "Doctrine, Technology, and Air Warfare: A Late Twentieth-century Perspective," *Airpower Journal* 1, no. 2 (Fall 1987). See also Robert F. Futrell, "The Influence of the Air Power Concept on Air Force Planning, 1945–1962," in *Military Planning in the Twentieth Century: Proceedings of the Eleventh Military History Symposium, 10–12 October 1984* [at the U.S. Air Force Academy], ed. Harry R. Borowski (Washington, D.C.: Office of Air Force History, 1986). The relevant Congressional hearings are U.S. Congress, House of Representatives, 81st Cong., 1st Sess., *The National Defense Program, Unification and Strategy,* Hearings before the Committee on Armed Services, October 6–8, 10–13, and 17–21, 1949 (Washington D.C.: GPO, 1949).

44. Alexander P. De Seversky, *Air Power: Key to Survival* (New York: Simon and Schuster, 1950).

45. For example, see Kahn, *On Thermonuclear War,* 3–13, 21, 27–39.

46. Jacob Neufeld, *The Development of Ballistic Missiles in the United States Air Force, 1945–1960* (Washington, D.C.: Office of Air Force History, 1990).

47. For the Air Force's general acceptance of the notion of atomic warfare, see Thomas L. Fisher II, "'Limited War'—What is It?" *Air University Quarterly Review* 9, no. 4 (Winter 1957–58): 127–42, esp. 135; and Frederic H. Smith, Jr.,

"Nuclear Weapons and Limited War," *Air University Quarterly Review* 12, no. 1 (Spring 1960): 3–27.

48. An idea first strongly encouraged (not surprisingly) by the von Kármán report. See the various articles in a special issue of the *Air University Quarterly Review* (11, nos. 3–4 [Fall and Winter, 1959]), which examined this matter in great detail. For the early gestation of the atomic airplane program, see Robert L. Perry, *The USAF Aircraft Nuclear Propulsion Program, 1944–1958* (Wright-Patterson AFB, Ohio: Air Research and Development Command, 1959), copy in the files of the History Office, Aeronautical Systems Division, Wright-Patterson AFB.

49. Futrell, "Influence of the Air Power Concept," 266–67.

50. See Richard P. Hallion, "A Troubling Past: Air Force Fighter Acquisition since 1945," *Airpower Journal* 4, no. 4 (Winter 1990): 4–23.

51. For two views of air power in Korea, see Robert F. Futrell, *The United States Air Force in Korea, 1950–1953* (Washington, D.C.: Office of Air Force History, 1983); and Richard P. Hallion, *The Naval Air War in Korea* (Baltimore: Nautical and Aviation Publishing Co., 1986). Victor Flintham's *Air Wars and Aircraft: A Detailed Record of Air Combat, 1945 to the Present* (New York: Facts on File, 1990), is an extremely useful reference for the many small conflicts that occurred after the Second World War.

52. The best account of Dien Bien Phu and the ill-fated air campaign on its behalf remains Bernard B. Fall's *Hell in a Very Small Place: The Siege of Dien Bien Phu* (New York: Vintage Books, 1966).

53. The best short analysis of the air war in Vietnam is Alan L. Gropman, "The Air War in Vietnam, 1961–1973," in *War in the Third Dimension: Essays in Contemporary Air Power,* ed. R. A. Mason (London: Brassey's Defence Publishers, 1986), 33–58. Five interesting analyses of the war are: U. S. Grant Sharp, *Strategy for Defeat: Vietnam in Retrospect* (San Rafael, Calif.: Presidio Press, 1978); Harry G. Summers, Jr., *On Strategy: A Critical Analysis of the Vietnam War* (New York: Dell, 1984); Robert A. Pape, Jr., "Coercive Air Power in the Vietnam War," *International Security* 15, no. 2 (Fall 1990): 103–46; John F. Guilmartin, Jr., "Bombing the Ho Chi Minh Trail," *Air Power History* 38, no. 4 (Winter 1991): 3–17; and Earl H. Tilford, Jr., *Setup: What the Air Force Did in Vietnam and Why* (Maxwell AFB, Ala.: Air University Press, 1991).

54. Joshua Muravchik, "End of the Vietnam Paradigm?" *Commentary* 91, no. 5 (May 1991): 17.

55. In the popular literature of the time, from newspapers through journals, Vietnam-era veterans were often criticized as dupes, probable war criminals, and losers; they became the "crazed vet" of popular culture, a common figure in novels, films, television, and pop psychology. Such accountings have become truisms, and as time passes tend to drift into an apocryphal fog—but they *did* occur—as did another distasteful episode, the posing of actress Jane Fonda with an antiair-

craft unit while on an "antiwar" trip to North Vietnam, at the same time that American airmen were being brutalized in the "Hanoi Hilton."

56. Drew Middleton, *Can American Win the Next War?* (New York: Charles Scribner's Sons, 1975), 7.

57. I have drawn on experiences I had as a visiting professor at the U.S. Army War College in 1987–88, and from numerous conversations and discussions with Air Force, Marine, and Navy colleagues through the years.

58. As Ball wrote in a national magazine, "We are considering air action against [North Vietnam] as the means to a limited objective—*the improvement of our bargaining position* with the North Vietnamese" (emphasis added). See George W. Ball, "How Valid Are the Assumptions Underlying Our Viet-Nam Policies?" *Atlantic Monthly* 230 (Oct. 5, 1964): 38. The clearest evidence of this can be seen in the various memos between senior administration officials reprinted in "The Air War in North Vietnam, 1965–1968," vol. 4 of The Senator Mike Gravel edition of *The Pentagon Papers: The Defense Department History of United States Decisionmaking on Vietnam* (Boston: Beacon Press, 1975), 1–276; for example, see the text of McNamara's July 20, 1965, memo to President Johnson, p. 26.

59. Despite a plethora of literature on the Vietnam air war, there are few definitive works. Four interesting perspectives are: Mark Clodfelter, *The Limits to Air Power: The American Bombing of North Vietnam* (New York: Free Press, 1989); Jack Broughton, *Going Downtown: The War Against Hanoi and Washington* (New York: Orion Books, 1988); John B. Nichols and Barrett Tillman, *On Yankee Station: The Naval Air War Over Vietnam* (Annapolis, Md.: Naval Institute Press, 1987); and William W. Momyer, *Air Power in Three Wars* (Washington, D.C.: HQ USAF, 1978). I acknowledge the very helpful contributions of Lt. Col. Ben Harvey, USAF, to my thinking on this subject.

60. Clodfelter, *The Limits to Air Power,* 121.

61. Ibid., 243.

62. Kenneth P. Werrell's *Archie, Flak, AAA and SAM: A Short Operational History of Ground-Based Air Defense* (Maxwell AFB, Ala.: Air University Press, 1988) is an outstanding monograph that examines the SAM impact on SEA air operations in detail. A good popular study is Larry Davis' *Wild Weasel: The SAM Suppression Story* (Carrollton, Tex.: Squadron/Signal Publications, 1986).

63. Bruce K. Holloway, "Air Superiority in Tactical Air Warfare," *Air University Review* 19, no. 3 (March–April 1968): 8–9.

64. David K. Mann, *The 1972 Invasion of Military Region I: Fall of Quang Tri and Defense of Hue* (Hickam AFB, Hawaii: HQ PACAF, Directorate of Operations Analysis, CHECO/Corona Harvest Division, March 15, 1973); John A. Doglione et al., *Airpower and the 1972 Spring Invasion,* Monograph 3 of the USAF Air University USAF Southeast Asia Monograph Series (Washington, D.C.: GPO, 1976).

65. Karl J. Eschmann, *Linebacker: The Untold Story of the Air Raids Over North Vietnam* (New York: Ivy Books, 1989).

66. John J. Tolson, *Airmobility, 1961–1971,* Vietnam Studies Series (Washington, D.C.: Dept. of the Army, 1973).

67. Ray L. Bowers, *Tactical Airlift,* The United States Air Force in Southeast Asia 1965–1973 Series (Washington, D.C.: Office of Air Force History, 1983), 691; conversation with Brig. Gen. James Cole, USAF, July 18, 1991.

68. Delbert Corum et al., *The Tale of Two Bridges,* Monograph 1 of the USAF Air University USAF Southeast Asia Monograph Series (Washington, D.C.: GPO, 1976), 79–92.

69. See John Schlight, *The War in South Vietnam: The Years of the Offensive, 1965–1968,* The United States Air Force in Southeast Asia 1965–1973 Series (Washington, D.C.: Office of Air Force History, 1988); and Bernard C. Nalty, *Air Power and the Fight for Khe Sanh* (Washington, D.C.: Office of Air Force History, 1973).

70. From a conversation with Lt. Col. Martin Andresen, USA, at the U.S. Army War College's Military History Institute, 1988. Andresen, as a Field Artillery officer, recalled several specific cases in which this was done.

71. Kinnard study results are quoted in Donald J. Mrozek, *Air Power and the Ground War in Vietnam: Ideas and Action* (Maxwell AFB, Ala.: Air University Press, 1988), 119, and are drawn from Kinnard's own *The War Managers* (Hanover, N.H.: University Press of New England, 1977), 63.

72. John J. Sbrega, "Southeast Asia," in *Case Studies,* ed. Cooling, 469.

73. Ibid.

74. Shelby L. Stanton, "Lessons Learned or Lost: Air Cavalry and Airmobility," *Military Review* 69, no. 1 (Jan. 1989): 74–86.

75. Kenneth R. Pierce, "The Battle of the Ia Drang Valley," *Military Review* 69, no. 1 (Jan. 1989): 88–97.

76. Stanton, "Lessons Learned or Lost," 84–85. Stanton, an Army veteran and distinguished commentator on the war, has written widely on airmobility operations. See his *Anatomy of a Division: The 1st Cav in Vietnam* (Novato, Calif.: Presidio Press, 1987); and his impressive *The Rise and Fall of an American Army: U.S. Ground Forces in Vietnam, 1965–1973* (Novato, Calif.: Presidio Press, 1985). See also Tolson, *Airmobility,* 18–24, 73–83.

77. U.S. Army Office of the Adjutant General, "Special Operational Report—Lessons Learned on the AH–1G Employment," HQ, 307th Combat Aviation Battalion (May 24, 1968), Military History Institute Library, U.S. Army War College, Carlisle Barracks, Pa. For a useful general survey of armed helicopter development and deployment, see Howard A. Wheeler, *Attack Helicopters: A History of Rotary-Wing Combat Aircraft* (Baltimore: Nautical and Aviation Publishing Co., 1987).

78. The best reference on fixed-wing gunship development is Jack S. Ballard's

Development and Employment of Fixed Wing Gunships, 1962–1972, The United States Air Force in Southeast Asia 1965–1973 Series (Washington, D.C.: Office of Air Force History, 1982); see p. 243 in particular. Additionally, see Henry Zeybel, "Truck Count," *Air University Review* 34, no. 2 (Jan.–Feb. 1983): 36–45.

79. For example, see Yossef Bodansky, "Air War Vietnam: What the Soviets Learned," *Air University Review* 34, no. 2 (Jan.–Feb. 1983): 83–91.

80. See Nadav Safran, *From War to War: The Arab-Israeli Confrontation, 1948–1967* (New York: Pegasus, 1969), 317–82, 435–52; John F. Kreis, *Air Warfare and Air Base Defense, 1914–1973* (Washington, D.C.: Office of Air Force History, 1988), 311–17.

81. Werrell, *Archie, Flak, AAA and SAM*, 138.

82. Ibid., 138–46; Edgar O'Ballance, *No Victor, No Vanquished: The Yom Kippur War* (San Rafael, Calif.: Presidio Press, 1978), 278–306; Hassan El Badri et al., *The Ramadan War, 1973* (Dunn Loring, Va.: T. N. Dupuy Associates, 1979), 21, 198–200.

83. Norman Podhoretz's excellent *Why We Were in Vietnam* (New York: Simon and Schuster, 1983) offers a brilliant and extremely disturbing analysis of how the media and the antiwar movement functioned in the war; it should be read by anyone interested in the war's larger issues.

84. Loren Baritz, *Backfire: A History of How American Culture Led Us into Vietnam and Made Us Fight the Way We Did* (New York: Ballantine Books, 1986), 153.

85. For a typical anti-airpower position prior to the war, see William S. Lind, "If We Fight This War, Can We Win?" *Washington Post*, August 19, 1990.

Chapter 2. Rebuilding Air Superiority

1. For example, see James E. Johnson, *Full Circle: The Tactics of Air Fighting, 1914–1964* (New York: Ballantine Books, 1964), 103; Alexis Dawydoff, "The Dogfight is Back!" *Air Trails* 13, no. 6 (March 1940): 16–17, 54–56; Nichols and Tillman, *On Yankee Station*, 72–86; and Holloway, "Air Superiority in Tactical Air Warfare," 9.

2. I have examined this issue in greater detail in "Between Scylla and Charybdis: The Acquisition of Air Force Fighter Aircraft Since 1945," a paper presented at the Triangle Universities' Security Seminar on Changing Technologies and New Weapons Systems, Quail Roost Conference Center, Durham, N.C., February 2–3, 1990; a shorter version of this paper appeared as "A Troubling Past" (see chap. 1, n. 50).

3. Richard G. Head, "Decision-Making on the A-7 Attack Aircraft Program," Ph.D. diss., Syracuse University, 1971; and Glenn E. Bugos, "Testing the F-4

Phantom II: Engineering Practice in the Development of American Military Aircraft, 1954–1969," Ph.D. diss., University of Pennsylvania, 1988.

4. Statistics from Nichols and Tillman, *On Yankee Station,* 169.

5. Ibid., 77; R. Frank Futrell et al., *Aces and Aerial Victories,* The United States Air Force in Southeast Asia 1965–1973 Series (Washington, D.C.: Office of Air Force History, 1976), 157.

6. Jacob Van Staaveren, *Air Operations in the Taiwan Crisis of 1958* (Washington, D.C.: USAF Historical Division Liaison Office, 1962), 38–39. For the background of Sidewinder, see the memoir of Ron Westrum and Howard A. Wilcox, "Sidewinder," *American Heritage of Invention and Technology* 2 (Fall 1989): 56–63; and Bill Gunston, "The AAM Story," *Air International* 32, no. 2 (Feb. 1987): 74–79.

7. I wish to acknowledge information from Lt. Col. William "Flaps" Flanagan, USAF (ret.), a former F-4E weapons system officer and noted authority on air-to-air and air-to-surface missiles.

8. See Eschmann, *Linebacker,* 128; Eschmann was an F-4 maintenance officer who witnessed missile mishandling and moved to stop it.

9. George Hall, *Top Gun: The Navy's Fighter Weapons School* (Novato, Calif.: Presidio Press, 1987).

10. Nichols and Tillman, *On Yankee Station,* 85–86.

11. First issued after Korea and then, unfortunately, quickly discarded as "obsolete" in the nuclear age, Frederick C. "Boots" Blesse's *No Guts, No Glory!* was reissued as a special publication by the Headquarters, 57th Tactical Training Wing, TAC, Nellis AFB, in 1977. Blesse's memoir, *Check Six: A Fighter Pilot Looks Back* (Mesa, Ariz.: Champlin Fighter Museum, 1987), offers a worthwhile perspective on jet age combat from Korea through Vietnam.

12. Michael Skinner, *Red Flag: Combat Training in Today's Air Force* (Novato, Calif.: Presidio Press, 1984), offers a useful survey.

13. John Joss, *Strike: U.S. Naval Strike Warfare Center* (Novato, Calif.: Presidio Press, 1989).

14. John Trotti, *Marine Air: First to Fight* (Novato, Calif.: Presidio Press, 1985).

15. Daniel P. Bolger, *Dragons at War: Land Battle in the Desert* (New York: Ivy Books, 1991).

16. And, indeed, this came to pass, not merely for designs but for individual aircraft, including the F-4. In 1990, the 6512th Test Squadron at Edwards AFB was still routinely flying a F-4C that the author had first seen on the ramp at Andrews AFB in 1963.

17. Cost data from Robert Frank Futrell, *Ideas, Concepts, Doctrine: Basic Thinking in the United States Air Force:* Vol. 2, 1961–1984 (Maxwell AFB, Ala.: Air University Press, 1989), 492.

18. The best sources of information on the F-111 are the two sets of Senate Committee on Government Operations hearings and a summary report: the ten-

volume *TFX Contract Investigation* (Washington, D.C.: GPO, 1963–64), the three-volume *TFX Contract Investigation (Second Series)* (Washington, D.C.: GPO, 1970); and the committee's summary report, *TFX Contract Investigation, Report 91–1496* (Washington, D.C.: GPO, 1970). The best introductory source is Robert F. Coulam's *Illusions of Choice: The F-111 and the Problem of Weapons Acquisition Reform* (Princeton: Princeton University Press, 1977). For Mc-Namara's views, see his *The Essence of Security: Reflections in Office* (New York: Harper and Row, 1968), 92–93.

19. For a more detailed examination of this issue, see my *The Evolution of Commonality in Fighter and Attack Aircraft Development and Usage* (Edwards AFB, Calif.: Air Force Flight Test Center History Office, 1985).

20. Jacob Neufeld, *The F-15 Eagle: Origins and Development, 1964–1972* (Washington, D.C.: Office of Air Force History, November 1974), 6–19; these are "sanitized" unclassified pages of a work that is still classified at the SECRET level. I with to thank Bill Heimdahl of the Office of Air Force History for making the sanitized version available.

21. Futrell, *Ideas, Concepts, Doctrine,* 2:471.

22. Ibid.; M. B. Rothman, *Aerospace Weapon System Acquisition Milestones: A Data Base,* N-2599-ACQ (Santa Monica, Calif.: Rand Corporation, 1987), 60, 62; I wish to acknowledge my appreciation to Gen. John M. "Mike" Loh, for insights he offered regarding the workings of the "Fighter Mafia" in the critical pre-F-15 and pre-F-16 days, while he served as Air Force vice chief of staff.

23. Holloway, "Air Superiority in Tactical Air Warfare," 8.

24. McCain quote from Daniel Guggenheim Medal Board of Award, *Pioneering in Aeronautics: Recipients of the Daniel Guggenheim Medal, 1929–1952* (New York: Daniel Guggenheim Medal Board of Award, 1952), 117.

25. Rothman, *Aerospace Weapon System Acquisition Milestones,* 58–59. The F-4 comparison to the F-14 is from James Perry Stevenson, *Grumman F-14 "Tomcat" (sic),* Aero Series (Fallbrook, Calif.: Aero Publishers, 1975), 62.

26. See Robert W. Drewes, *The Air Force and the Great Engine War* (Washington, D.C.: National Defense University Press, 1987), 51–67. Conversation with Lt. Col. David Deptula, September 23, 1991 (who experienced engine disintegration and fire on his very first F-15 flight, and, in an extraordinary feat of airmanship, successfully returned to base).

27. Rothman, *Aerospace Weapon System Acquisition Milestones,* 60–61; Tom Lennon and Jim Wray, *Bringing the F-15 to Operational Readiness* (Langley AFB, Calif.: 1st TFW, 1977).

28. Deborah L. Gable, "Acquisition of the F-16 Fighting Falcon (1972–1980)," Paper 87-0900, USAF Air Command and Staff College, Maxwell AFB, Ala., is a useful survey; Loh conversation.

29. Ibid.; also Rothman, *Aerospace Weapon System Acquisition Milestones,* 62–63.

30. Gable, "Acquisition of the F-16 Fighting Falcon"; Loh conversation;

Rothman, *Aerospace Weapon System Acquisition Milestones*. I have also bene-fited from conversations through the years with General Dynamics chief test pilot Phil Oestricher and Col. Bob Ettinger, USAF (ret.).

31. Rothman, *Aerospace Weapon System Acquisition Milestones*, 62–63. The annual histories of the Air Force Flight Test Center from 1974–82 have excellent summaries of the F-15, YF-16/F-16, and YF-17 flight test activities; they are on file with the History Office, Air Force Flight Test Center, Edwards AFB, Calif. See also Paul E. Ceruzzi, *Beyond the Limits: Flight Enters the Computer Age* (Cambridge: MIT Press, 1989). The F-104 comparison is from a personal experience. At Mach 1.2 and 3g in a TF-104G, the airframe buffet was so high that even reading the aft cockpit instrument panel proved very difficult. A decade later, on a hop in a F-16B, a positioning maneuver to 9.2g was rock-steady.

32. For the Navy–Air Force rivalry on the F-14 and F-15, see James W. Canan, *The Superwarriors* (New York: Weybright and Talley, 1975), 50–64.

33. Rothman, *Aerospace Weapon System Acquisition Milestones*, 64–65; I wish to acknowledge discussions I have had with George Spangenberg and, in particular, two memos that he sent to me: Memorandum for record, subject: Multi-Service Aircraft Procurements, August 30, 1974; and memorandum for record, subject: The VFAX/ACF Program—a Review, October 21, 1974.

34. Rothman, *Aerospace Weapon System Acquisition Milestones*, 65.

35. G. W. Lenox, "F-18 Multi-Mission Aircraft," in Society of Experimental Test Pilots, *1976 Report to the Aerospace Profession* 13, no. 2 (Sept. 22–25, 1976): 34–41; Ivan M. Behel and William G. McNamara, "F/A-18A High Angle of Attack/Spin Testing," in Society of Experimental Test Pilots, *1981 Report to the Aerospace Profession* 16, no. 2 (Sept. 23–26, 1981): 108–32; Barbara Amouyal and Robert Holzer, "Structural Flaws Halve Life of Early F/A–18 Hornets," *Defense News* (Nov. 20, 1989); for the details on the Hornet contract issue, see John F. Lehman, *Command of the Seas* (New York: Charles Scribner's Sons, 1989), 228–35.

36. Michael D. Hall and Richard L. Griffin, "Air-to-Air Missile Acquisition and Testing," in Society of Experimental Test Pilots, *1976 Report to the Aerospace Profession*, 168. P_{ssk} is the product of five factors: whether a fighter success-fully forces an opposing aircraft into an engagement (P_e); whether the pilot fires a missile (P_l); whether the missile guides successfully (P_g); whether the fuze works (P_f); and whether the warhead kills the target (P_k). Thus, probability of a single shot kill is expressed by the equation:

$$P_{ssk} = P_e \times P_l \times P_g \times P_f \times P_k$$

37. James A. McKinney and J. Thomas McWilliams, "The ACEVAL-AIMVAL Joint Test Program," in Society of Experimental Test Pilots, *1976 Report to the Aerospace Profession*, 128–37.

38. Rothman, *Aerospace Weapon System Acquisition Milestones*, 176–77;

Bill Gunston's *An Illustrated Guide to Modern Airborne Missiles* ([New York: Prentice-Hall, 1983], 58–61) is a useful reference.

39. Hall and Griffin, "Air-to-air Missile Acquisition and Testing," 165.

40. Rothman, *Aerospace Weapon System Acquisition Milestones,* 181–82; Gunston, *Modern Airborne Missiles,* 52–55.

41. Rothman, *Aerospace Weapon System Acquisition Milestones,* 183–84; Gunston, *Modern Airborne Missiles,* 40–41.

42. Rothman, *Aerospace Weapon System Acquisition Milestones,* 185–86; Jeffrey P. Rhodes, "The Next Round for Aerial Combat," *Air Force Magazine* 74, no. 2 (Feb. 1991): 46–51; personal recollections.

43. I acknowledge information received from Col. Doug Joyce, USAF, who reviewed the original Blitzfighter proposals for Air Force Systems Command, and who maintained an extensive file of "austere" fighter proposals.

44. See Fallows, *National Defense,* 95–106.

45. Michael Collins, *Carrying the Fire* (New York: Farrar, Straus and Giroux, 1974), 9. "In retrospect," Collins wrote, "it seems preposterous to endure such casualty rates without help from the enemy, but at the time the risk appeared perfectly acceptable."

46. What might seem a tall tale is confirmed by dramatic photos of the recovered aircraft; the author was present when this was briefed at an Air Force Flight Test Center flight safety meeting in 1982. Until the photos were shown, virtually no one believed that any aircraft could recover from such grievous damage. (Rumor had it that the Israeli air force subsequently demoted the pilot one grade for not maintaining sufficient alertness, and then promoted him *two* grades for his superb flying, a decision worthy of Solomon.)

47. A case in point is the P-47, which decimated the Luftwaffe over 1943–44, and then went on to become the most successful Allied fighter-bomber of the war—something that the much more vulnerable P-51, for all its air-to-air prowess, could not do (as Mustang losses on ground attack in 1944–45 and in Korea in 1950–52 clearly indicated). An ideal example of the "austere" philosophy would be the Fokker Dr I triplane of the First World War. Highly agile, it could not fulfill the kind of swing-role missions demanded by late World War I combat, and, further, could not engage or disengage on its own terms. More sophisticated opponents, even if less agile, were able to ignore it, or engage it on their own terms and destroy it in slashing attacks.

48. If imitation is the sincerest form of flattery, one could see in 1970s and 1980s Soviet fighter aircraft acquisition a tendency not to emphasize the defense critics' idealized austere fighters but, instead, to give their aircraft as much sophistication as possible—witness, for example, the MiG-23 Flogger, MiG-29 Fishbed, MiG-31 Foxhound, and Su-27 Flanker, clearly designed to confront sophisticated Western threats.

49. Mallin, *Tanks, Fighters, and Ships,* 199.

Chapter 3. Reforging Forces for General War

1. I have drawn on Gropman, "The Air War in Vietnam"; Doglione et al., *Airpower and the 1972 Spring Invasion;* Mann, *The 1972 Invasion of Military Region I;* and Werrell, *Archie, Flak, AAA and SAM,* as my principal sources for this account. For a ground view, see G. H. Turley, *The Easter Offensive: Vietnam, 1972* (New York: Warner, 1989).

2. Turley, *The Easter Offensive,* vii.

3. Doglione et al., *Airpower and the 1972 Spring Invasion,* 106–7, has excellent statistical summaries.

4. Werrell, *Archie, Flak, AAA and SAM,* 116.

5. Truong Nhu Tang, *A Viet Cong Memoir* (New York: Vintage Books, 1985), 211; see also Clodfelter, *Limits to Air Power,* 169.

6. Tang, *Viet Cong Memoir,* 168.

7. Doglione et al., *Airpower and the 1972 Spring Offensive,* 64–65.

8. Ibid., 74; see also Steven J. Zaloga and George J. Balin, *Anti-Tank Helicopters* (London: Osprey Publishing, 1986), 10–11.

9. See David R. Mets, *The Quest for a Surgical Strike: The United States Air Force and Laser Guided Bombs* (Eglin AFB, Fla.: Armament Division History Office, 1987); and Doglione et al., *Airpower and the 1972 Spring Offensive* studies.

10. Wellington quote from Robert Debs Heinl, *Dictionary of Military and Naval Quotations* (Annapolis, Md.: U.S. Naval Institute, 1966), 357. I have based this discussion on the 1973 Arab-Israeli war from O'Ballance, *No Victor, No Vanquished;* Badri, *The Ramadan War;* Kreis, *Air Warfare and Air Base Defense;* Futrell, *Ideas, Concepts, Doctrine* 2; David R. Mets, *Land-based Air Power in Third World Crises* (Maxwell AFB, Ala.: Air University Press, 1986); Ze'ev Schiff, *A History of the Israeli Army* (New York: Macmillan, 1985); Avraham Adan, *On the Banks of the Suez* (Novato, Calif.: Presidio Press, 1980); and Brereton Greenhous, "The Israeli Experience," in *Case Studies,* ed. Cooling, 513–24.

11. Adan, *On the Banks of the Suez,* 82–83; Adan's memoir is an unusually frank and thoughtful account of the war.

12. Orr Kelly, *King of the Killing Zone* (New York: Berkley Books, 1989), 225; the Soviet production figure is calculated on the basis of information in Department of Defense, *Soviet Military Power: 1983* (Washington, D.C.: GPO, 1983), 80.

13. Kreis, *Air Warfare and Air Base Defense,* 325–37; Futrell, *Ideas, Concepts, Doctrine* 2:484–85; and Mets, *Land-based Air Power,* 89–120; Schiff, *A History of the Israeli Army,* 207–29.

14. Yehuda Weinraub, "The Israel Air Force and the Air Land Battle," *Israeli Defense Forces Journal* 3, no. 3 (Summer 1986): 22–30; quote from p. 23.

15. Vannevar Bush, *Modern Arms and Free Men: A Discussion of the Role of Science in Preserving Democracy* (Cambridge: MIT Press, 1968), 31–32; "The tank," he wrote, "nearly met its match in the last war; perhaps it should have."

16. Adan, *On the Banks of the Suez*, 467–69.

17. Werrell, *Archie, Flak, AAA and SAM*, 119; testimony of Charles A. Horner and Buster C. Glosson regarding the performance of stealth in Desert Storm before the Committee on Appropriations, U.S. House of Representatives, 1991.

18. Werrell, *Archie, Flak, AAA and SAM*, 119–26. I have also benefited from conversations with Capt. Ray Grienke, USAF, who flew on Linebacker II as a B-52 crewman.

19. Meir quote from Christopher J. Bowie, *Airlift and U.S. National Security: The Case for the C-17* (Washington, D.C.: Staff Group, Office of the Secretary of the Air Force, 1991), 5; See also Mets, *Land-based Air Power*, 105–8; Chris J. Krisinger, "Operation Nickel Grass: Airlift in Support of National Policy," *Airpower Journal* 3, no. 1 (Spring 1989): 16–28; Dick J. Burkard, *Military Airlift Command: Historical Handbook, 1941–1984* (Scott AFB, Ill.: Military Airlift Command History Office, 1984), 11; Christopher J. Bowie, *The United States Air Force and U.S. National Security: A Historical Perspective, 1947–1990* (Washington, D.C.: Staff Group, Office of the Secretary of the Air Force, 1991), 25.

20. Bowie, *Airlift and U.S. National Security*, 8–13; also Rothman, *Aerospace Weapon System Acquisition Milestones*, 89–96; Gordon Swanborough and Peter M. Bowers, *United States Military Aircraft since 1909* (Washington, D.C.: Smithsonian Institution Press, 1989), 399–403.

21. Rothman, *Aerospace Weapon System Acquisition Milestones*, 98–99; Swanborough and Bowers, *U.S. Military Aircraft*, 143–50.

22. See Eschmann, *Linebacker*, 202–5, and Richard H. Kohn and Joseph P. Harahan, eds., *Strategic Air Warfare: An Interview with Generals Curtis E. LeMay, Leon W. Johnson, David A. Burchinal, and Jack J. Catton* (Washington, D.C.: Office of Air Force History, 1988), 126–27.

23. Rothman, *Aerospace Weapon System Acquisition Milestones*, 81–87.

24. See Nick Kotz, *Wild Blue Yonder: Money, Politics, and the B-1 Bomber* (New York: Pantheon Books, 1988); Kotz details the interesting interplay between the B-1A and the cruise missile issue.

25. Rothman, *Aerospace Weapon System Acquisition Milestones*, 78.

26. Winston S. Churchill II, *Defending the West* (Westport, Conn.: Arlington House, 1981), 46.

27. Data from Department of Defense, *Soviet Military Power: Prospects for Change—1989* (Washington, D.C.: GPO, 1989), 99.

28. Data from Department of Defense, *Soviet Military Power: An Assessment of the Threat—1988* (Washington, D.C.: GPO, 1988), 99–101.

29. Data from Department of Defense, *Soviet Military Power: 1989*, 107.

30. Ibid., 23.

31. The academic comment is from a personal recollection.

32. Three of these novels stand out: Sir John Hackett et al., *The Third World War, August 1985,* Harold Coyle's *Team Yankee* (based upon an episode in Hackett's work), and, of course, Tom Clancy's *Red Storm Rising.* Clancy's was thoughtful and the most successful, Hackett's the most provocative at the war college level, and Coyle's the most interesting in portraying armored warfare at the tactical level.

33. At least to this reader. I first heard this anecdote in a faculty discussion at the Army War College in 1988; subsequently it appeared in the recollections of one of the participants. See Romie L. Brownlee and William J. Mullen, eds., *Changing an Army: An Oral History of General William E. DuPuy, USA Retired* (Carlisle Barracks, Pa.: U.S. Army Military History Institute, 1988), 196.

34. Ibid., 173–75; Kelly, *King of the Killing Zone,* 88.

35. Copperhead Gulf War information from Department of the Army, "Army Weapons Systems Performance in Southwest Asia" (Washington, D.C.: Department of the Army, March 13, 1991), 3.

36. Personal recollection.

37. For one examination of American air support after FM 100-20, see my *Strike From the Sky.*

38. See Futrell, *USAF in Korea;* and Hallion, *Naval Air War in Korea.*

39. I have drawn extensivly upon David J. Stein's *The Development of NATO Tactical Air Doctrine,* R-3385-AF (Santa Monica, Calif.: Rand Corporation, 1987).

40. I have drawn upon personal recollection, as well as Richard G. Davis's monograph, *The 31 Initiatives: A Study in Air Force–Army Cooperation* (Washington, D.C.: Office of Air Force History, 1987). Futrell, *Ideas, Concepts, Doctrine* has a good summary of the A-X—Cheyenne—AAH battle. See 2:518–31.

41. Davis, *31 Initiatives,* 25–27.

42. Ibid.; Department of the Army, FM 100-5, *Operations* (Washington, D.C.: GPO, 1976); Brownlee and Mullen, eds., *Changing an Army,* 190–91.

43. The best study of Army doctrinal evolution in this time period is John L. Romjue's *From Active Defense to AirLand Battle: The Development of Army Doctrine, 1973–1982* (Washington, D.C.: GPO, 1984) For Starry's own perspective of where AirLand Battle fit within the evolution of Army thought, see Donn A. Starry, "A Perspective on American Military Thought," *Military Review* 69, no. 7 (July 1989): 2–11.

44. "New Army Doctrine Balances Offense and Defense," *Defense Electronics* 18, no. 8 (Aug. 1986): 43–44.

45. There is a brief but thoughtful discussion of what AirLand Battle meant in Air Force–Army terms in Edward Mann's "Desert Storm No Textbook for AirLand Battle."

46. Chief of Public Affairs, *AirLand Battle* (Ft. Monroe, Va.: TRADOC, n.d.); typescript copy in the library of the U.S. Army Military History Institute filed as U260.A3.

47. Department of the Army, *Operations;* I also wish to acknowledge information received in meetings with Lt. Col. Joe Shipes, and Col. M. J. Morin at the U.S. Army War College, in 1987–88. I have also drawn on TRADOC, "Tactical Air Support of Ground Forces on the AirLand Battle" (Ft. Monroe, Va.: TRADOC, April 1987).

48. Merrill A. McPeak, "TACAIR Missions and the Fire Support Coordination Line," *Air University Review* 36, no. 6 (Sept.–Oct. 1985).

49. See, for example, ALFA, *Air Land Bulletin,* 87–3 (Sept. 30, 1987).

50. Davis, *31 Initiatives.*

51. Ibid.

52. Robert Coram, "The Case Against the Air Force," *Washington Monthly* 19, nos. 7–8 (July–Aug. 1987): 17–24; quote from last page.

Chapter 4. Renewing Military Confidence

1. In tongue-in-cheek fashion, one might suggest that the stages through which American military experience proceeded in the 1970s and 1980s correspond in approximate fashion to those posited by Dr. Elizabeth Kübler-Ross: Denial, Isolation, Anger, Bargaining, Depression, Acceptance. For example, imagine the following: Period I, Denial, Isolation, Anger; Period II, Bargaining, Depression; Period III, Acceptance. See Elizabeth Kübler-Ross, *On Death and Dying* (New York: Macmillan, 1973). (I acknowledge the contributions of Margaret M. Kane of Sidwell Friends Middle School, Washington, D.C., to this "theory"). Perhaps it is more than mere accident that (at least to some) the Gulf war witnessed the "burying" of the "Vietnam syndrome."

2. Summers, *On Strategy,* 21.

3. Quoted in Lehman, *Command of the Seas,* 117.

4. See, for example, Vernon V. Aspaturian, "The Impact of the Grenada Events on the Soviet Alliance System," in *Grenada and Soviet/Cuban Policy: Internal Crisis and U.S./OECS Intervention,* ed. Jiri Valenta and Herbert J. Ellison (Boulder, Colo.: Westview Press, 1986), 49–50.

5. Benjamin F. Schemmer's *The Raid* (New York: Harper and Row, 1976), is a superb account of the planning and conduct of this ill-fated but noble affair.

6. Mets, *Land-based Air Power,* 58; his account of the crisis is the clearest and best short essay that has been done. Roy Rowan's *The Four Days of Mayaguez* (New York: W. W. Norton, 1975) is a useful account, and the presidential perspective is offered in Gerald R. Ford's autobiography *A Time to Heal* (New York: Berkley Books, 1979).

7. Hamilton Jordan, *Crisis: The Last Year of the Carter Presidency* (New York: G. P. Putnam's Sons, 1982), 278. Jordan's memoir is an excellent and surprisingly frank account of the Carter years.

8. There is a good summary of the problems in Les Aspin, "Desert One to Desert Storm: Making Ready for Victory," a speech delivered at the Center for Strategic and International Studies, June 20, 1991, Washington, D.C.

9. Paul B. Ryan, *The Iranian Rescue Mission: Why It Failed* (Annapolis, Md.: Naval Institute Press, 1985), 42–43; see also 36–42. Ryan's book is a good survey of the Iranian rescue attempt. See also Anthony Gambone's *Pave Low III: That Others May Live* (Wright-Patterson AFB, Ohio: ASD History Office, 1988), 227–29, and Luttwak, *The Pentagon and the Art of War,* 44–45.

10. The story of the defective helicopters is from Lehman, *Command of the Seas,* 389; see also Jordan, *Crisis,* 250–91. Charlie A. Beckwith, the commander of the rescue force, has left his own memoir (with Donald Knox), *Delta Force* (New York: Harcourt Brace Jovanovich, 1983); see 253–87. The on-scene ground commander has left his own account: see James H. Kyle, *The Guts to Try* (New York: Orion Books, 1990); he has an intriguing comment on the use of Pave Lows for post-rescue combat search-and-rescue over Iran from Dhahran.

11. I have drawn on my personal observations and recollections of this time period, and from discussions with other colleagues, notably Col. John Taylor, USAF (ret.). Polling data is from "Poll of Attitudes Toward American Institutions," *Washington Post,* January 31, 1991. Logistics figures are from John T. Correll, "Let's Hear it for the Loggies," *Air Force Magazine* 74, no. 8 (Aug. 1991): 7.

12. The observer is Lehman, *Command of the Seas,* 162–63; see also Aspin, "Desert One to Desert Storm." Hamilton Jordan's *Crisis* offers an excellent insider's perspective of an administration fighting to survive.

13. For example, see the doyen of Roosevelt biographers, James MacGregor Burns's *Roosevelt: The Lion and the Fox* (New York: Harcourt, Brace and World, 1956), 171: "Roosevelt was following no master program—no 'economic panaceas or fancy plans' as he later called them derisively. He not only admitted to, he boasted of, playing by ear. He was a football quarterback, he liked to tell reporters, calling a new play when he saw how the last one turned out."

14. For interesting perspectives on what the Reagan era meant for defense, see William P. Snyder and James Brown, eds., *Defense Policy in the Reagan Era* (Washington, D.C.: National Defense University Press, 1988).

15. Caspar W. Weinberger, *Fighting for Peace: Seven Critical Years in the Pentagon* (New York: Warner Books, 1990), 6–7.

16. Ibid., 36.

17. Ibid., 159.

18. For an excellent discussion of the implications of the Weinberger Doctrine,

see Alan Ned Sabrosky and Robert L. Sloane, eds., *The Recourse to War: An Appraisal of The "Weinberger Doctrine"* (Carlisle Barracks, Pa.: Strategic Studies Institute, U.S. Army War College, 1988).

19. As when he learned in 1986 of deficiencies in the B-1B's defensive avionics that seriously compromised its ability to fulfill its mission.

20. For example, the F-117, which entered the operational inventory in 1983.

21. For the Soviet reaction to SDI, see Benjamin S. Lambeth and Kevin N. Lewis, *The Strategic Defense Initiative in Soviet Planning and Policy*, R-3550-AF (Santa Monica, Calif.: Rand Corporation, 1988). See also Simon P. Worden's *SDI and the Alternatives* (Washington, D.C.: National Defense University Press, 1991); and Sanford Lakoff and Herbert F. York, *A Shield in Space? Technology, Politics, and the Strategic Defense Initiative* (Berkeley: University of California Press, 1989).

22. Source: Extracted data and computations based upon Tables A-3 and B-2, in Assistant Secretary of the Air Force (Financial Management and Comptroller of the Air Force), *USAF Statistical Digest (Abridged), FY 1991 Estimate* (Washington, D.C.: HQ USAF, 1990).

23. Korean war figures are from Mallin, *Tanks, Fighters and Ships*, 266.

24. Interview of Dimitri Simes on the Fred Fisk show, WAMU-FM, Washington, D.C., July 20, 1991.

25. And he remained loyal to the Communist ideal even after the August 1990 coup that nearly toppled him.

26. See Weinberger, *Fighting for Peace*, 176–77; Lehman, *Command of the Seas*, 361–62; and Robert L. Lawson, ed., *The History of U.S. Naval Air Power* (New York: Military Press, 1985), 210. When the F-14 crews returned to their ship, they were asked how good were the Libyans. "Not as good as we were," one crewman replied. The dogfight, incidentally, was the first in history between opposing airplanes equipped with variable-sweep wings. The polling data is from the chart "Washington Post Poll" in *Washington Post*, January 31, 1991, comparing selected polling results of Americans nationwide on institutions in 1981, 1983, 1990, and 1991,

27. Weinberger, *Fighting for Peace*, 203–17; Lehman's *Command of the Seas*, 269–90, has an excellent chapter on Falklands' "Lessons Learned."

28. From a conversation with the author; because of continued sensitivities in Argentina, I have elected to preserve his anonymity.

29. See Christopher J. Bowie, "Coping with the Unexpected: Great Britain and the War in the South Atlantic," *Conflict* 6, no. 2 (1985): 117–36; Tim Garden, "Technology Lessons of the Falklands Conflict," in *Low-Intensity Conflict and Modern Technology*, ed. David J. Dean (Maxwell AFB, Ala.: Air University Press, 1986), 113–21; and Joseph F. Udemi, "Modified to Meet the Need: British Aircraft in the Falklands," *Airpower Journal* 3, no. 1 (Spring 1989): 51–64. See also Harry D. Train II, "An Analysis of the Falkland/Malvinas Islands Cam-

paign," *Naval War College Review* 41, no. 1, Sequence 321 (Winter 1988): 33–50. The best popular account of the Falklands air war is Jeffrey Ethell and Alfred Price, *Air War South Atlantic* (New York: Jove Books, 1987); useful information is also contained in Roy Braybrook's *Battle for the Falklands:* Vol. 3, *Air Forces* (London: Osprey Publishing, 1984); Bruce W. Watson and Peter M. Dunn, eds., *Military Lessons of the Falkland Islands War: Views from the United States* (Boulder, Colo.: Westview Press, 1984); and British Aerospace Corporation, *V/ STOL in the Roaring Forties* (Titchfield, Eng.: Polygraphic Limited, 1982).

30. I have also benefited from conversations with Dr. John Fozard, the designer of the Sea Harrier.

31. Bowie, "Coping with the Unexpected," 134.

32. There are two good essays on the Bekaa Valley fighting; see Benjamin S. Lambeth, "Moscow's Lessons From the 1982 Lebanon Air War," in *War in the Third Dimension,* ed. Mason, 127–48; and Matthew M. Hurley's "The Bekaa Valley Air Battle, June 1982: Lessons Mislearned?" *Airpower Journal* 3, no. 4 (Winter 1989): 60–70.

33. Ibid. I also have drawn upon William L. Hamilton and Andrew M. Skow, "Operational Utility Survey: Supermaneuverability," Technical Report 84-04 (Torrance, Calif.: Eidetics International, Sept. 1984).

34. Soviet reaction is from Lambeth, "Moscow's Lessons," 134–48.

35. Weinberger, *Fighting for Peace,* 135–74; Lehman, *Command of the Seas,* 311–26. See also Luttwak, *The Pentagon and the Art of War,* 50–51. I will never forget driving down the coast of California one evening after this event, consumed with one thought: How, after Desert One, could we have done it to ourselves yet again?

36. There is an excellent collection of these assistance agreements (which were captured at Grenada) that is reprinted in Paul Seabury and Walter A. McDougall's *The Grenada Papers* (San Francisco: Institute for Contemporary Studies, 1984), 17–55, 181–243.

37. Though the Reagan administration protested the increasingly totalitarian character of the Grenadan government, Bishop and his followers could nevertheless count on some support in the U.S. Congress. See Joshua Muravchik, "Dellums' Dilemma," *New Republic* 204, no. 10 (March 11, 1991): 14–16, and Seabury and McDougall, *Grenada Papers,* Documents V-1 and V-3, 153–55, 162–71.

38. Literature on Grenada is voluminous. Weinberger, *Fighting for Peace,* 101–33; and Lehman, *Command of the Seas,* 291–305, offer good brief accounts. Other valuable works are: Richard D. Hooker, Jr., "Presidential Decisionmaking and Use of Force: Case Study Grenada," *Parameters* 21, no. 2 (Summer 1991): 61–72; Peter M. Dunn and Bruce W. Watson, eds., *American Intervention in Grenada: The Implications of Operation "Urgent Fury"* (Boulder, Colo.: Westview Press, 1985); Reynold A. Burrowes, *Revolution and Rescue*

in *Grenada: An Account of the U.S. Caribbean Invasion* (Westport, Conn.: Greenwood Press, 1983); Kai P. Schoenhals and Richard A. Melanson, eds., *Revolution and Intervention in Grenada: The New Jewel Movement, the United States, and the Caribbean* (Boulder, Colo.: Westview Press, 1985); Valenta and Ellison, eds., *Grenada and Soviet/Cuban Policy;* Mark Adkin, *Urgent Fury: The Battle for Grenada* (Lexington, Mass.: Lexington Books, D. C. Heath, 1989); and Ronald H. Spector, *U.S. Marines in Grenada, 1983* (Washington, D.C.: History and Museums Division, HQ USMC, 1987).

39. The best military account is Adkin, *Urgent Fury.*

40. For example, William Lind, a member of Sen. Gary Hart's staff, subsequently prepared the so-called Lind Report for Congressional reformers, based (as he claimed) on extensive barroom interviews, which generally denigrated the military's performance in the operation. The JCS issued its own report specifically rebutting Lind's allegations, likewise sending it to the Hill; so far as is known, the Chiefs did not submit it to the undoubtedly rigorous analysis of barroom experts.

41. Hooker, "Presidential Decisionmaking," 68.

42. Personal notes from a lecture given by Metcalf in 1987. See also Aspin, "Desert One to Desert Storm"; and Luttwak, *The Pentagon and the Art of War,* 51–58.

43. Weinberger, *Fighting for Peace,* 111 n. 3.

44. See, for example, Gabriel, *Military Incompetence,* 149–86. I have also drawn on discussions with students of mine at the U.S. Army War College who were Urgent Fury veterans.

45. Dov S. Zakheim, "The Grenada Operation and Superpower Relations: A Perspective from the Pentagon," in *Grenada and Soviet/Cuban Policy,* ed. Valenta and Ellison, 180.

46. Lehman, *Command of the Seas,* 335.

47. Ibid., 337. By chance, reporter George Wilson was on board one of the carriers, and has written a thorough account of the raids and their aftermath. See George C. Wilson, *Supercarrier: An Inside Account of Life aboard the World's Most Powerful Ship, the U.S.S. John F. Kennedy* (New York: Berkley Books, 1986), 133–67, 220–31.

48. Lehman, *Command of the Seas,* 337–56. See also Joss, *Strike.*

49. Gabriel, *Military Incompetence,* 199.

50. The best account of American-Libyan relations during this period is Brian L. Davis, *Qaddafi, Terrorism, and the Origins of the U.S. Attack on Libya* (New York: Praeger, 1990). The quotations are from pp. 184–85.

51. I have based this account on a superb memoir: Robert E. Stumpf, "Air War with Libya," *U.S. Naval Institute Proceedings,* 112/8/1002 (Aug. 1986): 42–48. See also Lehman, *Command of the Seas,* 364–76; Weinberger, *Fighting for Peace,* 182–201

52. Weinberger, *Fighting for Peace*, 189; Lehman, *Command of the Seas*, 171–72. There is an excellent discussion of the F-111 question in Davis, *Qaddafi*, 120–21.

53. Lehman, *Command of the Seas*, 373; for Mitterand remark, see Weinberger, *Fighting for Peace*, 192.

54. Lehman, *Command of the Seas*, 372–75; Weinberger, *Fighting for Peace*, 194–99; Stumpf, "Air War with Libya," 48. I have also benefited from discussions with Cmdr. Bill Readdy, USN.

55. Davis, *Qaddafi*, 133–43, has excellent coverage of the raid, though he differs on some particulars from Lehman. Davis's greatest service is his detailed analysis of the Hana story, about the alleged "adopted daughter" of Qaddafi, reputedly killed by an American bomb. "The Hana story," he writes, "stands on the word of the Qaddafi regime alone: no evidence for it was ever produced, yet the Western press inexplicably has continued to repeat it as established fact" (142).

56. Davis, *Qaddafi*, vii.

57. Ibid., 145.

58. For contrasting "think tank" views of the SW Asian situation in the mid-1980s, see Jeffrey Record, *The Rapid Deployment Force and U.S. Military Intervention in the Persian Gulf* (Washington, D.C.: Institute for Foreign Policy Analysis, 1983); and Christopher J. Bowie, *Concepts of Operations and USAF Planning for Southwest Asia*, R-3125-AF (Santa Monica, Calif.: Rand, 1984).

59. Lehman, *Command of the Seas*, 383.

60. Osman A. Eisa, *Iran-Iraq War (Background, Development and Regional Responses)*, AU-AWC-86–165 (Maxwell AFB, Ala.: Air University Press, March 1986), 20–21.

61. Davis C. Rohr, "Forging New Paths of Military Planning: Challenges of the Middle East/Persian Gulf," in *Military Planning in the Twentieth Century*, ed. Borowski, 416–22.

62. Weinberger, *Fighting for Peace*, 410. Michael A. Palmer, *On Course to Desert Storm* (Washington, D.C.: Naval Historical Center, 1992), 103–46.

63. Ibid., 403–26; Lehman, *Command of the Seas*, 392–95.

64. Weinberger, *Fighting for Peace*, 425–26. There is an excellent summary essay on the *Vincennes* episode written by an individual who was on the bridge of the ship during the engagement. See the comments of M. C. Agresti, "Comment and Discussion," *U.S. Naval Institute Proceedings*, 116/1/1,043 (Jan. 1990): 19–24. Rogers's wife, living in San Diego, was later targeted by unknown assailants who placed a bomb in a family car. Fortunately, when the bomb did go off, it misfired, and his wife escaped injury.

65. Thomas Donnelly, Margaret Roth, and Caleb Baker, *Operation Just Cause: The Storming of Panama* (New York: Lexington Books, 1991), is a good overall survey of the operation and its aftermath. Bob Woodward's *The Com-*

manders (New York: Simon and Schuster, 1991) also offers useful insight into the operation and decisionmaking involved.

66. See Mallin, *Tanks, Fighters and Ships,* 242.

67. Harry G. Summers, Jr., *On Strategy: A Critical Analysis of the Vietnam War* (Novato, Calif.: Presidio Press, 1982); subsequent citations are to the Dell edition of this work, cited above in chap. 1, n. 53. John A. Warden III, *The Air Campaign: Planning for Combat* (Washington, D.C.: National Defense University Press, 1988); subsequent citations are to the Pergamon-Brassey's edition, 1989.

68. Summers, *On Strategy,* 258.

69. Carl von Clausewitz, *On War,* trans. and ed. Michael Howard and Peter Paret (Princeton: Princeton University Press, 1976), 595.

70. Warden, *Air Campaign,* 125.

71. Ibid., 135.

72. Ibid., 128–40.

73. For interesting doctrinal viewpoints, see the collected essays in *Air Power,* ed. Vallance; R. A. Mason's "The Decade of Opportunity: Air Power in the 1990s," and my own "Doctrine, Technology, and Air Warfare," both in *Airpower Journal* 1, no. 2 (Fall 1987): 4–27; see also Dennis M. Drew, "Two Decades in the Air Power Wilderness: Do We Know Where We Are?" *Air University Review* 37, no. 6 (Sept.–Oct. 1986): 2–13.

74. For a useful discussion of George, Hansell, and A.W.P.D./1, see Futrell's *Ideas, Concepts, Doctrine:* Vol. 1, *1907–1960,* 109–11; Cate, "Development of United States Air Doctrine," 186–91; and Hansell, *Strategic Air War,* 30–41. See also James C. Gaston, *Planning the American Air War: Four Men and Nine Days in 1941—An Inside Narrative* (Washington, D.C.: National Defense University Press, 1982).

75. Lehman, *Command of the Seas,* 115–37.

76. Ibid., 144.

77. Report, Steven U. Ramsdell to Dean Allard (Naval Historical Center), May 14, 1991.

78. Office of the Secretary of the Air Force, *The Air Force and U.S. National Security: Global Reach—Global Power* (Washington, D.C.: HQ USAF, 1991).

79. See Office of the Secretary of the Air Force, *The United States Air Force and U.S. National Security: A Historical Perspective, 1947–1990* (Washington, D.C., HQ USAF, 1991), and Adam B. Siegel, *U.S. Navy Crisis Response Activity, 1946–1989: Preliminary Report,* CRM 89–315 (Alexandria, Va.: Center for Naval Analysis, 1989), iii; Barry Blechman and Stephen S. Kaplan, *Force Without War: U.S. Armed Forces as a Political Instrument* (Washington, D.C.: Brookings Institution, 1977); and Philip D. Zelikow's later "Force without War, 1975–82," *Journal of Strategic Studies* 7, no. 3 (March 1984): 29–54. See also OSAF, *Global Reach.*

Chapter 5. The Road to War

1. One luncheon speaker advanced this interpretation at a meeting of leading military historians at the Triangle Universities' Security Seminar on Changing Technologies and New Weapons Systems, Quail Roost Conference Center, Durham, N.C., February 3, 1990. At that time, according to the Stockholm International Peace Institute, there were at least 31 major wars, insurrections, and civil disorders occuring simultaneously around the world, and 75 smaller ones. The Carter Institute at Emory University listed an even higher figure of 115 armed conflicts underway in 1990.

2. This is, of course, my own strictly subjective interpretation.

3. For an excellent discussion of how Hussein rose to power and then used it, see Judith Miller and Laurie Mylroie, *Saddam Hussein and the Crisis in the Gulf* (New York: Times Books, 1990). See also Thomas Boylston Adams, "Removing the Virtue of Violence," *Boston Globe,* October 5, 1991.

4. Adams, "Removing the Virtue of Violence."

5. From an interview of H. Norman Schwarzkopf by David Frost, PBS, July 3, 1990.

6. There is a growing body of literature on the Gulf that is truly enormous in size; much of it falls outside the purpose and scope of this particular study. The following account is based upon Stephen C. Pelletiere and Douglas V. Johnson II, *Lessons Learned: The Iran-Iraq War* (Carlisle Barracks, Pa.: Strategic Studies Institute, U.S. Army War College, 1991); Eisa, *Iran-Iraq War;* and David Segal, "The Iran-Iraq War: A Military Analysis," *Foreign Affairs* 66, no. 5 (Summer 1988): 946–63. A very useful analytical reference that goes far beyond what its title would suggest is Ronald E. Bergquist's *The Role of Airpower in the Iran-Iraq War* (Maxwell AFB, Ala.: Air University Press, 1988).

7. Missile data from UN information presented in Lee Michael Katz, "U.N. Search Turns to Missiles, Superguns," *USA Today,* October 1, 1991.

8. Segal, "Iran-Iraq War," 960.

9. Comparable statistics of military spending per citizen for other regional nations in 1990 (in U.S. dollars) were:

Iran	$106
Egypt	126
Jordan	152
Syria	212
Saudi Arabia	1,089
Israel	1,400

For the record, the United States spent an average of $1,191 per citizen for defense in 1990. Table computed from data in Michael Widlanski, ed., *Can Israel Survive a Palestinian State?* (Jerusalem: Institute for Advanced Strategic and Political Studies, 1990), from the previously cited *USAF Statistical Digest (Abridged), FY 1991 Estimate;* and from information supplied by Gloria Mundo, U.S. Bureau of the Census, Population Division, August 6, 1991.

10. Widlanski, ed., *Can Israel Survive a Palestinian State?* 958–59; Katz, "U.N. Search Turns to Missiles."

11. There is a good useful summary of Iraq's build-up in Thomas B. Allen et al., *War in the Gulf* (Atlanta: Turner Publishing, 1991), 47–51.

12. I have drawn on Fredrick P. Smolar's excellent survey article, "The Arming of Saddam Hussein: Cynical Politics and Profiteering," *Dissent* 38, no. 3 (Summer 1991): 347–53, which itself made use of Adel Darwish and "Gregory Alexander" [pseud.], *Unholy Babylon: The Secret History of Saddam's War* (London: Victor Gollancz, 1991).

13. Iraqi 1980 data is from Record's *Rapid Deployment Force,* Table 2, p. 18.

14. Elaine Sciolino, "Soviet-Iraqi Tie: Marriage of Strained Convenience," *New York Times,* September 9, 1990. The $23.5 billion is between 22 and 29 percent of total Iraqi military expenditures during this time period.

15. Bergquist, *Role of Airpower.* Also, I have benefited from conversations with Col. John A. Warden III.

16. Eisa, *Iran-Iraq War,* 15.

17. Bergquist, *Role of Airpower,* 46. There is a revealing series of interviews in *Air Force Monthly,* nos. 35–37, with an Iraqi fighter pilot who defected from the Hussein regime. See Salvador Huertas, ed., "In His Own Words" (Feb. 1991): 10–11; "A Black Future" (March 1991): 30–31; and "A Doomed Air Force" (April 1991): 44–45.

18. Allegedly, the military commander of the Faw peninsula operation, which turned a stalemate into an Iraqi victory, was murdered by Saddam, who feared his popularity and initiative (he had ordered the attack on his own). Then, on the eve of the Gulf crisis, Saddam apparently killed over 100 officers who disagreed with his decision to invade Kuwait. Saddam, it is said by Iraqi propaganda, killed his first opponent at age 10.

19. Recollections from an unclassified briefing by Carl Duckett, the chief of science and technology for the Central Intelligence Agency, to the National Capitol Section, American Institute of Aeronautics and Astronautics c. fall 1979; the substance of his briefing was later printed by the *Washington Post.*

20. Dan McKinnon's *Bullseye Iraq* (New York: Berkley Books, 1988) is a useful account. See also Carol Berger, "Iraqi Files Seized by UN Inspectors Seen as Possible 'Hit Lists,'" *Christian Science Monitor,* October 10, 1991.

21. McKinnon, *Bullseye Iraq.*

22. William Lowther, *Arms and the Man: Dr. Gerald Bull, Iraq and the Supergun* (Novato, Calif.: Presidio Press, 1991), esp. 185–273. The Iraqi nuclear story is one that deserves a full-length book. See R. Jeffrey Smith, "Inspectors Say Iraq Had Key H-Bomb Item," *Washington Post,* October 9, 1991.

23. Eisa, *Iran-Iraq War,* 15, 17.

24. Dwight D. Eisenhower, *Waging Peace: The White House Years, 1956–1961* (Garden City, N.Y.: Doubleday, 1965), 278. See also Micah L. Sifry, "U.S. Intervention in the Middle East: A Case Study," in *The Gulf War Reader: History, Documents, Opinions,* ed. Micah L. Sifry and Christopher Cerf (New York: Times Books, 1991), 27–33.

25. For example, Gary Sick, a well-known Middle East advisor, considered an Iraqi invasion of Kuwait "extremely unlikely" on July 26. (Quotation from a PBS broadcast on July 26, 1990, and a replay on the PBS news program, "All Things Considered," August 3, 1991.)

26. OSAF, *Global Reach,* 2. The White Paper was echoing the earlier *National Security Strategy of the United States,* issued in March 1990.

27. Otto Friedrich and the Editors of *Time, Desert Storm: The War in the Persian Gulf* (Boston: Little, Brown, 1991), 16–23, has an excellent summary of the road to war. I have also relied on a chronology prepared by the U.S. Department of Defense of key events in the evolution of the crisis, and current through January 10, 1991; this is subsequently referred to as DoDC.

28. Amnesty International's *Iraq/Occupied Kuwait: Human Rights Violations since August 2, 1990* (New York: Amnesty International USA, Dec. 1990), offers a thorough and occasionally sickeningly graphic account of Iraqi atrocities in Kuwait. There is a good account of the invasion in Ralph Kinney Bennett and Rachel Flick's "The Rape of Kuwait: Why War Came to the Gulf," *Reader's Digest* (April 1991): 84–90; and in David A. Fulghum, "U.S. Mounts Swift Response to Iraq's Invasion of Kuwait," *Aviation Week and Space Technology* (hereafter cited as *AWST*) (Aug. 13, 1990): 18–22; see also "U.S. Hawks Were a Hit," *Defense News,* September 23, 1991, p. 2. Gibran quote from *The Garden of the Prophet* (1933).

29. Quoted in Joe Stork and Martha Wenger, "From Rapid Deployment to Massive Deployment," in *Gulf War Reader,* ed. Sifry and Cerf, 34.

30. For example, most notably in Bob Woodward's *The Commanders.*

31. For rates of advance of combat units, see Robert Helmbold, "Rates of Advance in Historical Land Combat Operations," CAA-RP-90-1 (Bethesda, Md.: U.S. Army Concepts Analysis Agency, 1990); David M. Glantz, *August Storm: The Soviet 1945 Strategic Offensive in Manchuria,* no. 7 of the *Leavenworth Papers* (Ft. Leavenworth, Kan.: Combat Studies Institute, 1983); R. P. Mulholland and R. D. Specht, *The Rate of Advance of the Front Line in Some World War II Campaigns,* RM-1072 (Santa Monica, Calif.: Rand Corporation, 16, 1953); and Alan Clark, *Barbarossa* (New York: New American Library, 1966), 70, 73. I have also benefited from a conversation with Robert Helmbold of the U.S. Army Concepts Analysis Agency, August 22, 1990, and from personal recollections of the "how fast can they go?" debate in early August.

32. From Schwarzkopf interview with David Frost, July 3, 1990.

33. Quoted in John M. Broder and Melissa Healy, "U.S. Ships, Planes Quickly Deployed to Troubled Area," *Los Angeles Times,* August 3, 1990.

34. DoDC, 2–3; Office of the Chief of Naval Operations, *The United States Navy in "Desert Shield" "Desert Storm"* (hereafter *USNDS*) (Washington, D.C.: USN, 1991), 11–12, A-2-3.

35. Quote is from Michael Dugan, "The Air War," *U.S. News and World Report* 110, no. 5 (Feb. 11, 1991): 27. See also Richard Mackenzie, "A Conversation with Chuck Horner," *Air Force Magazine* 74, no. 6 (June 1991): 58. The amount of munitions available is an important point, for some critics (who should have known better) alleged that tactical air wings lacked sufficient munitions for attacking Iraqi armor. (See, e.g., William Odom, "A Close-Run Thing," *The National Interest* 24 [Summer 1991]: 98.) I wish to acknowledge munitions information received from Dr. Alan L. Gropman of the Industrial College of the Armed Forces.

36. "An Interview with General Robert D. Russ," *TAC Attack* 31, no. 3 (March 1991): 4; personal recollection.

37. Interview of F–15 pilot by Phil McCombs, "War Stories," *Washington Post,* June 8, 1991.

38. Speech by Donald B. Rice to the Civil Reserve Air Fleet Air Carrier Executives, Bolling AFB, Washington, D.C., July 30, 1991. See also Mason, "The Air War in the Gulf," 211–29. The gunboat quote is from a conversation with Group Capt. Andrew Vallance, RAF, in August 1991.

39. Mason, "The Air War in the Gulf"; conversation with Vallance, RAF, in August 1991; also information supplied by Vallance in his manuscript "Air Power in the Gulf War—The Conduct of Operations," July 1991.

40. Mark E. Johnson, "Civilian Airlines: Partners in Defense Airlift," *Airman* 35, no. 6 (June 1991): 13.

41. DoDC, 2–7; see also HQ USAF White Paper, "Air Force Performance in Desert Storm" (April 1991): 2.

42. Remarks of Lt. Gen. Michael Carns, USAF, Director, The Joint Staff, before the D. W. Steele Chapter of the Air Force Association, Arlington, Va., December 10, 1990. I thank Ellen Piazza for making this available to me. See also OSAF, *Airlift and U.S. National Security: The Case for the C-17* (Washington, D.C.: HQ USAF, 1991), 4; comparative airlift data from information supplied by the History Office, Military Airlift Command, Scott AFB, Ill.

43. Gen. Merrill A. McPeak, Senior Statesmen briefing of March 15–19, 1991 (hereafter McPeak Senior Statesmen briefing); AF Desert Storm White Paper.

44. McPeak Senior Statesmen briefing; AF Desert Storm White Paper; *USNDS,* A-2–14.

45. *USNDS,* 19–23.

46. Friedrich et al., *Desert Storm,* 41.

47. Pelletiere and Johnson, *Lessons Learned,* xii.

48. Ibid., 67.

49. Despite a plethora of articles reflecting his status as media "star," the best insight into Schwarzkopf is found in C.D.B. Bryan's "Operation Desert Norm: Getting to Know the General," *New Republic* 204, no. 10 (March 11, 1991): 20–27.

50. William W. Mendel and Floyd T. Banks, Jr., *Campaign Planning: Final Report*, ACN 87003 (Carlisle Barracks, Pa.: Strategic Studies Institute, U.S. Army War College, Jan. 4, 1988), 20. See also Mackenzie, "Conversation with Chuck Horner," 57–58.

51. MacKenzie, "Conversation with Chuck Horner," 57–58.

52. Ibid., 58.

53. Reuter Transcript Report, Address of Charles Horner to the Business Executives for National Security Education Fund, May 8, 1991, Washington, D.C., p. B-2 (hereafter cited as Horner Reuter transcript).

54. Conversations with participants.

55. Horner Reuter transcript, p. B-4; conversations with participants.

56. The term *strategic air attacks* caused some discussions among air power traditionalists, for it did not fit within the established terms incorporated within AFM 1-1, the service's doctrinal "bible." Strategic air attack advocates argued cogently that the expression encapsulated the notion of "strategic aerospace offense" contained within 1-1, but without the strong implications that only "strategic bombers" could undertake such missions. In fact, during the subsequent attacks on the Iraqi leadership and key warmaking industries, strikes having genuine strategic importance were routinely undertaken by F-111s, F-117s, F-15Es, and F-16s, as well as B-52s. (Conversations with CENTAF planners.)

57. Department of Defense, Office of the Undersecretary of Defense for Policy, *Conduct of the Persian Gulf War: Final Report to Congress* (Washington, D.C.: Department of Defense, April 1992), 118–42 (hereafter abbreviated as *Title V*); personal information; and conversations with various participants.

58. James Adams, "Invasion Plans Ready as Build-up Continues," *London Sunday Times*, August 26, 1990.

59. See Woodward, *The Commanders*, particularly 74–80, 290–96, 308. See also Eliot Cohen's review of the book in the *New York Times Book Review*, May 26, 1991.

60. Michael J. Dugan, "Air Power: Concentration, Responsiveness and the Operational Art," *Military Review* 69, no. 7 (July 1989): 21. Despite aerospace technical press reports to the contrary, there was no "rewriting" of air campaign plans following the Dugan dismissal.

61. This discussion is based upon my own personal recollections, observations, and notes.

62. I have drawn extensively upon two documents: the McPeak brief of March 15, 1991 (hereafter McPeak media brief), and Lt. Gen. Charles A. Horner, "Re-

flections on Desert Storm" (*c.* June 1991). See also Mackenzie, "Conversation with Chuck Horner," 57. Scud information is from Katz, "U.N. Search Turns to Missiles." Scud totals for Iraq range up to 2,000. One "baseline" figure, from UN analysis after the war (including inspection of on-site records), is 819; allowing for those fired in testing and the Iran-Iraq war, a number of 600 thus seems reasonable for Iraq on the eve of the Gulf war. Future researchers will no doubt refine this further. I have also drawn on conversations with planning participants, and diverse published materials.

63. The exact number of Iraqi divisions remains uncertain, as the effective personnel strength of these divisions and associated formations fluctuated both before and during the war. I have relied on numbers supplied by Brig. Gen. Hal Nelson, Office of the Chief of Military History, U.S. Army.

64. See n. 42 above.

65. See W. Hays Parks, Memorandum of Law: Executive Order 12333 and Assassination," DAJA-IA (27–1a), November 2, 1989. The quote is from p. 8. I acknowledge with appreciation his bringing this memorandum to my attention.

66. Horner "Reflections on Desert Storm," and personal notes from discussions with members of the planning process.

67. Such niceties did not occur to Iraqi forces, who pillaged even Kuwait's museums and hospitals during their short but unforgettable occupation.

68. Interview with Dave Deptula, September 16, 1991.

69. Combined data from Horner, "Reflections on Desert Storm"; and McPeak media brief.

70. Mackenzie, "Conversation with Chuck Horner," 60.

71. Combined information from Horner, "Reflections on Desert Storm," McPeak media brief, and conversations with planning participants.

72. Horner, "Reflections on Desert Storm."

73. Conversation with Capt. Stanley J. Alluisi, USAF.

74. McPeak media brief, and conversations with crisis team participants.

75. Transcript of remarks of Pres. George Bush, White House press conference, November 8, 1990; NSC anecdote from a conversation with Col. Michael V. Hayden, USAF.

76. See William J. Taylor and James Blackwell, "The Ground War in the Gulf," *Survival* 33, no. 3 (May–June 1991): 232–33, 237; and Carns remarks (see n. 42, above).

77. Horner, "Reflections on Desert Storm."

78. For an excellent discussion of rhetoric and the Hussein regime, see James Gardner, "One with Nineveh and Tyre," *National Review* 43, no. 8 (May 13, 1991): 52–54.

79. For two excellent analyses of the antiwar movement, see David Horowitz, "Coalition against the U.S.," *National Review* 43, no. 3 (Feb. 25, 1991): 36–38; and Neal B. Freeman, "My Life in the Peace Movement," *National Review* 43,

no. 5 (April 1, 1991): 42–43. For a mix of antiwar viewpoints, see Michael Albert and Noam Chomsky, "The 'Logic' of War," and Michael Albert, "Shut It Down," both in *Z Magazine* (Feb. 1991): 54–68; and Michael Albert, "Loose Ends," Edward Herman, "Gulfspeak II," Lydia Sargent, "Birdtracks in the Sand," Barbara Ehrenreich, "War for War's Sake," and Zoltan Grossman, "Ecotide in the Gulf," *Z Magazine* (March 1991): 10–27. The "Airpower Chorus" anecdote is from personal recollection.

80. Kimberly Elliott et al., "The Big Squeeze: Why the Sanctions on Iraq Will Work," *Washington Post*, December 9, 1990. Though the authors argue otherwise (ignoring the Japanese sanctions issue entirely), the postwar evidence from Iraq strongly suggests that the historical record, had sanctions been imposed, would now be 40 successes out of *116* tries, a drop of 1 percent of the previously sobering indicator.

81. Personal recollection. This confusion persisted even into the war. At the time of the Gulf crisis, there were only three B-2s in existence, all extensively instrumented for flight test (and thus totally unsuited for war).

82. See Bob Drogin, "Dignity of Ancient City of Ur is Marred by Indignity of War," *Los Angeles Times*, March 28, 1991.

83. Transcript of statement by Secretary of State James A. Baker at news conference following Aziz meeting, January 9, 1991.

84. Don Kowet, "Desert Storm Hall of Shame," *Washington Times*, March 15, 1991.

85. From columnist Ray Kerrison, quoted in "What the Democrats Said," *National Review* 43, no. 5 (April 1, 1991): 14. F-16 pilot quote is from William Andrews, "Gulf War Journal (I)," *Code One* 6, no. 4 (Jan. 1992): 10.

86. Data from notes taken at Col. William Lawrence, USMC, "A Test Pilot's Visit to Desert Storm," a lecture presented to the East Coast Section Meeting, Society of Experimental Test Pilots, Naval Air Test Center, Patuxent River, Md., April 5, 1991.

87. Michael Walzer, "Perplexed," *New Republic* 204, no. 4 (Jan. 28, 1991).

Chapter 6. The Breaking Storm

1. At 3 A.M. in Baghdad, it was likewise 3 A.M. in Kuwait and Saudi Arabia, 7 P.M. East Coast United States time, and 0000 Zulu (Midnight Greenwich Mean Time). Its selection was not because of Zulu considerations but instead because planners believed that at 3 A.M., the greatest degree of surprise could be achieved.

2. *Title V,* 157; USAF, SAC news release 90-001, January 16, 1992; Tony Capaccio, "Displaying Global Reach, B-52s Made Combat History," *Defense Week,* January 21, 1992, p. 3; "Air Force Launched 35 ALCMs on First Night of

Gulf Air War," *Defense Daily,* January 17, 1992, p. 88; Frank Oliveri, "Conventional ALCM Revealed," *Air Force Magazine* 75, no. 3 (March 1992): 17. I acknowledge with appreciation information received from Sgt. William I. Chivalette, 2nd Bomb Wing historian.

3. This and subsequent discussions of F-117A operations are drawn from information in Harold P. Myers and Vincent C. Breslin, *Nighthawks over Iraq: A Chronology of the F-117A Stealth Fighter in Operations Desert Shield and Desert Storm,* Special Study 37FW/HO-91-1 (Tonopah, Nev.: Office of History, HQ 37th Fighter Wing, Jan. 9, 1992).

4. The account of the first night's activities is based on a variety of sources, including *Title V,* 151–55, the McPeak and Horner briefs (see chap. 5, nn. 43 and 62), the Lawrence talk, conversations with participants, the Air Force and Navy Desert Storm white papers, and various news accounts.

5. USCENTCOM statistics reprinted in James W. Canan, "Airpower Opens the Fight," *Air Force Magazine* (March 1991): 17; see also Friedrich et al., *Desert Storm,* 40; and McPeak media brief.

6. Quoted in David Evans, "With the Army and Air Force," *U.S. Naval Institute Proceedings,* 117/6/1,060 (June 1991): 63. See also Department of the Army, "Army Weapons System Performance," 3–4. There are generally useful accounts of this attack in *Title V,* 152; Douglas Waller's "Secret Warriors," *Newsweek* 117, no. 24 (June 17, 1991): 20–23; Benjamin F. Schemmer's "USAF MH-53J Pave Lows Led Army Apaches Knocking Out Iraqi Radars to Open Air War," *Armed Forces Journal* (July 1991): 34; and Richard Mackenzie's "Apache Attack," *Air Force Magazine* 74, no. 10 (Oct. 1991): 54–60. Readers should also read Casey Anderson's "War Planner: Civilians Didn't Change Target List," *Air Force Times,* July 8, 1991, for necessary corrective statements by campaign planner Brig. Gen. Buster C. Glosson.

7. Anderson, "War Planner."

8. Fred Barnes, "Winners and Losers: A Postwar Balance Sheet," *The National Interest* 24 (Summer 1991): 49.

9. Eugene Burdick and Harvey Wheeler, *Fail-Safe* (New York: Dell Books, 1963), 280.

10. Transcript from Allen et al., *War in the Gulf,* 119; Black Hole recollection is from participants, and also from Evans, "With the Army and Air Force," 63.

11. *Title V,* 156–57.Jeffrey P. Rhodes, "Aerospace World," *Air Force Magazine* 74, no. 3 (March 1991): 24; see also *USNDS,* p. A-15; and Stanley W. Kandebo, "U.S. Fires Over 25% of Its Conventional Land Attack Tomahawks in First Week of War," *AWST* (Jan. 28, 1991): 29; Capaccio, "Displaying Global Reach," 3; Oliveri, "Conventional ALCM Revealed," 17.

12. "Mid-East Carrier War," *The Hook* 19, no. 1 (Spring 1991): 50.

13. Canan, "Airpower Opens the Fight," 17; James W. Canan, "The Electronic Storm," *Air Force Magazine* 74, no. 6 (June 1991): 26. Pilot comment

from Bruce D. Nordwall, "Electronic Warfare Played Greater Role in Desert Storm than Any Conflict," *AWST* (April 22, 1991): 68.

14. Data from George Muellner, "TAF's New Technology in Desert Storm," Seventh Washington Symposium, Society of Experimental Test Pilots, April 26, 1991, Alexandria, Va. Decoy information from Frank Oliveri, "Aerospace World," *Air Force Magazine* 74, no. 10 (Oct. 1991): 21. ALARM information from Graham Thompson of British Aerospace Ltd., and British Aerospace Defence Corporation, *Cause for ALARM: Executive Summary for the British Aerospace ALARM Weapon System* (hereafter British Aerospace, *Cause for ALARM*) (Stevenage, Eng.: British Aerospace Ltd., 1991).

15. British Aerospace, *Cause for ALARM;* I have also benefited from data furnished by Graham Thompson of British Aerospace (Dynamics) Ltd.

16. Canan, "Airpower Opens the Fight," 20; information from participants.

17. McPeak media brief. See also "F-117 Fact Sheet—Desert Storm," in HQ USAF, *Air Force Stealth Technology Review,* June 10–14, 1991 (Washington, D.C.: HQ USAF, 1991), Tab B; the "ghost" story is from a statement by Secretary of Defense Dick Cheney.

18. Horner Reuter transcript, p. B-13; Zoe Schofield, "Gulf Flyers," *Aircraft Illustrated* 24, no. 4 (April 1991): 187; Glenn Ashley, *Panavia Tornado in Action* (Carrollton, Tex.: Squadron/Signal Publications, 1991), 44.

19. *Title V,* 158; Allen et al., *War in the Gulf,* 124; David A. Fulghum, "Lack of Opposition Puzzles Pilots Who Flew First Missions," *AWST* (Jan. 21, 1991): 23.

20. "Iraqi MiG-29 Shot Down Partner," *AWST* (Feb. 18, 1991): 63.

21. *Title V,* 167; McPeak Senior Statesmen brief.

22. *Title V,* 227–29; McPeak media brief; see also Perry, "Desert Storm and Deterrence," 76. F-117 discussion based on analysis of data in Myers and Breslin, *Nighthawks over Iraq.* I have benefited from discussions with F-117 pilots and mission planners during the Air Force's "Stealth Week" exhibition at Andrews AFB, June 10–14, 1991, and from conversations with Col. John A. Warden III.

23. Philip Finnegan and Neil Munro, "DoD Molds Strategy to Destroy Missile Launchers," *Defense News* (July 1991). See also Mark D. Mandeles, "Between a Rock and a Hard Place: Implications for the U.S. of Third World Nuclear Weapon and Ballistic Missile Proliferation," *Security Studies* 1, no. 2 (Winter 1991): 235–69.

24. Thomas L. McNaugher, "Ballistic Missiles and Chemical Weapons: The Legacy of the Iran-Iraq War," *International Security* 15, no. 2 (Fall 1990): 5–34, is an excellent survey. See also Segal, "Iran-Iraq War," 958–59; details on Scud from Bill Gunston, *The Illustrated Encyclopedia of the World's Rockets and Missiles* (New York: Crescent Books, 1979), 26–27; and Bruce A. Smith, "Scud Propulsion Designs Help Patriot System Succeed," *AWST* (Jan. 28, 1991): 28.

25. McPeak media brief; see also Horner Reuter transcript, pp. B-6, B-7.

26. From Schwarzkopf interview with David Frost, July 3, 1990.

27. Ibid.

28. Ibid.

29. Ibid.; Rick Atkinson and David S. Broder, "Iraq Retaliates with Missile Attacks against Israeli Cities, Saudi Air Base," and Molly Moore, "U.S. Missile Intercepts Iraqi Scud," in *Washington Post*, January 18, 1991; see also Waller, "Secret Warriors," 28. Thomas A. Rose, "Surviving the Scuds, Fearing the Fallout," *Global Affairs* 6, no. 4 (Fall 1991): 123–35, is a provocative account by an American who survived Scud attacks during the war.

30. McPeak media brief; Mason, "The Air War in the Gulf," 216–17; Lt. Gen. Thomas S. Moorman, Jr., "Military Space Systems Utility," address delivered to the 28th Space Congress, Cocoa Beach, Fla., April 24, 1991. I thank Capt. Jon Watkins, USAF, for making this material available to me. See also *Title V*, 223–26.

31. McPeak media brief.

32. Benjamin F. Schemmer, "Special Ops Teams Found 29 Scuds Ready to Barrage Israel 24 Hours Before Cease-Fire," *Armed Forces Journal International* (July 1991): 36. The comparison that comes to mind is Lt. Cmdr. C. Wade McClusky's detection of the Japanese fleet at Midway, triggering the immensely successful air strikes that essentially destroyed Japan's carrier aviation forces.

33. Ibid.

34. Waller, "Secret Warriors," 28.

35. Numbers of exact Scud launches are still uncertain. See Donald R. Baucom, "Providing High Technology Systems for the Modern Battlefield: The Case of Patriot's ATBM Capability," a paper presented to the Conference of the American Military Institute, Durham, N.C., March 23, 1991; Augustine, "How We Almost Lost the Technological War"; David Hughes, "Patriot Antimissile Successes Show How Software Upgrades Help Meet New Threats," *AWST* (Jan. 28, 1991); and Department of the Army, "Army Weapons Systems Performance." See also Norman Friedman, *Desert Victory: The War for Kuwait* (Annapolis, Md.: Naval Institute Press, 1991), 365; James Kitfield, "Weapons under Fire," *Government Executive* (June 1991): 21; Friedrich, *Desert Storm*, 155–65; and Allen et al., *War in the Gulf*, 149–58. Patriot engagement doctrine statement is from a conversation with Tom Forburger of the Raytheon corporation, September 23, 1991.

36. The best-known "revisionist" viewpoint on Patriot is Theodore A. Postol's thoughtful "Lessons of the Gulf War Experience with Patriot," *International Security* 16, no. 3 (Winter 1991–92): 119–71, together with his earlier *Lessons for SDI from the Gulf War Patriot Experience: A Technical Perspective* (Cambridge: MIT, April 16, 1961). I thank Professor Postol for making these documents and some supporting research materials available to me.

37. The casualties are from DoD figures as of August 19, 1991; 615 Ameri-

cans were killed or wounded in the Gulf war, 113 killed by enemy action, and 394 wounded by enemy action. "Friendly" fire casualties were 35 killed and 73 wounded, while 77 Army, 10 USMC, 6 USN, and 20 USAF personnel died from enemy action; 289 Army, 85 USMC, 11 USN, and 9 USAF personnel were wounded by enemy action. See Mason, "The Air War in the Gulf," 217. I have also benefited from articles in a locally (Saudi) produced satirical journal; see Godel E. Escherbach [pseud.], "Scud Watching: A New Sport for the '90's!" *Banana Republic Gazette* 3, no. 2 (April 1, 1991): 3–4, and from conversations with Capt. Stanley J. Alluisi, USAF, who was present during many Scud engagements.

38. Source data is from R. V. Jones, *The Wizard War* (New York: Coward, McCann and Geoghegan, 1978), 459; David Irving, *The Mare's Nest* (London: William Kimber, 1965), 295; Frederick I. Ordway III and Mitchell R. Sharpe, *The Rocket Team* (New York: Thomas Y. Crowell, 1979), 243–48, 252; Friedrich et al., *Desert Storm*, 159; and Allen, *War in the Gulf*, 158. There is disagreement on the number of precise casualties caused by the Scuds; I have selected the figures I found most reliable, and have also relied on figures supplied by an American AWACS crewman stationed in Riyadh who lived through several Scud attacks, and from Postol, *Lessons for SDI*, 4–5. The precise number of homes and buildings damaged from Scud attacks is unclear; approximately 130 apartment complexes (including 10,476 individual apartments destroyed or damaged) and 100 homes were damaged or destroyed. Riyadh suffered significantly less damage because of its lesser density. Including schools, buildings not used as residential housing, homes, and individual apartments that were hit as part of the total, data supports a general estimate of 10,750 for combined Arab-Israeli Scud damage and destruction. Numbers are rounded to closest whole number where appropriate.

39. I am grateful to Dr. Donald Baucom, historian of the Strategic Defense Initiative Organization, for furnishing me with this information on the "counter V-2" effort.

40. McPeak media brief, and the Senior Statesmen brief. Where discrepancies have occurred between the two briefings, I have relied upon the Senior Statesmen document, as it is a later one. The McPeak media brief shows the following breakdown for the various American services as follows: CENTAF: 65,318 sorties, 45% of which were combat (defined as offensive counter air, interdiction, CAS, and electronic warfare; 5% defensive counter air; 24% CENTAF support; and 26% other support. NAVCENT: 17,160 sorties, consisting of 36% strike (and not defined more precisely than this), 30% fleet air defense, and 34% support. MARCENT: 10,207 sorties, consisting of 84% combat (not defined with greater precision), and 16% support. The sum total of all U.S. sorties from D-day to ceasefire is thus 92,685, 44,145 of which were combat, as defined by the various services. There are minor discrepancies between this document and the Navy's

previously cited *USNDS*, Table 1 and 2, pp. D-5–D-9, where the Navy lists only 16,899 sorties as combat or direct combat-support missions.

41. Conversation with Chip Setnor, August 1991.

42. Ibid.

43. Sources are: "Final Report of Chief of Air Service, AEF," reprinted in Maurer Maurer, ed., *The U.S. Air Service in World War I:* Vol. 1, *The Final Report and A Tactical History* (Washington, D.C.: Office of Air Force History, 1978), 17. (The figure of 137.5 tons is expressed in the report as 275,000 pounds; while it sounds low, readers should remember that most bombing planes of World War I vintage had payloads no greater than 500 pounds, and often flew with considerably smaller bombs). Statistics for World War II, Korea, and Vietnam are from Appendix IV: "USAF Air Munitions Consumption WW II, Korea, and Southeast Asia," in Carl Berger, ed., *The United States Air Force in Southeast Asia, 1961–1973: An Illustrated Account* (Washington, D.C.: Office of Air Force History, 1984), 368. Gulf figures are computed on the basis of statistics released by Air Force Chief of Staff Gen. Merrill A. McPeak from his so-called Senior Statesmen briefing of the same period.

44. For example, at the height of the war, the Reverend Jesse Jackson proclaimed on a Sunday morning discussion show he hosted that the United States had dropped more bombs on Iraq than in World War II and Vietnam.

45. National Public Radio interview of a physician with Physicians for Social Responsibility, following his return from Iraq; I thank Col. John A. Warden III for making this citation available to me. See also McPeak media and Senior Statesmen briefs; Horner, "Reflections on Desert Storm;" and *Title V,* 199–203.

46. Speech by General Ron Yates, Commander, AFSC, at the annual meeting of the East Coast Section, Society of Experimental Test Pilots, Alexandria, Va., April 26, 1991. I thank Maj. Brian Hoey for making this available.

47. *Title V,* 200. Briefing and information from Col. John A. Warden III, Lt. Col. Dave Deptula, and Lt. Col. Phillip S. Meilinger; I have drawn the statistics on the Eighth Air Force in Europe from Hansell, *Strategic Air War,* 280–81. I have also drawn upon an interview of Col. Chris Christon, CENTAF/IN, on the PBS news program "Talk to the Nation," March 5, 1992.

48. *Title V,* 209; Warden, Deptula, and Meilinger information.

49. *Title V,* 210–11; Warden, Deptula, and Meilinger information. For example, consider famous bridge campaigns such as the "Battle of Carlson's Canyon" in the Korean War (the model for James Michener's fine novel *The Bridges at Toko-ri*), and the Vietnam era's Thanh Hoa and Paul Doumier bridges, which claimed dozens of strike aircraft.

50. Quote from Fulghum, "Lack of Opposition"; see also "Mid-East Carrier War," 50. The Hornet story is from a McDonnell-Douglas summary by Tom Downey entitled "F/A-18 Hornet War Stories," 1991. See also *Title V,* 163.

51. London comparison is from Vallance, "Air Power in the Gulf War"; the Dulles comparison is from data furnished by Bonnie Mattingly of the Dulles Airport staff; in 1990, Dulles covered 10,000 acres, ranking it within the top ten largest airports in the world.

52. McPeak media brief; Horner Reuter transcript, p. B–12; see also *USNDS,* pp. A-15–19.

53. *Title V,* 169–71. McPeak media brief; Horner, "Reflections on Desert Storm"; and information from participants.

54. Ibid. See also Horner Reuter transcript, p. B-5; and Mason, "The Air War in the Gulf," 213–14; and Frederic T. Case et al., *Analysis of Air Operations during Desert Shield/Desert Storm* (USAF Studies and Analysis Agency, 1991), vii, 5.

55. These statistics are based on the following: Robert Saundby, "The Uses of Air Power in 1939–1945," in *Impact of Air Power,* ed. Emme, 225; Futrell, *USAF in Korea,* 688–92; Hallion, *Naval Air War in Korea,* 205–6; Nichols and Tillman, *On Yankee Station,* 163; Maurer, ed., *The U.S. Air Service in World War I,* 1:17–27; and the McPeak Senior Statesmen brief. Two caveats are in order: The World War I data does not include actual sortie numbers, but states that 35,000 combat flight hours were flown. I have based the loss rate on the assumption of an average flight of 1.25 hours, based on previous research on World War I aviation, thus giving a total of 28,000 sorties. Also, the figures for Korea are for Air Force fighters only, for other numbers are contradictory and/or missing. However, fighter sorties accounted for the preponderance of AF combat sorties in Korea; fighters flew 341,269 sorties in Korea, 87 percent of the total of 392,139 total Air Force combat sorties (strategic bombers—B-29s—only flew 994 sorties, less than .0025). Therefore, the figures for fighters are considered completely representative for the service's overall record in the war. Overall, including noncombat operational losses, the Air Force in Korea lost 1,466 aircraft on 720,980 sorties, a loss rate per sortie of .0020, or .20 percent (one-fifth of 1 percent).

56. From McPeak Senior Statesmen brief.

57. This transformation of thought is admirably documented in William M. Arkin et al., *On Impact: Modern Warfare and the Environment—A Case Study of the Gulf War,* a Greenpeace study prepared for a "Fifth Geneva" Convention on the Protection of the Environment in Time of Conflict (London: Centre for Defence Studies, Kings College; Greenpeace International; and the London School of Economics, May 1991).

58. Michael Kelly, "Blitzed," *New Republic* 204, no. 6 (Feb. 11, 1991): 21.

59. Ibid., 22.

60. Ibid.

61. Milton Viorst, "Report from Baghdad," *New Yorker* 67, no. 18 (June 24, 1991): 55–73.

62. Ibid., 57.

63. Ibid., 58.

64. Ibid., 72.

65. DoD Interim Report, p. 24–1, and *Title V*, 189.

66. From testimony of Gen. Colin L. Powell before the Senate Committee on Appropriations, March 5, 1991.

67. Viorst, "Report from Baghdad," 61.

68. Quoted in Allen et al., *War in the Gulf*, 141.

69. Letter, UN Secretary General to President of UN Security Council, S22366, March 20, 1991, and attached trip report.

70. Erika Monk, "The New Face of Techno-War," *Nation* (May 6, 1991): 583.

71. Transcript notes from the PBS morning show, "Morning Edition," broadcast on WAMU-FM, Washington, D.C., on May 27, 1991.

72. Joost R. Hiltermann, "Bomb Now, Die Later," *Mother Jones* 16, no. 4 (July–Aug. 1991): 46.

73. Paul Lewis, "Effects of War Begin to Fade in Iraq," *New York Times*, May 12, 1991.

74. As I myself encounted when discussing the potential use of "smart" weapons against Iraq on news shows and with colleagues prior to the war.

Chapter 7. Air Power and the Conclusion of the Gulf War

1. McPeak media brief.

2. Horner Reuter transcript, p. B-7.

3. Muellner, "TAF's New Technology"; Air Force Desert Storm White Paper, 4, 7; conversations with JFACC planning staff.

4. Ibid.

5. Quoted in George Lardner, Jr., "In a Changing World, CIA Reorganizing to Do More with Less," *Washington Post*, July 5, 1991. See also *Title V*, appendix C.

6. Perhaps the best example of this was the bitter battle among a variety of individuals over the magnitude and veracity of the V-2 threat against Great Britain during the Second World War. For the general question of intelligence and its role in wartime planning, see R. V. Jones's excellent *Reflections on Intelligence* (London: William Heinemann, 1989). Jones, one of the twentieth century's remarkable figures, was Churchill's Director of Scientific Intelligence, for which the citizens of Allied nations can be thankful.

7. Lardner, "In a Changing World"; McPeak media brief; and conversations with Black Hole and Checkmate planners. I have also relied on analytical data supplied by Maj. Rich King, AF/XOXW-G, June 27, 1991. There is a summary of the intelligence problem in the DoD Interim Report, pp. 14-1–14-3.

8. Conversations with JFACC planning staff.

9. Ibid.

10. Ibid.; quote from Horner Reuter transcript, p. B-8.

11. Conversations with JFACC planning staff; *Title V,* 182–97.

12. Ibid.

13. Ibid.

14. Ibid.

15. Quote from a sign posted in the Black Hole on January 29, 1991.

16. Office of the Secretary of Defense, *Conduct of the Persian Gulf Conflict: An Interim Report to Congress* (Washington, D.C.: Department of Defense, 1991), 4–5 (hereafter cited as DoD Interim Report).

17. Letter, Charles "Buck" Wyndham to Brian Nicklas, February 10, 1991, transmitted to the author by Brian Nicklas.

18. *Title V,* appendix T, 8–11; AF Gulf War White Paper. There is an interesting perspective on A-10 operations in Breck W. Henderson's "A-10 'Warthogs' Damaged Heavily in Gulf War But Survived to Fly Again," *AWST* (Aug. 5, 1991): 42–43. A-10 weapons data from information supplied by Maj. Rich King, AF/XOXW-G, June 27, 1991.

19. Ibid. See also *Title V,* 243.

20. AF Gulf War White Paper; Muellner, "TAF's New Technology"; F-16 Maverick and bomb data is from information supplied by Maj. Rich King, AF/XOXW-G, June 27, 1991.

21. Ibid.; also conversations with JFACC planning staff.

22. I have drawn upon information from Lt. Col. Bob Hilton, the commanding officer of the 69th TFS, presented during a Warrior briefing at the Pentagon, September 11, 1991.

23. There is good account of RAF Tornado operations in Group Captain Andrew "Andy" Vallance's essay "Air Power in the Gulf War: The RAF Contribution," *Air Clues: The Royal Air Force Magazine* 45, no. 7 (July 1991): 251–54; the quoted text is from p. 251.

24. David A. Fulghum, "Saudis Claim Air Strikes Still May Break Iraq's Will," *AWST* (Feb. 4, 1991): 66–67.

25. The Tornado issue merely confirmed that, for a country which has always benefited from NATO's protective shield, Germany was distinctly unhelpful during the Gulf war, though both international pressure and that of public opinion eventually forced some limited German support of the coalition. To be fair, one country was even worse: Belgium refused to sell 155mm artillery shells to Great Britain—a country that had gone to war in 1914 precisely to guarantee Belgium's freedom. Some payback! For an excellent review of the German situation, see Alan Sked, "Cheap Excuses: Germany and the Gulf Crisis," *National Interest* 24 (Summer 1991): 51–60.

26. Vallance, "Air Power in the Gulf War." I am also grateful for information

furnished by AVM Tony Mason, RAF (ret.), Group Captain Andy Vallance, and Group Captain Neil E. Taylor.

27. Vallance, "Air Power in the Gulf War," 253; quote is from p. 252. There is a good summation of British Gulf activity in "Aerospace Analysis: Gulf Air War," *Aerospace* 18, no. 3 (March 1991): 4–5.

28. Jeffrey M. Lenorovitz, "French Use Jaguar Fighter/Bombers to Strike Desert Storm Targets," *AWST* (Jan. 28, 1991): 22–23; Jeffrey M. Lenorovitz, "French Air Force Mirage F1CRs Join Attacks on Iraqi Targets," *AWST* (Feb. 4, 1991): 65–66

29. Vallance, "Air Power in the Gulf War," 253; see also Mike Rondot, "Jaguar Sortie," and "UK in the Gulf," *Aircraft Illustrated* 24, no. 4 (April 1991): 177–79, 184–85.

30. "Kuwaiti Mirage F1s Fly Missions against Targets in Occupied Homeland," *AWST* (Feb. 18, 1991): 61.

31. See Fulghum, "Saudis Claim Air Strikes," 66.

32. Horner Reuter transcript, pp. B-7–B-8; conversations with JFACC and CENTCOM planning staff.

33. Fulghum, "Saudis Claim Air Strikes," 67; *Title V*, appendix T, 24–27.

34. Allen et al., *War in the Gulf,* 162.

35. For this discussion, I have drawn on the AF Gulf War White Paper; Horner, "Reflections on Desert Storm"; also EPW interrogation information furnished by Dr. Christopher J. Bowie and a campaign summary prepared by Lt. Col. Phillip S. Meilinger, and a "Warrior" briefing on BLU-82 drops by personnel of the 8th Special Operations Squadron at the Pentagon on September 11, 1991.

36. Ibid.

37. See Paul Taylor, "At 85%, Confidence in Military Strikes Highest Point in Years," and Edward Cody, "Allies Claim to Bomb Iraqi Targets at Will," *Washington Post,* January 31, 1991.

38. Friedman, *Desert Victory,* 197.

39. Armies are always reluctant to accept such claims by air personnel, often believing them to be dubious and extravagant exaggerations. So, it is worth noting that the 58 of 71 figure is from the Department of the Army summary "Army Weapons Systems Performance," 5, and not from an Air Force document. I have also drawn upon Muellner's "TAF's New Technology," and a conversation with him on April 26, 1991.

40. *Title V,* 174–75. See Taylor and Blackwell, "Ground War in the Gulf," 235–36; R. A. Padilla, "F/A-18D's Go to War," *U.S. Naval Institute Proceedings,* 118/8/1,062 (Aug. 1991): 40; Friedman, *Desert Victory,* 197–203. I have also relied upon information furnished by Capt. Stanley J. Alluisi, USAF.

41. Ibid.

42. *Washington Post,* January 31, 1991; see also Caryle Murphy and Molly Moore, "Attacks at Saudi Border Kill 12 U.S. Marines; Iraqis Lose 24 Tanks,

Suffer 'Heavy' Casualties," and Henry Allen, "Numbers That Numb," in the same issue.

43. Ironically, one of the major figures in Bryan's book had been then-Lt. Col. H. Norman Schwarzkopf; it was the story of one family's coming to grips with the death of a son caused by "friendly" artillery fire. See also Rowan Scarborough, "U.S. Confirms 'Friendly Fire' Killed Marines," *Washington Times,* February 4, 1991.

44. The best—that is, most rational and balanced—account of Cobra is found in John J. Sullivan, "The Botched Air Support of Operation *Cobra,*" *Parameters* 18, no. 1 (March 1988); see also Hallion, *Strike from the Sky,* 206–14.

45. Over time, a distressing number of incidents—particularly of ground units firing on ground units—have come to light; see Stewart M. Powell, "Investigators Detail Fatal Errors in Gulf War," *Albany Times Union,* July 21, 1991; Richard H. P. Sia, "Friendly Fire Cited in 13% of U.S. Losses," *Baltimore Sun,* August 10, 1991; Barton Gellman, "Gulf War's Friendly Fire Tally Triples," *Washington Post,* August 14, 1991; and Steve Vogel, "VII Corps Soldiers Describe Incidents," *Army Times,* August 19, 1991.

46. Ibid.; see also DoD Interim Report, 17-1–17-3.

47. The best account of this debacle is Ronald Millar's thorough *Death of an Army: The Siege of Kut, 1915–1916* (Boston: Houghton Mifflin, 1970). Curiously, in all the "scare" literature that came out before the war, Kut was almost never mentioned.

48. This statement may seem unusually inflammatory, so I will buttress it with an anecdote. On March 9, 1991, PBS broadcast a media symposium sponsored by KCRW from the Guest Quarters Suite Hotel, Santa Monica, Calif., entitled "The Press Goes to War: Vietnam and the Persian Gulf." The symposium followed the airing of a play about the *Washington Post*'s leaking the Pentagon Papers. A question from the panel moderator—on whether the media would have published details of Schwarzkopf's "Hail Mary" maneuver had reporters known of it—elicited no responses that such a revelation would have been, at the least, ethically wrong. Indeed, participants generally conceded that the media "probably" would have published it. With sentiments like this, it is understandable why the relationship between the media and the military is often strained; one has a duty to keep secrets to save lives, and the other believes its duty is to ferret them out, consequences be damned. Several other international media representatives—for example, CNN's Peter Arnett—have commented since the war that even had they known of information that could have saved Allied lives, they believed their journalistic code would have compelled them not to take action, thus overriding any obligations they might have had as citizens of various coalition nations. Times have changed since the days of Ernie Pyle, Hanson Baldwin, Richard Tregaskis, Jim Lucas, Maggie Higgins, and Claire Booth Luce, although, to be fair, there *are* others who hold to the same values as these legendary journal-

ists. For a good, balanced survey, see Lloyd J. Matthews, ed., *Newsmen and National Defense: Is Conflict Inevitable?* (McLean, Va.: Brassey's, 1991).

49. From Frost interview of Schwarzkopf.

50. Transcript of remarks, Gen. Colin L. Powell, Pentagon press conference, January 23, 1991.

51. Notably by Congressman Les Aspin, chairman of the House Armed Services Committee, who wisely voiced reservations about launching a ground campaign too soon. For a good example of the media war on this issue, see strategist Edward N. Luttwak's provocative essay "Ground Nuts: The Army's Fatal War Strategy," *New Republic* 204, no. 8 (Feb. 25, 1991): 20–21.

52. Conversations with Checkmate, NSC, JFACC, and CENTAF planning staffs, and personal recollections; The Bush-McPeak-Scowcroft incident is from a commencement speech by Pres. George Bush at the Air Force Academy, May 29, 1991; see also transcript of remarks by Pres. George Bush, White House press conference, February 5, 1991.

53. Conversations with JFACC and CENTAF planning staff; see also Rick Atkinson and Ann Devroy, "Bush: No Immediate Plans to Start Ground War," *Washington Post,* February 12, 1991.

54. Transcript of testimony of Colin Powell before the Senate Armed Services Committee, February 21, 1991.

55. The surrender video of this episode, taken from a hovering Apache helicopter, is dramatic; copy in the film archives of the National Air and Space Museum, Smithsonian Institution, Washington, D.C. The Harrier story is from Atkinson and Devroy, "Bush."

56. Ibid.; also transcript of Schwarzkopf's CENTCOM briefing to the media on February 27, 1991, and eighth SOS briefing on BLU-82 operations, September 11, 1991. The Abrams move figure is from Department of the Army, "Army Weapons Systems Performance," 1. Tim Ripley's *Land Power: The Coalition and Iraqi Armies* (London: Osprey, 1991), is a useful introduction to the land power elements and forces employed in the Gulf war.

57. DoD Interim Report, p. 4-6. There are some discrepancies between units listed in official documents and units listed in popular sources; therefore, I have relied upon DoD information.

58. Michael Dobbs and Rick Atkinson, "Soviets Say Iraq's Response 'Positive'; Bush Calls Pullout Plan Unacceptable," *Washington Post,* February 22, 1991.

59. Conversations with members of the national security staffs of the Executive Branch.

60. Transcripts of statements by Pres. George Bush and Marlin Fitzwater, White House press conference, February 22, 1991.

61. Lawrence, "A Test Pilot's Visit to Desert Storm."

62. R. P. D. Folkes, ed., "The Gulf War: Granby Reflections from 4 Regiment

Army Air Corps," *The Army Air Corps Journal*, 1991, p. 19; see also Friedrich, *Desert Storm*, 77. The known actual prisoner breakdown was as follows: captured or interned by American forces, 63,080; captured by Britain and France, 5,849; captured by coalition forces: approximately 17,300. The total is thus approximately 86,229. Prisoner data from DoD Interim Report, p. 12-4.

63. Christina Barnes, "Bringing Home Hard Lessons from Gulf," *Prince Georges Journal Weekly* [Maryland], September 4–5, 1991.

64. *Title V,* 359–407; DoD Interim Report, pp. 4-7–4-8; Charles Lindbergh noticed the same problem in Germany in 1945, when troops were wantonly destroying German jet aircraft at the very time that Allied technical intelligence teams were desperately trying to recover them for postwar analysis. British accounts of the Falklands indicate that the same problem occurred there as well. Soldiers, it seems, can't resist shooting at airplanes—in the air or on the ground.

65. Department of the Army, "Army Weapons Systems Performance," 3–4; see also John G. Roos, "Sergeant Pilot Recalls First Hit Delivered by France's 'Iron Fist,'" *Armed Forces Journal International* (Aug. 1991): 35. The Hellfire statistic is from a conversation with Terry Gordy of the Rockwell Corporation, September 23, 1991.

66. Department of the Army, "Army Weapons Systems Performance," 5; DoD Interim Report, p. 4-8. See also Bill Turque et al., "The Day We Stopped the War," *Newsweek* (Jan. 20, 1992): 20–23.

67. P. J. O'Rourke, "Hoo-Ah!" *Rolling Stone* (May 2, 1991): 63.

68. Michael Kelly, "Highway to Hell," *New Republic* 204, no. 13 (1991): 11–14. See also William Claiborne and Caryle Murphy, "Retreat Down Highway of Doom," *Washington Post,* March 2, 1991. I also have benefited from the previously cited Muellner conversation.

69. Kelly, "Highway to Hell," 12.

70. Lord Byron (George Gordon), "The Destruction of Sennacherib," second stanza. The story of Sennacherib is in the Old Testament, 2 Kings 19:35–37; he invaded Judea and besieged Jerusalem. Like Hussein, his forces were shattered by air power—allegedly suffering 185,000 dead at the hands of the Angel of Death (cynics credit a plague, but a miraculous intervention of some sort cannot be denied). He returned to Assyria in disorder, dying at the hands of his overly ambitious and impatient sons years later. (I acknowledge the help of Jack Neufeld in tracing the history of this Saddam-like "wanna-be.")

71. DoD Interim Report, pp. 4-8–4-9; *Washington Post* columnist Rick Atkinson gave a moving and detailed examination of one such firefight in his graduation banquet address to the cadets of the Class of 1991, U.S. Military Academy, West Point, June 1991. See also Taylor and Blackwell, "Ground War in the Gulf." The statistics on Abrams and Bradley are from a briefing on friendly fire incidents issued in August 1991 by the Department of the Army and released on August 13 with the DoD news release, "Military Investigations Probe Friendly Fire Inci-

dents," August 13, 1991. The friendly fire story is detailed in the following chapter.

72. Trevor N. Dupuy, "How the War Was Won," *National Review* 53, no. 5 (April 1, 1991): 30. By way of comparison, the following are statistics for annual deaths to Americans from various other causes (sources are the U.S. Centers for Disease Control, National Safety Council, and National Center for Health Statistics): smoking: 434,000; alcohol/drunk driving: 105,000; AIDS: 31,000; homicide: 22,000; drug overdoses: 5,700.

73. DoD Interim Report, p. 4–10.

Chapter 8. Questions, Answers, and Conjectures

1. Speech by Gen. Ron Yates, Commander, AFSC, at the annual meeting of the East Coast Section, Society of Experimental Test Pilots, Alexandria, Va., April 26, 1991. I thank Maj. Brian Hoey for making this available. The British examples are drawn from M. C. Brooke, "Aeroplane and Armament Experimental Establishment Boscombe Down's Test Flying Support for Operation Desert Storm," paper presented at the 35th Symposium, Society of Experimental Test Pilots, Beverly Hills, Calif., September 1991.

2. Clausewitz, *On War*, 117.

3. Muellner, "TAF's New Technology."

4. Strategic Defense Initiative Organization, *Global Protection against Limited Strikes* (Washington, D.C.: SDIO, July 18, 1991), 1–15. For example, the Israeli-American Arrow, THAAD (Theater High Altitude Area Defense), and Brilliant Pebbles. These are all controversial, and time will tell if they do, in fact, lead to deployable systems.

5. Data from DoD news release, "Military Investigations Probe Friendly Fire Incidents," and the previously cited Army briefing on friendly fire (see chap. 7, n. 71). See also *Title V*, appendix M.

6. One stealth critic, Norman Friedman, has repeatedly suggested that stealth did *not* work, arguing that the F-117 was detected by a Royal Navy destroyer, variously claimed to be H.M.S. *London,* then H.M.S. *Gloucester,* using a Type 1022 radar, which then "was able to pass F-117 tracks to her Sea Wolf missile system, which locked on quite successfully." (The original source for this allegation appears to have been a story in a British newspaper.) In fact, the ships in question were never in a position where they could have detected F-117s even if they had been conventional (i.e., nonstealthy) airplanes! This is simply another of the growing Gulf war myths which, over time, will muddy rather than clarify what occurred in the war. For Friedman's allegations, see his "Did Stealth Really Work?" *U.S. Naval Institute Proceedings,* 118/9/1,063 (Sept. 1991): 124, as well as his *Desert Storm,* 403–4.

7. Transcript of speech by Pres. George Bush at the commencement of the Air Force Academy, May 29, 1991, reprinted in the *Weekly Compilation of Presidential Documents* 27, no. 22 (June 3, 1991): 683–86. The "virus" story first appeared in "The Gulf War Flu," *U.S. News and World Report* (Jan. 20, 1992): 50.

8. HQ USAF, "Stealth, the F-117, the B-2, and Desert Storm" (Washington, D.C.: HQ USAF, n.d.).

9. Both examples were drawn from the Gulf war. See statement of Lt. Gen. Charles A. Horner and Brig. Gen. Buster C. Glosson before the House Committee on Appropriations, U.S. Congress, n.d. (Spring 1991).

10. This statistic is computed in the following fashion: each TLAM costs approximately $1.2 million (other sources suggest an even higher figure, $1.5 million, but I have selected the lower one). Each TLAM delivers a 1,000-pound warhead. Just to match a ton of high explosive delivered by an airplane means using two TLAMS. Therefore:

$$(\$1,200,000) \times (2) = \$2,400,000$$

F-117s dropped approximately 2,000 tons of smart bombs. Therefore:

$$(2,000) \times (\$2,400,000) = \$4,800,000,000$$

Each F-117A costs $42,600,000. Therefore:

$$(\$4,800,000,000) / (\$42,600,000) = 112.676 \ aircraft$$

I have rounded this number off to 112 aircraft. As an aside, if one accepts the figure of $1.5 million per TLAM, then the total cost to match the tonnage dropped by the F-117 rises to $6 billion dollars, equivalent to purchasing 140 F-117s.

11. Total precision tonnage dropped by American forces was approximately 7,400 tons. Therefore:

$$(7,400) \times (2 \times \$1,200,000) = \$17,760,000,000$$

12. And, if ground proponents had to do it all over again, would they prefer a more ground-oriented strategy—say, attacking on the ground for 39 days, followed by 4 days of air attack?

13. Transcript of Secretary of Defense Dick Cheney speaking on the CNN television program, "Newsmaker Saturday," March 2, 1991.

14. Transcript of comments of Dick Cheney when interviewed on the CBS Morning News by reporter Harry Smith, August 2, 1991.

15. Fernando Serna, "Eye of the Rolling Storm: Air Force–Army Ground Teams," *Airman* (July 1991): 48.

16. McPeak media brief.

17. See, for example, Rowan Scarborough, "Tight Lips Sank Ships' Role in Gulf," *Washington Times,* October 6, 1991; R. F. Dunn, "After the Storm," *U.S. Naval Institute Proceedings,* 117/6/1,060 (June 1991): 60–61. The CNN comment is from a JFACC planner.

18. The source of subsequent statistics is the previously cited Chief of Naval Operations report, *USNDS,* Table 2, p. D-9. There are some variations between these and the statistics in the McPeak Senior Statesmen brief (see chap. 5, n. 43), but analysis indicates relatively close agreement between them.

19. Navy squadrons are significantly smaller than their Air Force counterparts; a Navy fighter squadron numbers between nine and twelve aircraft, while an Air Force fighter squadron numbers twenty-four.

20. This discussion is based on taking "per deck per day" sortie figures for defensive counter air, plus one-half of tanking, EW, and Maritime sorties. Incidentally, the figure of 30 percent for fleet air defense is independently verified by the McPeak Senior Statesmen brief. The 50-percent figure is from Riley D. Mixson, "Where We Must Do Better," *U.S. Naval Institute Proceedings,* 118/8/1,062 (Aug. 1991): 39.

21. Again, this figure is based on data in Table 2 of the CNO Desert Storm report.

22. The carrier cost $40 million (in 1958 dollars) and was damaged by a $1,000 mine that forced $5 million of emergency repairs to get the ship back on temporary duty before more permanent—and costly—repairs were done. The $948.3 million AEGIS-class cruiser was damaged by a $3,000 mine; final repair time and cost estimates are unknown. See Charles F. Horne III, "Mine Warfare Is with Us and Will Be with Us," J. M. Martin, "We Still Haven't Learned," and Frank Evans, "*Princeton* Leaves the War," in *U.S. Naval Institute Proceedings,* 117/7/1,061 (July 1991): 63–72.

23. See Dennis Palzkill, "Making Interoperability Work," *U.S. Naval Institute Proceedings,* 118/9/1,063 (Sept. 1991): 50.

24. Mixson, "Where We Must Do Better," 38.

25. Ibid.

26. Pilots of Ready Room 3, VFA-87, CVN-71 (U.S.S. *Theodore Roosevelt*), "Naval Aviation's Triad for Success: Aircraft-Tactics-Weapons" (1991), p. 1. A smoothed-over version of this manuscript was subsequently published as "Aircraft—Yes, Tactics—Yes, WEAPONS—NO," in *U.S. Naval Institute Proceedings,* 118/9/1,063 (Sept. 1991): 55–57.

27. See the previously cited report, Ramsdell to Allard, May 14, 1991.

28. Ibid.

29. Ibid.

30. James Blackwell et al., *The Gulf War: Military Lessons Learned—Interim Report of the CSIS Study Group on Lessons Learned from the Gulf War* (Washington, D.C.: The Center for Strategic and International Studies, 1991), 21.

31. Dov S. Zakheim, "Top Guns," *Policy Review* 57 (Summer 1991): 16. I do not agree, however, with his subsequent statement that "naval aviation played a relatively minor role in the Gulf War."

32. See Aspin, "Desert One to Desert Storm." See also U.S. Congress, House of Representatives, *Goldwater-Nichols Department of Defense Reorganization Act of 1986,* Report 99-284 (Washington, D.C.: House of Representatives, 1986). For the defense climate from whence Goldwater-Nichols sprang, see David C. Hendrickson, *Reforming Defense: The State of American Civil-Military Relations* (Baltimore: Johns Hopkins University Press, 1988). I also acknowledge with appreciation information on Goldwater-Nichols furnished by Col. George Sumrall, USA, of the Joint Staff, and Dr. Will Webb, the JCS historian. For an interesting examination of the relationship between the JCS and the civilian defense leadership, see Mark Perry, *Four Stars* (Boston: Houghton Mifflin, 1989), esp. 326–44.

33. Eliot A. Cohen, "After the Battle," *New Republic* 204, no. 13 (April 1, 1991): 26. For a contrary view, see Warren A. Trest, "Military Unity and National Policy: Some Past Effects and Future Implications," CADRE Paper Special Series, Report AU-ARI CPSS 91-7 (Maxwell AFB, Ala.: Air University, Dec. 1991).

34. I acknowledge with grateful appreciation very helpful information received from Air Vice Marshal R. A. "Tony" Mason, RAF (ret.), Dr. Mary C. FitzGerald of the Hudson Institute, and Lt. Col. Barbara McColgan, AF/XOXWD. FitzGerald's *Soviet Views of Future War: The Impact of New Technologies,* HI-4138 (Washington, D.C.: Hudson Institute, March 1991) is a good compilation of Soviet statements from 1990 through the Gulf war.

35. See his "Tanks Will Not Save the Day," *Izvestiya,* January 21, 1991.

36. Quoted in TASS, March 3, 1991.

37. See his "Gulf War: Initial Conclusions—Air Power Predetermined the Outcome," *Krasnaya Zvezda,* March 14, 1991. I thank Barbara McColgan for making this available.

38. See his "Smarter than Two Generals?" *Pravda* (Moscow edition), April 11, 1991.

39. From a statement on Moscow Central TV, February 28, 1991.

40. Yazov quoted from *Krasnaya Zvezda,* April 2, 1991; Moiseyev from *Izvestiya,* April 6, 1991; and Lobov from *Der Morgen,* February 18, 1991.

41. Private communication, Mason to author, August 1991.

42. Quoted in Fred Hiatt, "Soviet Generals Feared Each Other during Coup," *Washington Post,* September 13, 1991.

43. J. F. C. Fuller, *Armament and History: A Study of the Influence of Arma-*

ment on History: from the Dawn of Classical Warfare to the Second World War (New York: Charles Scribner's Sons, 1945), xv.

44. Ibid., xiii

45. Ibid., 7.

46. The best account of attempts to regulate air power is W. Hays Parks' brilliantly argued "Air War and the Law of War," *Air Force Law Review* 32, no. 1 (1990): 1–225.

47. See the previously cited Vallance, "Air Power in the Gulf Conflict—Learning the Lessons," 8.

48. Ibid., 7.

49. For a cogent discussion of this, see FitzGerald, *Soviet Images of Future War,* 9–10.

50. See HQ USAF, *Air Force Restructure White Paper* (Washington, D.C.: HQ USAF, 1991), and remarks of Secretary of the Air Force Donald B. Rice at the Air Force Association's Washington National Convention, Washington, D.C., September 17, 1991.

51. See Friedman, *Desert Victory,* 204. For a contrary view, see Benjamin F. Schemmer, "Six Navy Carriers Launch only 17% of Attack Missions in Desert Storm," *Armed Forces Journal* (Jan. 1992): 12–13.

52. I am indebted to John A. Warden III for pointing this out.

53. Aram Bakshian, Jr., quoting "an old Austrian friend of mine," in "New Paradigm or Old Paradox?" *National Review* 43, no. 11 (June 24, 1991): 36.

Appendix Introduction

1. See, for example, Lewis Mumford, *The Myth of the Machine: The Pentagon of Power* (New York: Harcourt Brace Jovanovich, 1970); Herbert Marcuse, *One-Dimensional Man: Studies in the Ideology of Advanced Industrial Society* (Boston: Beacon Press, 1964); and Jacques Ellul, *The Technological Society* (New York: Random House, 1964).

2. E. F. Schumacher, *Small Is Beautiful: Economics as If People Mattered* (New York: Harper and Row, 1973).

Appendix A. Air Superiority Technology

1. Paul F. Crickmore, *Lockheed SR-71 Blackbird* (London: Osprey Publishing, 1986), 47–48; Crickmore's book is the without question the best of the many on the Blackbird and its predecessors.

2. Drewes, *The Air Force and the Great Engine War,* 37; this is an excellent study of modern military systems acquisition.

3. The F100's test experience, coupled with lingering problems with the earlier TF30, led to a grim joke among 1970s fighter test pilots: "If the engines say Pratt & Whitney, the seats should say Martin-Baker," a reference to a manufacturer of excellent ejection seats. This anecdote was relayed to me in the early 1980s by the late Charles "Chuck" Sewell.

4. See Augustine, "How We Almost Lost the Technological War."

5. I have computed these figures from data in the following works: William Green and Gordon Swanborough, *The Observer's Basic Military Aircraft Directory* (New York: Frederick Warne and Co., 1974); William Green, *The Observer's Book of Aircraft* (London: Frederick Warne and Co., 1982); and Chris Chant, ed., *Concise Guide to Military Aircraft of the World* (Feltham, Eng.: Temple Press, 1985).

6. See Robert L. Shaw, *Fighter Combat: Tactics and Maneuvering* (Annapolis, Md.: Naval Institute Press, 1985), 394–95; W. B. Herbst, "Dynamics of Air Combat," *AIAA Journal of Aircraft* 20, no. 7 (July 1983): 594–98; and Klaus Huenecke, *Modern Combat Aircaft Design* (Annapolis, Md.: Naval Institute Press, 1987), 202–8. For an interesting "speed is life" counterpoint to the energy maneuverability notion, see Mike Straight, "Being Fast," *USAF Fighter Weapons Review* (Spring 1989): 4–7.

7. The specific energy of an aircraft is expressed by the equation:

$$E_s = H + V^2 / 2g$$

where E_s is specific energy in feet, H is the altitude above sea level in feet, V is the true airspeed of the aircraft in feet per second, and g is the acceleration of gravity in feet per second. Specific excess power is expressed by the equation:

$$P_s = \frac{(T - D)}{W} V$$

where P_s is specific excess power in feet per second, T is engine thrust in pounds, D is total drag in pounds, W is aircraft weight in pounds, and V is velocity in feet per second.

8. I have drawn heavily from Tuck McAtee's "Agility: Its Nature and Need in the 1990s," in Society of Experimental Test Pilots, *1987 Report to the Aerospace Profession* (Beverly Hills, Calif.: SETP, Sept. 23–26, 1987): 53–75.

9. From notes taken at a Department of Defense "Program Analysis and Evaluation Fighter Performance Metrics Conference" held at the Pentagon on July 22, 1987. Further, I have benefited from conversations with the technical staff of Eidetics International, Torrance, California.

Appendix B. Battlefield Attack Technology

1. I have based this on various materials, but particularly HQ USAF, "Air Power Lethality and Precision: Then and Now" (1990). I thank Col. John A. Warden III and Lt. Col. Dave Deptula for making this chart available to me, as well as additional CEP data. The number of aircraft calculations are my own.

2. Seymour J. Deitchman, *Military Power and the Advance of Technology: General Purpose Military Forces for the 1980s and Beyond* (Boulder, Colo.: Westview Press, 1983), 46. Deitchman based his World War II data on the 1944 Operation Strangle interdiction campaign in Italy.

3. See Rothman, *Aerospace Weapon System Acquisition Milestones,* 73–74; and George M. Watson, Jr., *The A-10 Close Air Support Aircraft: From Development to Production, 1970–1976* (Andrews AFB, Md.: History Office, Air Force Systems Command, n.d.). There is a good popular account in Bill Gunston, *Attack Aircraft of the West* (London: Ian Allen, 1974), 249–71.

4. Rothman, *Aerospace Weapon System Acquisition Milestones,* 164–66; AGM-65 System Program Office, *Program Management Plan for AGM-65 Missile System (WS-319) (Maverick)* (Wright-Patterson AFB: Deputy for Tactical Systems, Aeronautical Systems Division, 1984). I wish to thank Mr. Albert Misenko, ASD History Office, for making this latter document available to me. See also Mike Isherwood, "Combat Hammer: Tactical Maverick Execution," *USAF Fighter Weapons Review* (Winter 1988): 5–8.

5. I have based much of this discussion upon conversations with Col. Alan Todd, Maj. Austin Omlie, and CW4 Mark Metzger of the U.S. Army Aviation Engineering Flight Activity, Edwards AFB, Calif. I greatly appreciate their introduction to the world of attack helicopters on August 20, 1987. See also Rothman, *Aerospace Weapon System Acquisition Milestones,* 125–26, 173, and Zaloga and Balin, *Anti-Tank Helicopters,* 19–20.

6. Ibid.; also Al Adcock, *AH-64 Apache in Action, Aircraft* series, no. 95 (Carrolton, Tex.: Squadron/Signal Publications, 1989) offers much useful technical information.

7. Again, I have benefited from conversations with John Fozard, and from personal recollections of YAV-8B flight testing at Edwards in the 1980s (including an unfortunate string of engine-related in-flight emergencies). The best reference sources on the AV-8B are Bill Gunston, *Modern Fighting Aircraft: Harrier,* Aviation Fact File series (London: Salamander Books, 1984); and Don Linn, *AV-8 Harrier:* Vol. 1, *USMC Versions* (London: Airlife Publishing, 1988). See also Rothman, *Aerospace Weapon System Acquisition Milestones,* 75.

Appendix C. Strike Warfare Technology

1. Jones quote is from Futrell, *Ideas, Concepts, Doctrine,* 2:495.
2. Recollections of Col. William J. "Pete" Knight, USAF (ret.) to the author.

3. I have drawn on personal memories of the fly-off, and conversations with members of both the F-15 and F-16XL test forces.

4. Gary L. Jennings and Pat Henry, "F-15 Synthetic Aperture Radar," in Society of Experimental Test Pilots, *1981 Report to the Aerospace Profession* (Beverly Hills, Calif.: SETP, 1981), 182–91; Stephen D. Stowe and Gary Jennings, "F-15E Initial Flight Test Results," in Society of Experimental Test Pilots, *1987 Report to the Aerospace Profession,* 171–86.

5. I have relied for this account on Harold C. Farley, Jr., and Richard Abrams, "F-117A Flight Test Program," in Society of Experimental Test Pilots, *1990 Report to the Aerospace Profession* (Beverly Hills, Calif.: SETP, Sept. 1990), 141–67. The single best source of information on radar cross-section reduction is Eugene F. Knott, John F. Shaeffer, and Michael T. Tuley, *Radar Cross Section: Its Prediction, Measurement and Reduction, The Artech House Radar Library* series (Norwood, Mass.: Artech House, 1985), particularly 155–219.

Appendix D. Missile Technology

1. Kenneth P. Werrell, *The Evolution of the Cruise Missile* (Maxwell AFB: Air University Press, 1985), 150–51; Rothman, *Aerospace Weapon System Acquisition Milestones,* 169; McDonnell-Douglas Missile Systems Company (McDDMSC), "Harpoon Weapon System," document E 08/90 P 05K H 1 (Aug. 28, 1990); and McDDMSC, "Standoff Land Attack Missile—SLAM," document E 08/90 P 05K S 1, n.d. Iraqi war details from anon., "SLAMs Hit Iraqi Target in First Combat Firing," *Aviation Week and Space Technology* 134, no. 4 (Jan. 28, 1991): 31, 34.

2. The definitive study of cruise missile development is Werrell's *The Evolution of the Cruise Missile;* see also Rothman, *Aerospace Weapon System Acquisition Milestones,* 192.

3. Ibid.

4. See Kotz, *Wild Blue Yonder,* 165.

5. Ibid. See also USN, *Annual Report of the Secretary of the Navy,* February 1992, pp. 120–21.

6. This early—and fascinating—history of rocketry is treated in Frank H. Winter's encyclopedia *The First Golden Age of Rocketry: Congreve and Hale Rockets of the Nineteenth Century* (Washington, D.C.: Smithsonian Institution Press, 1990), esp. 1–42, and 215–24.

7. The Army's role in rocketry has never received its proper attention. A useful memoir is John B. Medaris's *Countdown for Decision* (New York: G. P. Putnam's Sons, 1960); and Wernher von Braun's "The Redstone, Jupiter, and Juno," in *The History of Rocket Technology: Essays on Research, Development, and Utility,* ed. Eugene M. Emme (Detroit: Wayne State University Press, in cooperation with

the Society for the History of Technology, 1964), 107–21. There is a collection of interesting rocket transport studies in the library of the Military History Institute, Carlisle Barracks, Pa.

8. See Department of the Army, "Army Weapons Systems Performance," 2; and Taylor and Blackwell, "Ground War in the Gulf," 242–43. I have also drawn upon briefing notes on the MLRS from the U.S. Army War College, 1987–88, and from information supplied by the U.S. Army Missile Command Public Affairs Office.

9. Department of the Army, "Army Weapons Systems Performance," 2–3. See also Charles Rabb, "ATACMS Adds Long-Range Punch," *Defense Electronics* 18, no. 8 (Aug. 1986): 69–75. The figure on total ATACMS used is from the U.S. Army Missile Command Public Affairs Office.

10. I wish to acknowledge with grateful appreciation information from a paper by Donald R. Baucom entitled "Providing High Technology Systems for the Modern Battlefield: The Case of Patriot's ATBM Capability," presented to the Conference of the American Military Institute, Durham, N.C., March 23, 1991. This is the single best analysis done to date of how the Patriot was developed to confront ballistic missile threats. For an interesting perspective on the ATBM debate and NATO, see Robert M. Soofer, "Antitactical Ballistic Missile Defense in NATO," *Military Review* 68, no. 3 (March 1988): 14–23.

11. Baucom, "Providing High Technology Systems"; Ralph Kinney Bennett, "The Vision Behind the Patriot," *Reader's Digest* (May 1991): 76–80.

12. Quote from Baucom, "Providing High Technology Systems," 6; other data from Bennett, "The Vision Behind the Patriot," 79; and Rothman, *Aerospace Weapon System Acquisition Milestones,* 209.

13. See n. 12, above.

14. See n. 12, above. See also the following articles on the Patriot, its supporters, and its critics, all in *New Dimensions* 5, no. 5 (May 1991): David Kuperlian and Mark Masters, "Patriot Demolishes Congressional Scuds," 16–27; and Ken Adelman, "Missile Defense Foresight," 19.

15. Kuperlian and Masters, "Patriot Demolishes Congressional Scuds," 16–17; Department of the Army, "Army Weapons Systems Performance," 3; and Hughes, "Patriot Antimissile Successes," 26–28. See also Augustine, "How We Almost Lost the Technological War."

Appendix E. The "Smart" Bomb

1. From transcription notes of the Public Broadcast System morning broadcast of "Morning Edition," May 27, 1991, 8:48 A.M.–8:51 A.M., WAMU-FM (Washington, D.C.), with peace activist Erika Monk.

2. The single best discussion of the evolution of the smart bomb is David R.

Mets' impressive *Quest for a Surgical Strike;* for an interesting profile of one of the "fathers" of the laser-guided bomb, see "Weldon Wood," *People Weekly* (Spring–Summer 1991): 40–41. See also Kahn, *On Thermonuclear War,* 386–87.

3. Mets, *Quest for a Surgical Strike,* 43–56. (The "Zero CEP" information is from a comment made by former Secretary of Defense Harold Brown regarding smart bomb development and its use in Desert Storm, June 21, 1991.)

4. Mets, *Quest for a Surgical Strike,* 56–68. I have also benefited from information furnished by Dr. Wayne Thompson. Pave Nail, while it worked, was a high-risk system for the OV-10. One Nail crew miraculously survived a SA-7 hit that destroyed one engine and left it in flames. (Conversation with Lt. Col. John R. Houle, USAF, May 1982.)

5. Mets, *Quest for a Surgical Strike,* 77–92; Doglione et al., *Airpower and the 1972 Spring Invasion,* 54, 66, 73.

6. Mets, *Quest for a Surgical Strike,* 93–107; Lehman, *Command of the Seas,* 353.

7. Mets, *Quest for a Surgical Strike,* 107–24. Statistics are from a GBU-15 and GBU-24 display at Headquarters, Air Force Systems Command, Andrews AFB, Maryland, in May 1991, and from information received from Texas Instruments and Rockwell International, at the 1991 Air Force Association convention and trade show. Roy Braybrook's "Tactical Air-to-Surface Guided Weapons," *Air International* 40, no. 5 (May 1991): 241–46, is an excellent survey article.

8. Remarks of Gen. Bernard P. Randolph, Commander of Air Force Systems Command, at the joint Air Force Association-Tactical Air Command Tactical Air Warfare Symposium, Orlando, Florida, January 22, 1988, p. 8. I thank Ellen Piazza for making this available to me.

9. Computed on the basis of information in the aforementioned HQ AFSC GBU-15 exhibit.

Appendix F. Battlefield Information and Control

1. HQ USAF White Paper, "Air Force Performance in Desert Storm," 11–12. For additional information, see remarks of Gen. Ronald W. Yates, commander of Air Force Systems Command, at the Armed Forces Communications and Electronics Association, February 13, 1991. I thank Maj. Brian Hoey for making this available to me. See also remarks of Maj. Gen. John Fairfield, commander of Air Force Communications Command, at the AFCEA/Executive C³ Logistics Review Dinner, September 11, 1991. I thank Col. Wayne Corbett for making this available.

2. A claim made by the Cinc of the Pakistani air force, Air Marshal Rahim Khan; see "Airscene," *Air Enthusiast* 2, no. 3 (March 1972): 111.

3. AWACS information is from Terence R. St. Louis, *An Interview with Col. Kenneth R. McKean, E-3A Test Director* (Holloman AFB, N.M.: History Office, Air Force Operational Test and Evaluation Center, n.d., *c.* 1982); and unclassified portions of Vincent C. Breslin, *Development of the Airborne Warning and Control System (AWACS) and the E-3A Brassboard* (Hanscom AFB, Mass.: History Office, Electronic Systems Division, 1983). See also *DMS Market Intelligence Reports (Electronic Systems* and *Military Aircraft)* issued by the Jane's Information Group (Alexandria, Va., 1989). See also HQ USAF, "Air Force Performance in Desert Storm," 12; and Peter M. Bowers, *Boeing Aircraft since 1916* (Annapolis, Md.: Naval Institute Press, 1989), 454–59.

4. William E. DuPuy, "For the Joint Specialist: Five Steep Hills to Climb," *Parameters* 19, no. 3 (Sept. 1989): 10–11.

5. Joshua M. Epstein, quoted in "Army Banks on Joint STARS for AirLand Battle Management," *Defense Electronics* 18, no. 8 (Aug. 1986): 77–85. For JSTARS's promise, see Frederick A. Tarantino, "A Substitute for NATO's Nuclear Option?" *Military Affairs* (March 1988): 24–35.

6. Epstein, quoted in "Army Banks on Joint STARS for AirLand Battle Management"; Tarantino, "A Substitute for NATO's Nuclear Option?"; Air Force Systems Command, Electronic Systems Division, "J-STARS Talking Paper," n.d. (*c.* 1990); "Joint STARS Pinpoints Targets as U.S., NATO Generals Watch," *Leading Edge* (Andrews AFB, Md.: Public Affairs Office, HQ AFSC, 1990), 9; "J-STARS Joins Desert Storm," *Leading Edge* (Andrews AFB, Md.: Public Affairs Office, HQ AFSC, 1991), 7; DMS JSTARS information (Jane's, 1989); Mark Lambert et al., *Jane's All the World's Aircraft* (81st ed.), *1990–91* (Alexandria, Va.: Jane's Information Group, 1991); HQ USAF, "Air Force Performance in Desert Storm," 12.

7. Information on Pioneer and Pointer are from Lehman, *Command of the Seas,* 177–78; and from "Storm Warning," and "Low-Tech Surveillance," *U.S. Naval Institute Proceedings,* 117/3/1,057 (March 1991): 61, 157. See also Brian P. Tice, "Unmanned Aerial Vehicles: The Force Multiplier of the 1990s," *Airpower Journal* 5, no. 1 (Spring 1991): 41–55. The Weinberger story is from his *Fighting for Peace,* 149. As unbelievable as it seems, the surrender story is a true one. The Pioneer's ship controllers were amazed to see Iraqi soldiers desperately waving anything white they had at the drone, which wandered on until it ran out of fuel and crashed.

Appendix G. Space-based Systems, LANTIRN, and Pave Low

1. HQ USAF, "Air Force Performance in Desert Storm," 10 (see Appendix F, n. 1). See also Vincent Kiernan, "War Tests Satellites' Prowess," *Space News,* February 3, 1991. I have also drawn from the following sources for background

information, and I gratefully acknowledge the help of Capt. Jon Watkins, USAF, in making them available to me. General Donald J. Kutyna, Testimony before the Senate Armed Services Committee, U.S. Congress, April 23, 1991; Air Force Space Command, "Remarks on Space and Space Systems" (Peterson AFB, Colo.: AFSpaceCom Commander's Group, April 1991); Lt. Gen. Thomas S. Moorman (AFSpaceCom/CC), "Space: A New Strategic Frontier," April 1991; Lt. Gen. Thomas S. Moorman, "Future Space Systems Support to the War-Fighter," remarks for the AFCEA Space Symposium, July 31, 1991; Maj. Gen. Jay W. Kelley, "Space Launch Operations: An Operator's View," September 1991; and AFSpaceCom, "Space Support to Desert Storm," September 1991.

2. HQ USAF, "Air Force Performance in Desert Storm," 10–11; Yates remarks (Feb. 13, 1991). For an excellent introduction to GPS, see Daniel K. Malone, "GPS/NAVSTAR," *Military Review* (March 1988): 37–43. I have also relied on information acquired during acquisitions research at Headquarters Air Force Systems Command in 1989.

3. HQ USAF, "Air Force Performance in Desert Storm," 11, and information from acquisitions research at HQ AFSC in 1989.

4. Deborah C. Meyer and Benjamin F. Schemmer, interview with Wilbur Creech, *Armed Forces Journal International* (Jan. 1983): 32.

5. HQ USAF, "Air Force Performance in Desert Storm," 3–4; I have drawn on information contained in the 1983–84 annual history of the Air Force Flight Test Center, History Office, Edwards AFB; and from personal recollection. The Martin information comes from a speech by Gen. Bernard P. Randolph (see Appendix E, n. 8, above).

6. This discussion is based extensively upon Leo Anthony Gambone's *Pave Low III;* Gambone was project engineer on the Pave Low III program.

7. USAF ASD Office of Information, "Pave Low III," OIP 79-081 (March 1979).

8. See Kenneth M. Page, "U.S. Air Force Special Operations: Charting a Course for the Future," *Airpower Journal* 1, no. 2 (Fall 1987): 58–69; and HQ USAF, "Air Force Performance in Desert Storm," 6.

Index

air combat (*continued*)
  likelihood of "blue-on-blue" encoun-
    ters, 37
  rediscovering techniques for, 30–33
Air Combat Command, 265
aircraft. *See also* bombers; engines; fighters; flight control systems; helicopters;
  individual aircraft model number; sorties
  available to Iraq at start of Gulf war,
    146–47
  AWACS, 98, 155, 242, 309–10
  civilian used in Desert Shield/Desert
    Storm, 137
  and energy maneuverability, 30, 35,
    278–80
  proliferation of Soviet style, 68–69,
    127, 128
  used in Desert Storm, 153, 155, 157,
    158f, 165–66
  used on G-day operations, 226, 227
  versus missiles for air operations,
    250–51
  vulnerability to missiles, 59–62
aircraft carriers
  as base for air power, 254–56,
    265–66
  CAFMS and ATO not electronically
    available, 156–57, 256
  in support of Desert Shield, 135, 136,
    139, 165
aircraft maintenance, 155–56, 196, 197t,
  211
aircraft shelters in Iraq, 131, 195, 205
air defense networks
  destroyed by Desert Storm, 169, 170f,
    172, 176
  developed by Egypt and Syria, 25–26
  in Iraq, 131, 147, 153, 248
  Iraqi in Kuwait, 154
  in Libya, 104, 106–7
  proliferation of Soviet style, 68–69,
    81, 128
  technology to defeat, 62
air doctrine. *See also* air superiority; military doctrine
  and AFM, 1-1, 118
  AirLand Battle concept, 74, 76, 77–
    79, 120, 243, 252
  battlefield air interdiction, 6, 8, 75,
    78, 117
  CAS (close **air support**), **6, 8,** 78, 117

for NATO, 74, 81
offensive and defensive, 6–8, 11
soundness of, 243
airfields
  of Desert Storm coalition forces, 157
    (*map*)
  Iraqi, 147, 148–49 (*map*), 176, 194
Air Force, 31, 72–75, 188, 264–65
Air-Ground Combat Center, 33
AirLand Battle doctrine, 74, 76, 77–79,
  120, 243, 252
airlift
  coalition air strength on eve of war,
    158f
  in Desert Shield/Desert Storm, 137–
    39, 156, 226, 227
  in Grenada, 100
  need for, 63–64
  in Vietnam, 21, 22
Air Mobility Command, 265
air power, 4. *See also* air doctrine; air superiority; battlefield attack; confidence
  in military effectiveness; Desert Storm
  air campaign
  advantages and capabilities of, 1, 12,
    13, 25, 119–20, 264
  carrier-based, 254–56, 265–66
  as cavalry, 23
  prewar lack of confidence in, 1–4,
    140–41, 159
  role for the future, 266–68
  role in atomic era, 13–17
  role in June 1967 Arab-Israeli war, 2,
    24–26
  role in Second World War, 8–13
  role in Vietnam, 17–24
  versus ground power, 251–54
air reconnaissance, value of, 5
air refueling. *See* tankers (air refueling)
air superiority. *See also* air power
  in air combat techniques, 30–33
  with missiles, 46–51
  with new fighters, 33–38, 39–46,
    51–54
  perceived need for, 5, 13, 73, 117
  potential European irrelevancy of, 73
  proven need for, 243
  rebuilding after Vietnam, 27–30
  technologies, 275–81
air transport, 6, 8, 63, 64, 137, 227
ALARM anti-radar missile, 173, 291

ALCMs (air-launched cruise missiles), 163, 297

angle of attack (AOA), 279, 280

antiaircraft defenses. *See also* air defense networks; missiles
    Arab, 59
    German, 9
    Iraqi, 128, 130, 167, 171, 202
    Vietnamese, 20

antitank weapons, 59, 72

Arab-Israeli wars
    Bekaa Valley air campaign, 97–99
    June 1967, 2, 24–26
    Yom Kippur 1973, 58–62

Army, 32, 70–75

Arnett, Peter, 170, 199

artillery
    directed by GPS, 233
    importance of destroying in Desert Storm, 150, 154, 201

assassination
    of Gerald Bull, 132
    Saddam Hussein not target for, 150
    of Vahia al-Mashad?, 130

ATACMS (Army Tactical Missile System), 299–300

ATO (Air Tasking Order), 143, 155, 256, 258. *See also* targets

Augustine, Norman R., 3, 277–78

Ault, Frank, 30–31

austere fighters, 42, 51–54

AV-8B Harrier II, 221, 287–88

AWACS (airborne warning aircraft), 98, 155, 242, 309–10

'Aziz, Tariq, 160

B-1B bomber, 90

B-1 bomber, 66–67

B-2 stealth bomber, 90–91

B-52 Stratofortress
    at battle of Khafji, 221
    in Desert Storm, 154, 174
    longevity of, 65–67
    over Baghdad, 163–64, 171
    in Vietnam, 22, 58, 65

B-57, 22

Baathism in Iraq, 125, 129

Bahraini forces on eve of G-day, 228, 229*t*, 230 *(map)*

Baker, James, 159–60

Banks, Donald, 300

battlefield air interdiction, 6, 8, 75, 78, 117

battlefield air support, 13, 21, 73

battlefield attack
    information and control technologies, 308–12
    missile technologies, 282–88
    rocket artillery, 298–300

Beirut incident, 99

Bekaa Valley air campaign, 97–99

Berlin airlift, compared to Desert Shield airlift, 138

BGM-109 Tomahawk TLAM land attack missile, 171, 251, 296, 297–98

Black Hole planning cell, 143, 169, 170

"blue-on-blue" combat, 37, 216. *See also* friendly fire

bombers. *See also* B-series aircraft models
    development of, 65–67
    susceptibility to enemy defenses, 8
    as symbol of air power, 8, 67, 163

bombing
    1940s improved precision of, 10
    civilian reaction to, 7, 8, 9, 199
    early vision of long-range strategic, 7, 8–9
    effect on morale of troops, 218–19, 227, 232
    improvements in precision of, 282–83
    supposed failure of strategic, 11

Bowie, Christopher J., 97

Boyd, John, 38, 42, 278–79

Bradley fighting vehicle, 227, 237, 247–48

bridges, difficulty of destroying, 21, 154, 193, 303, 304

"Bud lights," 223

Buffs. *See* B-52 Stratofortress

Bull, Gerald, 131, 132

Bush, George, 124, 159–60, 274

C-5B Galaxy airlifter, 64, 137

C-17, 64

C-130, 137, 227

C-141, 63, 137

carriers. *See* aircraft carriers

Carter Doctrine, 109–10

CAS (close air support), 6, 8, 78, 117

casualties
    from friendly fire, 221–22, 237, 247
    suffered by U.S. Army, 237, 238*t*

Cate, James L., 10

electrical power generation facilities, 191–92
expected failure of sanctions, 158–59
fuel and lubricant production facilities, 192–93
historic treasures, 151, 159
invasion of Kuwait, 133–34
military capabilities, 128, 146–47
morale of troops, 218–19, 227, 232
naval forces, 216
potential for invasion of Saudi Arabia, 134–35
recipient of Soviet military doctrine and equipment, 81, 127, 128
response to Shiite and Kurdish resistance, 198–99, 239
transportation infrastructure, 193
treatment of POWs, 239
Iraqi prisoners, 199, 221, 233, 236
Israel, 130–31, 179–80. *See also* Arab-Israeli wars

Jaguar (Anglo-French), 136, 166, 215, 216, 243, 290
jamming (electronic countermeasures), 172
Jedi Knights, 144
"jointness"
accelerated by Powell, 259
advocated by Air Force, 120
advocated by Michael Dugan, 145
fostered by Lehman, 118–19
and Goldwater-Nichols Act, 259–60
for Libyan incident, 106
problems revealed by Grenada, 101–2
and USCENTCOM (U.S. Central Command), 109, 110, 136, 141–42
JSTARS (E-8A), 154–55, 183, 202, 220, 242, 310
JTACMS (Joint Tactical Missile System), 299
June 1967 Arab-Israeli war, importance of air power in, 2, 24–26

KC-10 Extender, 64–65, 139, 165
KC-130 tanker, 165
KC-135 Stratotankers, 64, 139, 165
Kelly, Michael, 197, 198, 235–36
Khafji battle, 219–23
"kill boxes", 155

Kurdish resistance to Iraqi government, 239
Kuwait
air strength on eve of war, 158*f*
forces on eve of G-day, 228, 229*t*, 230 *(map)*
Hussein's timing of invasion, 123–24
importance to Iraq, 132

LANTIRN (Low Altitude Navigation Targeting Infrared for Night), 155, 243, 314–15
laser-guided bombs. *See* "smart" bombs
Lebanon, 97, 99
Lehman, John, 32, 94, 103, 106, 107, 118
Lewis, Paul, 200
LGB (laser-guided bombs). *See* "smart" bombs
LGM-118A Peacekeeper missile, 91–92
Libya, 94–95, 104–9
Loh, John M., 38, 42, 143, 146

McCurdy, Dave, 169
McNamara, Robert, 35–36
McPeak, Merrill A., 145, 201, 225, 254, 264
maintenance of aircraft, 155–56, 196, 197*t*, 211
Mallin, Maurice A., 115
Marine Corps
aircraft used in Desert Storm, 155
and amphibious "invasion" of Kuwait, 227–28
in battle of Khafji, 221
establishment of Air-Ground Combat Center, 33
forces on eve of G-day, 228, 229*t*, 230 *(map)*
percent of sorties by, 188
role in Desert Storm, 244
Maritime Strategy, 118, 119, 120
Mason, R. A., 1, 263
Maverick missile, 62, 203, 285
MH-53H Pave Low III helicopter, 87, 166–67, 315–17
MiG-series Soviet aircraft, 27, 28, 29, 30, 36, 37, 172
military doctrine. *See also* air doctrine and AFM 1-1, 118

Tapline Road, 227
targets. *See also* ATO (Air Tasking Order); intelligence estimates
  by-service separation of, 20
  controversy over priorities, 206–9
  identifying, 202
  identifying with drones, 312
  Saddam Hussein not specifically included, 150
  visual identification requirement, 177
Task Force Normandy, 166–67
TDF (Tactical Digital Facsimile), 308–9
technologies
  for air superiority, 275–81
  for battlefield attack, 282–88
  for battlefield information and control, 308–12
  for missiles, 295–302
  overall success of, 242–43, 273–74
  of "smart" bombs, 303–7
  of space-based and night-capable systems, 313–17
  for strike warfare, 289–94
TEL (transporter, erector, and launcher) for Scuds, 178
TERCOM (terrain contour matching) guidance systems, 171, 297
terror-bombing of civilian populations, 7, 8, 9
Terry, Ronald W., 316
theater-strike sorties, 255
31 Initiatives, 74, 78–80
thrust-to-weight ratios, 278
TLAM missiles, 171, 251, 296, 297–98
Tomahawk BGM-109 TLAM land attack missile, 171, 251, 296, 297–98
"Top Gun" Fighter Weapons School, 31
Tornado (Anglo/German/Italian), 136–37, 165, 175, 213–15, 243, 290–91
TOW (tube-launched/optically tracked/wire-guided) missiles, 58, 286
TR-1, 202
Trenchard, Hugh, 6, 7
Trident missile, 92

U-2R, 202
UAVs (Unmanned Air Vehicles), 311. *See also* drones
UH-1 Huey helicopter gunship, 23–24
United Arab Emirates, forces on eve of G-day, 228, 229t, 230 *(map)*
United Nations, 239
United States military services. *See also* confidence in military effectiveness; "jointness"; military doctrine
  and Goldwater-Nichols Defense Reorganization Act, 104
  report card on eve of Gulf crisis, 122–24
unmanned air vehicles (drones), 23, 98, 173, 293, 311–12
USCENTCOM (U.S. Central Command), 109, 110, 136, 141–42
USS *Mayaguez* incident, 86
USS *Samuel B. Roberts,* 111
USS *Stark,* 111, 126
USS *Vincennes,* 111–12

videotape reports, 204, 206, 209, 235, 245
Vietnam, 17–24, 56–58, 65, 83, 84–85
Viorst, Milton, 198–99
V/STOL aircraft, 96, 97, 98, 287

Walzer, Michael, 160
Warden, John A., III, 115, 116, 117, 118, 142–43, 243, 264
weather
  and DMSP (Defense Meteorological Support Program), 314
  as factor for Desert Storm, 176–77, 231, 234, 235, 237
Weinberger, Caspar W., 89, 90, 102, 312
Weinberger Doctrine, 90, 99
wing loadings, 278

Yom Kippur 1973 Arab-Israeli war, 58–62

Zakheim, Dov S., 102, 259
Zeppelin airship, 5, 8